SALEM WITCHCRAFT

first published in 1867, will long remain the standard work on seventeenth-century Salem and its notorious trials, with all that the era holds of "the pitiable and tragical, the mysterious and awful."

The work of a historian who was a Mayor of modern Salem, these comprehensive volumes present a memorable picture of the time and the people who were so deeply involved in searching out purveyors of witchcraft.

Volume One gives a full background and history of Salem, revealing how the witchcraft hysteria grew out of a dark and despondent period—"the triumphant age of superstition"—when the struggling colonists were oppressed by debts, piracy on the coasts, the passing of their leading citizens, etc. Volume Two contains details of the prosecutions of 1692 including depositions which, in line with an earlier Massachusetts ruling, were to be preserved *in perpetuum*. Modernized for spelling and punctuation but otherwise unchanged, these fascinating documents take us into the inmost recesses of Salem life.

A large fold-in map of Salem Village and plates showing documents and other items of special interest add to the unique value of this extraordinary work.

SALEM
WITCHCRAFT

THE TOWNSEND BISHOP HOUSE.—Vol. I., 70, 96; Vol. II., 294, 467.

Charles W. Upham.

AMERICAN CLASSICS

SALEM WITCHCRAFT

*With an Account of Salem Village
and
A History of Opinions on
Witchcraft and Kindred Subjects*

CHARLES W. UPHAM

Volume I

FREDERICK UNGAR PUBLISHING CO.
New York

Third Printing, 1966

Printed in the United States of America

Library of Congress Catalog Card No. 59-10887

DEDICATED

TO

OLIVER WENDELL HOLMES,

PROFESSOR OF ANATOMY AND PHYSIOLOGY IN
HARVARD UNIVERSITY.

CONTENTS.

VOLUME I.

VOLUME II.

PREFACE.

THIS work was originally constructed, and in previous editions appeared, in the form of Lectures. The only vestiges of that form, in its present shape, are certain modes of expression. The language retains the character of an address by a speaker to his hearers; being more familiar, direct, and personal than is ordinarily employed in the relations of an author to a reader.

The former work was prepared under circumstances which prevented a thorough investigation of the subject. Leisure and freedom from professional duties have now enabled me to prosecute the researches necessary to do justice to it.

The "Lectures on Witchcraft," published in 1831, have long been out of print. Although frequently importuned to prepare a new edition, I was unwilling to issue again what I had discovered to be an insufficient presentation of the subject. In the mean time,

it constantly became more and more apparent, that
much injury was resulting from the want of a complete and correct view of a transaction so often referred to, and universally misunderstood.

The first volume of this work contains what seems
to me necessary to prepare the reader for the second,
in which the incidents and circumstances connected
with the witchcraft prosecutions in 1692, at the village
and in the town of Salem, are reduced to chronological
order, and exhibited in detail.

As showing how far the beliefs of the understanding, the perceptions of the senses, and the delusions
of the imagination, may be confounded, the subject
belongs not only to theology and moral and political
science, but to physiology, in its original and proper
use, as embracing our whole nature; and the facts
presented may help to conclusions relating to what is
justly regarded as the great mystery of our being, —
the connection between the body and the mind.

It is unnecessary to mention the various well-known
works of authority and illustration, as they are referred to in the text. But I cannot refrain from bearing
my grateful testimony to the value of the " Collections of the Massachusetts Historical Society" and the
" New-England Historical and Genealogical Register."
The "Historical Collections" and the "Proceedings" of
the Essex Institute have afforded me inestimable assistance. Such works as these are providing the materials

that will secure to our country a history such as no
other nation can have.   Our first age will not be
shrouded in darkness and consigned to fable, but, in
all its details, brought within the realm of knowledge.
Every person who desires to preserve the memory of
his ancestors, and appreciate the elements of our institutions and civilization, ought to place these works,
and others like them, on the shelves of his library, in
an unbroken and continuing series.   A debt of gratitude is due to the earnest, laborious, and disinterested
students who are contributing the results of their
explorations to the treasures of antiquarian and genealogical learning which accumulate in these publications.

A source of investigation, especially indispensable
in the preparation of the present work, deserves to
be particularly noticed.   In 1647, the General Court
of Massachusetts provided by law for the taking of
testimony, in all cases, under certain regulations, in
the form of depositions, to be preserved *in perpetuam
rei memoriam*.   The evidence of witnesses was prepared
in writing, beforehand, to be used at the trials; they
to be present at the time, to meet further inquiry, if
living within ten miles, and not unavoidably prevented.
In a capital case, the presence of the witness, as well
as his written testimony, was absolutely required.
These depositions were lodged in the files, and constitute the most valuable materials of history.   In our

day, the statements of witnesses ordinarily live only in the memory of persons present at the trials, and are soon lost in oblivion. In cases attracting unusual interest, stenographers are employed to furnish them to the press. There were no newspaper reporters or " court calendars" in the early colonial times; but these depositions more than supply their place. Given in, as they were, in all sorts of cases, — of wills, contracts, boundaries and encroachments, assault and battery, slander, larceny, &c., they let us into the interior, the very inmost recesses, of life and society in all their forms. The extent to which, by the aid of WILLIAM P. UPHAM, Esq., of Salem, I have drawn from this source is apparent at every page.

A word is necessary to be said relating to the originals of the documents that belong to the witchcraft proceedings. They were probably all deposited at the time in the clerk's office of Essex County. A considerable number of them were, from some cause, transferred to the State archives, and have been carefully preserved. Of the residue, a very large proportion have been abstracted from time to time by unauthorized hands, and many, it is feared, destroyed or otherwise lost. Two very valuable parcels have found their way into the libraries of the Massachusetts Historical Society and the Essex Institute, where they are faithfully secured. A few others have come to light among papers in the possession of individuals. It is to be hoped, that, if any more should be found, they will be lodged in some public institution; so that, if thought best, they may all be collected, arranged, and placed beyond wear, tear, and loss, in the perpetual custody of type.

The papers remaining in the office of the clerk of this county were transcribed into a volume a few years since; the copyist supplying, conjecturally, headings to the several documents. Although he executed his work in an elegant manner, and succeeded in giving correctly many documents hard to be deciphered, such errors, owing to the condition of the papers, occurred in arranging them, transcribing their contents, and framing their headings, that I have had to resort to the originals throughout.

As the object of this work is to give to the reader of the present day an intelligible view of a transaction of the past, and not to illustrate any thing else than the said transaction, no attempt has been made to preserve the orthography of that period. Most of the original papers were written without any expectation that they would ever be submitted to inspection in print; many of them by plain country people, without skill in the structure of sentences, or regard to spelling; which, in truth, was then quite unsettled. It is no uncommon thing to find the same word spelled differently in the same document. It is very questionable whether it is expedient or just to perpetuate blemishes, often the result of haste or carelessness, arising from mere inadvertence. In some instances, where the interest of the passage seemed to require it, the antique style is preserved. In no case is a word changed or the structure altered; but the now received spelling is generally adopted, and the punctuation made to express the original sense.

It is indeed necessary, in what claims to be an exact reprint of an old work, to imitate its orthography precisely, even at the expense of difficulty in apprehending at once the meaning, and of perpetuating errors of carelessness and ignorance. Such modern reproductions are valuable, and have an interest of their own. They deserve the favor of all who desire to examine critically, and in the most authentic form, publications of which the original copies are rare, and the earliest editions exhausted. The enlightened and enterprising publishers who are thus providing facsimiles of old books and important documents of past ages ought to be encouraged and rewarded by a generous public. But the present work does not belong to that class, or make any pretensions of that kind.

My thanks are especially due to the Hon. ASAHEL HUNTINGTON, clerk of the courts in Essex County, for his kindness in facilitating the use of the materials in his office; to the Hon. OLIVER WARNER, secretary of the Commonwealth, and the officers of his department; and to STEPHEN N. GIFFORD, Esq., clerk of the Senate.

DAVID PULSIFER, Esq., in the office of the Secretary of State, is well known for his pre-eminent skill and experience in mastering the chirography of the primitive colonial times, and elucidating its peculiarities. He has been unwearied in his labors, and most earnest in his efforts, to serve me.

Mr. SAMUEL G. DRAKE, who has so largely illustrated our history and explored its sources, has, by spontaneous and considerate acts of courtesy rendered me important help. Similar expressions of friendly interest by Mr. WILLIAM B. TOWNE, of Brookline, Mass.; Hon. J. HAMMOND TRUMBULL, of Hartford, Conn.; and GEORGE H. MOORE, Esq., of New-York City, — are gratefully acknowledged.

SAMUEL P. FOWLER, Esq., of Danvers, generously placed at my disposal his valuable stores of knowledge relating to the subject. The officers in charge of the original papers, in the Historical Society and the Essex Institute, have allowed me to examine and use them.

I cordially express my acknowledgments to the Hon. BENJAMIN F. BROWNE, of Salem, who, retired from public life and the cares of business, is giving the leisure of his venerable years to the collection, preservation, and liberal contribution of an unequalled amount of knowledge respecting our local antiquities.

CHARLES W. PALFRAY, Esq., while attending the General Court as a Representative of Salem, in 1866,

gave me the great benefit of his explorations among
the records and papers in the State House.

Mr. MOSES PRINCE, of Danvers Centre, is an embodi-
ment of the history, genealogy, and traditions of that
locality, and has taken an active and zealous interest
in the preparation of this work. ANDREW NICHOLS,
Esq., of Danvers, and the family of the late Colonel
PERLEY PUTNAM, of Salem, also rendered me much
aid.

I am indebted to CHARLES DAVIS, Esq., of Beverly,
for the use of the record-book of the church, composed of " the brethren and sisters belonging to Bass
River," gathered Sept. 20, 1667, now the First
Church of Beverly; and to JAMES HILL, Esq., town-
clerk of that place, for access to the records in his
charge.

To GILBERT TAPLEY, Esq., chairman of the committee of the parish, and AUGUSTUS MUDGE, Esq., its
clerk, and to the Rev. Mr. RICE, pastor of the church,
at Danvers Centre, I cannot adequately express my
obligations. Without the free use of the original
parish and church record-books with which they intrusted me, and having them constantly at hand, I
could not have begun adequately to tell the story of
Salem Village or the Witchcraft Delusion.

C. W. U.

MAP AND ILLUSTRATIONS.

THE map, based upon various local maps and the Coast-Survey chart, is the result of much personal exploration and perambulation of the ground. It may claim to be a very exact representation of many of the original grants and farms. The locality of the houses, mills, and bridges, in 1692, is given in some cases precisely, and in all with near approximation. The task has been a difficult one. An original plot of Governor Endicott's Ipswich River grant, No. III., is in the State House, and one of the Swinnerton grant, No. XIX., in the Salem town-books. Neither of them, however, affords elements by which to establish its exact location. A plot of the Townsend Bishop grant, No. XX., as its boundaries were finally determined, is in the State House, and another of the same in the court-files of the county. This gives one fixed and known point, Hadlock's Bridge, from which, following the lines by points of compass and distances, as indicated on the plot and described in the Colonial Records, all the sides of the grant are laid out with accuracy, and its place on the map determined with absolute certainty. A very perfect and scientifically executed plan of a part of the boundary between Salem and Reading in

1666 is in the State House; of which an exact tracing was kindly furnished by Mr. H. J. COOLIDGE, of the Secretary of State's office. It gives two of the sides of the Governor Bellingham grant, No. IV., in such a manner as to afford the means of projecting it with entire certainty, and fixing its locality. There are no other plots of original or early grants or farms on this territory; but, starting from the Bishop and Bellingham grants thus laid out in their respective places, by a collation of deeds of conveyance and partition on record, with the aid of portions of the primitive stone-walls still remaining, and measurements resting on permanent objects, the entire region has been reduced to a demarkation comprehending the whole area. The locations of then-existing roads have been obtained from tl e returns of laying-out committees, and other evidence in the records and files. The construction of the map, in all its details, is the result of the researches and labors of W. P. UPHAM.

The death-warrant is a photograph by E. R. PERKINS, of Salem. The original, among the papers on file in the office of the clerk of the courts of Essex County, having always been regarded as a great curiosity, has been subjected to constant handling, and become much obscured by dilapidation. The letters, and in some instances entire words, at the end of the lines, are worn off. To preserve it, if possible, from further injury, it has been pasted on cloth. Owing to this circumstance, and the yellowish hue to which the paper has faded, it does not take favorably by photograph; but the exactness of imitation, which can only thus be obtained with absolute certainty, is more important than any other consideration. Only so much as contains the body of the warrant, the sheriff's return, and the seal, are given.

The tattered margins are avoided, as they reveal the cloth, and impair the antique aspect of the document. The original is slowly disintegrating and wasting away, notwithstanding the efforts to preserve it; and its appearance, as seen to-day, can only be perpetuated in photograph. The warrant is reduced about one-third, and the return one-half.

The Townsend Bishop house and the outlines of Witch Hill are from sketches by O. W. H. Upham. The English house is from a drawing made on the spot by J. R. Penniman of Boston, in 1822, a few years before its demolition, for the use of which I am indebted to James Kimball, Esq., of Salem. The view of Salem Village and of the Jacobs' house are reduced, by O. W. H. Upham, from photographs by E. R. Perkins.

The map and other engravings, including the autographs, were all delineated by O. W. H. Upham.

INDEX TO THE MAP.

DWELLINGS IN 1692.

[The Map shows all the houses standing in 1692 within the bounds of Salem Village; some others in the vicinity are also given. The houses are numbered on the Map with Arabic numerals, 1, 2, 3, &c., beginning at the top, and proceeding from left to right. In the following list, against each number, is given the name of the occupant in 1692, and, in some cases, that of the recent occupant or owner of the locality is added in parenthesis.]

ABBREVIATIONS USED IN THIS LIST.

s. The same house believed to be still standing.

s.m. The same house standing within the memory of persons now living

t.r. Traces of the house remain.

c. The site given is conjectural.

1. John Willard. *c.*
2. Isaac Easty.
3. Francis Peabody. *c.*
4. Joseph Porter.
   (John Bradstreet.)
5. William Hobbs. *t.r.*
6. John Robinson.
7. William Nichols. *t.r.*
8. Bray Wilkins. *c.*
9. Aaron Way.
   (A. Batchelder.)
10. Thomas Bailey.
11. Thomas Fuller, Sr.
    (Abijah Fuller.)
12. William Way.
13. Francis Elliot. *c.*
14. Jonathan Knight. *c.*
15. Thomas Cave.
    (Jonathan Berry.)
16. Philip Knight.
    (J. D. Andrews.)
17. Isaac Burton.
18. John Nichols, Jr.
    (Jonathan Perry and Aaron Jenkins.) *s.*
19. Humphrey Case. *t.r.*

20. Thomas Fuller, Jr.
    (J. A. Esty.) *s.*
21. Jacob Fuller.
22. Benjamin Fuller.
23. Deacon Edward Putnam. *s.m.*
24. Sergeant Thomas Putnam.
    (Moses Perkins.) *s.*
25. Peter Prescot.
    (Daniel Towne.)
26. Ezekiel Cheever.
    (Chas. P. Preston.) *s.m.*
27. Eleazer Putnam.
    (John Preston.) *s.m.*
28. Henry Kenny.
29. John Martin.
    (Edward Wyatt.)
30. John Dale.
    (Philip H. Wentworth.)
31. Joseph Prince.
    (Philip H. Wentworth.)
32. Joseph Putnam.
    (S. Clark.) *s.*
33. John Putnam 3d.
34. Benjamin Putnam.
35. Daniel Andrew.
    (Joel Wilkins.)

36. John Leach, Jr. *c.*
37. John Putnam, Jr.
    (Charles Peabody.)
38. Joshua Rea.
    (Francis Dodge.) *s.*
39. Mary, wid. of Thos. Putnam.
    (William R. Putnam.) *s.*
    [Birthplace of Gen. Israel Put-
    nam. Gen. Putnam also
    lived in a house, the cellar
    and well of which are still
    visible, about one hundred
    rods north of this, and just
    west of the present dwell-
    ing of Andrew Nichols.]
40. Alexander Osburn and James
    Prince.
    (Stephen Driver.) *s.*
41. Jonathan Putnam.
    (Nath. Boardman.) *s.*
42. George Jacobs, Jr.
43. Peter Cloyse. *t.r.*
44. William Small. *s.m.*
45. John Darling.
    (George Peabody.) *s.m.*
46. James Putnam.
    (Wm. A. Lander.) *s.m.*
47. Capt. John Putnam.
    (Wm. A. Lander.)
48. Daniel Rea.
    (Augustus Fowler.) *s.*
49. Henry Brown.
50. John Hutchinson.
    (George Peabody.) *t.r.*
51. Joseph Whipple. *s.m.*
52. Benjamin Porter.
    (Joseph S. Cabot.)
53. Joseph Herrick.
    (R. P. Waters.)
54. John Phelps. *c.*
55. George Flint. *c.*
56. Ruth Sibley. *s.m.*
57. John Buxton.
58. William Allin.
59. Samuel Brabrook. *c.*
60. James Smith.
61. Samuel Sibley. *t.r.*
62. Rev. James Bayley.
    (Benjamin Hutchinson.)
63. John Shepherd.
    (Rev. M. P. Braman.)
64. John Flint.
65. John Rea. *s.m.*
66. Joshua Rea.
    (Adam Nesmith.) *s.m.*
67. Jeremiah Watts.
68. Edward Bishop, the sawyer.
    (Josiah Trask.)

69. Edward Bishop, husbandman.
70. Capt. Thomas Rayment.
71. Joseph Hutchinson, Jr.
    (Job Hutchinson.)
72. William Buckley.
73. Joseph Houlton, Jr. *t.r.*
74. Thomas Haines.
    (Elijah Pope.) *s.*
75. John Houlton.
    (F. A. Wilkins.) *s.*
76. Joseph Houlton, Sr.
    (Isaac Demsey.)
77. Joseph Hutchinson, Sr. *t.r.*
78. John Hadlock.
    (Saml. P. Nourse.) *s.m.*
79. Nathaniel Putnam.
    (Judge Putnam.) *t.r.*
80. Israel Porter. *s.m.*
81. James Kettle.
82. Royal Side Schoolhouse.
83. Dr. William Griggs.
84. John Trask.
    (I. Trask.) *s.*
85. Cornelius Baker.
86. Exercise Conant.
    (Subsequently, Rev. John
    Chipman.)
87. Deacon Peter Woodberry. *t.r.*
88. John Rayment, Sr.
    (Col. J. W. Raymond.)
89. Joseph Swinnerton.
    (Nathl. Pope.)
90. Benjamin Hutchinson. *s.m.*
91. Job Swinnerton.
    (Amos Cross.)
92. Henry Houlton.)
    (Artemas Wilson.)
93. Sarah, widow of Benjamin
    Houlton.
    (Judge Houlton.) *s.*
94. Samuel Rea.
95. Francis Nurse.
    (Orin Putnam.) *s.*
96. Samuel Nurse.
    (E. G. Hyde.) *s.*
97. John Tarbell. *s.*
98. Thomas Preston.
99. Jacob Barney.
100. Sergeant John Leach, Sr.
     (George Southwick.) *s.m.*
101. Capt. John Dodge, Jr.
     (Charles Davis.) *t.r.*
102. Henry Herrick.
     (Nathl. Porter.)
     [This had been the homestead
     of his father, Henry Her-
     rick.]

103. Lot Conant.
    [This was the homestead of his father, Roger Conant.]
104. Benjamin Balch, Sr.
    (Azor Dodge.) *s.*
    [This was the homestead of his father, John Balch.]
105. Thomas Gage.
    (Charles Davis.) *s.*
106. Families of Trask, Grover, Haskell, and Elliott.
107. Rev. John Hale.
108. Dorcas, widow of William Hoar.
109. William and Samuel Upton. *c.*
110. Abraham and John Smith.
    (J. Smith.) *s.*
    [This had been the homestead of Robert Goodell.]
111. Isaac Goodell.
    (Perley Goodale.)
112. Abraham Walcot.
    (Jasper Pope.) *s. m.*
113. Zachariah Goodell.
    (Jasper Pope.)
114. Samuel Abbey.
115. John Walcot.
116. Jasper Swinnerton. *s. m.*
117. John Weldon. Captain Samuel Gardner's farm.
    (Asa Gardner.)
118. Gertrude, widow of Joseph Pope.
    (Rev. Willard Spaulding.) *s.m.*
119. Capt. Thomas Flint. *s.*
120. Joseph Flint. *s.*
121. Isaac Needham. *c.*
122. The widow Sheldon and her daughter Susannah.
123. Walter Phillips.
    (F. Peabody, Jr.)

124. Samuel Endicott. *s.m.*
125. Families of Creasy, King, Batchelder, and Howard.
126. John Green.
    (J. Green) *s.*
127. John Parker.
128. Giles Corey. *t.r.*
129. Henry Crosby.
130. Anthony Needham, Jr.
    (E. and J. S. Needham.)
131. Anthony Needham, Sr.
132. Nathaniel Felton.
    (Nathaniel Felton.) *s.*
133. James Houlton.
    (Thorndike Procter.)
134. John Felton.
135. Sarah Phillips.
136. Benjamin Scarlett.
    (District Schoolhouse No. 6.)
137. Benjamin Pope.
138. Robert Moulton.
    (T. Taylor.) *c.*
139. John Procter.
140. Daniel Epps. *c.*
141. Joseph Buxton. *c.*
142. George Jacobs, Sr.
    (Allen Jacobs.) *s.*
143. William Shaw.
144. Alice, widow of Michael Shaflin.
    (J. King.)
145. Families of Buffington, Stone, and Southwick.
146. William Osborne.
147. Families of Very, Gould, Follet, and Meacham.

+   Nathaniel Ingersoll.
¶   Rev. Samuel Parris. *t.r.*
☐   Captain Jonathan Walcot. *t.r.*

TOWN OF SALEM.

[For the sites of the following dwellings, &c., referred to in the book, see the small capitals in the lower right-hand corner of the Map.]

A. Jonathan Corwin.
B. Samuel Shattock, John Cook, Isaac Sterns, John Bly.
C. Bartholomew Gedney.
D. Stephen Sewall.
E. Court House.
F. Rev. Nicholas Noyes.
G. John Hathorne.
H. George Corwin, High-sheriff.
I. Bridget Bishop.
J. Meeting-house.
K. Gedney's "Ship Tavern."
L. The Prison.
M. Samuel Beadle.
N. Rev. John Higginson.
O. Ann Pudeator, John Best.
P. Capt. John Higginson.
Q. The Town Common.
R. John Robinson.
S. Christopher Babbage.
T. Thomas Beadle.
U. Philip English.
W. Place of execution, "Witch Hill."

GRANTS.

NOTE. — The grants are numbered on the Map with Roman numerals, the bounds being indicated by broken lines. They were all granted by the town of Salem, unless otherwise stated.

I. JOHN GOULD.

Sold by him to Capt. George Corwin, March 29, 1674; and by Capt. Corwin's widow sold to Philip Knight, Thomas Wilkins, Sr., Henry Wilkins, and John Willard, March 1, 1690.

II. ZACCHEUS GOULD.

Sold by him to Capt. John Putnam before 1662; owned in 1692 by Capt. Putnam, Thomas Cave, Francis Elliot, John Nichols, Jr., Thomas Nichols, and William Way.

The above, together, comprised land granted by the General Court to Rowley, May 31, 1652, and laid out by Rowley to John and Zaccheus Gould.

III. Gov. John Endicott.

Ipswich-river Farm, 550 acres, granted by the General Court, Nov. 5, 1639; owned in 1692 by his grandsons, Zerubbabel, Benjamin, and Joseph.

The General Court, Oct. 14, 1651, also granted to Gov. Endicott 300 acres on the southerly side of this farm, in "Blind Hole," on condition that he would set up copper-works. As the land appears afterwards to have been owned by John Porter, it is probable that the copper-mine was soon abandoned; but traces of it are still to be seen there.

IV. Gov. Richard Bellingham.

Granted by the General Court, Nov. 5, 1639.

V. Farmer John Porter.

Owned in 1692 by his son, Benjamin Porter. This includes a grant to Townsend Bishop, sold to John Porter in 1648; also 200 acres granted to John Porter, Sept. 30, 1647. That part in Topsfield was released by Topsfield to Benjamin Porter, May 2, 1687.

VI. Capt. Richard Davenport.

Granted Feb. 20, 1637, and Nov. 26, 1638; sold, with the Hathorne farm, to John Putnam, John Hathorne, Richard Hutchinson, and Daniel Rea, April 17, 1662.

VII. Capt. William Hathorne.

Granted Feb. 17, 1637; sold with the above.

VIII. John Putnam the Elder.

This comprises a grant of 100 acres to John Putnam, Jan. 20, 1641; 80 acres to Ralph Fogg, in 1636; 40 acres (formerly Richard Waterman's) to Thomas Lothrop, Nov. 29, 1642; and 30 acres to Ann Scarlett, in 1636. The whole owned by James and Jonathan Putnam in 1692.

IX. Daniel Rea.

Granted to him in 1636; owned by his grandson, Daniel Rea, in 1692.

X. Rev. Hugh Peters.

Granted Nov. 12, 1638; laid out June 15, 1674, being then in the possession of Capt. John Corwin; sold by Mrs. Margaret Corwin to Henry Brown, May 22, 1693.

XI. Capt. George Corwin.

Granted Aug. 21, 1648; sold (including 30 acres formerly John Bridgman's) to Job Swinnerton, Jr., and William Cantlebury, Jan. 18, 1661.

XII. Richard Hutchinson, John Thorndike, and Mr. Freeman.

Granted in 1636 and 1637; owned in 1692 by Joseph, son of Richard Hutchinson, and by Sarah, wife of Joseph Whipple, daughter of John, and grand-daughter of Richard Hutchinson.

XIII. Samuel Sharpe.

Granted Jan. 23, 1637; sold to John Porter, May 10, 1643; owned by his son, Israel Porter, in 1692.

XIV. John Holgrave.

Granted Nov. 26, 1638; sold to Jeffry Massey and Nicholas Woodberry, April 2, 1652; and to Joshua Rea, Jan. 1, 1657.

XV. William Alford.

Granted in 1636; sold to Henry Herrick before 1653.

XVI. Francis Weston.

Granted in 1636; sold by John Pease to Richard Ingersoll and William Haynes, in 1644.

XVII. Elias Stileman.

Granted in 1636; sold to Richard Hutchinson, June 1, 1648.

XVIII. Robert Goodell.

504 acres laid out to him, Feb. 13, 1652: comprising 40 acres granted to him "long since," and other parcels bought by him of the original grantees; viz., Joseph Grafton, John Sanders, Henry Herrick, William Bound, Robert Pease and his brother, Robert Cotta, William Walcott, Edmund Marshall, Thomas Antrum, Michael Shaflin, Thomas Venner, John Barber, Philemon Dickenson, and William Goose.

XIX. Job Swinnerton.

300 acres laid out, Jan. 5, 1697, to Job Swinnerton, Jr.; having been owned by his father, by grant and purchase, as early as 1650.

XX. Townsend Bishop.

Granted Jan. 11, 1636; sold to Francis Nurse, April 29, 1678.

XXI. Rev. Samuel Skelton.

Granted by the General Court, July 3, 1632; sold to John Porter, March 8, 1649; owned by the heirs of John Porter in 1692.

XXII. John Winthrop, Jr.

Granted June 25, 1638; sold by his daughter to John Green, Aug. 9, 1683.

XXIII. Rev. Edward Norris.

Granted Jan. 21, 1640: sold to Elleanor Trusler, Aug. 7, 1654; to Joseph Pope, July 18, 1664.

XXIV. Robert Cole.

Granted Dec. 21, 1635; sold to Emanuel Downing before July 16th, 1638; conveyed by him to John and Adam Winthrop, in trust for himself and wife during their lives, and then for his son, George Downing, July 23, 1644; leased to John Procter in 1666; occupied by him and his son Benjamin in 1692.

XXV. Col. Thomas Reed.

Granted Feb. 16, 1636; sold to Daniel Epps, June 28, 1701, by Wait Winthrop, as attorney to Samuel Reed, only son and heir of Thomas Reed.

XXVI. John Humphrey.

Granted by the General Court, Nov. 7, 1632, May 6, 1635, and March 12, 1638, 1,500 acres, part in Salem and part in Lynn; sold, on execution, to Robert Saltonstall, Dec. 6, 1642, and by him sold to Stephen Winthrop, June 7, 1645, whose daughters — Margaret Willie and Judith Hancock — owned it in 1692: that part within the bounds of Salem is given in the Map according to the report of a committee, July 11, 1695.

Orchard Farm.

Granted by the General Court to Gov. Endicott; owned by his grandsons, John and Samuel, in 1692.

The Governor's Plain.

Granted to Gov. Endicott, Jan. 27, 1637, Dec. 23, 1639, and Feb. 5, 1644; including land granted under the name of " small lots."

Johnson's Plain.

Granted to Francis Johnson, Jan. 23, 1637.

FARMS.

[The bounds of farms are indicated by dotted lines, except where they coincide with the bounds of grants. The following are those given on the Map.]

1st, Between grants No. XI. and VII., and extending north of the Village bounds, and south as far as Andover Road, — about 500 acres; bought by Thomas and Nathaniel Putnam of Philip Cromwell, Walter Price and Thomas Cole, Jeffry Massey, John Reaves, Joseph and John Gardner, and Giles Corey; owned, in 1692, by Edward Putnam, Thomas Putnam, and John Putnam, Jr. This includes also 50 acres granted to Nathaniel Putnam, Nov. 19, 1649.

2d, At the northerly end of Grant No. VII., and extending north of the Village bounds, — 100 acres, known as the "Ruck Farm;" granted to Thomas Ruck, May 27, 1654, and sold to Philip Knight and Thomas Cave, July 24, 1672.

3d, North of the "Ruck Farm," — 100 acres; sold by William Robinson to Richard Richards and William Hobbs, Jan. 1, 1660, and owned, in 1692, by William Hobbs and John Robinson.

4th, Next east, bounded northeast by Nichols Brook, and extending within the Village bounds, — 200 acres; granted to Henry Bartholomew, and sold by him to William Nichols before 1652.

5th, East of the "Ruck Farm," and extending across the Village bounds, — about 150 acres; granted to John Putnam and Richard Graves. Part of this was sold by John Putnam to Capt. Thomas Lothrop, June 2, 1669, and was owned by Ezekiel Cheever in 1692: the rest was owned by John Putnam.

6th, East of the above, and south of the Nichols Farm, — 60 acres, owned by Henry Kenny; also 50 acres granted to Job Swinnerton, given by him to his son, Dr. John Swinnerton, and sold to John Martin and John Dale, March 20, 1693.

7th, South of the above, and east of Grant No. VII., — 150 acres; granted to William Pester, July 16, 1638, and sold by Capt. William Trask to Robert Prince, Dec. 20, 1655.

8th, East of Grant No. VI., and extending north to Smith's Hill and south to Grant No. IX., — about 400 acres; granted to Allen Kenniston, John Porter, and Thomas Smith, and owned, in 1692, by Daniel Andrew and Peter Cloyse.

9th, East and southeast of Smith's Hill, — 500 acres; granted to Emanuel Downing in 1638 and 1649, and sold by him to John Porter, April 15, 1650. John Porter gave this farm to his son Joseph, upon his marriage with Anna daughter of William Hathorne.

10th, East of Frost-fish River, including the northerly end of Leach's Hill, and extending across Ipswich Road, — about 250 acres, known as the "Barney Farm;" originally granted to Richard Ingersoll, Jacob Barney, and Pascha Foote.

11th, South of the "Barney Farm," — about 200 acres; granted to Lawrence, Richard, and John Leach; owned, in 1692, by John Leach.

12th, North of the "Barney Farm," and between grants No. XIII. and XIV., — about 250 acres, known as "Gott's Corner;" granted to Charles Gott, Jeffry Massey, Thomas Watson, John Pickard, and Jacob Barney, and by them sold to John Porter. (Recently known as the "Burley Farm.")

13th, Eastward of the "Barney Farm," — 40 acres; originally granted to George Harris, and afterwards to Osmond Trask; owned, in 1692, by his son, John Trask.

14th, Next east, and extending across Ipswich Road, — 40 acres; granted to Edward Bishop, Dec. 28, 1646; owned, in 1692, by his son, Edward Bishop, "the sawyer."

15th, At the northwest end of Felton's Hill, and extending across the Village line, — about 60 acres; owned by Nathaniel Putnam.

16th, Southeast of Grant No. XXIII., — a farm of about 150 acres; owned by Giles Corey, including 50 acres bought by him of Robert Goodell, March 15, 1660, and 50 acres bought by him of Ezra and Nathaniel Clapp, of Dorchester, heirs of John Alderman, July 4, 1663.

17th, Northeast of the above, — 150 acres granted to Mrs. Anna Higginson in 1636; sold by Rev. John Higginson to John Pickering, March 23, 1652; and by him to John Woody and Thomas Flint, Oct. 18, 1654; owned in 1692 by Thomas and Joseph Flint.

GENERAL INDEX.

Orchard Farm, 24, 87.
Orne, John, 57.
Osborne, Hannah, ii. 272.
Osborne, William, 152, 227; ii. 272.
Osburn, Alexander, ii. 18.
Osburn, John, ii. 19.
Osburn, Sarah, ii. 11, 17; examination, 20; death, 32.
Osgood, Mary, ii. 349, 404, 406.
Osgood, William, 432.

P.

Page, Abraham, 139.
Paine, Elizabeth, ii. 208.
Paine, Stephen, ii. 208.
Paine, Robert, 423; ii. 449.
Palfrey, Peter, 63, 129.
Palfrey, John G., 125.
Palisadoes, 31.
Parker, Alice, ii. 179–185; trial and execution, 324.
Parker, John, ii. 179, 181.
Parker, John, 189; ii. 38, 48, 124.
Parker, Mary, trial and execution, ii. 324, 325, 480.
Parris, Elizabeth, ii. 3.
Parris, Samuel, 170, 172, 278; autograph, 280, 286–320; ii. 1, 7, 9, 25, 31, 43, 49, 55, 92, 275, 290, 485–503, 515, 545–553.
Parris, Thomas, 286; ii. 499.
Parsonage of Salem Village, 243, 386; ii. 74, 466, 493.
Parsons, Hugh, 419.
Parsons, Mary, 418.
Partridge, John, ii. 150.
Payson, Edward, ii. 218, 494, 553.
Peabody, John, ii. 475.
Peach, Barnard, ii. 414.
Pease, Robert, ii. 208.
Peele, William, ii. 267.
Peine forte et dure, ii. 338, 484.
Peirce, Joseph, 123.
Pendleton, Bryan, 256.
Penn, William, 414.
Perkins, Isaac, ii. 306.
Perkins, Nathaniel, ii. 306.
Perkins, Thomas, ii. 475.
Perkins, William, 362.
Perley, Samuel, ii. 216.
Perley, Thomas, ii. 475.
Peters, Elizabeth, 50–53, 57.
Peters, Hugh, 47, 50, 51–59.
Pettingell, Richard, 40.
Phelps, Henry, 237.
Phelps, John, 187.

Phips, Sir William, 131, 451; ii. 99, 250; autograph, 314, 345.
Phips, Spencer, ii. 482.
Phillips, Margaret, ii. 272.
Phillips, Samuel, 299; ii. 218, 494, 553.
Phillips, Tabitha, ii. 272.
Phillips, Walter, ii. 272.
Pickering, John, 46.
Pickering, Timothy, 46, 227.
Pierpont, James, 384.
Pike, John, ii. 226, 229.
Pike, Robert, ii. 226, 228, 250, 449, 538–544.
Pikeworth, 123; ii. 329.
Pitcher, Moll, ii. 521.
Pit-saw, 191.
Poindexter, ii. 185.
Poland, James, 188.
Pope, Gertrude, 236.
Pope, Joseph, 237, 238; ii. 65, 496.
Pope Innocent VIII., 342.
Porter, Benjamin, 141.
Porter, Elizabeth, ii. 272.
Porter, Israel, 141; ii. 59, 272, 550.
Porter, John, 40, 136.
Porter, John, Jr., 219.
Porter, John, ii. 207.
Porter, Joseph, 270, 296, 319.
Porter, Moses, 223, 230.
Post, Hannah, ii. 349.
Post, Mary, ii. 349, 480.
Powell, Caleb, 439.
Pratt, Francis, 428.
Prescott, Peter, 129, 316; ii. 153.
Preston, Thomas, 80, 91; ii. 11, 57, 496, 550.
Price, Walter, 226.
Prince, James, ii. 17.
Prince, Joseph, ii. 17.
Prince, Robert, ii. 17.
Prison, ii. 254.
Procter, Benjamin, ii. 207.
Procter, Elizabeth, arrest and examination, ii. 101–111; trial and condemnation, 296, 312, 466.
Procter, John, 179, 184, 227; ii. 4, 106, 111; trial and execution, 296, 304–312; autograph, 313, 458, 480.
Procter, Joseph, ii. 306.
Procter, Sarah, ii. 207.
Procter, William, ii. 208, 311.
Procter's Corner, 49.
Pronunciation, ii. 233.
Pudeator, Ann, ii. 179, 185, 300; trial and execution, 324, 329.
Pudeator, Jacob, ii. 185, 329.
Puppets, 408, ii. 12, 266.

T.

SALEM VILLAGE.

INTRODUCTION.

———◆———

IT is one of the distinguishing characteristics of the human being, that he loves to contemplate the scenes of the past, and desires to have his own history borne down to the future. This, like all the other propensities of our nature, is accompanied by faculties to secure its gratification. The gift of speech, by which the parent can convey information to the child — the old transmit intelligence to the young — is an indication that it is the design of the Author of our being that we should receive from those passing away the narrative of their experience, and communicate the results of our own to the generations that succeed us. All nations have, to a greater or less degree, been faithful to their trust in using the gift to fulfil the design of the Giver. It is impossible to name a people who do not possess cherished traditions that have descended from their early ancestors.

Although it is generally considered that the invention of a system of arbitrary and external signs to communicate thought is one of the greatest and most

arduous achievements of human ingenuity, yet so
universal is the disposition to make future generations
acquainted with our condition and history,—a disposition the efficient cause of which can only be found
in a sense of the value of such knowledge,—that you
can scarcely find a people on the face of the globe, who
have not contrived, by some means or other, from the
rude monument of shapeless rock to the most perfect alphabetical language, to communicate with posterity; thus declaring, as with the voice of Nature
herself, that it is desirable and proper that all men
should know as much as possible of the character,
actions, and fortunes of their predecessors on the stage
of life.

It is not difficult to discern the end for which this
disposition to preserve for the future and contemplate
the past was imparted to us. If all that we knew
were what is taught by our individual experience, our
minds would have but little, comparatively, to exercise
and expand them, and our characters would be the result of the limited influences embraced within the
narrow sphere of our particular and immediate relations and circumstances. But, as our notice is extended in the observation of those who have lived
before us, our materials for reflection and sources of
instruction are multiplied. The virtues we admire in
our ancestors not only adorn and dignify their names,
but win us to their imitation. Their prosperity and
happiness spread abroad a diffusive light that reaches
us, and brightens our condition. The wisdom that

guided their footsteps becomes, at the same time, a lamp to our path. The observation of the errors of their course, and of the consequent disappointments and sufferings that befell them, enables us to pass in safety through rocks and ledges on which they were shipwrecked; and, while we grieve to see them eating the bitter fruits of their own ignorance and folly as well as vices and crimes, we can seize the benefit of their experience without paying the price at which they purchased it.

In the desire which every man feels to learn the history, and be instructed by the example, of his predecessors, and in the accompanying disposition, with the means of carrying it into effect, to transmit a knowledge of himself and his own times to his successors, we discover the wise and admirable arrangement of a providence which removes the worn-out individual to a better country, but leaves the acquisitions of his mind and the benefit of his experience as an accumulating and common fund for the use of his posterity; which has secured the continued renovation of the race, without the loss of the wisdom of each generation.

These considerations suggest the true definition of history. It is the instrument by which the results of the great experiment of human action on this theatre of being are collected and transmitted from age to age. Speaking through the records of history, the generations that have gone warn and guide the generations that follow. History is the Past, teaching Philosophy to the Present, for the Future.

Since this is the true and proper design of history, it assumes an exalted station among the branches of human knowledge. Every community that aspires to become intelligent and virtuous should cherish it. Institutions for the promotion and diffusion of useful information should have special reference to it. And all people should be induced to look back to the days of their forefathers, to be warned by their errors, instructed by their wisdom, and stimulated in the career of improvement by the example of their virtues.

The historian would find a great amount and variety of materials in the annals of this old town, — greater, perhaps, than in any other of its grade in the country. But there is one chapter in our history of pre-eminent interest and importance. The witchcraft delusion of 1692 has attracted universal attention since the date of its occurrence, and will, in all coming ages, render the name of Salem notable throughout the world. Wherever the place we live in is mentioned, this memorable transaction will be found associated with it; and those who know nothing else of our history or our character will be sure to know, and tauntingly to inform us that they know, that we hanged the witches.

It is surely incumbent upon us to possess ourselves of correct and just views of a transaction thus indissolubly connected with the reputation of our home, with the memory of our fathers, and, of course, with the most precious part of the inheritance of our children. I am apprehensive that the community is very superficially acquainted with this transaction. All have heard of the Salem witchcraft; hardly any are aware of the real character of that event. Its mention creates a smile of astonishment, and perhaps a sneer of contempt, or, it may be, a thrill of horror for the innocent who suffered; but there is reason to fear, that it fails to suggest those reflections, and impart that salutary instruction, without which the design of Providence in permitting it to take place cannot be accomplished. There are, indeed, few passages in the history of any people to be compared with it in all that constitutes the pitiable and tragical, the mysterious and awful. The student of human nature will contemplate in its scenes one of the most remarkable developments which that nature ever assumed; while the moralist, the statesman, and the Christian philosopher will severally find that it opens widely before them a field fruitful in instruction.

Our ancestors have been visited with unmeasured reproach for their conduct on the occasion. Sad, indeed, was the delusion that came over them, and shocking the extent to which their bewildered imaginations and excited passions hurried and drove them on. Still, however, many considerations deserve to be well weighed before sentence is passed upon them. And while I hope to give evidence of a readiness to have every thing appear in its own just light, and to expose to view the very darkest features of the transaction, I am confident of being able to bring forward

such facts and reflections as will satisfy you that no
reproach ought to be attached to them, in consequence
of this affair, which does not belong, at least equally,
to all other nations, and to the greatest and best men
of their times and of previous ages ; and, in short,
that the final predominating sentiment their conduct
should awaken is not so much that of anger and
indignation as of pity and compassion.

Let us endeavor to carry ourselves back to the state
of the colony of Massachusetts one hundred and
seventy years ago. The persecutions our ancestors
had undergone in their own country, and the privations, altogether inconceivable by us, they suffered
during the early years of their residence here, acting
upon their minds and characters, in co-operation with
the influences of the political and ecclesiastical occurrences that marked the seventeenth century, had
imparted a gloomy, solemn, and romantic turn to
their dispositions and associations, which was transmitted without diminution to their children, strengthened and aggravated by their peculiar circumstances.
It was the triumphant age of superstition. The imagination had been expanded by credulity, until it
had reached a wild and monstrous growth. The
Puritans were always prone to subject themselves
to its influence; and New England, at the time to
which we are referring, was a most fit and congenial
theatre upon which to display its power. Cultivation
had made but a slight encroachment on the wilderness. Wide, dark, unexplored forests covered the

hills, hung over the lonely roads, and frowned upon the scattered settlements. Persons whose lives have been passed where the surface has long been opened, and the land generally cleared, little know the power of a primitive wilderness upon the mind. There is nothing more impressive than its sombre shadows and gloomy recesses. The solitary wanderer is ever and anon startled by the strange, mysterious sounds that issue from its hidden depths. The distant fall of an ancient and decayed trunk, or the tread of animals as they prowl over the mouldering branches with which the ground is strown ; the fluttering of unseen birds brushing through the foliage, or the moaning of the wind sweeping over the topmost boughs, — these all tend to excite the imagination and solemnize the mind. But the stillness of a forest is more startling and awe-inspiring than its sounds. Its silence is so deep as itself to become audible to the inner soul. It is not surprising that wooded countries have been the fruitful fountains and nurseries of superstition.

> " In such a place as this, at such an hour,
>   If ancestry can be in aught believed,
>   Descending spirits have conversed with man,
>   And told the secrets of the world unknown."

The forests which surrounded our ancestors were the abode of a mysterious race of men of strange demeanor and unascertained origin. The aspects they presented, the stories told of them, and every thing connected with them, served to awaken fear, bewilder the imagination, and aggravate the tendencies of the general condition of things to fanatical enthusiasm.

It was the common belief, sanctioned, as will appear in the course of this discussion, not by the clergy alone, but by the most learned scholars of that and the preceding ages, that the American Indians were the subjects and worshippers of the Devil, and their powwows, wizards.

In consequence of this opinion, the entire want of confidence and sympathy to which it gave rise, and the provocations naturally incident to two races of men, of dissimilar habits, feelings, and ideas, thrown into close proximity, a state of things was soon brought about which led to conflicts and wars of the most distressing and shocking character. A strongly rooted sentiment of hostility and horror became associated in the minds of the colonists with the name of Indian. There was scarcely a village where the marks of savage violence and cruelty could not be pointed out, or an individual whose family history did not contain some illustration of the stealth, the malice or the vengeance of the savage foe. In 1689, John Bishop, and Nicholas Reed a servant of Edward Putnam; and, in 1690, Godfrey Sheldon, were killed by Indians in Salem. In the year 1691, about six months previous to the commencement of the witchcraft delusion, the county of Essex was ordered to keep twenty-four scouts constantly in the field, to guard the frontiers against the savage enemy, and to give notice of his approach, then looked for every hour with the greatest alarm and apprehension.

Events soon justified the dread of Indian hostilities

felt by the people of this neighborhood. Within six years after the witchcraft delusion, incursions of the savage foe took place at various points, carrying terror to all hearts. In August, 1696, they killed or took prisoners fifteen persons at Billerica, burning many houses. In October of the same year, they came upon Newbury, and carried off and tomahawked nine persons ; all of whom perished, except a lad who survived his wounds. In 1698, they made a murderous and destructive assault upon Haverhill. The story of the capture, sufferings, and heroic achievements of Hannah Dustin, belongs to the history of this event. It stands by the side of the immortal deed of Judith, and has no other parallel in all the annals of female daring and prowess. On the 3d of July, 1706, a garrison was stormed at night in Dunstable ; and Holyoke, a son of Edward Putnam, with three other soldiers, was killed. He was twenty-two years of age. In 1708, seven hundred Algonquin and St. Francis Indians, under the command of French officers, fell again upon Haverhill about break of day, on the 29th of August ; consigned the town to conflagration and plunder ; destroyed a large amount of property ; massacred the minister Mr. Rolfe, the commander of the post Captain Wainwright, together with nearly forty others ; and carried off many into captivity. On this occasion, a troop of horse and a foot company from Salem Village rushed to the rescue ; the then minister of the parish, the Rev. Joseph Green, seized his gun and went with them. They pursued the flying Indians for some distance. So deeply were the people of Haverhill impressed by the valor and conduct of Mr. Green and his people, that they sent a letter of thanks, and desired him to come and preach to them. He complied with the invitation, spent a Sunday there, and thus gave them an opportunity to express personally their gratitude. On other occasions, he accompanied his people on similar expeditions.

These occurrences show that the fears and anxieties of the colonists in reference to Indian assaults were not without grounds at the period of the witchcraft delusion. They were, at that very time, hanging like a storm-cloud over their heads, soon to burst, and spread death and destruction among them.

There was but little communication between the several villages and settlements. To travel from Boston to Salem, for instance, which the ordinary means of conveyance enable us to do at present in less than an hour, was then the fatiguing, adventurous, and doubtful work of an entire day.

It was the darkest and most desponding period in the civil history of New England. The people, whose ruling passion then was, as it has ever since been, a love for constitutional rights, had, a few years before, been thrown into dismay by the loss of their charter, and, from that time, kept in a feverish state of anxiety respecting their future political destinies. In addition to all this, the whole sea-coast was exposed to danger : ruthless pirates were continually prowling along the shores. Commerce was nearly extinguished, and great losses had been experienced by men in business. A recent expedition against Canada had exposed the colonies to the vengeance of France.

The province was encumbered with oppressive taxes, and weighed down by a heavy debt. The sum assessed upon Salem to defray the expenses of the country at large, the year before the witchcraft prosecutions, was £1,346. 1s. Besides this, there were the town taxes. The whole amounted, no doubt, inclusive of the support of the ministry, to a weight of taxation, considering the greater value of money at that time, of which we have no experience, and can hardly form an adequate conception. The burden pressed directly upon the whole community. There were then no great private fortunes, no moneyed institutions, no considerable foreign commerce, few, if any, articles of luxury, and no large business-capitals to intercept and divert its pressure. It was borne to its whole extent by the unaided industry of a population of extremely moderate estates and very limited earnings, and almost crushed it to the earth.

The people were dissatisfied with the new charter. They were becoming the victims of political jealousies, discontent, and animosities. They had been agitated by great revolutions. They were surrounded by alarming indications of change, and their ears were constantly assailed by rumors of war. Their minds were startled and confounded by the prevalence of prophecies and forebodings of dark and dismal events. At this most unfortunate moment, and, as it were, to crown the whole and fill up the measure of their affliction and terror, it was their universal and sober belief, that the Evil One himself was, in a special manner, let loose, and permitted to descend upon them with unexampled fury.

The people of Salem participated in their full share of the gloom and despondency that pervaded the province, and, in addition to that, had their own peculiar troubles and distresses. Within a short time, the town had lost almost all its venerable fathers and leading citizens, the men whose councils had governed and whose wisdom had guided them from the first years of the settlement of the place. Only those who are intimately acquainted with the condition of a community of simple manners and primitive feelings, such as were the early New-England settlements, can have an adequate conception of the degree to which the people were attached to their patriarchs, the extent of their dependence upon them, and the amount of the loss when they were removed.

In the midst of this general distress and local gloom and depression, the great and awful tragedy, whose incidents, scenes, and characters I am to present, took place.

PART FIRST.

PART FIRST.

SALEM VILLAGE.

IT is necessary, before entering upon the subject of the witchcraft delusion, to give a particular and extended account of the immediate locality where it occurred, and of the community occupying it. This is demanded by justice to the parties concerned, and indispensable to a correct understanding of the transaction. No one, in truth, can rightly appreciate the character of the rural population of the towns first settled in Massachusetts, without tracing it to its origin, and taking into view the policy that regulated the colonization of the country at the start.

"The Governor and Company of the Massachusetts Bay in New England" possessed, by its charter from James the First, dated Nov. 3, 1620, and renewed by Charles the First, March 4, 1629, the entire sovereignty over all the territory assigned to it. Some few conditions and exceptions were incorporated in the grant, which, in the event, proved to be merely nominal. The company, so far as the crown and sovereignty of England were concerned, became absolute owner of the whole territory within its limits, and exercised its powers accordingly. It adopted wise and efficient measures to promote the settlement of the country by emigrants of the best description. It gave to every man who transported himself at his own charge fifty acres of land, and lots, in distinction from farms, to those who should choose to settle and build in towns. In 1628, Captain John Endicott, one of the original patentees, was sent over to superintend the management of affairs on the spot, and carry out the views of the company. On the 30th of April, 1629, the company, by a full and free election, chose said Endicott to be " Governor of the Plantation in the Massachusetts Bay," to hold office for one year " from the time he shall take the oath," and gave him instructions for his government. In reference to the disposal of lands, they provided that persons " who were adventurers," that is, subscribers to the common stock, to the amount of fifty pounds, should have two hundred acres of land, and, at that rate, more or less, " to the intent to build their houses, and to improve their labors thereon." Adventurers who carried families with them were to have fifty acres for each member of their respective families. Other provisions were made, on the same principles, to meet the case of servants taken over; for each of whom an additional number of acres was to be allowed. If a person should choose " to build on the plot of ground where the town is intended to be built," he was to have half an acre for every fifty pounds subscribed by him to the common stock. A general discretion was given to Endicott and his council to make grants to particular persons, " according to their charge and quality ; " having reference always to the ability of the grantee to improve his allotment. Energetic and intelligent men, having able-bodied sons or servants, even if not adventurers, were to be favorably regarded. Endicott carried out these instructions faithfully and judiciously during his brief administration. In the mean time, it had been determined to transfer the charter, and the company bodily, to New England. Upon this being settled, John Winthrop, with others, joined the company, and he was elected its governor on the 29th of October, 1629. On the 12th of June, 1630, he arrived in Salem, and held his first court at Charlestown on the 28th of August.

There was some irregularity in these proceedings. The charter fixed a certain time, " yearly, once in the year, for ever hereafter," for the election of governor, deputy-governor, and assistants. Matthew Cradock had been elected accordingly, on the 13th of May, 1629, governor of the company " for the year following." He presided at the General Court of the company when Winthrop was elected governor. There does not appear to have been any formal resignation of his office by Cradock. In point of fact, the charter made no provision for a resignation of office, but only for cases where a vacancy might be occasioned

3

by death, or removal by an act of the company. It would have been more regular for the company to have removed Cradock by a formal vote ; but the great and weighty matter in which they were engaged prevented their thinking of a mere formality. Cradock had himself conceived the project they had met to carry into effect, and labored to bring it about. He vacated the chair to his successor, on the spot. Still forgetting the provisions of the charter, they declared Winthrop elected " for the ensuing year, to begin on this present day," the 20th of October, 1629. By the language of the charter, he could only be elected to fill the vacancy " in the room or place " of Cradock ; that is, for the residue of the official year established by the express provision of that instrument, namely, until the " last Wednesday in Easter term" ensuing. All usage is in favor of this construction. The terms of the charter are explicit ; and, if persons chosen to fill vacancies during the course of a year could thus be commissioned to hold an entire year from the date of their election, the provision fixing a certain day " yearly " for the choice of officers would be utterly nullified. Whether this subsequently occurred to Winthrop and his associates is not known ; but, if it did, it was impossible for them to act in conformity to the view now given ; for, in the ensuing " last Wednesday of Easter term," he was at sea, in mid ocean, and the several members of the company dispersed throughout his fleet. When he arrived in Salem, he found Endicott — who, in the records of the company before its transfer to New England, is styled "the Governor beyond the seas"—with his year of office not yet expired. The company had not chosen another in his place, and his commission still held good. It was so evident that the vote extending the term of Winthrop's tenure to a year from the day on which he was chosen, Oct. 20, 1629, was illegal, that when that year expired, in October, 1630, no motion was made to proceed to a new election. In the mean time, however, Endicott's year had expired; and, for aught that appears, there was not, for several months, any legal governor or government at all in the colony. When the next "last Wednesday of Easter term" came round, on the 18th of May, 1631, Winthrop was chosen governor, as the record says, "according to the meaning of the patent;" and all went on smoothly afterwards. If the difficulty into which they had got was apprehended by Winthrop, Endicott, or any of their associates, they were wise enough to see that nothing but mischief could arise from taking notice of it; that no human ingenuity could disentangle the snarl; and that all they could do was to wait for the lapse of time to drift them through. The conduct of these two men on the occasion was truly admirable. Endicott welcomed Winthrop with all the honors due to his position as governor; opened his doors to receive him and his family; and manifested the affectionate respect and veneration with which, from his earliest manhood to his dying day, Winthrop ever inspired all men in all circumstances. Winthrop performed the ceremony at Endicott's marriage. They each went about his own business, and said nothing of the embarrassments attached to their official titles or powers. After a few months, Winthrop held his courts, as though all was in good shape ; and Endicott took his seat as an assistant. They proved themselves sensible, high-minded men, of true public spirit, and friends to each other and to the country, which will for ever honor them both as founders and fathers. They entered into no disputes — and their descendants never should — about which was governor, or which first governor.

The disposal of lands, at the expiration of Endicott's delegated administration, passed back into the hands of the company, and was conducted by the General Court upon the policy established at its meetings in London. On the 3d of March, 1635, the General Court relinquished the control and disposal of lands, within the limits of towns, to the towns themselves. After this, all grants of lands in Salem were made by the people of the town or their own local courts. The original land policy was faithfully adhered to here, as it probably was in the other towns.

The following is a copy of the Act : —

" Whereas particular towns have many things which concern only themselves, and the ordering of their own affairs, and disposing of businesses in their own towns, it is therefore ordered, that the freemen of any town, or the major part of them, shall only have power to dispose of their own lands and woods, with all the privileges and appurtenances of the said towns, to grant lots, and make such orders as may concern the well ordering of their own towns, not repugnant to the laws and orders here established by the General Court; as also to lay mulcts and penalties for the breach of these orders, and to levy and distress the same, not exceeding the sum of twenty shillings; also to choose their own particular officers, as constables, surveyors of the high-ways, and the like; and because much business is like to ensue to the constables of several towns, by reason they are to make distress, and gather fines, therefore that every town shall have two constables, where there is need, that so their office may not be a burthen unto them, and they may attend more carefully upon the discharge of their office, for which they shall be liable to give their accounts to this court, when they shall be called thereunto."

The reflecting student of political science will probably regard this as the most important legislative act in our annals. Towns had existed before, but were scarcely more than local designations, or convenient divisions of the people and territories. This called them into being as depositories and agents of political power in its mightiest efficacy and most vital force. It remitted to the people their original sovereignty. Before, that sovereignty had rested in the hands of a remote central deputation; this returned it to them in their primary capacity, and brought it back, in its most important elements, to their immediate control. It gave them complete possession and absolute power over their own lands, and provided the machinery for managing their own neighborhoods and making and executing their own laws in what is, after all, the greatest sphere of government, — that which concerns ordinary, daily, immediate relations. It gave to the people the power to do and determine all that the people can do and determine, by themselves. It created the towns as the solid foundation of the whole political structure of the State, trained the people as in a perpetual school for self-government, and fitted them to be the guardians of republican liberty and order.

Large tracts were granted to men who had the disposition and the means for improving them by opening roads, building bridges, clearing forests, and bringing the surface into a state for cultivation. Men of property, education, and high social position, were thus made to lead the way in developing the agricultural resources of the country, and giving character to the farming interest and class. In cases where men of energy, industry, and intelligence presented themselves, if not adventurers in the common stock, with no other property than their strong arms and resolute wills, particularly if they had able-bodied sons, liberal grants were made. Every one who had received a town lot of half an acre was allowed to relinquish it, receiving, in exchange, a country lot of fifty acres or more. Under this system, a population of a superior order was led out into the forest. Farms quickly spread into the interior, seeking the meadows, occupying the arable land, and especially following up the streams.

I propose to illustrate this by a very particular enumeration of instances, and by details that will give

us an insight of the personal, domestic, and social
elements that constituted the condition of life in the
earliest age of New England, particularly in that part
of the old township of Salem where the scene of our
story is laid.   I shall give an account of the persons
and families who first settled the region included in,
and immediately contiguous to, Salem Village, and
whose children and grandchildren were actors or suf-
ers in, or witnesses of, the witchcraft delusion.   I am
able, by the map, to show the boundaries, to some degree of precision, of their farms, and the spots on or
near which their houses stood.

The first grant of land made by the company, after
it had got fairly under way, was of six hundred acres
to Governor Winthrop, on the 6th of September, 1631,
" near his house at Mystic."   The next was to the deputy-governor, Thomas Dudley, on the 5th of June, 1632,
of two hundred acres " on the west side of Charles
River, over against the new town," now Cambridge.
The next, on the 3d of July, 1632, was three hundred
acres to John Endicott.   It is described, in the record, as " bounded on the south side with a river,
commonly called the Cow House River, on the north
side with a river, commonly called the Duck River, on
the east with a river, leading up to the two former
rivers, known by the name of Wooleston River, and on
the west with the main land."   The meaning of the
Indian word applied to this territory was " Birch-
wood."   At the period of the witchcraft delusion, and
for some time afterwards, " Cow House River " was

called "Endicott River." Subsequently it acquired
the name of "Waters River."

This grant constituted what was called "the Governor's Orchard Farm." In conformity with the policy
on which grants were made, Endicott at once proceeded to occupy and improve it, by clearing off the
woods, erecting buildings, making roads, and building
bridges. His dwelling-house embraced in its view the
whole surrounding country, with the arms of the sea.
From the more elevated points of his farm, the open
sea was in sight. A road was opened by him, from
the head of tide water on Duck, now Crane, River,
through the Orchard Farm, and round the head of Cow
House River, to the town of Salem, in one direction,
and to Lynn and Boston in another. A few years
afterwards, the town granted him two hundred acres
more, contiguous to the western line of the Orchard
Farm. After this, and as a part of the transaction,
the present Ipswich road was made, and the old
road through the Orchard Farm discontinued. This
illustrates the policy of the land grants. They were
made to persons who had the ability to lay out roads.
The present bridge over Crane River was probably
built by Endicott and the parties to whom what is now
called the Plains, one of the principal villages of Danvers, had been granted. The tract granted by the
town was popularly called the "Governor's Plain."
By giving, in this way, large tracts of land to men of
means, the country was opened and made accessible to
settlers who had no pecuniary ability to incur large

outlays in the way of general improvements, but had the requisite energy and industry to commence the work of subduing the forest and making farms for themselves. To them, smaller grants were made.

The character of the population, thus aided at the beginning in settling the country, cannot be appreciated without giving some idea of what it was to open the wilderness for occupancy and cultivation. This is a subject which those who have always lived in other than frontier towns do not perhaps understand.

How much of the land had been previously cleared by the aboriginal tribes, it may be somewhat difficult to determine. They were but slightly attached to the soil, had temporary and movable habitations, and no bulky implements or articles of furniture. They were nomadic in their habits. On the coast and its inlets, their light canoes gave easy means of transportation, for their families and all that they possessed, from point to point, and, further inland, over intervening territory, from river to river. They probably seldom attempted, in this part of the country, to clear the rugged and stony uplands. In some instances, they removed the trees from the soft alluvial meadows, although it is probable that in only a very few localities they would have attempted such a persistent and laborious undertaking. There were large salt marshes, and here and there meadows, free from timber. There were spots where fires had swept over the land and the trees disappeared. On such spots they probably planted their corn; the land being made at once fertile

and easily cultivable, by the effects of the fires. Near
large inland sheets of water, having no outlets passa-
ble by their canoes, and well stocked with fish, they
sometimes had permanent plantations, as at Will's Hill.
With such slight exceptions, when the white settler
came upon his grant, he found it covered by the pri-
meval wilderness, thickly set with old trees, whose
roots, as well as branches, were interlocked firmly
with each other, the surface obstructed with tangled
and prickly underbrush; the soil broken, and mixed
with rocks and stones, — the entire face of the country hilly, rugged, and intersected by swamps and winding streams.

Among all the achievements of human labor and
perseverance recorded in history, there is none more
herculean than the opening of a New-England forest
to cultivation. The fables of antiquity are all suggest-
ive of instruction, and infold wisdom. The earliest
inhabitants of every wooded country, who subdued its
wilderness, were truly a race of giants.

Let any one try the experiment of felling and eradi-
cating a single tree, and he will begin to approach an
estimate of what the first English settler had before
him, as he entered upon his work. It was not only a
work of the utmost difficulty, calling for the greatest
possible exercise of physical toil, strength, patience,
and perseverance, but it was a work of years and generations. The axe, swung by muscular arms, could,
one by one, fell the trees. There was no machinery to
aid in extracting the tough roots, equal, often, in

size and spread, to the branches. The practice was to level by the axe a portion of the forest, managing so as to have the trees fall inward, early in the season. After the summer had passed, and the fallen timber become dried, fire would be set to the whole tract covered by it. After it had smouldered out, there would be left charred trunks and stumps. The trunks would then be drawn together, piled in heaps, and burned again. Between the blackened stumps, barley or some other grain, and probably corn, would be planted, and the lapse of years waited for, before the roots would be sufficiently decayed to enable oxen with chains to extract them. Then the rocks and stones would have to be removed, before the plough could, to any considerable extent, be applied. As late as 1637, the people of Salem voted twenty acres, to be added within two years to his previous grant, to Richard Hutchinson, upon the condition that he would, in the mean time, " set up ploughing." The meadow to the eastward of the meeting-house, seen in the head-piece of this Part, probably was the ground where ploughing was thus first " set up." The plough had undoubtedly been used before in town-lots, and by some of the old planters who had secured favorable open locations along the coves and shores ; but it required all this length of time to bring the interior country into a condition for its use.

The opening of a wilderness combined circumstances of interest which are not, perhaps, equalled in any other occupation. It is impossible to imagine a more exhilarating or invigorating employment. It developed the muscular powers more equally and effectively than any other. The handling of the axe brought into exercise every part of the manly frame. It afforded room for experience and skill, as well as strength; it was an athletic art of the highest kind, and awakened energy, enterprise, and ambition; it was accompanied with sufficient danger to invest it with interest, and demand the most careful judgment and observation. He who best knew how to fell a tree was justly looked upon as the most valuable and the leading man. To bring a tall giant of the woods to the ground was a noble and perilous achievement. As it slowly trembled and tottered to its fall, it was all-important to give it the right direction, so that, as it came down with a thundering crash, it might not be diverted from its expected course by the surrounding trees and their multifarious branches, or its trunk slide off or rebound in an unforeseen manner, scattering fragments and throwing limbs upon the choppers below. Accidents often, deaths sometimes, occurred. A skilful woodman, by a glance at the surrounding trees and their branches, could tell where the tree on which he was about to operate should fall, and bring it unerringly to the ground in the right direction. There was, moreover, danger from lurking savages; and, if the chopper was alone in the deep woods, from the prowling solitary bear, or hungry wolves, which, going in packs, were sometimes formidable. There were elements also, in the work, that awakened

the finer sentiments. The lonely and solemn woods
are God's first temples. They are full of mystic influences; they nourish the poetic nature; they feed the
imagination. The air is elastic, and every sound
reverberates in broken, strange, and inexplicable in-
tonations. The woods are impregnated with a health-
giving and delightful fragrance nowhere else experienced. All the arts of modern luxury fail to produce
an aroma like that which pervades a primitive forest
of pines and spruces. Indeed, all trees, in an original
wilderness, where they exist in every stage of growth
and decay, contribute to this peculiar charm of the
woods. It was not only a manly, but a most lively,
occupation. When many were working near each
other, the echoes of their voices of cheer, of the sharp
and ringing tones of their axes, and of the heavy con-
cussions of the falling timber, produced a music that
filled the old forests with life, and made labor joyous
and refreshing.

The length of time required to prepare a country
covered by a wilderness, on a New-England soil, for
cultivation, may be estimated by the facts I have
stated. A long lapse of years must intervene, after
the woods have been felled and their dried trunks and
branches burned, before the stumps can be extracted,
the land levelled, the stones removed, the plough introduced, or the smooth green fields, which give such
beauty to agricultural scenes, be presented. An
immense amount of the most exhausting labor must
be expended in the process. The world looks with

wonder on the dykes of Holland, the wall of China, the pyramids of Egypt. I do not hesitate to say that the results produced by the small, scattered population of the American colonies, during their first century, in tearing up a wilderness by its roots, transforming the rocks, with which the surface was covered, into walls, opening roads, building bridges, and making a rough and broken country smooth and level, converting a sterile waste into fertile fields blossoming with verdure and grains and fruitage, is a more wonderful monument of human industry and perseverance than them all. It was a work, not of mere hired laborers, still less of servile minions, but of freemen owning, or winning by their voluntary and cheerful toil, the acres on which they labored, and thus entitling themselves to be the sovereigns of the country they were creating. A few thousands of such men, with such incentives, wrought wonders greater than millions of slaves or serfs ever have accomplished, or ever will.

It was not, therefore, from mere favoritism, or a blind subserviency to men of wealth or station, that such liberal grants of land were made to Winthrop, Dudley, Endicott, and others, but for various wise and good reasons, having the welfare and happiness of the whole people, especially the poorer classes, in view. In illustration of the one now under consideration, a few facts may be presented. They will show the amount of labor required to bring the "Orchard Farm" into cultivation, and which must have been procured at a large outlay in money by the proprietor. In the court-files are many curious papers, in the shape of depositions given by witnesses in suits of various kinds, arising from time to time, showing that large numbers of hired men were kept constantly at work. Nov. 10, 1678, Edmund Grover, seventy-eight years old, testified, " that, above forty-five years since, I, this deponent, wrought much upon Governor Endicott's farm, called Orchard, and did, about that time, help to cut and cleave about seven thousand palisadoes, as I remember, and was the first that made improvement thereof, by breaking up of ground and planting of Indian-corn." The land was granted to Endicott in July, 1632; and the work in which Grover, with others, was engaged, commenced undoubtedly forthwith. Palisadoes were young trees, of about six inches in diameter at the butt, cut into poles of about ten feet in length, sharpened at the larger end, and driven into the ground; those that were split or cloven were used as rails. In this way, lots were fenced in. In some cases, the upright posts were placed close together, as palisades in fortifications, to prevent the escape of domestic animals, and as a safeguard against depredations upon the young cattle, sheep, and poultry, by bears, wolves, foxes, the loup-cervier, or wild-cat, with which the woods were infested. Grover seems to have wrought on the Orchard Farm for a short time. We find, that, a few years after the point to which his testimony goes back, he had a farm of his own. Some wrought there for a longer time, and were permanent retainers on the farm. In 1635, the widow Scarlett apprenticed her son Benjamin, then eleven years of age, to Governor Endicott. The following document, recorded in Essex Registry of Deeds, tells his story : —

" To all christian people to whom these presents shall come, I, Benjamin Scarlett of Salem, in New England, sendeth Greeting — Know ye, that I, the said Benjamin Scarlett, having lived as a servant with Mr. John Endicott, Esq, sometimes Governor in New England, and served him near upon thirty years, for, and in consideration whereof, the said Governor Endicott gave unto me, the said Benjamin Scarlett, a certain tract of land, in the year 1650, being about 10 acres, more or less, the which land hath ever since been possessed by me, the said Benjamin Scarlett, and it lyeth at the head of Cow House River, bounded on the north with the land of Mr. Endicott called Orchard Farm, on the South with the high way leading to the salt water, on the West with the road way leading to Salem, on the East with the salt water, which tract of land was given to me, as aforesaid, during my life, and in case I should leave no issue of my body, to give it to such of his posterity as I should see cause to bestow it upon; Know ye, therefore, that I, the said Benjamin Scarlett, for divers considerations me thereunto moving, have given, granted, and by these presents do give and grant, assign, sett over, and bestow the aforesaid tract of land, with all the improvements I have made thereon, both by building, fencing, or otherwise, unto Samuel Endicott, second son to Zerubabel Endicott deceased, and unto Hannah his wife, to have and to hold the said ten acres of land, more or less, with all the privileges and appurtenances thereunto belonging, unto the said Samuel

Endicott and Hannah his wife, to his and her own proper use and behoof forever; and after their decease I give the said tract of land to their son Samuel Endicott. In case he should depart this life without issue, then to be given to the next heir of the said Samuel and Hannah. — In witness whereof I have hereunto set my hand and seal. — Dated the ninth of January one thousand six hundred and ninety one. — BENJAMIN SCARLETT, his mark."

It is to be observed, that Governor Endicott had died twenty-six years, and his son Zerubabel seven years, before the date of the foregoing deed. No writings had passed between them in reference to the final disposition Scarlett was conditionally to make of the estate. There were no living witnesses of the original understanding. But the old man was true to the sentiments of honor and gratitude. The master to whom he had been apprenticed in his boyhood had been kind and generous to him, and he was faithful to the letter and spirit of his engagement. He evidently made a point to have the language of the deed as strong as it could be. He did not leave the matter to be settled by a will, but determined to enjoy, while living, the satisfaction of being true to his plighted faith. He was known, in his later years, as " old Ben Scarlett." He did not feel ashamed to call himself a servant. But humble and unpretending as he was, I feel a pride in rescuing his name from oblivion. Old Ben Scarlett will for ever hold his place among nature's nobles, — honest men.

The extent to which Endicott went in improving his

lands is shown in the particular department which gave the name to his original grant. In 1648, he bought of Captain Trask two hundred and fifty acres of land, in another locality, giving in exchange five hundred apple-trees, of three years' growth. Such a number of fruit-trees of that age, disposable at so early a period, could only be the result of a great expenditure of labor and money. So many operations going on under his direction and within his premises made his farm a school, in which large numbers were trained to every variety of knowledge needed by an original settler. The subduing of the wilderness; the breaking of the ground; the building of bridges, stone-walls, " palisadoes," houses, and barns; the processes of planting; the introduction of all suitable articles of culture; the methods best adapted to the preparation of the rugged soil for production; the rearing of abundant orchards and bountiful crops; the smoothing and levelling of lands, and the laying-out of roads, — these were all going at once, and it was quite desirable for young men to work on his farm, before going out deeper into the wilderness to make farms for themselves. There were many besides Grover who availed themselves of the advantage. John Putnam was a large landholder, and an original grantee; but we find his youngest son, John, attached to Endicott's establishment, and working on his farm about the time of his maturity. In a deposition in court, in a land case of disputed boundaries, August, 1705, " John Putnam. Sr., of full age, testifieth and saith that — being a re-

tainer in Governor Endicott's family, about fifty years
since, and being intimately acquainted with the governor himself and with his son, Mr. Zerubabel Endicott, late of Salem, deceased, who succeeded in his
father's right, and lived and died on the farm called
Orchard Farm, in Salem — the said Governor Endicott
did oftentimes tell this deponent," &c. The same
John Putnam, in a deposition dated 1678, says that
he was then fifty years old, and that, thirty-five years
before, he was at Mr. Endicott's farm, and went out to
a certain place called " Vine Cove," where he found Mr.
Endicott; and he testifies to a conversation that he
heard between Mr. Endicott and one of his men, Walter Knight. I mention these things to show that a lad
of fifteen, a son of a neighbor of large estate in lands,
was an intimate visitor at the Orchard Farm ; and that,
when he became of age, before entering upon the work
of clearing lands of his own, given by his father, he
went as " a retainer" to work on the governor's farm.
He went as a voluntary laborer, as to a school of agricultural training. This was done on other farms, first
occupied by men who had the means and the enterprise
to carry on large operations. It gave a high character, in their particular employment, to the first settlers
generally.

I cannot leave this subject of Endicott on his farm,
without presenting another picture, drawn from a wilderness scene. In 1678, Nathaniel Ingersol, then
forty-five years of age, in a deposition sworn to in
court, describes an incident that occurred on the east-

ern end of the Townsend Bishop farm as laid out on
the map, when he was about eleven years of age. His
father, Richard Ingersol, had leased the farm. It was
contiguous to Endicott's land, and controversies of
boundary arose, which subsequently contributed to
aggravate the feuds and passions that were let loose in
the fury of the witchcraft proceedings. Nathaniel Ingersol says, —

"This deponent testifieth, that, when my father had fenced
in a parcel of land where the wolf-pits now are, the said Governor Endicott came to my father where we were at plough,
and said to my father he had fenced in some of the said Governor's land. My father replied, then he would remove
the fence. No, said Governor Endicott, let it stand; and,
when you set up a new fence, we will settle in the bounds."

This statement is worthy of being preserved, as it
illustrates the character of the two men, exhibiting
them in a most honorable light. The gentlemanly
bearing of each is quite observable. Ingersol manifests an instant willingness to repair a wrong, and set
the matter right; Endicott is considerate and obliging
on a point where men are most prone to be obstinate
and unyielding, — a conflict of land rights: both are
courteous, and disposed to accommodate. Endicott
was governor of the colony, and a large conterminous
landowner; Ingersol was a husbandman, at work
with his boys on land into which their labor had incorporated value, and with which, for the time being,
he was identified. But Endicott showed no arrogance,

and assumed no authority; Ingersol manifested no resentment or irritation. If a similar spirit had been everywhere exhibited, the good-will and harmony of neighborhoods would never have been disturbed, and the records of courts reduced to less than half their bulk.

To his dying day, John Endicott retained a lively interest in promoting the welfare of his neighbors in the vicinity of the Orchard Farm.

Father Gabriel Druillettes was sent by the Governor of Canada, in 1650, to Boston, in a diplomatic charac ter, to treat with the Government here. He kept a journal, during his visit, from which the following is an extract: " I went to Salem to speak to the Sieur Indicatt who speaks and understands French well, and is a good friend of the nation, and very desirous to have his children entertain this sentiment. Find- ing I had no money, he supplied me, and gave me an invitation to the magistrates' table." Endicott had undoubtedly received a good education. His natural force of character had been brought under the influ- ence of the knowledge prevalent in his day, and invigorated by an experience and aptitude in practical affairs. There is some evidence that he had, in early life, been a surgeon or physician.

He was a captain in the military service before leaving England. Although he was the earliest who bore the title of governor here, having been deputed to exercise that office by the governor and company in England, and subsequently elected to that station for a greater length of time than any other person in our history, had been colonel of the Essex militia, commandant of the expedition against the Indians at Block Island, and, for several years, major-general, at the head of the military forces of the colony, the title of captain was attached to him, more or less, from beginning to end; and it is a singular circumstance, that it has adhered to the name to this day. His descendants early manifested a predilection for maritime life. During the first half of the present century, many of them were shipmasters. In our foreign, particularly our East-India, navigation, the title has clung to the name; so much so, that the story is told, that, half a century ago, when American ships arrived at Sumatra or Java, the natives, on approaching or entering the vessels to ascertain the name of the captain, were accustomed to inquire, "Who is the Endicott?" The public station, rank, and influence of Governor Endicott required that he should first be mentioned, in describing the elements that went to form the character of the original agricultural population of this region.

The map shows the farm of Emanuel Downing. The lines are substantially correct, although precise accuracy cannot be claimed for them, as the points mentioned in this and other cases were marked trees, heaps of stones, or other perishable or removable objects, and no survey or plot has come down to us. A collation of conterminous grants or subsequent conveyances, with references in some of them to

permanent objects, enables us to approximate to a
pretty certain conclusion. This gentleman was one of
the most distinguished of the early New-England colonists. He was a lawyer of the Inner Temple. He
married, in the first instance, a daughter of Sir James
Ware, a person of great eminence in the learned lore
of his times. His second wife was Lucy, sister of
Governor Winthrop of Massachusetts, who was born
July 9, 1601. They were married, April 10, 1622.
There seems to have been a very strong attachment
between Emanuel Downing and his brother Winthrop;
and they went together, with their whole heart, into
the plan of building up the colony. They devoted to
it their fortunes and lives. Downing is supposed to
have arrived at Boston in August, 1638, with his family. On the 4th of November, he and his wife were
admitted to the Church at Salem. So great had been
the value of his services in behalf of the colony, in
defending its interests and watching over its welfare
before leaving England, that he was welcomed with
the utmost cordiality to his new home. His nephew,
John Winthrop, Jr., afterwards Governor of Connecticut, was associated with John Endicott to administer
to him the freeman's oath. The General Court
granted him six hundred acres of land. He was
immediately appointed a judge of the local court in
Salem, and, for many years, elected one of its two
deputies to the General Court. In anticipation of his
arrival in the country, the town of Salem, on the 16th
of July, granted him five hundred acres. He after-

wards purchased the farm on which he seems to have lived, for the most part, until he went to England in 1652. The condition of public affairs, and his own connection with them, detained him in the mother-country much of the latter part of his life. While in this colony, he was indefatigable in his exertions to secure its prosperity. His wealth and time and faculties were liberally and constantly devoted to this end.

The active part taken by Mr. Downing in the affairs of the settlement is illustrated in the following extract from the Salem town records: —

"At a general Town meeting, held the 7th day of the 5th month, 1644 — ordered that two be appointed every Lord's Day, to walk forth in the time of God's worship, to take notice of such as either lye about the meeting house, without attending to the word and ordinances, or that lye at home or in the fields without giving good account thereof. and to take the names of such persons, and to present them to the magistrates, whereby they may be accordingly proceeded against. The names of such as are ordered to this service are for the 1st day, Mr Stileman and Philip Veren Jr 2d day, Philip Veren Sr and Hilliard Veren. 3d day, Mr Batter and Joshua Veren. 4th day, Mr Johnson and Mr Clark. 5th day, Mr Downing and Robert Molton Sr 6th day, Robert Molton Jr and Richard Ingersol. 7th day, John Ingersol and. Richard Pettingell. 8th day, William Haynes and Richard Hutchinson. 9th day, John Putnam and John Hathorne. 10th day, Townsend Bishop and Daniel Rea. 11th day, John Porter and Jacob Barney."

Each patrol, on concluding its day's service, was to notify the succeeding one; and they were to start on their rounds, severally, from "Goodman Porter's near the Meeting House."

The men appointed to this service were all leading characters, reliable and energetic persons. It was a singular arrangement, and gives a vivid idea of the state of things at the time. Its design was probably, not merely that expressed in the vote of the town, but also to prevent any disorderly conduct on the part of those not attending public worship, and to give prompt alarm in case of fire or an Indian assault. The population had not then spread out far into the country; and the range of exploration did not much extend beyond the settlement in the town. None but active men, however, could have performed the duty thoroughly, and in all directions, so as to have kept the whole community under strict inspection.

Mr. Downing probably expended liberally his fortune and time in improving his farm, upon which there were, at least, four dwelling-houses prior to 1661, and large numbers of men employed. He was a ready contributor to all public objects. His education had been superior and his attainments in knowledge extensive. He was of an enlightened spirit, and strove to mitigate the severity of the procedures against Antinomians and others. He seems to have had an ingenious and enterprising mind. At a General Court held at Boston, Sept. 6, 1638, it was voted that, "Whereas Emanuel Downing, Esq., hath brought

over, at his great charges, all things fitting for taking
wild fowl by way of duck-coy, this court, being desirous to encourage him and others in such designs as
tend to the public good," &c., orders that liberty shall
be given him to set up his duck-coy within the limits
of Salem; and all persons are forbidden to molest
him in his experiments, by "shooting in any gun
within half a mile of the ponds," where, by the regulations of the town, he shall be allowed to place the
decoys. The court afterwards granted to other towns
liberty to set up duck-coys, with similar privileges.
What was the particular structure of the contrivance,
and how far it succeeded in operation, is not known;
but the thing shows the spirit of the man. He at
once took hold of his farm with energy, and gathered
workmen upon it. Winthrop in his journal has this
entry, Aug. 2, 1645: —

"M.ʳ Downing having built a new house at his farm, he
being gone to England, and his wife and family gone to the
church meeting on the Lord's day, the chimney took fire and
burned down the house, and bedding, apparel and household,
to the value of 200 pounds."

This proves that his family resided on the farm; and
it indicates, that, when he first occupied it, he had
only such a house as could have been seasonably put
up at the start, but that a more commodious one had
been erected at his leisure: the expression "having
built a new house" appears to carry this idea. On his
return from England, he undoubtedly built again, and

had other houses for his workmen and tenants; for we find that one of them, in 1648, was allowed to keep an ordinary, "as Mr. Downing's farm, on the road between Lynn and Ipswich, was a convenient place" for such an accommodation to travellers. Public travel to and from those points goes over that same road to-day. That it was so early laid out is probably owing to the fact, that such men as Emanuel Downing were on its route, and John Winthrop, Jr., at Ipswich. Downing called his farm "Groton," in dear remembrance of his wife's ancestral home in "the old country."

Originally, travel was on a track more interior. The opening of roads did not begin until after the more immediate and necessary operations of erecting houses and bringing the land, on the most available spots near them at the points first settled, under culture. Originally, communication from farm to farm, through the woods, was by marking the trees, — sometimes by burning and blackening spots on their sides, and sometimes by cutting off a piece of the bark. The traveller found his way step by step, following the trees thus marked, or "blazed," as it was called whichever method had been adopted. When the branches and brush were sufficiently cleared away, horses could be used. At places rendered difficult by large roots, partly above ground, intercepting the passage, or by rough stones, the rider would dismount, and lead the horse. From this, it was called a "bridle-path." After the way had become sufficiently opened for ox-carts or other vehicles to pass, it would begin to receive the name of a road. On reaching a cleared and fenced piece of land, the traveller would cross it, opening and closing gates, or taking down and replacing bars, as the case might be. There were arrangements among the settlers, and, before long, acts of the General Court, regulating the matter. This was the origin of what were called " press-roads," or " farm-roads," or " gate-roads." When a proprietor concluded it to be for his interest to do so, he would fence in the road on both sides where it crossed his land, and remove the gates or bars from each end. Ultimately, the road, if convenient for long travel, would be fenced in for a great distance, and become a permanent " public highway." In all these stages of progress, it would be called a " highway." The fee would remain with the several proprietors through whose lands it passed ; and, if travel should forsake it for a more eligible route, it would be discontinued, and the road-track, enclosed in the fields to which it originally belonged, be obliterated by the plough. Many of the " highways," by which the farmers passed over each other's lands to get to the meeting-house or out to public roads, in 1692, have thus disappeared, while some have hardened into permanent public roads used to this day. When thus fully and finally established, it became a " town road," and if leading some distance into the interior, and through other towns, was called a " country road." The early name of " path " continued some time in use long after it had got to be worthy of a more pretentious title. The old " Boston Path," by which the country was originally penetrated, long retained that name. It ran through the southern and western part of Salem Village by the Gardners, Popes, Goodales, Flints, Needhams, Swinnertons, Houltons, and so on towards Ipswich and Newbury.

On the 30th of September, 1648, Governor Winthrop, writing to his son John, says " they are well at Salem, and your uncle is now beginning to distil. Mr. Endicott hath found a copper mine in his own ground. Mr. Leader hath tried it. The furnace runs eight tons per week, and their bar iron is as good as Spanish." Whatever may be thought by some of the logic which infers that " all is well " in Salem, because they are beginning " to distil ; " and however little has, as yet, resulted here from the discovery of copper-mines, or the manufacture of iron, the foregoing extract shows the zeal and enthusiasm with which the wealthier settlers were applying themselves to the development of the capabilities of the country.

Mr. Downing seems to have resided permanently on his farm, and to have been identified with the agricultural portion of the community. His house-lot in the town bounded south on Essex Street, extending from Newbury to St. Peter's Street. He may not, perhaps, have built upon it for some time, as it long continued to be called " Downing's Field." Two of his daughters married sons of Thomas Gardner: Mary married Samuel; and Ann, Joseph. They came into possession of the " Downing Field." Mary was the mother of John, the progenitor of a large branch of the Gardner family. Mr. Downing had another large lot in the town, which, on the 11th of February, 1641, was sold to John Pickering, described in the deed as follows : " All that parcel of ground, lying before the now dwelling-house of the said John Pickering, late in the occupation of John Endicott, Esq., with all the appurtenances thereunto belonging, abutting on the east and south on the river commonly called the South River, and on the west on the land of William Hathorne, and on the north on the Town Common." The deed is signed by Lucy Downing, and by Edmund Batter, acting for her husband in his absence. On the 10th of February, 1644, he indorsed the transaction as follows : " I do freely agree to the sale of the said Field in Salem, made by my wife to John Pickering : witness my hand," &c. The attesting witnesses were Samuel Sharpe and William Hathorne. This land was then called " Broad Field." On his estate, thus enlarged, Pickering, a few years afterwards, built a house, still standing. The estate has remained, or rather so much of it as was attached to the homestead, in that family to this day, and is now owned and occupied by John Pickering, Esq., son of the eminent scholar and philologist of that name, and grandson of Colonel Timothy Pickering, of Revolutionary fame, — the trusted friend of Washington.

Emanuel Downing was the father of Sir George Downing, one of the first class that graduated at Harvard College, — a man of extraordinary talents and wonderful fortunes. After finishing his collegiate

course, in 1642, he studied divinity, probably under the
direction of Hugh Peters; went to the West Indies,
acting as chaplain in the vessel; preached and received
calls to settle in several places; went on to England;
entered the parliamentary service as chaplain to a regiment; was rapidly drawn into notice, and promoted
from point to point, until he became scoutmaster-
general in Cromwell's army. This office seems to have
combined the functions of inspector and commissary-
general, and head of the reconnoitering department.
In 1654, he was married to Frances, sister of Viscount
Morpeth, afterwards Earl of Carlisle; thus uniting
himself with "the blood of all the Howards," one of
the noblest families in England. The nuptials were
celebrated with great pomp, an epithalamium in Latin,
&c. All this, within eleven years after he took his
degree at Harvard, is surely an extraordinary instance
of rising in the world. He was a member of Parliament for Scotland. Cromwell sent him to France on
diplomatic business, and his correspondence in Latin
from that court was the beginning of a career of great
services in that line. He was soon commissioned ambassador to the Hague, then the great court in Europe.
Thurlow's state papers show with what marvellous vigilance, activity, and efficiency he conducted, from that
centre, the diplomatic affairs of the commonwealth.
At the restoration of the monarchy, he made the quick-
est and the loftiest somersault in all political history.
It was done between two days. He saw Charles the
Second at the Hague, on his way to England to re-

sume his crown: and the man who, up to that moment, had been one of the most zealous supporters of
the commonwealth, came out next morning as an
equally zealous supporter of the king.   He accompanied this wonderful exploit by an act of treachery to
three of his old associates, — including Colonel Oakey,
in whose regiment he had served as chaplain, — which
cost them their lives.   He was forthwith knighted,
and his commission as ambassador renewed.   After a
while, he returned to England; went into Parliament
from Morpeth, and ever after the exchequer was in
his hands.   By his knowledge, skill, and ability, he
enlarged the financial resources of the country, multiplied its manufactures, and extended its power and
wealth.   He was probably the original contriver of
the policy enforced in the celebrated Navigation Act,
having suggested it in Cromwell's time.   By that single short act of Parliament, England became the great
naval power of the world; her colonial possessions,
however widely dispersed, were consolidated into one
vast fountain of wealth to the imperial realm; the
empire of the seas was fixed on an immovable basis,
and the proud Hollander compelled to take down the
besom from the mast-head of his high-admiral.

Sir George Downing did one thing in favor of the
power of the people, in the British system of government, which may mitigate the resentment of mankind
for his execrable seizure and delivery to the royal
vengeance of Oakey, Corbett, and Barkstead.   He
introduced into Parliament and established the prin-

ciple of Specific Appropriations. The House of Commons has, ever since, not only held the keys of the treasury, but the power of controlling expenditures. The fortune of Sir George, on the failure of issue in the third generation, went to the foundation of Downing College, in Cambridge, England. It amounted to one hundred and fifty thousand pounds sterling. It is not improbable, that Downing Street, in London, owes its name to the great diplomatist.

This remarkable man spent his later youth and opening manhood on Salem Farms. In his college vacations and intervals of study, he partook, perhaps, in the labors of the plantation, mingled with the rural population, and shared in their sports. The crack of his fowling-piece re-echoed through the wild woods beyond Procter's Corner ; he tended his father's duck-coys at Humphries' Pond, and angled along the clear brooks. It is an observable circumstance, as illustrating the transmission of family traits, that the same ingenious activity and versatility of mind, which led Emanuel Downing, while carrying on the multifarious operations of opening a large farm in the forest, presiding in the local court at Salem, and serving year after year in the General Court as a deputy, to contrive complicated machinery for taking wild fowl and getting up distilleries, re-appeared in his son, on the broader field of the manufactures, finances, and foreign relations of a great nation.

A tract of three hundred acres, next eastward of the Downing farm, was granted to Thomas Read. He became a freeman in 1634, was a member of the Salem Church in 1636, received his grant the same year, and was acknowledged as an inhabitant, May 2, 1637. The farm is now occupied and owned by the Hon. Richard S. Rogers. It is a beautiful and commanding situation, and attests the taste of its original proprietor. Mr. Read seems to have had a passion for military affairs. In 1636, he was ensign in a regiment composed of men from Saugus, Ipswich, Newbury, and Salem, of which John Endicott was colonel, and John Winthrop, Jr., lieutenant-colonel. In 1647, he commanded a company. During the civil wars in England, he was attracted back to his native country. He commanded a regiment in 1660, and held his place after the Restoration. He died about 1663.

Our antiquarians were long at a loss to understand a sentence in one of Roger Williams's letters to John Winthrop, Jr., in which he says, " Sir, you were not long since the son of two noble fathers, Mr. John Winthrop and Mr. Hugh Peters." How John Winthrop, Jr., could be a son of Hugh Peters was the puzzle. Peters was not the father of either of Winthrop's two wives; and there was nothing in any family records or memorials to justify the notion. On the contrary, they absolutely precluded it. By the labors and acumen of the Hon. James Savage and Mr. Charles Deane, of Cambridge, who have no superiors in grappling with such a difficulty, its solution seems, at last, to be reached. " After long fruitless search," Mr. Savage has expressed a conviction that Mr. Deane has " ac-

quired the probable explication." The clue was thus
obtained: Mr. Savage says, "This approach to explanation is gained from 'the Life and Death of Hugh
Peters, by William Yonge, Dᴿ. Med. London. 1663,'
a very curious and more scarce tract." The facts discovered are that Peters taught a free school at Maldon,
in Essex; and that a widow lady with children and an
estate of two or three hundred pounds a year be-
friended him. She was known as "Mistress Read."
Peters married her. The second wife of John Winthrop, Jr., was Elizabeth, daughter of Colonel Read,
of Essex. By marrying Mrs. Read, Peters became the
step-father of the younger Winthrop's wife; and, by
the usage of that day, he would be called Winthrop's
father.

A few additional particulars, in reference to Peters
and our Salem Read, may shed further light on the
subject. While a prisoner in the Tower of London,
awaiting the trial which, in a few short days, consigned him to his fate, Peters wrote "A Dying Father's
Last Legacy to an only Child," and delivered it to his
daughter just before his execution. This is one of the
most admirable productions of genius, wisdom, and
affection, anywhere to be found. In it he gives a
condensed history of his life, which enables us to settle
some questions, which have given rise to conflicting
statements, and kept some points in his biography in
obscurity. In the first place, the title proves that he
had, at the time of his death, no other child. In the
course of it, he tells his daughter, that, when he was

fourteen years of age, his mother, then a widow, removed with him to Cambridge, and connected him
with the University there. His elder brother had
been sent to Oxford for his education. After residing
eight years in Cambridge, he took his Master's degree,
and then went up to London, where he was " struck
with the sense of his sinful estate by a sermon he
heard under Paul's, which was about forty years since,
which text was the *burden of Dumah or Idumea,* and
stuck fast. This made me to go into Essex ; and after
being quieted by another sermon in that country, and
the love and labors of Mr. Thomas Hooker, I there
preached, there married with a good gentlewoman, till
I went to London to ripen my studies, not intending
to preach at all." He then relates the circumstances
which subsequently led him again to engage in preaching. He is stated to have been born in 1599 : his
death was in 1660. Putting together these dates and
facts, it becomes evident that he could not have been
more than twenty-two years of age when he married
" Mistress Read." The " Last Legacy " shows, not
merely in the manner in which he speaks of her, —
" a good gentlewoman," — but, in its express terms,
that she was not the mother of the " only child " to
whom it was addressed. " Besides your mother," he
states that he had had " a godly wife before." There
is no indication that there were children by the earlier
marriage. If there were, they died young. He married, for his second wife, Deliverance Sheffield, at
Boston, in March, 1639.

His first wife, the time of whose death is unknown, had left the children by her former husband in his hands and under his care. He evidently cherished the memory of the "good gentlewoman of Essex" with the tenderest and most sacred affection. She had not only been the dear wife of his youth, but her property placed him above want. No wonder that the strongest attachment existed between him and her children. John Winthrop, Jr., and his wife, called him father, not merely in conformity with custom, being their step-father in point of fact, but with the fondness and devotion of actual children. It was on account of this intimate and endeared connection, and in consideration of the pecuniary benefit he had derived from his marriage to the mother of the younger Winthrop's wife, that he made arrangements, in case he should not return to America, that his Salem property should go to her and her husband. Having married a second wife, and there being issue of said marriage, he would not have alienated so considerable a part of his property from the legal heir without some good and sufficient reason. The foregoing view of the case explains the whole. The solution of the mystery which had enveloped Roger Williams's language is complete. Elizabeth, the daughter of the second marriage, to whom the "Last Legacy" was addressed, was baptized in the First Church at Salem, on the 8th of March, 1640. It does not appear, that, during her subsequent life, there was any intimacy, or even acquaintance, between her and the

Winthrops, as there was no ground for it, she being in no way connected with them.

May not Thomas Read, of Salem, have been a son of Colonel Read, of Maldon in Essex, and a brother of the wife of the younger Winthrop? Peters says, in the "Last Legacy," "Many of my acquaintances, going for New England, had engaged me to come to them when they sent, which accordingly I did." Thomas Read came over some time before him; so did John Winthrop, Jr., and wife. They were the same as children to him. They sent for him, and he came. After it was ascertained and determined that Peters should settle in Salem, Read joined the church here, and became a full inhabitant. Peters located his grant of land in sight of Read's residence, on the next then unappropriated territory, at a distance of about two and a half miles. When Read returned to England, he left his property here in the care of the Winthrops. Wait Winthrop, as the agent and attorney of his heirs, sold it to Daniel Eppes. If, as I conjecture, Thomas Read was a son of Colonel Read, of Essex, his coming here with Peters, and his connection with the Winthrops, are accounted for. His strong predilection for military affairs was natural in a son of a colonel of the English army. It led him back to the mother-country, on the first sound of the great civil war reaching these shores, and raised him to the rank he finally attained. The conjecture that he was a brother of the wife of the younger Winthrop is favored by the fact, that her son, Fitz John Winthrop, was a captain in Read's regiment, at the time of the restoration of the Stuarts.

During the short period of the residence of Hugh Peters in America, professional duties, and the extent to which his great talents were called upon in ecclesiastical and political affairs, in all parts of the colony, left him but little opportunity to attend to his two-hundred-acre grant. It was to the north of the present village of Danvers Plains, on the eastern side and adjoining to Frost-Fish Brook. The history of this grant confirms the supposition of his particular connection with the family of the younger Winthrop. It seems that it had not been formally laid out by metes and bounds while Peters was here. Owing to this circumstance, perhaps, it escaped confiscation at the time of his condemnation and execution. Some years afterwards, June 4, 1674, a committee of the town laid out the grant " to Mr. Peters." The record of this transaction says, " The land is in the possession of John Corwin." Captain John Corwin had married, in May, 1665, Margaret, daughter of John Winthrop, Jr. She survived her husband, and sold the same land, May 22, 1693, to " Henry Brown, Jr., of Salisbury, yeoman." These facts show that this portion of Mr. Peters's lands did go, according to the agreement when he left America, to the family of John Winthrop, Jr.

Whether he had erected a house on this grant is not known. From his characteristic energy, activity, and promptitude, it is probable that he had begun to clear

it. In agriculture, as in every thing else, he gave a
decisive impulse. It is stated that he had a particular
design to attempt the culture of hemp. He introduced
many implements of labor, and started new methods
of improvement. He disclosed to the producer of agricultural growths the idea of raising what the land
was most capable of yielding in abundance, in greater
quantities than were needed for local consumption, and
finding for the surplus an outside market. He is allowed to have introduced the coasting and foreign
trade on an intelligent and organized basis, and to
have promoted ship-building and the export of the
products of the forests and the fields generally to
the Southern plantations, the West Indies, and even
more distant points. If he had remained longer
in the country, the farming interests, and the settlers in
what was afterwards called Salem Village, within
which his tract was situated, would have felt his great
influence. As it was, he undoubtedly did much to in-
spire a zeal for improvement. His town residence was
on the south-western corner of Essex and Washington
Street, then known as "Salem Corner," where the
office of the Horse-railroad Company now is. The lot
was a quarter of an acre. Roger Williams probably
had resided there, and sold to Peters, who was his
successor in the ministry of the First Church, and
whose attorney sold it to Benjamin Felton, in 1659.
The range of ground included within what are now
Washington, Essex, Summer, and Chestnut Streets,
and extending to the South River, as it was before any

dam or mills had been erected over or across it, was a beautiful swell of land, with sloping surfaces, intersected by a creek from near the foot of Chestnut Street to its junction with the South River under the present grade of Mill Street. To the south of the corner, occupied successively by Roger Williams and Hugh Peters, Ralph Fogg, the Lady Deborah Moody, George Corwin, Dr. George Emory, Thomas Ruck, Samuel Skelton, Endicott, Pickering, Downing, and Hathorne, each had lots, extending in order to the foot of what is now Phelps Street. Most, if not all of them, had houses on their lots. Elder Sharp had what was called " Sharp's Field," bordering on the north side of Essex Street, extending from Washington to North Streets. His house was at the north corner of Lynde and Washington Streets. Edmund Batter, Henry Cook, Dr. Daniel Weld, Stephen Sewall, and Edward Norris, were afterwards on his land. Hugh Peters also owned the lot, consisting of a quarter of an acre, on the north-eastern corner of Essex and Washington Streets, now occupied by what is known as Stearns's Building, and was preparing to erect a house upon it when he was sent to England. His attorney sold it, in 1652, to John Orne, the founder of the family of that name.

The daughter of Mr. Peters came over to America shortly after his death, bringing with her her mother, who, for many years, had been subject to derangement. They were kindly received ; and some of his property, particularly a valuable farm in the vicinity of Marblehead, which the daughter sold to the American ancestor of the Devereux family, was recovered from the effect of his attainder. She probably soon went back to England, where she spent her days. Papers on file in the county court show that Elizabeth Barker, widow, " daughter of Mr. Hugh Peters," was living, in March, 1702, in good health, at Deptford, Kent, in the immediate vicinity of London, and had been living there for about forty years.

In consequence, perhaps, of the intimate connection between Mr. Peters and the family of John Winthrop, Jr., the name of the latter is to be added to the cluster of eminent men who, at that time, were drawn to reside in Salem. He was here, it is quite certain, from 1638 to 1641, if not for a longer period. There are indications of his presence as early as March of the former year, when he was appointed with Endicott to administer the freeman's oath to his uncle Downing. On the 25th of the next June, he had liberty to set up a salt-house at Royal Neck, on the east side of Wooleston River. There he erected a dwelling-house and other buildings, as appears by the depositions of sundry persons in a land suit about thirty years afterwards, who state that they worked for him, and were conversant with him there for several years. His first experiments and enterprises in the salt-manufacture, which he subsequently conducted on a very extensive scale in Connecticut, were performed at Royal Neck. His daughter, the widow successively of Antipas Newman and Zerubabel Endicott, in the suit just mentioned, recovered possession of that property, comprising forty acres, with the buildings and improvements. In 1646, John Winthrop, Jr., accompanied by a brother of Hugh Peters, Rev. Thomas Peters from Cornwall in England, began a plantation at Pequot River; and Trumbull, in his "History of Connecticut," says that "Mr. Thomas Peters was the first minister of Saybrook." The fortunes and families of Hugh Peters and John Winthrop, Jr., seem all along to have been linked together.

Downing, Read, and Peters, three of the original planters of Salem Farms, were drawn back to England and kept there by the engrossing interest which the wonderful revolution then breaking out in that kingdom could not but awaken in such minds as theirs. Here and everywhere, a great check was given to the early progress of the country by the turn of the tide which carried such men back to England, and prevented others from coming over. If the Parliament had not attempted to arrest the usurpations of the crown at that time, and the Stuarts been suffered to establish an absolute monarchy, the eyes and hearts of all free spirits would have remained fixed on America, and a perpetual stream of emigration brought over, for generations and for ever, thousands upon thousands of such men as came at the beginning. The effects that would have been thus produced in America and in England, in accelerating the progress of society here, and sinking it into debasement there; and thereby upon the fortunes of mankind the world

over, is a subject on which a meditative and philosophical mind may well be exercised.

But, although these men were lost, others are
worthy of being enumerated, in forming an estimate
of the elements that went to make the character of
the people, a chapter in whose history, of awful import, we are preparing ourselves to explore.

Francis Weston was a leading man at the very beginning. In 1634, with Roger Conant and John Holgrave, he represented Salem in the first House of Deputies ever assembled. His land grant was some little
distance to the west of the meeting-house of the village. He must have been a person of more than
ordinary liberality of spirit; for he discountenanced
the intolerance of his age, and kept his mind open to
receive truth and light. He did not conceal his sympathy with those who suffered for entertaining Antinomian sentiments. He was ordered to quit the colony
in 1638. For the same offence, his wife, who probably
had refused to go, was placed in the stocks " two hours
at Boston and two at Salem, on a lecture day." Weston, having ventured back, five years afterwards, was
put in irons, and imprisoned to hard labor. But, as
he stood to his principles, and there was danger to be
apprehended from his influence, he was again driven
out of the colony.

Richard Waterman came over from England in
1629, recommended to Governor Endicott by the governor and deputy in London. He was a noted hunter.
" His chief employment," says the letter introducing

him to Endicott, "will be to get you good venison."
A land grant was assigned him near Davenport's Hill.
But he, too, had a spirit that resisted the severe and
arbitrary policy of the times. He became a dissenter
from the prevalent creed, and sympathized with those
who suffered oppression. In 1664, he was brought
before the court, condemned to imprisonment, and
finally banished. Weston and Waterman subsequently were conspicuous in Rhode-Island affairs.
While residing in the village, the latter probably devoted himself to the opening of his land, and the pursuit of game through the forests. I find but one
notice of him as connected with public affairs.

For some years, the settlements were necessarily
confined to the shores of bays or coves, and the banks
of rivers. There were no wheel-carriages of any kind,
for transportation or travel, until something like roads
could be made ; and that was the work of time. A
few horses had been imported ; but it was long before
they could be raised to meet the general wants, or come
much into use. Every thing had to be water-borne.
The only vehicles were boats or canoes, mostly the
latter. There were two kinds of canoes. Large white-
pine logs were scooped or hollowed out, and wrought
into suitable shape, about two and a half feet in
breadth and twenty in length. These were often
quite convenient and serviceable, but not to be compared with the Indian canoes, which were made of
the bark of trees, wrought with great skill into a beautiful shape. The birch canoe was an admirable struc-

ture, combining elements and principles which modern
naval architecture may well study to imitate. In light-
ness, rapidity, freedom and ease of motion, it has not
been, and cannot be, surpassed. Its draft, even when
bearing a considerable burden, was so slight, that it
would glide over the shallowest bars. It was strong,
durable, and easily kept in repair. Although dangerous to the highest degree under an inexperienced and
unskilful hand, no vessel has ever been safer when
managed by persons trained to its use. The cool and
quick-sighted Indian could guide it, with his exquisitely
moulded paddle, in perfect security, through whirling
rapids and over heavy seas, around headlands and
across bays. The settlers early supplied themselves
with canoes, by which to thread the interior streams,
and cross from shore to shore in the harbors. One
great advantage of the light canoe, before roads were
opened through the woods, was, that it could be un-
loaded, and borne on the shoulders across the land, at
any point, to another stream or lake, thus cutting off
long curves, and getting from river to river. The
lading would be transported in convenient parcels,
the canoe launched, loaded, and again be floated on its
way. Canoes soon came into universal use, particularly in this neighborhood. Wood, in his " New-England's Prospect," speaking of Salem, says, " There
be more canowes in this town than in all the whole
Patent, every household having a water horse or two."
It was so important for the public safety to have them
kept in good condition, that the town took the matter

in hand. The quarterly court records have the following entry under the date of June 27, 1636 : —

"It was ordered and agreed, that all the canoes of the
north side of the town shall be brought the next second day,
being the 4th day of the 5th month, about 9 o'clock, A.M.,
unto the cove of the common landing place of the North
River, by George Harris his house — And that all the
canoes of the south side are to be brought before the port-
house in the South River, at the same time, then and there to
be viewed by J. Holgrave, P. Palfrey, R. Waterman, R.
Conant, P. Veren, or the greater number of them. And
that there shall be no canoe used (upon penalty, of forty shillings, to the owner thereof) than such as the said surveyors
shall allow of and set their mark upon ; and if any shall
refuse or neglect to bring their canoes to the said places at
the time appointed, they shall pay for said fault 10 shillings."

The names of the men associated with Waterman
prove that he was ranked among the chief citizens of
the town. The austere manners of the age, among
communities like that established here ; the exclusion,
at that time, by inexorable laws, of many forms of
amusement ; and the general sombre aspect of society,
kept down the natural exhilaration of life to such a
degree, that, when the pressure was occasionally removed, the whole people bounded into the liveliest
outbursts of glad excitement. It was no doubt a gala
day. Ceremony, sport, and festivity, in all their
forms, took full effect. The surveyors performed their
functions with the utmost display of authority, examined the canoes with the gravest scrutiny, and affixed

their marks with all due formality. A light, graceful, and most picturesque fleet swarmed, from all directions, to the appointed rendezvous. The harbor glittered with the flashing paddles, and was the scene of swift races and rival feats of skill, displaying manly strength and agility. It must have been an aquatic spectacle of rare gayety and beauty, not surpassed nor equalled in some respects, when, more than a century afterwards, the " Grand Turk " or the " Essex " frigate was launched, or when Commodore Forbes, still later, swept into our peaceful waters with his boat flotilla. It was the first Fourth of July ever celebrated in America.

Thomas Scruggs was an early inhabitant of Salem; often represented the town as deputy in the General Court; was one of the judges of the local court, and always recognized among the rulers of the town. In January, 1636, he received a grant of three hundred acres on the south-west limits of its territory. The next month, an exchange took place, which is thus recorded in the town-book of grants: " It was ordered, that, whereas Mr. Scruggs had a farm of three hundred acres beyond Forest River, and that Captain Trask had one of two hundred acres beyond Bass River, and Captain Trask freely relinquishing his farm of two hundred acres, it was granted unto Mr. Thomas Scruggs, and he thereupon freely relinquished his farm of three hundred acres." This brought Scruggs upon the Salem Farms, between Bass River and the great pond, Wenham Lake. The real object in making this arrangement was to advance a project which the leading people of Salem at that time had much at heart. They were very desirous to have the college established on the tract relinquished by Scruggs. What would have been the effect of placing it there, in the immediate neighborhood of the sea-shore, in full view of the spacious bay, its promontories, islands, and navigation, is a question on which we may speculate at our leisure. The effort failed : Captain Trask and Mr. Scruggs had done all they could to accomplish it, and gave their energies to the welfare of the community in other directions. From the little that is recorded of Scruggs, it is quite evident that he was an intelligent and valuable citizen. The event that brought his career as a public man to a close proves that his mind was enlightened, liberal, and independent ; that he was in advance of the times in which he lived. When the bitter and violent persecution of the celebrated Anne Hutchinson, on account of her Antinomian sentiments, took place, Mr. Scruggs disapproved and denounced it. He gave his whole influence, earnestly and openly, against such attempts to suppress freedom of inquiry and the rights of conscience. He, with others in Salem, was proscribed, disarmed, and deprived of his public functions. He appears to have been suffered to remain unmolested on his estate, and died there in 1654. He had but one child, Rachel ; and the name, as derived from him, became extinct. The inventory of his property is dated on the 24th of June of that year. The items mentioned in it amount to £244. 10s. 2d. Considering the rates of value at that time, it was a large property. At the same date, an agreement is recorded by which his widow, Margery, conveys to her son-in-law, John Raymond, all her real estate, upon these conditions: She to have the use of her house during her life, the bedding, and other " household stuff; " and he to pay her five pounds " in hand," twenty pounds per annum, and five pounds " at the hour of her death." This was an ample provision, in those times, for her comfort while she lived, and for her funeral charges. I do not remember to have found this last point arranged for, in such a form of expression, in any other instance.

William Alford was an early settler. He was a member of the numerous and wealthy society, or guild, of Skinners, in the city of London, and probably came here with the view of establishing an extensive trade in furs. He received accordingly, in 1636, a grant of two hundred acres, including what was for some time called Alford's Hill, afterwards Long Hill, now known as Cherry Hill. It is owned and occupied by R. P. Waters, Esq. Alford sympathized in religious views with his neighbor Scruggs, and with him was subjected to censure, and disarmed by order of the General Court. He sold his lands to Henry Herrick, and left the jurisdiction.

One of the most enlightened, and perhaps most accomplished, men among the first inhabitants of Salem Village, was Townsend Bishop. He was admitted a freeman in 1635. The next year, he appears on the list of members of the Salem Church. He was one of the judges of the local court, and, almost without intermission from his first coming here, a deputy to the General Court. In 1645, as his attention had been led to the subject, he conceived doubts in reference to infant baptism; and it was noticed that he did not bring forward a child, recently born, to the rite. Although himself on the bench, and ever before the object of popular favor and public honors, he was at once brought up, and handed over for discipline. The next year, he sold his estates, and probably removed elsewhere. He appears no more in our annals. Where he went, I have not been able to learn. It is to be hoped that he found somewhere a more congenial and tolerant abode. It is evident that he could not breathe in an atmosphere of bigotry; and it was difficult to find one free from the miasma in those days.

Five of the most valuable of the first settlers of the village — Weston, Waterman, Scruggs, Alford, and Bishop — were thus early driven into exile, or subdued to silence, by the stern policy on which the colony was founded. It is an error to characterize this as religious bigotry. It was not so much a theological as a political persecution. Its apparent form was in reference to tenets of faith, but the policy was deeper than this. Any attempt to make opposition to the existing administration was treated with equal severity, whatever might be the subject on which it ventured to display itself.

The men who sought this far-off " nook and corner of the world," crossing a tempestuous and dangerous ocean, and landing on the shores of a wilderness, leaving every thing, however dear and valuable, behind, came to have a country and a social system for themselves and of themselves alone. Their resolve was inexorable not to allow the mother-country, or the whole outside world combined, to interfere with them. And it was equally inexorable not to suffer dissent or any discordant element to get foothold among them. Sir Christopher Gardner's rank and title could not save him: he was not of the sort they wanted, and they shipped him back. Roger Williams's virtues, learning, apostolic piety, could not save him; and they drove him into a wintry wilderness, hunting him beyond their borders. It was not so much a question whether Baptists, Antinomians, or Quakers were right or wrong, as a preformed determination not to have any dissentients of any description among them. They had sacrificed all to find and to make a country for themselves, and they meant to keep it to themselves. They had gone out of everybody else's way, and they did not mean to let anybody else come into their way. They did not understand the great truth which Hugh Peters preached to Parliament, " Why," said he, " cannot Christians differ, and yet be friends? All children should be fed, though they have different faces and shapes: unity, not uniformity, is the Christian word." They admitted no such notion as this. They thought uniformity the only basis of unity. They meant to make and to keep this a country after their own pattern, a Congregational, Puritan, Cambridge-Platformman's country. The time has not yet come when we can lift up clean hands against them. Two successive chief-magistrates of the United States have opened the door and signified to one-eighth part of our whole people, that it will be best for them to walk out. So long as the doctrine is maintained that this is the white man's country, or any man's, or any class or kind of men's country, it becomes us to close our lips against denunciation of the Fathers of New England because they tried to keep the country to themselves. The sentiment or notion on which they acted, in whatever form it appears, however high the station from which it emanates, or however long it lasts in the world, is equally false and detestable in all its shapes. It is a defiant rebellion against that law which declares that "all nature's difference is all nature's peace;" that there can be no harmony without variety of sound, no social unity without unlimited freedom, and no true liberty where any are deprived of equal rights; that differences ought to bring men together, rather than keep them apart; and that the only government that can stand against the shocks of time, and grow stronger and dearer to all its people, is one that recognizes no differences of whatever kind among them. The only consistent or solid foundation on which a republic or a church can be built, is an absolute level, with no enclosures and no exclusion.

Townsend Bishop's grant of three hundred acres was made on the 16th of January, 1636. When he sold it, Oct. 18, 1641, it appears by the deed, that there were on it edifices, gardens, yards, enclosures, and meadows. A large force must have been put and kept upon it, from the first, to have produced such results in so short a time. Orchards had been planted. The manner in which the grounds were laid out is still indicated by embankments, with artificial slopes and roadways, which exhibit the fine taste of the proprietor, and must have required a large expenditure of money and labor. Although the estate has always been in the hands of owners competent to take care of it and keep it in good preservation, none but the original proprietor would have been likely to have made the outlay apparent on its face, on the plan adopted. The mansion in which he resided stands to-day. Its front, facing the south, has apparently been widened, at some remote intermediate date since its original erection, by a slight extension on the western end, beyond the porch. It has been otherwise, per_ haps, somewhat altered in the course of time by repairs; but its general aspect, as exhibited in the frontispiece of this volume, and its original strongly com‾ pacted and imperishable frame, remain. No saw was used in shaping its timbers; they were all hewn, by the broad-axe, of the most durable oak: they are massive, and rendered by time as hard to penetrate almost as iron. The walls and stairway of the cellar, the entrance to which is seen by the side of the porch, constructed of such stones as could be gathered on the surface of a new country, bear the marks of great antiquity. A long, low kitchen, with a stud of scarcely six feet, extended originally the whole length of the lean-to, on the north side of the house. The rooms of the main house were of considerably higher stud. The old roadway, the outlines of which still remain, approached the house from the east, came up to its north-east corner, wound round its front, and continued from its north-west corner, on a track still visible, over a brook and through the apple-orchard planted by Bishop, to the point where the burial-ground of the village now is; and so on towards the lands then occupied by Richard Hutchinson, also to the lands afterwards owned by Nathaniel Ingersol, towards Beaver Dam, and the first settlements in that direction and to the westward. In general it may be said, that the structural proportions and internal arrangements of the house, taken in its relations to the vestiges and indications on the face of the grounds, show that it is coeval with the first occupancy of the farm. But we do not depend, in this case, upon conjectural considerations, or on mere tradition, which, on such a point, is not always reliable. It happens to be demonstrated, that this is the veritable house built and occupied by Townsend Bishop, in 1636, by a singular and irrefragable chain of specific proof. A protracted land suit, hereafter to be described, gave rise to a great mass of papers, which are preserved in the files of the county courts and the State Department; among them are several plots made by surveyors, and adduced in evidence by the parties. Not only the locality but a diagram of the house, as then standing, are given.

The spot on which it stood is shown. Further, it appears, that, in the deeds of transference of the estate, the homestead is specially described as the house in which Townsend Bishop lived, called "Bishop's Mansion." This continues to a period subsequent to the style of its architecture, and within recent tradition and the memory of the living. In the old Salem Commoner's records, it is called "Bishop's Cottage," which was the name generally given to dwelling-houses in those early times. Having, as occasion required, been seasonably repaired, it is as strong and good a house to-day as can be found. Its original timbers, if kept dry and well aired, are beyond decay; and it may stand, a useful, eligible, and comely residence, through a future as long as the past. It may be doubted whether any dwelling-house now in use in this country can be carried back, by any thing like a similar strength of evidence, to an equal antiquity. Its site, in reference to the surrounding landscape, was well chosen. Here its hospitable and distinguished first proprietor lived, in the interims of his public and official service, in peace and tranquillity, until ferreted out by the intrusive spirit of an intolerant age. Here he welcomed his neighbors, — Endicott, Downing, Peters, John Winthrop, Jr., Read, and other kindred spirits.*

* Not only the storms of two hundred and thirty years, but the bolts of heaven, have beat in vain upon this mansion. The view given of it in the frontispiece is from a sketch taken in winter. The leafless branches of a tall elm at its western end are represented. At noon on Saturday, July 28, 1866, during a violent thunder-storm,

In the course of a mysterious providence, this venerable mansion was destined to be rendered mem-

the electric fluid seems to have passed down the tree, rending and tearing some of its branches, and leaving its traces on the trunk. It flashed into the house. It tore the roof, knocking away one corner, displacing in patches the mortar that coated the old chimney top and sides, hacking the edges of the brick-work, splitting off the side of an extension to the building at the western end, entering a chamber at that point, where two children were sitting at a window, and throwing upon the floor, within two or three feet of them, a considerable portion of the plastered ceiling. It then scattered all through the apartments. What looked like perforations, as if made by shot or pistol-balls, were found in many places; but there were no corresponding marks on the opposite sides of the walls or partitions. Portions of the paper-hangings were stripped off, and small slivers ripped up from the floors. It struck the frames of looking-glasses, cracking off small pieces of the wood, but only in one instance breaking the mirror. It cut a velvet band by which one was hung; and it was found on the floor, the mirror downward and unbroken, as if it had been carefully laid there. In the attic, fragments of the old gnarled and knotted rafters, of different lengths, — from four or five feet to mere chips, — were scattered in quantities upon the floor, and grooves made lengthwise along posts and implements of household use. Large cracks were left in the wooden casings of some of the doors and windows. A family of eight persons were seated around the dinner-table. All were more or less affected. They were deprived for the time of the use of their feet and ancles; were stunned, paralyzed, and rendered insensible for a few moments by the shock; and felt the effects, some of them, for a day or two in their lower limbs. In front of each person at the table was a tall goblet, which had just been filled with water. As soon as they were able to notice, they found the water dripping on all sides to the floor, the whole table-cloth wet, seven of the goblets entirely empty, the eighth half emptied, and not one of them thrown over, or in the slightest manner displaced. The whole house was filled with what seemed, to the sight and smell, to be smoke; but no combustion, scorch, discoloration, or the least indication of heat, could be found on any of the objects struck. The building, in its thirteen orable by its connection with the darkest scene in our annals. As that scene cannot otherwise be comprehended in all the elements that led to it, it is necessary to give the intermediate history of the Townsend Bishop farm and mansion. In 1641, Bishop sold it to Henry Chickering, who seems to have been residing for some time in Salem, and to whom, in January, 1640, a grant of land had been made by the town. He continued to own it until the 4th of October, 1648; although he does not appear to have resided on the farm long, as he soon removed to Dedham, from which place he was deputy to the General Court in 1642, and several years afterwards. He sold the farm at the above-mentioned date to Governor Endicott for one hundred and sixty pounds. In 1653, John Endicott, Jr., the eldest son of the Governor, married Elizabeth, daughter of Jeremiah Houchins, an eminent citizen of Boston, who had before resided in Hingham, which place he represented as deputy for six years. The name was pronounced "Houkins," and so perhaps was finally spelled "Hawkins." By agreement, or "articles of marriage contract," Endicott bestowed the farm upon his son. "Present possession" was given. How long, or how much of the time, the young couple lived on the estate, is not known. Their principal residence was in Boston. The General Court, in 1660, granted John Endicott,

rooms, from the garret to the ground-floor, had been flooded with lightning; but, with all its inmates, escaped without considerable or permanent injury.

Jr., four hundred acres of land on the eastern side of the upper part of Merrimac River. After the purchase of the farm from Chickering, the Endicott property covered nearly a thousand acres in one tract, extending from the arms of the sea to the centre of the present village of Tapleyville. On the 10th of May, 1662, the Governor executed a deed, carrying out the engagements of the marriage contract, giving to his son John, his heirs, and assigns for ever, the Bishop farm. Governor Endicott died in 1665. A will was found signed and sealed by him, dated May 2, 1659, in which, referring to the marriage gift to John, he bequeathes the aforesaid farm to "him and his heirs," but does not add, "and assigns." Another item of the will is, "The land I have bequeathed to my two sons, in one place or another, my will is that the longest liver of them shall enjoy the whole, except the Lord send them children to inherit it after them." Unfortunately, there were no witnesses to the will. It was not allowed in Probate. The matter was carried up to the General Court; and it was decided Aug. 1, 1665, that the court "do not approve of the instrument produced in court to be the last will and testament of the late John Endicott, Esq., governor." In October of the same year, John Endicott, Jr., petitioned the General Court to act on the settlement of his father's estate; and the court directs administration to be granted to "Mrs. Elizabeth Endicott and her two sons, John and Zerubabel," and that they bring in an inventory to the next county court at Boston, and to dispose of the same as the law directs. Upon this, the widow of the Governor, and his son Zerubabel, again appeal to the General Court; and on the 23d of May, 1666, "after a full hearing of all parties concerned in the said estate, i.e., the said Mrs. Elizabeth Endicott and her two sons, Mr. John and Mr. Zerubabel Endicott, Mr. Jeremiah Houchin being also present in court, and respectively presenting their pleas and evidences in the case," it was finally decided and ordered by the court, that the provisions of the document purporting to be the will of Governor Endicott should be carried into effect, with these exceptions: that the Bishop or Chickering farm shall go to his son John "to him, his heirs and assigns for ever;" and that Elizabeth, the wife of said son John, if she should survive her husband, shall enjoy during her life all the estate of her husband in all the other houses and lands mentioned in the instrument purporting to be his father's will. The court adjudge that this must have been "the real intent of the aforesaid John Endicott, Esq., deceased, who had during his life special favor and respect for her." They give the widow of the Governor "the goods and chattels" of the said John Endicott, Esq., her late husband, provided that, if "she shall die seized to the value of more than eighty pounds sterling" thereof, the surplus shall be divided between her two sons: John to have a double portion thereof. Finally, they appoint the widow sole administratrix, and require her to bring in a true inventory to the next court for the county of Suffolk, and to pay all debts.

John and his father-in-law had it all their own way.
The decision of the court was perhaps correct, according to legal principles; although it is not so certain
that it was, in all respects, in conformity with the
intent of Governor Endicott. Undoubtedly, as the
language of the deed shows, he had made up his mind
to give to his son John and "his assigns" absolute, full,
and final possession of the Bishop farm. But it seems
equally certain, that he meant to have the rest of his
landed estate, including the Orchard Farm and the
Ipswich-river farm, go directly and wholly to the survivor, if either of his sons died without issue. The
facts and dates are as follows: His son John was
married in 1653. The Governor's will was made in
1659. It had then become quite probable that John
might not have issue. The will gives him and his
heirs, but not his assigns, the Bishop farm. In the
event of his death without issue, his widow would
have her dower and legal life right in it, but the final
heir would be Zerubabel. In 1662, the Governor,
who had, some years before, removed to Boston, where
he resided the remainder of his life, executed a deed,
giving to his son John, "his heirs and assigns," a full
and permanent title to the Bishop farm. This was a
variation of the plan for the disposition of his estate
as shown in his will. He probably designed to make
a new will, securing to his natural heirs, so far as his
other landed property was concerned, what he had
thus permitted to pass away from them in the Bishop
farm; that is, the full and immediate possession by

the survivor, if either of the sons died without issue.
It was a favorite idea, almost a sacred principle, in
those days, to have lands go in the natural descent.
The sentiment is quite apparent in the tenor of the
Governor's will. When he deprived, by his deed to
John in 1662, Zerubabel's family of the right to the
final possession of the Bishop farm, it can hardly be
doubted that he relied upon the provisions of his will
to secure to them the immediate, complete possession
of all his other lands, without the incumbrance of any
claim of dower or otherwise of John's widow. But
the pressure of public duties prevented his duly executing his will, and putting it into a new shape, in
conformity with the circumstances of the case. The
troubles that followed teach the necessity of the utmost caution and carefulness in that most difficult
and most irremediable of all business transactions, —
the attempt to continue the control of property, after
death, by written instruments.

John Endicott, Jr., died in February, 1668, without
issue; leaving his whole estate to his widow, " her
heirs and assigns for ever." His will is dated Jan.
27, 1668, and was offered to Probate on the 29th of
February, 1668. His widow married, Aug. 31,
1668, the Rev. James Allen, one of the ministers of
the First Church in Boston, whose previous wife,
Hannah Dummer, by whom he received five hundred
acres of land, had died in March, 1668. His Endicott
wife died April 5, 1673, leaving the Townsend-
Bishop farm and all her other property to him; and

on the 11th of September, of the same year, he married Sarah Hawlins. By his two preceding wives he received twelve hundred acres of land. How much he got by the last-mentioned, we have no information. Besides these matrimonial accumulations, the accounts seem to indicate that he was rich before.

It may well be imagined, that it could not have been very agreeable to the family at the Orchard Farm to see this choice and extensive portion of their estate, which was within full view from their windows, swept into the hands of utter strangers in so rapid and extraordinary a manner, by a series of circumstances most distasteful and provoking. But this was but the beginning of their trouble.

On the 29th of April, 1678, Allen sold the Bishop farm to Francis Nurse, of the town of Salem, for four hundred pounds. Nurse was an early settler, and, before this purchase, had lived, for some forty years, " near Skerry's," on the North River, between the main part of the settlement in the town of Salem and the ferry to Beverly. He is described as a " tray-maker." The making of these articles, and similar objects of domestic use, was an important employment in a new country remote from foreign supply. He appears to have been a very respectable person, of great stability and energy of character, whose judgment was much relied on by his neighbors. No one is mentioned more frequently as umpire to settle disputes, or arbitrator to adjust conflicting claims. He was often on committees to determine boundaries or estimate

valuations, or on local juries to lay out highways and
assess damages. The fact that he was willing to encounter the difficulties connected with such a heavy
transaction as the purchase of the Bishop farm at
such a price at his time of life proves that he had a
spirit equal to a bold undertaking. He was then fifty-
eight years of age. His wife Rebecca was fifty-seven
years of age. We shall meet her again.

They had four sons, — Samuel, John, Francis, and
Benjamin ; and four daughters, — Rebecca, married to
Thomas Preston, Mary to John Tarbell, Elizabeth to
William Russell, and Sarah, who remained unmarried
until after the death of her mother. With this strong
force of stalwart sons and sons-in-law, and their industrious wives, Francis Nurse took hold of the farm.
The terms of the purchase were so judicious and ingenious, that they are worthy of being related, and
show in what manner energetic and able-bodied men,
even if not possessed of capital, particularly if they
could command an effective co-operation in the labor
of their families, obtained possession of valuable
landed estates. The purchase-money was not required
to be paid until the expiration of twenty-one years.
In the mean time, a moderate annual rent was fixed
upon ; seven pounds for each of the first twelve years,
and ten pounds for each of the remaining nine years.
If, at the end of the time, the amount stipulated had
not been paid, or Nurse should abandon the undertaking, the property was to relapse to Allen. Disinterested and suitable men, whose appointment was

provided for, were then to estimate the value added to
the estate by Nurse during his occupancy, by the clearing of meadows or erection of buildings or other permanent improvements, and all of that value over and
above one hundred and fifty pounds was to be paid to
him. If any part of the principal sum should be paid
prior to the expiration of twenty-one years, a proportionate part of the farm was to be relieved of all obligation to Allen, vest absolutely in Nurse, and be
disposable by him. By these terms, Allen felt authorized to fix a very high price for the farm, it not being
payable until the lapse of a long period of time. If not
paid at all, the property would come back to him, with
one hundred and fifty pounds of value added to it. It
was not a bad bargain for him, — a man of independent
means derived from other sources, and so situated as
not to be able to carry on the farm himself. It was a
good investment ahead. To Nurse the terms were
most favorable. He did not have to pay down a dollar
at the start. The low rent required enabled him to
apply almost the entire income from the farm to improvements that would make it more and more
productive. Before half the time had elapsed, a
value was created competent to discharge the whole
sum due to Allen. His children severally had good
farms within the bounds of the estate, were able to
assume with ease their respective shares of the obligations of the purchase; and the property was thus
fully secured within the allotted time. Allen gave, at
the beginning, a full deed, in the ordinary form, which

was recorded in this county. Nurse gave a duly executed bond, in which the foregoing conditions are carefully and clearly defined. That was recorded in Suffolk
County; and nothing, perhaps, was known in the
neighborhood, at the time or ever after, of the terms
of the transaction. When the success of the enterprise was fully secured, Nurse conveyed to his children
the larger half of the farm, reserving the homestead
and a convenient amount of land in his own possession. The plan of this division shows great fairness
and judgment, and was entirely satisfactory to them all.
They were required, by the deeds he gave them, to
maintain a roadway by which they could communicate
with each other and with the old parental home.

Here the venerable couple were living in truly patriarchal style, occupying the "mansion" of Townsend
Bishop, when the witchcraft delusion occurred. They
and their children were all clustered within the limits
of the three-hundred-acre farm. They were one family.
The territory was their own, secured by their united action, and made commodious, productive, valuable, and
beautiful to behold, by their harmonious, patient,
and persevering labor. Each family had a homestead,
and fields and gardens; and children were growing up
in every household. The elder sons and sons-in-law
had become men of influence in the affairs of the
church and village. It was a scene of domestic happiness and prosperity rarely surpassed. The work of
life having been successfully done, it seemed that a
peaceful and serene descent into the vale of years was

secured to Francis and Rebecca Nurse. But far otherwise was the allotment of a dark and inscrutable providence.

There is some reason to suspect that the prosperity of the Nurses had awakened envy and jealousy among the neighbors. The very fact that they were a community of themselves and by themselves, may have operated prejudicially. To have a man, who, for forty years, had been known, in the immediate vicinity, as a farmer and mechanic on a small scale, without any pecuniary means, get possession of such a property, and spread out his family to such an extent, was inexplicable to all, and not relished perhaps by some. There seems to have been a disposition to persist in withholding from him the dignity of a landholder; and, long after he had distributed his estate among his descendants, it is mentioned in deeds made by parties that bounded upon it, as " the farm which Mr. Allen, of Boston, lets to the Nurses." Not knowing probably any thing about it, they call it, even after Nurse's death, " Mr. Allen's farm." This, however, was a slight matter. When Allen sold the farm to Nurse, he bound himself to defend the title ; and he was true to his bond. What was required to be done in this direction may, perhaps, have exposed the Nurses to animosities which afterwards took terrible effect against them.

In granting lands originally, neither the General Court nor the town exercised sufficient care to define boundaries. There does not appear to have been any well-arranged system, based upon elaborate, accurate, scientific surveys. Of the dimensions of the area of a rough, thickly wooded, unfrequented country, the best estimates of the most practised eyes, and measurements resting on mere exploration or perambulation, are very unreliable. The consequence was, that, in many cases, grants were found to overlap each other. This was the case with the Bishop farm; and soon after Nurse came into possession, and had begun to operate upon it, a conflict commenced; trespasses were complained of; suits were instituted; and one of the most memorable and obstinately contested land-controversies known to our courts took place. In that controversy Nurse was not formally a principal. The case was between James Allen and Zerubabel Endicott, or between Allen and Nathaniel Putnam.

An inspection of the map, at this point, will enable us to understand the grounds on which the suit was contested. The Orchard Farm was granted to Endicott, as has been stated, July 3, 1632, by the General Court. The grant states the bounds on the south and on the north to be two rivers; on the east, another river, into which they both flow; and, on the west, the mainland. Where this western line was to strike the rivers on the north and south is not specified; but the natural interpretation would seem to be, in the absence of any thing to the contrary, that it was to strike them at their respective heads. The evidence of all persons who were conversant with the premises during the life of the Governor as connected with the farm was unanimous and conclusive to this point; that is, that he and they always supposed that the west line was, as drawn on the map, from the head of one river to the head of the other; that the farm embraced all between them as far up as the tide set. It was objected, on the other side, that this made the farm much more than three hundred acres; but as an offset to that was the fact, that a considerable part of the area was swamp or marsh, not usually taken into the account in reckoning the extent of a grant, and the additional fact, that the language of the General Court in reference to quantity was not precise, — " about " three hundred acres. At the same date with the grant to Endicott, the General Court granted two hundred acres to Mr. Skelton, which tract is given on the map.

As has been stated, the General Court conferred upon the towns the exclusive right to dispose of the lands within their limits, March 3, 1635. On the 10th of December of that year, the town of Salem granted to Robert Cole the tract of three hundred acres subsequently purchased by Emanuel Downing, which is indicated on the map. On the 11th of January, 1636, the grant of three hundred acres was made to Townsend Bishop. Its language is unfortunately obscure in some expressions; but it is clear, that the tract was to be four hundred rods in length, one hundred and twenty-four rods in width at the western end, and one hundred and sixteen rods at the eastern. At the north-east corner it was to meet the water or brook that separated it from the grant to Skelton; and it

was also to " but " upon, or touch, at the eastern end,
the land granted to Endicott by the General Court.
After the grant to Bishop, the town, from time to time,
made grants to Stileman of land north of the Bishop
grant. Stileman's grants adjoined Skelton's at the
north-eastern corner of the Bishop farm. That part
of Stileman's land had come into possession of Nathaniel Putnam, and the residue westwardly, together
with the grant to Weston, into the possession of
Hutchinson, Houlton, and Ingersol. Still further
west, the town had made grants to Swinnerton. Their
respective locations are given in the map. The point
of difficulty which gave rise to litigation was this:
The Bishop farm was required, by the terms of the
grant, to be one hundred and sixteen rods wide at its
eastern end. But there was no room for it. The
requisite width could not be got without encroaching
upon either Putnam or Endicott, or both. As Endicott stood upon an earlier title than that of Bishop,
and from a higher authority, and Putnam upon a later
title from an inferior authority, the court of trials
might have disposed of the matter, at the opening, on
that ground, and Putnam been left to suffer the encroachment. But it did not so decide ; and the case
went on. The struggle was between Endicott to push
it north, and thereby save his Orchard Farm, and
the land between it and the Bishop grant, given by the
town to his father, called the Governor's Plain, and
Nathaniel Putnam to push it south, and thereby save
the land he had received from his wife's father, Rich-

ard Hutchinson, who had purchased from Stileman. Allen stood on the defensive against both of them. The Nurses had nothing to do but to attend to their own business, carrying on their farming operations up to the limits of their deed, looking to Allen for redress, if, in the end, the dimensions of their estate should be curtailed. But, being the occupants, and, until finally ousted, the owners of the land, if there was any intrusion to be repelled, or violence to be met, or fighting to be done, they were the ones to do it. They were equal to the situation.

After various trials in the courts of law in all possible shapes, the whole subject was carried up to the General Court, where it was decided, in conformity with the report of a special commission in May, 1679, substantially in favor of Putnam and Allen. Endicott petitioned for a new hearing. Another commission was appointed; and their report was accepted in May, 1682. It was more unfavorable to Endicott than the previous one. He protested against the judgment of the court in earnest but respectful language, and petitioned for still another hearing. They again complied with his request, and appointed a day for once more examining the case; but, when the day came, Nov. 24, 1683, he was sick in bed, and the case was settled irrevocably against him.

The map gives the lines of the Bishop farm as finally settled by the General Court. It will be noticed, that it is laid directly across the Governor's Plain, and runs far into the Orchard Farm " up to the rocks

near Endicott's dwelling-house," or, as it is otherwise
stated, " within a few rods of Guppy's ditch, near to "
the said house.   It may be said to have been a necessity, as the original three hundred acres of the grant
to Townsend Bishop had to be made up.   It could not
go north; for Houlton and Ingersol stood upon the
Weston grant, and Hutchinson and Nathaniel Putnam
stood upon Stileman's grants, to push it back.   It
could not go west or south-west, for there Swinnerton
stood to fend off upon his grants; and there, too, was
Nathaniel Putnam, upon his own grant, and lands he
had purchased of another original grantee.   It could
not be swung round to the south without jamming up
the lands of Felton and others, or pushing them over
the grants, made to Robert Cole — under which Downing had purchased — and to Thomas Read.   All these
parties were combined to force it south-eastwardly over
the grounds of Endicott.   Nathaniel Putnam was his
most fatal antagonist.   He was a man of remarkable
energy, of consummate adroitness, and untiring resources in such a transaction; and he so managed to
press in the bounds of the Bishop farm, at the north-
east, as to gain a valuable strip for himself.   With this
strong man against him, acting in combination with
the rich and influential James Allen, minister of the
great metropolitan First Church, and licenser of the
press, who brought the whole power of his clerical
and social connections in Boston and throughout the
colony to bear upon the General Court, Zerubabel
Endicott had no chance for justice, and no redress for

wrong. In vain he invoked the memory of his father, or of Winthrop, the grandfather of his wife. His father and both the Winthrops had long before left the scene: a new generation had risen, and there was none to help him.

One would have supposed, that the General Court, which had granted the Orchard Farm to Governor Endicott, would have felt bound, in self-respect and in honor, to have protected it against any overlapping grants subsequently made by an inferior authority. Under the circumstances of the case, it was its duty to have held the Orchard Farm intact, and made it up to the satisfaction of Allen and Nurse by a grant elsewhere, or an equitable compensation in money. It owed so much to the son of Endicott and the grand-daughter of Winthrop, the first noble Fathers of the colony. Perhaps the court found its justification in the phraseology of the deed of conveyance of the Bishop farm from Governor Endicott to his son John. After reciting or referring to the original town grant to Bishop, and the deeds from Bishop to Chickering, and from Chickering to himself, the Governor conveys to his son John all the houses, &c., and every part and parcel of the land " to the utmost extent thereof, according as is expressed or included in either of the forecited deeds, or town grant." It was maintained, and justly, by Allen, that he held all that was conveyed to John Endicott, Jr. But the Court had no right to encroach upon the Orchard Farm, which had been granted to the Governor by them prior to all deeds and to the town grant to Bishop.

Never did that deep and sagacious observation on the mysteries of human nature, " Men's judgments are a parcel of their fortunes," receive a more striking or melancholy illustration than in the case of Zerubabel Endicott. With his falling fortunes, his judgment and discretion fell also; his mind, maddened by a sense of wrong, seemed bent upon exposing itself to new wrongs. Having been broken down by lawsuits, that had wasted his estate, he seemed to have acquired a blind passion for them. Having destroyed his peace and embarrassed his affairs in attempts to resist the adjudications of the Court, he persisted in struggling against them. He had tried to push the Bishop grant west, over the land of Nathaniel Putnam in that quarter. The highest tribunal had settled it against him. But he appeared to be incapable of realizing the fact. He sent his hired men to cut timber on that land. They worked there some days, felled a large number of trees, and hewed them into beams and joists for the frame of a house. One morning, returning to their work, there was no timber to be found; logs, frame-work, and all, were gone. They were carefully piled up a mile away, by the side of Putnam's dwelling-house, who had sent two teams, one of four oxen, the other of two oxen and a horse, with an adequate force of men, and in two loadings had cleaned out the whole. Endicott of course sued him, and of course was cast.

When the General Court had consented to give him

a rehearing of the case of the Bishop farm, they expressly forbade his making any "strip" of the land in the mean while. But with the infatuation which seemed to possess him, and not heeding how fatally it would prejudice his cause at the impending hearing to violate the order of the Court, he again sent a gang of men to cut wood on the land in controversy. The following shows the result: —

" Hugh Jones, aged 46 years, and Alexius Reinolds, aged 25 years, testify and say, that we, these deponents, being desired by Mr. Zerubabel Endicott to cut up some wood, for his winter firewood, accordingly went with our teams, which had four oxen and a horse; and there we met with several other teams of our neighbors, which were upon the same account, that is to say, to help carry up Mr. Endicott some wood for his winter firewood, and when we had loaded our sleds, Thomas Preston and John Tarbell came in a violent manner, and hauled the wood out of our sleds; and Francis Nurse, being present, demanded whose men we were. Mr. Endicott, being present, answered, they were his men."

These witnesses testify that this " battle of the wilderness " lasted two days, — Endicott's men cutting the wood and loading the teams, and Nurse's men pitching it off. The altercations and conflicts that took place between the parties during those two days may easily be imagined. Whether there was a final, decisive pitched battle, we are not informed. Perhaps there was. The woods rang with rough echoes, we may be well assured. A lawsuit followed; the result could not be in doubt. Endicott had no right there;

he was there in direct violation of the order of Court. Nurse was in possession, had a right, and was bound, to keep the land from being stripped.

Shortly after this, Endicott broke down, under the difficulties that had accumulated around him. On the 24th of November, 1683, as we have seen, he was " sick in bed." Two days before, — that is, on the 22d of November, — he had made his will, which was presented in court on the 27th of March, 1684. He was game to the last; for this is an item of the will: —

" Whereas my late father, by his last will, bequeathed to me his farm called Bishop's or Chickering's farm, I do give the said farm to my five sons, to be equally divided among them."

The will of his father had been declared invalid on that point, and others. The whole thing had been conclusively settled for years; but he never would recognize the fact. It is a singular instance of an obstinacy of will completely superseding and suppressing the reason and the judgment. He lost the perception of the actual and real, in clinging to what he felt to be the right.

Every association and sentiment of his soul had been shocked by the wrongs he had suffered. He could not walk over his fields, or look from his windows, without feeling that a property which his father had given to his brother had, in a manner that he knew would have been as odious to that father as it was to him, passed into the hands of strangers, and been used as a wedge on which everybody had conspired to deal blows, driving it into the centre of his patrimonial acres, splitting and rending them through and through. He brooded over the thought, until, whenever his mind was turned to it, his reason was dethroned, his heart broken, and under its weight he fell into his grave.

An argument addressed by him to the court and jury, in one of the innumerable trials of the Bishop-farm case, is among the papers on file. It appears to be a verbatim report of the speech as it was delivered at the time, and proves him to have been a man of talents. It is courteous, gentlemanly, and, I might say, schol-arly in its diction and style, skilful in its statements, and forcible in its arguments.

In all the earlier trials, the juries uniformly gave verdicts in favor of Endicott; but Allen carried the cases up to the General Court, which exercised a final and unrestrained jurisdiction in all matters referred to it. It usually appointed committees or commis-sioners to examine such questions, accepted their reports, and made them binding. Lands were thus disposed of without the agency, and against the de-cisions, of juries. In his arguments addressed to the General Court, Zerubabel Endicott protested against this jurisdiction, by which his lands were taken from him " by a committee, in an arbitrary way, being neither bound nor sworn by law or evidence." He boldly denounced it.

" To be disseized of my inheritance ; to be judged by three or four committee-men, who are neither bound to law nor evi-dence, — who are, or may be, mutable in their apprehensions, doing one thing to-day, and soon again undoing what they did, — I conceive, to be judged in such an arbitrary way is repugnant to the fundamental law of England contained in Magna Charta, chap. 29, which says no freeman shall be dis-seized of his freehold but by the lawful judgment of his peers, — that is to say, by due process of law; which was also con-firmed by the Petition of Right, by Act of Parliament, *tertio Caroli I.* And also such arbitrary jurisdiction was exploded in putting down the Star-Chamber Court; and the excessive fines imposed upon all such actings. See 'English Liberties,' as also the fourth and sixth articles against the Earl of Straf-ford in Baker's 'Chronicle,' folio 518."

He closes one of his remonstrances thus: —

"The humble request of your petitioner to the Hon. Gen. Court, that, as an Englishman, — as a freeman of this juris-diction; as descended from him who, in his time, sought the welfare of this commonwealth, — I may have the benefit and protection of the wholesome laws established in this jurisdic-tion: that, in my extreme wrong, I may have liberty to seek relief in a way of law, and may not, contrary to Magna Charta, be disseized of my freehold by the arbitrary act of two or three committee-men; the fundamental law of England knowing no such constitution, abhorring such administrations: and that the Hon. Court would release your petitioner from the injurious effects of the said committee's act, and explode so pernicious a precedent."

Zerubabel Endicott was an imprudent and obstinate man, but had the traits of a generous, ardent, and noble character. He was a physician by profession. His second wife — the widow, as has been stated, of Rev. Antipas Newman, of Wenham, and daughter of

John Winthrop, Jr., governor of Connecticut — survived him. Although he left five sons, the name, at one time, was borne by a single descendant only, a lad of seven years of age, — Samuel, a grandson of Zerubabel. On him it hung suspended, but he saved it. From that boy, those who bear the name in New England have been derived. We rejoice to believe that they will preserve it, and keep its honor bright.

Winthrop was recognized as the great leader in the early history of the Colony. He had a combination of qualities that marked him as a wise and good man, and gave him precedence. The eminent dignity of his character was admired and revered by all. No one was more ready to admit this than Endicott. Never were men placed towards each other in relations more severely testing their magnanimity, and none ever bore the test more perfectly. But Endicott was, after all, the most complete representative man of that generation. He was thoroughly identified with the people, participating in their virtues and in their defects. He was a strict religionist, a sturdy Puritan, a firm administrator of the law; at the same time, there are indications that he was of a genial spirit. He was personally brave, and officially intrepid. His administration of the government required nerve, and he had it. Sometimes the ardor of his temperament put him for a moment off his guard; but he was quick to acknowledge his error. He was true to the people, who never faltered in their fidelity to him. The author of "Wonder-working Providence" described him as " a fit instrument to begin the wilderness worke, of courage bold undaunted, yet sociable and of a cheerful spirit." I have presented some instances of his kind and pleasant relations with his workmen and neighbors. His name will ever be held in honored remembrance in this vicinity, where his useful enterprise was appreciated ; and his descendants in our day, and to the present time, have contributed to the prosperity and the adornment of the community.

It is not unlikely, that hostile feelings towards the Nurses, which contributed afterwards to serious results, may have been engendered in this long-continued land quarrel. There is evidence that no such feeling existed on the part of the Endicotts : but there were many others interested ; for, by testimony at the trials and in outside discussions, the whole community had become more or less implicated in the strife. The Nurses, as holding the ground and having to bear the brunt of defending it in all cases of intrusion, had a difficult position, and may have made some enemies. At any rate, this controversy was one of the means of stirring up animosities in the neighborhood ; and an account of it has been deemed necessary, as contributing to indicate the elements of the awful convulsions which soon afterwards desolated Salem Village.

When we reach the story, for which this account of the farms of the village and the population that grew up on them is a preparative, we shall come back to the Townsend-Bishop grant, and to the house, still standing, that he built and dwelt in, upon it. It may be well to pause, and view its interesting history prior to 1692. While occupied by its original owner, the "mansion," or "cottage," was the scene of social intercourse among the choicest spirits of the earliest age of New England. Here Bishop, and, after him, Chickering, entertained their friends. Here the fine family of Richard Ingersoll was brought up. Here Governor Endicott projected plans for opening the country; and the road that passes its entrance-gate was laid out by him. To this same house, young John Endicott brought his youthful Boston bride. Here she came again, fifteen years afterwards, as the bride of the learned and distinguished James Allen, to show him the farm which, received as a "marriage gift" from her former husband, she had brought as a "marriage gift" to him. Here the same Allen, in less than six years afterwards, brought still another bride. In all these various, and some of them rather rapid, changes, it was, no doubt, often the resort of distinguished guests, and the place of meeting of many pleasant companies. During the protracted years of litigation for its possession, frequent consultations were held within it; and now, for twelve years, it had been the home of a happy, harmonious, and prosperous family, exemplifying the industry, energy, and enterprise of a New England household. A new chapter was destined, as we shall see, to be opened in its singular and diversified history. But we must return to the enumeration of the original landholders of the village.

George Corwin came to Salem in 1638. He had large tracts of land in various places. He lived, a part of his time, on his farm in the village; is found to have taken an active part in the proceedings of the people, particularly in military affairs; and was captain of a company of cavalry. His great mercantile transactions probably led him to have his residence mostly in the town, first on a lot on Washington Street, near the corner of Norman Street, where his grandson the sheriff lived in 1692. In 1660, he bought of Ann, the relict of Nicholas Woodbury, a lot on Essex Street, next east of the Browne Block, with a front of about one hundred and fifty feet. Here he built a fine mansion, in which he lived the remainder of his days. He died Jan. 6, 1685, leaving an estate inventoried at £5,964. 10s. 7d.,—a large fortune for those times. His portrait is preserved by his descendants, one of whom, the late George A. Ward, describes his dress as represented in the picture: " A wrought flowing neckcloth, a sash covered with lace, a coat with short cuffs and reaching half-way between the wrist and elbow; the skirts in plaits below; an octagon ring and cane." The last two articles are still preserved. His inventory mentions " a silver-laced cloth coat, a velvet ditto, a satin waistcoat embroidered with gold, a trooping scarf and silver hat-band, golden-topped and embroidered, and a silver-headed cane." His farms in the vicinity contained fifteen hundred acres. His connections were distinguished, and his descendants have included many eminent persons. The name, by male descent, disappeared for a time in this part of the country; but in the last generation it was restored in the female descent by an act of the Legislature, and is honorably borne by one of our most respectable families, who inherit his blood, and cherish the memorials which time has spared of their first American ancestor.

William Hathorne appears on the church records as early as 1636. He died in June, 1681, seventy-four years of age. No one in our annals fills a larger space. As soldier commanding important and difficult expeditions, as counsel in cases before the courts, as judge on the bench, and in innumerable other positions requiring talent and intelligence, he was constantly called to serve the public. He was distinguished as a public speaker, and is the only person, I believe, of that period, whose reputation as an orator has come down to us. He was an Assistant, that is, in the upper branch of the Legislature, seventeen years. He was a deputy twenty years. When the deputies, who before sat with the assistants, were separated into a distinct body, and the House of Representatives thus came into existence, in 1644, Hathorne was their first Speaker. He occupied the chair, with intermediate services on the floor from time to time, until raised to the other House. He was an inhabitant of Salem Village, having his farm there, and a dwelling-house, in which he resided when his legislative, military, and other official duties permitted. His son John, who succeeded him in all his public honors, also lived on his own farm in the village

a great part of the time. The name is indelibly
stamped on the hills and meadows of the region, as
it was in the civil history of that age, and has been in
the elegant literature of the present.

William Trask was one of what are called the
" First Planters." He came over before Endicott,
had his residence on Salem Farms, was a most energetic, enterprising, and useful citizen, and filled a
great variety of public stations. He brought large
tracts of land under culture, planted orchards, and
established mills at the head of tide-water on the
North River. He was the military leader of the first
age of the plantations in this neighborhood, was captain of the train-band from the beginning, and, by his
gallantry and energy in action, commanded the applause of his contemporaries. For his services in the
Pequot Expedition, the General Court gave him and
his associates large grants of land. His obsequies
were celebrated, on the 16th of May, 1666, with great
military parade ; and the people of the town and the
whole surrounding country followed his honored remains to the grave.

Richard Davenport came to Salem in 1631. His
first residence was in the town ; but soon he was led
to the Farms. In 1636, he received a grant of eighty
acres ; in 1638, of two hundred and twenty acres ;
and, in 1642, eighty acres more, to be divided between
him and Captain Lothrop. Besides these, he received
several smaller grants of meadow and salt marsh.
Such grants were made only with the view of having

them duly improved; and it cannot be doubted that
he was zealously engaged in agricultural operations.
His town residence was on a lot reaching from Essex
Street to the North River. Its front extended from
the grounds now the site of the North Church to
North Street. His house stood at some distance back
from Essex Street. This estate was sold by his administrators, in 1674, to Jonathan Corwin, whose
family occupied it until a very recent period. He left
the town in 1643, and subsequently lived in what was
afterwards Salem Village, until the public service
called him away. He sold some of his estates, but
retained others, on the Farms and in the town, to the
time of his death. He continued the superintendence
of his country estate, which seems to have been his
family home, to the last. His military career gave
him early distinction, and closed only with his life.
In 1634, the General Court chose him " Ensign to
Capt. Trask." He was concerned with Endicott in
cutting out the cross from the king's colors. The following is from the record of a meeting of the court,
Nov. 7, 1634: " It is ordered that Ensign Davenport shall be sent for by warrant, with command to
bring his colors with him to the next court, as also
any other that hath defaced the said colors." Davenport did not seem anxious to cover up his agency in
this matter; for, when he offered his next child to
baptism, he signified to the assembly that he was determined to commemorate and perpetuate the memory
of the transaction, by having her christened " True

Cross." It was necessary to make a show of punishing Endicott and Davenport on this occasion, to prevent trouble from the home government. Soon after, we find the General Court heaping honors upon Davenport, and finally, in 1639, making him a grant of one hundred and fifty acres of land, specially noticing his services in the Pequot War, which appear to have elicited general applause. In some desperate encounters with the savages, seventeen arrows were shot " into his coat of mail," and he was wounded in unprotected parts of his person. He was twice deputy to the General Court. In 1644, the General Court organized an elaborate system of external defence, the whole based upon Castle Island, now Fort Independence, in Boston Harbor. From that point, hostile invasion by a naval force was to be repelled. Every vessel, on entering, was to report to the castle, be examined and subject to the orders of the commandant. It became the military headquarters of the colony, the protection and oversight of whose commerce were intrusted to the officer in command. This was the highest military station and trust in the gift of the Government. It was assigned to Richard Davenport; and he held it for twenty-one years, to the moment of his death. The country reposed in confidence upon his watchful fidelity. He put and kept the castle in an efficient condition. In 1659, as evidence of their satisfaction and approval of his official conduct, the General Court made him a grant of five hundred acres of land laid out in Lancaster. On the 15th of July, 1665, he was killed by lightning, at his post. The records of the General Court speak of " the solemn stroke of thunder that took away Captain Davenport." The whole country mourned the loss of the veteran soldier ; and the Court granted his family an additional tract of one hundred acres of land on the Merrimac River. He was in his sixtieth year at the time of his death. Of the company required to be raised in Salem for the Block-Island Expedition, in 1636, the three commissioned officers were furnished from the Farms, — Trask, Davenport, and Read. They were soldiers by nature and instinct, and to the end. The volleys of devoted, faithful, and mourning comrades were fired over their graves, with no great interval of time. United in early service, separated by the course of their lives, they were united again in death.

Thomas Lothrop originally lived in the town, between Collins Cove and the North River. He became a member of the First Church in Salem, and was admitted a freeman in 1634. He soon removed to the Farms; and his name appears among the rate-payers at the formation of the village parish. For many years he was deputy from Salem to the General Court; and after Beverly was set off, as his residence at the time was on that side of the line, he was always in the General Court, as deputy from the new town, when his other public employments permitted. No man was ever more identified with the history of the Salem Farms. He contributed to form the structure of its society, and the character of its population, by all that

a wise and good man could do. During his whole life
in America, he was more or less engaged in the military service, in arduous, difficult, and dangerous positions and operations; acting sometimes against
Indians, and sometimes against the French, or, as was
usually the case, against them both combined. He
was occasionally sent to distant posts; commanding
expeditions to the eastward as far as Acadia. He
was at one time in charge of a force at Port Royal,
now Annapolis, Nova Scotia. Increase Mather calls
him a " godly and courageous commander." When
the last decisive struggle with King Philip was approaching, and aid was needed from the eastern part
of the colony to rescue the settlements on the Connecticut River from utter destruction, the " Flower of
Essex " was summoned to the field. It was a choice
body of efficient men, " all culled out of the towns
belonging to this county," numbering about one hundred men. Lothrop, of course, was their captain. In
August, 1675, they were on the ground at Hadley, the
place of rendezvous. On the 26th of that month,
Captain Lothrop, with his company, and Captain
Beers, of Watertown, with his, after a vigorous pursuit, attacked the Indians in a swamp, about ten miles
from Hatfield, at the foot of Sugar-Loaf Hill. Ten
were killed on the side of the English, and twenty-six
on the side of the Indians, who were driven from the
swamp, and scattered in their flight; to fall, as was
their custom, upon detached settlements; and continuing to waste and destroy, by fire and sword, with

hatchet, scalping-knife, torch, and gun. On the 18th
of September, Lothrop, with his company, started from
Deerfield, to convoy a train of eighteen wagons, loaded
with grain, and furniture of the inhabitants seeking refuge from danger, with teamsters and others.
Moseley, with his men, remained behind, to scout the
woods, and give notice of the approach of Indians;
but the stealthy savages succeeded in effecting a complete surprise, and fell upon Lothrop as his wagons
were crossing a stream. They poured in a destructive
fire from the woods, in all directions. They were
seven to one. A perfect carnage ensued. Lothrop
fell early in the unequal fight, and only seven or eight
of his whole party were left to tell the story of the
fatal scene. The locality of this disastrous and sanguinary tragedy has ever since been known as "Bloody
Brook." In the list of those who perished by bullet,
tomahawk, or arrow, on that fearful morning, we read
the names of many village neighbors of the brave and
lamented commander, — Thomas Bayley, Edward
Trask, Josiah Dodge, Peter Woodbury, Joseph Balch,
Thomas Buckley, Joseph King, Robert Wilson, and
James Tufts. One of Lothrop's sergeants, who was
among the slain, Thomas Smith, then of Newbury,
originated in the village. His family had grants of
land, including the hill called by their name.

Captain Lothrop was as remarkable for the benevolence of his spirit and the tenderness of his nature as
for his wisdom in council, energy in command, or gallantry in battle. Indeed, his character in private life

was so beautiful and lovable, that I cannot refrain
from leading you into the recesses of his domestic
circle. It presents a picture of rare attractiveness.
He had no children. His wife was a kind and amiable
person. They longed for objects upon which to gratify
the yearnings of their affectionate hearts. He had a
large estate. His character became known to the
neighbors and the country people around. If there
was an occurrence calling for commiseration anywhere in the vicinity, it was managed to bring it to
his notice. Orphan children were received into his
household, and brought up with parental care and tenderness. Many were, in this way, the objects of his
charity and affections. Persons especially, who were
in any degree connected with his wife's family, naturally conceived the desire to have him adopt their
children. This was the case particularly with those
who were in straitened circumstances. Others, knowing his disposition, would bring tales of distress and
destitution to his ears. Some, perhaps, turned out
to be unworthy of his goodness. In one instance,
at least, where he had taken a child into his family
in its infancy, touched by appeals made to his compassion by the parents, brought it up carefully,
watched over its education, and become attached to it,
when it had reached an age to be serviceable, the
parents claimed and insisted on their right to it, and
took it away, much against his will. But the good
man's benevolence was not impaired, nor the stream
of his affectionate charities checked, by the misconduct

or ingratitude of his wards or of their friends. His plan was to do all the good in his power to the children thus brought into his family, to prepare them for usefulness, and start them favorably in life. In the case of boys, he would get them apprenticed to worthy people in useful callings. At the time of his death, there were two grown-up members of his family, who appear to have been foisted upon his care in their earliest childhood. But there was no blame to be attached to them in the premises; and they were regarded by him with much affection. There were no relations of his own in this country in need of charitable aid or without adequate parental protection; and it was not strange that several of his wife's connections should have availed themselves of the benefit of his generous disposition. She herself gives a very interesting account of an instance of this sort, in a deposition found wrapped up among some old papers in the county court-house. The object of the statement was to explain how a connection of hers became domesticated in the family.

"When the child's mother was dead, my husband being with me at my cousin's burial, and seeing our friends in so sad a condition, the poor babe having lost its mother, and the woman that nursed it being fallen sick, I then did say to some of my friends, that, if my husband would give me leave, I could be very willing to take my cousin's little one for a while, till he could better dispose of it; whereupon the child's father did move it to my husband. My dear husband, considering my weakness, and the incumbrance I had in the family.

was pleased to return this answer, — that he did not see how it was possible for his wife to undergo such a burden. The next day there came a friend to our house, a woman which gave suck, and she understanding how the poor babe was left, being intreated, was willing to take it to nurse, and forthwith it was brought to her : but it had not been with her three weeks before it pleased the Lord to visit that nurse with sickness also ; and the nurse's mother came to me desiring I would take the child from her daughter, and then my dear husband, observing the providence of God, was freely willing to receive her into his house."

At the time when this addition was made to his family, there was certainly already in it another of his wife's connections, who had been brought there when an infant in a manner perhaps equally singular, and who had grown up to maturity. The particular " incumbrance," however, spoken of by her, related to another matter. She was an only daughter. Her father had died many years before, at quite an advanced age. Her mother, who was sickly and infirm as well as aged, was taken immediately into her family, and remained under her roof until her death. In her weak and helpless condition, much care and exertion were thrown upon her daughter. The only objection the captain seemed to have to increasing the burden of the household, by receiving into it this additional child with its nurse, resulted from conjugal tenderness and considerateness. It must be confessed that there are some indications of well-arranged management in the foregoing account. The friend who happened to

call at the house the "next day," and who was able
to supply what the "poor babe" needed, certainly
came very opportunely; and there was altogether a
remarkable concurrence and sequence of circumstances. But all that he saw was a case of suffering,
helpless innocence, and an opportunity for benevolence
and charity; and in these, with a true theology, he
read "a providence of God." That child continued,
to the hour when he took his last farewell of his
family, beneath his roof, and was an object of affectionate care, and in her amiable qualities a source of
happiness to him and his good wife. It is stated that
the children, thus from time to time domesticated in
the family, called him father, and that he addressed
them as his children. While they were infants, he
was "a tender nursing father" to them. When fond-
ling them in his arms, in the presence of his wife, he
would solemnly take notice of the providence of God
that had "disposed of them from one place to another" until they had been brought to him; and
"would present them in his desires to God, and
implore a blessing upon them."

The picture presented in the foregoing details is
worth rescuing from oblivion. Such instances of actual life, exhibited in the most private spheres, constitute a branch of history more valuable, in some
respects, than the public acts of official dignitaries.
History has been too exclusively confined, in its materials, to the movements of states and of armies. It
ought to paint the portraits of individual men and

women in their common lives; it ought to lead us into the interior of society, and introduce us to the family circles and home experiences of the past. It cannot but do us good to know Thomas Lothrop, not only as an early counsellor among the legislators of the colony, and as having immortalized by his blood a memorable field of battle and slaughter, but as the centre of a happy and virtuous household on a New England farm. He made that home happy by his benignant virtue. Although denied the blessing of children of his own, his fireside was enlivened with the prattle and gayeties of the young. Joy and hope and growth were within his walls. He was not a parent; but his heart was kept warm with parental affections. He had a home where dear ones waited for him, and rushed out to meet and cling round him with loving arms, and welcome him with merry voices, when he returned from the sessions of the General Court, or from campaigns against the French and Indians.

Besides these offices of beneficence in the domestic sphere, we find traces, in the local records, of constant usefulness and kindness among his rural neighbors. He was called, on all occasions, to advise and assist. As a judicious friend, he was relied upon and sought at the bedside of the sick and dying, and in families bereaved of their head. His name appears as a witness to wills, appraiser of estates, trustee and guardian of the young. He was the friend of all. I know not where to find a more perfect union of the hero and the Christian; of all that is manly and chivalrous with all that is tender, benevolent, and devout.

Somewhere about the year 1650, after he had been married a considerable time, he revisited his native country. A sister, Ellen, had, in the mean while, grown up from early childhood; and he found her all that a fond brother could have hoped for. With much persuasion, he besought his mother to allow her to return with him to America. He stated that he had no children; that he would be a father to her, and watch over and care for her as for his own child. At length the mother yielded, and committed her daughter to his custody, not without great reluctance, trusting to his fraternal affection and plighted promise. He brought her over with him to his American home. She was worthy of his love, and he was true to his sacred and precious trust.

Ellen Lothrop became the wife of Ezekiel Cheever, the great schoolmaster; and I should consider myself false to all good learning, if I allowed the name of this famous old man to slip by, without pausing to pay homage to it. His record, as a teacher of a Latin Grammar School, is unrivalled. Twelve years at New Haven, eleven at Ipswich, nine at Charlestown, and more than thirty-eight at Boston, — more than seventy in all, — may it not be safely said that he was one of the very greatest benefactors of America? With Elijah Corlett, who taught a similar school at Cambridge for more than forty years, he bridged over the wide chasm between the education brought with them

by the fathers from the old country, and the education
that was reared in the new. They fed and kept alive
the lamp of learning through the dark age of our
history. All the scholars raised here were trained by
them. One of Cotton Mather's most characteristic
productions is the tribute to his venerated master. It
flows from a heart warm with gratitude. "Although
he had usefully spent his life among children, yet he
was not become twice a child," but held his faculties
to the last. "In this great work of bringing our sons
to be men, he was my master seven and thirty years
ago, was master to my betters no less than seventy
years ago ; so long ago, that I must even mention my
father's tutor for one of them. He was a Christian of
the old fashion, — an old New England Christian ; and
I may tell you, that was as venerable a sight, as the
world, since the days of primitive Christianity, has
ever looked upon. He lived, as a master, the term
which has been, for above three thousand years, assigned for the life of a man." Mather celebrated his
praises in a poetical effusion : —

> " He lived, and to vast age no illness knew,
>   Till Time's scythe, waiting for him, rusty grew.
>   He lived and wrought ; his labors were immense,
>   But ne'er declined to preterperfect tense.
>   .   .   .   .
>   'Tis Corlett's pains, and Cheever's, we must own,
>   That thou, New England, art not Scythia grown."

To our early schoolmasters, as Mather says, and
the later too, I may add, it is owing, that the whole
country did not become another Scythia.

Ezekiel Cheever was in this country as early as 1637. He was then in New Haven, sharing in the work of the first settlement of that colony, teaching school as his ordinary employment, but sometimes preaching, and in other ways helping to lay the foundations of church and commonwealth. While there, he had a family of several children. The first-born, Samuel, became the minister of Marblehead. In 1650, he was keeping a school at Ipswich. About this time, he lost his wife. On the 18th of November, 1652, he married Ellen, the sister whom Captain Lothrop had brought with him from England. They had several children; one of them, Thomas, was ordained first at Malden, and afterwards at Chelsea. The old schoolmaster died on the 21st of August, 1708, aged ninety-three years and seven months. His son Thomas reached the same age. Samuel, the minister at Marblehead, was eighty-five years old at his death. The name of Ezekiel, jr., appears on the rate-list of the village parish as late as 1731, so that he must have reached the age of at least seventy-seven years.

The antiquarians have been sorely perplexed in determining the relationship of the Cheevers and Reas, as they appear to be connected together as heirs of the Lothrop property, in an order of the General Court of the 11th of June, 1681.

The facts are these: Captain Lothrop married Bethia, daughter of Daniel Rea. He died without issue, and had made no will. As he was killed in battle, his widow undertook to set up a nuncupative will. A snow-storm, on the day appointed to act upon the matter, so blocked up the roads, that neither Ezekiel Cheever nor his son Thomas, who had charge of his mother's rights, could get to Salem; and the court granted administration to the widow. The Cheevers demanded a rehearing: it was granted; and quite an interesting and pertinacious law-suit arose, which was finally carried up to the General Court, who decided it in 1681. The widow does not appear to have been actuated by merely selfish motives, but sought to divert a portion of the landed estate from the only legal heir, Ellen, the wife of Ezekiel Cheever, to other parties, in favor of whom her feelings were much enlisted. There is no indication of any un-friendliness between her and her "sister Cheever."

Lothrop's wife had become much attached to one of her connections, who had been brought into the family. Her husband, having been fond of children, had often expressed great affection for those of her brother, Joshua Rea. He had also sometimes, in expressing his interest in the Beverly Church, evinced a disposition to leave to it "his ten acre lot and his house upon the same," as a parsonage. Perhaps, if he had not been suddenly called away, he might have done something, particularly for the latter object. It appeared in evidence, from her statements and from others, that he had been importuned to make a will, and that it was much on his mind, particularly when recovering from a long and dangerous sickness the winter before his death; but he never could be brought to do it. There was no evidence that he had ever absolutely determined on any thing positively or specifically. His widow, who seems to have been a perfectly honest and truthful woman, testified to a conversation that passed between them on the subject, as they were riding " together towards Wenham, the last spring, in the week before the Court of election." In passing by particular pieces of property owned by him, he indulged in some speculations as to what disposal he should make of this or that pasture or plain or woodland. But she did not represent that his expressions were absolute and determinate, but rather indicative of the then inclination of his mind. In another part of her statement, she said, " I did desire him to make his will, which, when he was sick, I did more than once or twice; and his answer to me was, that he did look upon it as that which was very requisite and fit should be done. But, dear wife, thou hast no cause to be troubled; if I should die and not make a will, it would be never the worse for thee; thyself would have the more." It is not difficult to understand the case as it probably stood in the mind of Captain Lothrop. Whenever the subject of making a will, and doing kind things for the Beverly parish, and the individuals in whose behalf his wife was so anxious, was brought up, he felt the force, as he expressed it, " of the duty which God required of a master of a family to set his house in order; " and he was no doubt strongly moved, and sometimes almost resolved, to gratify her wishes : but he remembered the

solemn promise he had made to his mother, as he
parted from her for ever, and received his sister from
her hands, and every sentiment of honor, and of
filial and fraternal love, restrained him; and his mind
settled into a conviction that it was his duty to allow
his sister the benefit of the final inheritance of his
property. As the particular persons to whom his wife
wished him to make bequests were her relatives, and
the law would give her an ample allowance in the use,
for life, of his large landed property, she would be
able to provide for them after his death, as he had
been in the habit of doing.

The General Court took a just view of the case, and
decided that she should have the whole movable estate
for her own " use and dispose," and the " use and
benefit " for life of the houses and lands, " making no
strip nor waste;" after her death, the same to go to
Ellen, the wife of Ezekiel Cheever. The widow was
to pay all debts due from the estate, and also twenty
pounds to the children of her brother, Joshua Rea.
The Court seemed to think, that, if any expectations
had been excited in that quarter, she was fully as responsible for it as her late husband; and, as the
Cheevers were to get nothing, while she lived, out of
the estate, the Court required her to pay the sum just
named to her nephews and nieces. They ordered
Ezekiel Cheever to pay five pounds as costs for their
hearing the case, which he did on the spot.

It may be mentioned, by the way, that the widow
of Captain Lothrop was married again within eight

months of his death; but that was quite usual in those days. She and her new husband concluded that it would be troublesome to take care of Captain Lothrop's several farms. They preferred to live in the town. She was probably over sixty years of age. The conclusion of the whole matter was, that, in consideration of sixty pounds paid down, they surrendered all claim whatever to the "houseing and lands" left by Captain Lothrop, to Cheever and his wife. They conveyed them "free and clear of and from all debts owing from the estate of said Lothrop, and gifts or bequests pretended to be made by him, or by any ways or means to be had, claimed, or challenged therefrom by any person or persons whomsoever." The relict of Captain Lothrop died in 1688.

Ezekiel Cheever and his wife, having thus become possessed of all her brother's real estate, conveyed the lands belonging to it in Salem Village to their son, Ezekiel Cheever, Jr. He had, for some years, been living in the town of Salem, carrying on the business of a tailor. He was a member of the First Church, and appears to have been a respectable person. His dwelling-house stood on the lot in Washington Street occupied by the late Robert Brookhouse. He sold it to the Rev. Nicholas Noyes, on the 14th of April, 1684, removed to the village, took possession of the Lothrop farm, and was there in time to bear a share in the witchcraft delusion.

In 1636, a grant of land was made to Thomas Gardner of one hundred acres. He came to this country as early as 1624, and resided at Cape Ann. Subsequently he removed to Salem, and, with his wife, was admitted to the church. He was deputy to the General Court in 1637. His grant was in the western part of the township, and embraced land included within the limits of Salem Village. The name still remains on the same territory. His sons became proprietors of several additional tracts in the neighborhood. One of them, Joseph, is connected, in the most conspicuous and interesting manner, with our military history.

The destruction of Captain Lothrop and his company, on the 18th of September, filled the country with grief and consternation ; and, as the year 1675 drew towards a close, the conviction became general, that the crisis of the fate of the colonies was near at hand. The Indians were carrying all before them. Philip was spreading conflagration, devastation, and slaughter around the borders, and striking sudden and deadly blows into the heart of the country. It was evident that he was consolidating the Indian power into irresistible strength. Among papers on file in the State House is a letter addressed to the governor and council, dated at Mendon, Oct. 1, 1675, from Lieutenant Phinehas Upham, of Malden. In command of a company, acting under Captain Gorham of Barnstable, who had also a company of his own, he had been on a scout for Indians beyond Mendon, which was a frontier town. Their route had been over a sweep of territory then an almost un-

broken wilderness, embracing the present sites of Grafton, Worcester, Oxford, and Dudley. The result of
the exploration is thus given : " Now, seeing that in
all our marches we find no Indians, we verily think
that they are drawn together into great bodies far
remote from these parts." From other scouting parties, it became evident that this opinion was correct,
and that the Indians were collecting stores and as-
sembling their warriors somewhere, to fall upon the
colonies at the first opening of spring. Further information made it certain, that their place of gathering
was in the Narragansett country, in the south-westerly
part of the colony of Rhode Island. There was no
alternative but, as a last effort, to strike the enemy at
that point, with the utmost available force. A thousand men were raised, 527 by Massachusetts, 315 by
Connecticut, and 158 by Plymouth. Massachusetts
organized a company of cavalry and six companies of
foot soldiers, Connecticut five and Plymouth two companies of foot. All were placed under the command
of Governor Winslow, of Plymouth. The winter had
set in earlier than usual ; much snow had fallen, and
the weather was extremely cold. The seven companies of Massachusetts, under the command of Major
Samuel Appleton of Ipswich, started on their march,
Dec. 10. On the evening of the 12th, having
effected a junction with the Plymouth companies, they
reached the rendezvous, on the north side of Wickford
Hill, in North Kingston, R.I. On the 13th, Winslow
commenced his move upon the enemy. On the 18th,

the Connecticut troops joined him. His army was complete; the enemy was known to be near, and all haste made to reach him. The snow was deep. The Narragansetts were intrenched on a somewhat elevated piece of ground of five or six acres in area, surrounded by a swamp, within the limits of the present town of South Kingston. The Indian camp was strongly fortified by a double row of palisades, about a rod apart, and also by a thick hedge. There was but a single entrance known to our troops, which could only be reached, one at a time, over a slanting log or felled tree, slippery from frost and falling snow, about six feet above a ditch. There were other passages, known only to the Indians, by which they could steal out, a few at a time, and get a shot at our people in the flank and rear. Many of our men were cut off in this way. The allied forces had expected to pass the night, previous to reaching the hostile camp, at a garrison about fifteen miles distant from that point; but the Indians had destroyed the buildings, and slaughtered the occupants, seventeen in number, two days before. Here the troops passed the night, unsheltered from the bitter weather. The next day, Dec. 19, was Sunday; but their provisions were exhausted, and the supply they had expected to find had been destroyed with the garrison-house. There could be no delay. They recommenced their march, at half-past five o'clock in the morning, through the deep snow, which continued falling all day, and reached the borders of what was described, by a

writer well acquainted with it, as " a hideous swamp."
Fortunately, the early and long-continued extreme
cold weather of that winter had rendered it more pass-
able than it otherwise would have been. But the
ground was rough, and very difficult to traverse. They
were chilled and worn by their long march, following
winding paths through thick woods, across gullies, and
over hills and fields. It was between one and two
o'clock in the afternoon, and the short winter day was
wearing away. Winslow saw the position at a glance,
and, by the promptness of his decision, proved himself a great captain. He ordered an instant assault.
The Massachusetts troops were in the van; the Plymouth, with the commander-in-chief, in the centre;
the Connecticut, in the rear. The Indians had erected
a block-house near the entrance, filled with sharp-
shooters, who also lined the palisades. The men
rushed on, although it was into the jaws of death,
under an unerring fire. The block-house told them
where the entrance was. The companies of Moseley
and Davenport led the way. Moseley succeeded in
passing through. Davenport fell beneath three fatal
shots, just within the entrance. Isaac Johnson, captain of the Roxbury company, was killed while on the
log. But death had no terrors to that army. The centre
and rear divisions pressed up to support the front and
fill the gaps; and all equally shared the glory of the
hour. Enough survived the terrible passage to bring
the Indians to a hand-to-hand fight within the fort.
After a desperate struggle of nearly three hours, the

savages were driven from their stronghold ; and, with the setting of that sun, their power was broken. Philip's fortunes had received a decided overthrow, and the colonies were saved. In all military history, there is not a more daring exploit. Never, on any field, has more heroic prowess been displayed. By the best computations, the Indian loss was at least one thousand, including the large numbers who perished from cold, as they scattered in their flight without shelter, food, or place of refuge. Of the colonial force, over eighty were killed, and one hundred and fifty wounded. Three of the Massachusetts captains — Johnson, Gardner, and Davenport — were killed on the spot. Three of the Connecticut captains — John Gallop, Samuel Marshall, and Robert Seely — also fell in the fight. Captain William Bradford, of Plymouth, was wounded by a musket-ball, which he carried in his body to his grave. Captain John Gorham, also of the Plymouth colony, was shortly after carried off by a fever, occasioned by the over-exhaustion of the march and the battle. Lieutenant Phinehas Upham, of Johnson's company, was mortally wounded. Great value appears to have been attached to the services of this officer. In the hurried preparation for the campaign, Captain Johnson had nominated his brother as his lieutenant. The General Court overruled the appointment. Johnson cheerfully acquiesced, and, in a paper addressed to the Court, assured them that he " most readily submitted to their choice of Lieutenant Upham." This single passage is an imperishable eulogium upon the characters of the two brave men who gave their lives to the country on that fatal but glorious day.

Captain Gardner's company was raised in this neighborhood. Joseph Peirce and Samuel Pikeworth of Salem, and Mark Bachelder of Wenham, were killed before entering the fort. Abraham Switchell of Marblehead, Joseph Soames of Cape Ann, and Robert Andrews of Topsfield, were killed at the fort. Charles Knight, Thomas Flint, and Joseph Houlton, Jr., of Salem Village; Nicholas Hakins and John Farrington, of Lynn; Robert Cox, of Marblehead; Eben Baker and Joseph Abbot, of Andover; Edward Harding, of Cape Ann; and Christopher Read, of Beverly, — were wounded. An account of the death of Captain Gardner, in detail, has been preserved. The famous warrior, and final conqueror of King Philip, Benjamin Church, was in the fight as a volunteer, rendered efficient service, and was wounded. His "History of King Philip's War" is reprinted, by John Kimball Wiggin, as one of his series of elegant editions of rare and valuable early colonial publications entitled "Library of New England History." In the second number, Part I. of Church's history is edited by Henry Martyn Dexter. Church's account of what came within his observation in this fight, with the notes of the learned editor, is the most valuable source of information we have in reference to it. He says, that, in the heat of the battle, he came across Gardner, "amidst the wigwams in the east end of the fort, making towards him; but, on a sudden, while they were looking each other in the face, Captain Gardner settled down." He instantly went to him. The blood was running over his cheek. Church lifted up his cap, calling him by name. " Gardner looked up in his face, but spoke not a word, being mortally shot through the head." The widow of Captain Gardner (Ann, sister of Sir George Downing) became the successor of Ann Dudley, the celebrated poetess of her day, by marrying Governor Bradstreet, in 1680. She died in 1713.

There is a curious parallelism between the first and the last great victory over the Indian power in the history of America. An interval of one hundred and sixty one years separates them. On the 19th of December, 1836, — the anniversary of the day when Winslow stormed the Narragansett fort, — Colonel Taylor received his orders to pursue the Florida Indians. It was a last attempt to subdue them. They had long baffled and defied the whole power of the United States. Every general in the army had laid down his laurels in inglorious and utter failure. He started on the 20th, with an army of about one thousand men. On the 25th, he found himself on the edge of a swamp, impassable by artillery or horses. On the opposite side were the Indian warriors, ready to deal destruction, if he should attempt to cross the swamp. He had the same question to decide which Winslow had; and he decided it in the same way, with equal promptness. The struggle lasted about the same time; and the loss, in proportion to the numbers engaged, was about the same. The results were alike permanently decisive. Okee-cho-bee stands by the side of Narragansett, and the names of Josiah Winslow and Zachary Taylor are imperishably inscribed together on the tablets of military glory.

Dr. Palfrey says that Captain Nathaniel Davenport was a son of "Davenport of the Pequot War." He was born in Salem, and brought up in the village. His name, with those of his brave father, and his associate in youth and in death Joseph Gardner, belongs to our local annals. They were both the idols of their men. Davenport was dressed, when he fell, in a "full buff suit," and was probably thought by the Indians to be the commander-in-chief. On receiving his triple wound, he called his lieutenant, Edward Tyng, to him, gave him his gun in charge, delivered over to him the command of his company, and died.

There has been some uncertainty on the point whether Nathaniel Davenport was a son of Richard, the commandant at the castle. The fact that he was associated with William Stoughton, and Stephen Minot whose wife was a daughter of Richard Davenport, as an administrator of the estate of the latter, has been regarded as rendering it probable. Dr. Palfrey's unhesitating statement to that effect is, of itself, enough to settle the question. There is, moreover, a document on file which proves that he is correct. Nathaniel's widow had some difficulty in settling his estate, and applied to the General Court for its interposition.

Quite a mass of papers belong to the case. Among them is a bill of expenses incurred by her in connection with his funeral charges, such as, " twenty-one rings to relatives," and to those " who took care to bring him off slain, eight pounds ; " and " for mourning for my mother Davenport, sisters Minot and Elliot, and myself, sixteen pounds." This latter item is decisive, as we know that two of Richard Davenport's daughters married persons of those names. It is a circumstance of singular interest, as showing by how slight an accident — for it is a mere accident — important questions of history are sometimes determinable. This item, so far as I have been able to find, is the only absolute evidence we have to the point that Richard was the father of Nathaniel Davenport ; and it would not have been in existence, had not questions arisen in the settlement of the estate of the latter requiring the action of the General Court. The record of baptisms in the First Church at Salem, prior to 1636, is lost. The names of Richard Davenport's children, baptized subsequent to that date, are in the records of the Salem or Boston churches. As Nathaniel is understood to have been one of the earliest born, the record of his baptism was probably in the lost part of the Salem book.

It may be thought surprising, that so little appears to have been known concerning an officer of his rank and parentage, and whose death has rendered his name so memorable. To account for it, I must recur to the history of the Narragansett expedition. No military organization was ever more rapidly effected, or more thoroughly and promptly executed its work. The commissioners of the three united colonies were satisfied that the Indian rendezvous at Narragansett, where their forces and stores were being collected and their resources concentrated, must be struck at without a moment's delay; that the blow must be swift and decisive; that it must be struck then, in the depth of winter; that, if deferred to the spring, all would be lost; that, if the Indian power was allowed to remain and to gather strength until the next season, nothing could save the settlements from destruction. Early in November, they formed their plan, and put the machinery for summoning all their utmost resources into instant action. On the 30th of November, the officers appointed for the purpose made return, that they had impressed the required number in the several counties and towns, fitted them out with arms, ammunition, clothes, and all necessary equipments; that the men were on the ground, ready to go forward. There was no time for recruiting, or raising bounties, or substitute brokerage; no time for electioneering to get commissions. The rank and file were ready: they had been brought in by a process that gave no time for canvassing for offices. A summons had been left at the house of every drafted man, to report himself the next morning. If any one failed to appear, some other member of the family, brother or father, had to take his place. The organizing and officering of this force must be done instanter. All depended upon suitable officers being selected. A company was waiting at Boston for a captain, and a captain must be found. Some one in authority happened to think of Nathaniel Davenport. His childhood and youth had been passed at Salem Village and on Castle Island: on reaching maturity, he had removed to New York, and been there for years in commercial pursuits. A short time before, he had returned to Boston, and engaged in business there. His father had been dead since 1665, and not many persons knew him, — only, perhaps, a few of his early associates, and the old friends of his father: but they knew, that, from his birth to his manhood, he had breathed a military atmosphere, — was a soldier, by inheritance, of the school of Lothrop, Read, and Trask; and it was determined at once to hunt him up. He was serving at Court; taken out of the jury-box in a pending trial; and placed at the head of the company. The accurate historian of Boston, Samuel G. Drake, says, "Captain Davenport's men were extremely grieved at the death of their leader; he having, by his courteous carriage, much attached them to himself, although he was a stranger to most of them when he was appointed their captain. On which occasion he made 'a very civil speech,' and allowed them to choose their sergeants themselves." He had no time to settle his accounts, arrange his affairs, or confer with any one, but led his company at once to the rendezvous. These circumstances, perhaps, partially explain why so little seems to have been known of him in Boston, or to local writers.

Besides Captains Gardner and Davenport and the men whose names have been mentioned as killed or wounded, there were in the Narragansett fight the following from Salem Village and its farming neighborhood : John Dodge, William Dodge, William Raymond, Thomas Raymond, John Raymond, Joseph Herrick, Thomas Putnam, Jr., Thomas Abbey, Robert Leach, and Peter Prescott. There may have been others : no full roll is on record. The foregoing are gathered from partial returns miscellaneously collected in the files at the State House. The Dodges (sometimes the name is written Dodds, which appears, I think, to have been its original form), and the Raymonds (sometimes written Rayment), were, from the first, conspicuous in military affairs. A few words explanatory of their relation to the village may be here properly given.

On the 25th of January, 1635, the town of Salem voted to William Trask, John Woodbury, Roger Conant, Peter Palfrey, and John Balch, a tract of land, as follows : " Two hundred acres apiece together lying, being at the head of Bass River, one hundred and twenty-four poles in breadth, and so running northerly to the river by the great pond side, and so in breadth, making up the full quantity of a thousand acres." These men were original settlers, having been in the country for some time before Endicott's arrival. This circumstance gave to them and others the distinguishing title of " old planters." The grant of a thousand acres, comprising the five farms above mentioned, was always known as " the Old Planters' Farms." The

first proprietors of them, and their immediate successors, appear to have arranged and managed them in
concert, — to have had homesteads near together between the head of Bass River and the neighborhood of
the "horse bridge," where the meeting-house of the
Second Congregational Society of Beverly, or of the
"Precinct of Salem and Beverly" now stands. Their
woodlands and pasture lands were further to the north
and east. An inspection of the map will give an idea
of the general locality of the "Old Planters' Farms"
in the aggregate — above the head of Bass River, extending northerly towards "the river," as the Ipswich
River was called, and easterly to the "great pond,"
that is, Wenham Lake. Conant, Woodbury, and
Balch occupied their lands at once. I have stated how
Trask's portion of the grant went into the hands of
Scruggs, and then of John Raymond. Palfrey is
thought never to have occupied his portion. He sold
it to William Dodge, the founder of the family of that
name, known by way of eminence as "Farmer Dodge,"
whose wife was a daughter of Conant. A portion of
the grant assigned to Conant was sold by one of his
descendants to John Chipman, who, on the 28th of
December, 1715, was ordained as the first minister
of the "Second Beverly Society." He was the grandfather of Ward Chipman, Judge of the Supreme Court,
and for some time President, of the Province of New
Brunswick, and whose son of the same name was
chief-justice of that court. He was also grandfather
of the wife of the great merchant, William Gray,

whose family has contributed such invaluable service
to the literature, legislation, judicial learning, and general welfare of the country. The Rev. Mr. Chipman
was the ancestor of many other distinguished persons.
The house in which he lived is still standing, near the
site of the church in which he preached. It is occupied by his descendants, bearing his name, and, although much time-worn, has the marks of having been
a structure of a very superior order for that day.
The venerable mansion stands back from the road,
on a smooth and beautiful lawn, bordered by a solid
stone wall of even lines and surfaces. In these respects it well compares with any country residence
upon which taste, skill, and wealth have, in more
recent times, been bestowed.

The dividing line between Beverly and Salem Village, as seen on the map, finally agreed upon in 1703,
ran through the " Old Planters' Farms," particularly
the portions belonging to the Dodges, Raymonds, and
Woodbury. It went through " Captain John Dodge's
dwelling-house, six foot to the eastward of his brick
chimney as it now stands." At the time of the witchcraft delusion, the Raymonds and Dodges mostly
belonged to the Salem Village parish and church.
They continued on the rate-list, and connected with
the proceedings entered on the record-books, until the
meeting-house at the " horse bridge " was opened for
worship, in 1715, when they transferred their relations
to the " Precinct of Salem and Beverly."

When Sir William Phipps got up his expedition

against Quebec, in 1690, William Raymond raised a company from the neighborhood ; and so deep was the impression made upon the public mind by his ability and courage, and so long did it remain in vivid remembrance, that, in 1735, the General Court granted a township of land, six miles square, " to Captain William Raymond, and the officers and soldiers " under his command, and " to their heirs," for their distinguished services in the " Canada Expedition." The grant was laid out on the Merrimack, but, being found within the bounds of New Hampshire, a tract of equivalent value was substituted for it on the Saco River. Among the men who served in this expedition was Eleazer, a son of Captain John Putnam, who afterwards, for many years, was one of the deacons of the Salem Village Church.

The short, rapid, sharp, and sanguinary campaign against the Narragansetts seems to have tried to the utmost, not only the courage and spirit of the men, but the powers of human endurance. The constitutions of many were permanently impaired. As much fatigue and suffering were crowded into that short month as the physical forces of strong men could bear. We find such entries as this in the town-books : — " Salem, 1683. Samuel Beadle, who lost his health in the Narragansett Expedition, is allowed to take the place of Mr. Stephens as an innkeeper." A petition, dated in 1685, is among the papers in the State House, signed by men from Lynn, the Village, Beverly, Reading, and Hingham, praying for a grant of land, for their services and sufferings in that expedition. The petition was granted. The following extract from it tells the story: " We think we have reason to fear our days may be much shortened by our hard service in the war, from the pains and aches of our bodies, that we feel in our bones and sinews, and lameness thereby taking hold of us much, especially in the spring and fall."

While there is " reason to fear " that the days of many were shortened, there were some so tough as to survive the strain, and bid defiance to aches and pains, and almost to time itself. In a list of fourteen who went from Beverly, six, including Thomas Raymond and Lott, a descendant of Roger Conant, were alive in 1735!

The grants of land made to these gallant men and their heirs amounted in all, and ultimately, to seven distinct tracts, called "Narragansett Townships." They were made in fulfilment of an express public promise to that effect. It is stated in an official document, that " proclamation was made to them, when mustered on Dedham Plain " on the 9th of December, just as they took up their march, " that, if they played the man, took the fort, and drove the enemy out of the Narragansett country, which was their great seat, they should have a gratuity in land, besides their wages." The same document, which is in the form of a message from the House of Representatives to the Council of the Province of Massachusetts, dated Jan. 10, 1732, goes on to say, " And as the condition has been performed, certainly the promise, in all equity and justice,

ought to be fulfilled.   And if we consider the difficulties these brave men went through in storming the
fort in the depth of winter, and the pinching wants
they afterwards underwent in pursuing the Indians
that escaped, through a hideous wilderness, known
throughout New England to this day by the name of
the *hungry march;* and if we further consider, that,
until this brave though small army thus played the
man, the whole country was filled with distress and fear,
and we trembled in this capital, Boston itself; and that
to the goodness of God to this army we owe our
fathers' and our own safety and estates," — therefore
they urge the full discharge of the obligations of public justice and gratitude.   They did not urge in vain.
The grants were made on a scale, that finally was
liberal and honorable to the government.

I have dwelt at this great length on the Narragansett campaign and fight, partly because the details
have not been kept as familiar to the memory of the
people as they deserve, but chiefly because they de-
monstrate the military genius of the community with
whose character our subject requires us to be fully
acquainted.   The enthusiasm of the troops, when
Winslow gave the order for the assault, was so great,
that they rushed over the swamp with an eagerness
that could not be restrained, struggling as in a race to
see who could first reach the log that led into the fiery
mouth of the fort.   A Salem villager, John Raymond,
was the winner.   He passed through, survived the
ordeal, and came unharmed out of the terrible fight.

He was twenty-seven years of age. He signed his name to a petition to the General Court, in 1685, as having gone in the expedition from Salem Village, and as then living there. Some years afterwards, he removed to Middleborough, joined the church in that place in 1722, and died in 1725. The fact that his last years were spent there has led to the supposition that he went from Middleborough to the Narragansett fight; but no men were drafted into that army from Middleborough. It was not a town at the time, but was organized some years afterwards. It had no inhabitants then. Philip had destroyed what few houses had been there, and slaughtered or dispersed their occupants.

Thus far our attention has been directed to that portion of the population of Salem Village drawn there by the original policy of the company in London to attract persons of superior social position, wealth, and education to take up tracts of land, and lead the way into the interior. It operated to give a high character to the early agriculture of the country, and facilitate the settling of the lands. Without taking into view the means they had to make the necessary outlays in constructing bridges and roads, and introducing costly implements of husbandry and tasteful improvements, but looking solely at the social, intellectual, and moral influence they exerted, it must be acknowledged that the benefit derived from them was incalculable. They gave a powerful impulse to the farming interest, and introduced a high tone to the spirit of the community. They were early on the ground, and remained more or less through the period of the first generation. Their impress was long seen in the manners and character of the people. There was surely a goodly proportion of such men among the first settlers of this neighborhood.

I come now to another class drawn along with and after the preceding, — the permanent, substantial yeo-manry with no capital but their sturdy industry, doing hard work with their strong arms, and striking the roots of the settlement down deep into the soil by mix-ing their own labor with it. A glance at the map will be useful, at this point, showing the general direction by which the farming population advanced to the inte-rior. All between the North and Cow House Rivers was, as now, called North Fields, and is still for the most part a farming territory. All north of Cow House River, westwardly to Reading and eastwardly to the sea, was originally known as the "Farms" or "Salem Farms." When the First Beverly Parish was set off in 1667, it took from the "Farms" all east of Bass River. As Topsfield and other townships were established, they were more or less encroached upon. The "Farmers" as they were called, although un-organized, regarded themselves as one community, having a common interest. The tide of settlement flowed up the rivers and brooks, sought out the meadows, and was drawn into the valleys among the hills.

John Porter, called "Farmer Porter," came with

his sons from Hingham, and bought up lands to the
north of Duck or Crane River. His family before long
held among them more land, it is probable, than any
other. He served many years as deputy in the General Court, first from Hingham and then from Salem.
He is spoken of in the colonial records of Massachusetts as "of good repute for piety, integrity, and
estate." The Barneys, Leaches, and others went eastwardly towards Bass River. The Putnams followed
up Beaver Brook to Beaver Dam, and spread out towards the north and west; while Richard Hutchinson
turned southerly to the interval between Whipple
and Hathorne Hills, bought the Stileman grant, and
cleared the beautiful meadows where the old village
meeting-house afterwards stood. He was a vigorous
and intelligent agriculturist, and a man of character.
He died in 1681, at eighty years of age, leaving a
large and well-improved estate. His will has this
item: I give "five acres of land to Black Peter, my
servant." He had given fine farms to his children
severally, many years before his death. His second
wife, who survived him, had no children. He had
come by her into possession of a valuable addition to
his estate. After distributing his property, and providing legacies for children and grandchildren, his will
left it to the option of his widow to spend the residue of her days either in the family of his son Joseph,
or elsewhere; if she should prefer to live elsewhere,
then she should receive back, in her own right, all the
property she had originally owned; if she continued

to live to her death in Joseph's family, then her property was to go to him and his heirs. This, I think, shows that he was as sagacious as he was just.

Richard Ingersoll came from Bedfordshire in England in 1629, bringing letters of recommendation from Matthew Cradock to Governor Endicott. After living awhile in town, a tract of land of eighty acres was granted to him, on the east side of Wooleston River, opposite the site of Danversport, at a place called, after him, Ingersoll's Point. He there proceeded to clear and break ground, plant corn, fence in his land, and make other improvements. He also carried on a fishery. Subsequently he leased the Townsend Bishop farm, where he lived several years. He died in 1644. Not long before his death, he purchased, jointly with his son-in-law Haynes, the Weston grant. His half of it he bequeathed to his son Nathaniel. He was evidently a man of real dignity and worth, enjoying the friendship of the best men of his day. Governor Endicott and Townsend Bishop were with him in his last sickness, and witnesses to his will. His widow married John Knight of Newbury. In a legal instrument filed among the papers connected with a case of land title, dated twenty-seven years after her first husband's death, she expresses in very striking language the tender affection and respect with which she still cherished his memory.

William Haynes married Sarah, daughter of Richard Ingersoll, and occupied his half of the Weston grant. In company with his brother, Richard Haynes, he had before bought of Townsend Bishop five hundred and forty acres, covering a considerable part of the northern end of the village territory. They sold one-third part of it to Abraham Page. Page sold to Simon Bradstreet, and John Porter bought all the three parts from the Hayneses and Bradstreet. It long constituted a portion of the great landed property of the Porter family. These facts show that William Haynes was a person of means; and the manner in which he is uniformly spoken of proves that he was regarded with singular respect and esteem. He died about 1650, and his son Thomas became subsequently a leading man in the village.

There has been uncertainty where William Haynes came from, or to what family of the name he belonged. Among the papers of the Ingersoll family, it has recently been found that he is mentioned as " brother to Lieutenant-Governor Haynes." There seems to be no other person to whom this language can refer than John Haynes, who, after being Governor of Massachusetts, removed to Connecticut where he was governor and deputy-governor, in alternate years, to the day of his death. John Haynes, as Winthrop informs us, was a gentleman of " great estate." His property in England is stated to have yielded a thousand pounds per annum. Dr. Palfrey says he was " a man of family as well as fortune; and the dignified and courteous manners, which testified to the care bestowed on his early nurture, won popularity by their graciousness, at the same time that they diffused a refining

influence by their example." If William of the village
was brother to John of Connecticut, the fact that he
and his brother Richard could make such large purchases of lands, and the remarkable respect manifested towards him, are well accounted for. The
Ingersoll family traditions and entries would seem to
be the highest authority on such a point.

Job Swinnerton was a brother of John who for
many years was the principal physician in the town of
Salem. He had several grants of land, and was a
worthy, peaceable, unobtrusive citizen. He seems to
have kept out of the heat of the various contentions
that occurred in the village; and, although his influence was sometimes decisively put forth, he evidently
did nothing to aggravate them. He died April 11,
1689, over eighty-eight years of age. He had a
large family, and his descendants continue the name
in the village to this day. Daniel Rea came originally to Plymouth, and in 1630 bought a dwelling-
house, garden, and " all the privileges thereunto
belonging," in that town. In 1632 he removed
to Salem, and at once became a leading man in the
management of town affairs. He had a grant of
one hundred and sixty acres, which he occupied and
cultivated till his death in 1662. He had but two children: one, the wife of Captain Lothrop; the other,
Joshua Rea, became the founder of a large family who
acted conspicuously in the affairs of the village for
several generations. Jacob Barney was an original
grantee, and for several years a deputy. His son of

the same name became a large landholder, and, on
the 5th of April, 1692, at the very moment when the
witchcraft delusion was at its height, gave two acres
conveniently situated for the erection of a schoolhouse. He conveyed it to inhabitants of the neighborhood to be used for that purpose, mentioning
them severally by name. I give the list, as it shows
who were the principal people thereabouts at the time:
" Mr. Israel Porter; Sergeant John Leach; Cornet
Nathaniel Howard, Sr.; Corporal Joseph Herrick,
Sr.; Benjamin Porter; Joshua Rea, Sr.; Thomas
Raymond, Sr.; Edward Bishop, *secundus;* John Trask,
Jr.; John Creesy; Joshua Rea, Jr.; John Rea; John
Flint, Sr." Lawrence Leach received a grant of one
hundred acres; and others of the same name and
family had similar evidence that they were regarded
as valuable accessions to the population. William
Dodge and Richard Raymond had grants of sixty
acres each; Humphrey and William Woodbury had
forty each. The families of Leach, Raymond, Dodge,
and Woodbury, still remain in the community of
which their ancestors were the founders. John Sibley
had a grant of fifty acres. Robert Goodell was a
grantee, and became a large landholder.

The descendants of the two last-named persons are
very numerous, and have maintained the respectability of their family names. They are each, at this
day, represented by gentlemen whose enthusiastic
interest in our antiquities is proved by their invaluable labors and acquisitions in the interesting depart-

ments of genealogy and local history, — John L. Sibley, Librarian of Harvard University; and Abner C. Goodell, Register of Probate for the County of Essex.

Besides Townsend Bishop, there were two other persons of that name among the original inhabitants of Salem. They do not appear to have been related to him or to each other. Richard Bishop, whose wife Dulcibell had died Aug. 6, 1658, married the widow Galt, July 22, 1660. He died Dec. 30, 1674.

Edward Bishop was in Salem in 1639, and became a member of the church in 1645. In 1660 he was one of the constables of Salem, an original member of the Beverly Church in 1667, and died in January, 1695. He was an early settler on the Farms; his lands were on both sides of Bass River, the parcels on the west side being above and below the Ipswich road. His own residence was on the Beverly side; and he was not usually connected with the concerns of the village. His name appears but once in the witchcraft proceedings, and then in favor of an accused person.

Edward Bishop, commonly called "the sawyer," from the tenor of conveyances of land, dates, and other evidences, appears to have been a son of the preceding. In his earlier life, he was somewhat notable for irregularities and aberrations of conduct. With his wife Hannah, he was fined by the local court, in 1653, for depredating upon the premises of his neighbors. During the subsequent period of his history, he bore

the character of an industrious and reputable person.
At some time previous to 1680, he married Bridget,
widow of Thomas Oliver. On the 9th of March, 1693,
he married Elizabeth Cash. He lived originally in
Beverly ; afterwards, at different times, on the land
belonging to his father in Salem Village, — the estate
he occupied being on both sides of the Ipswich road.
His last years were passed in the town of Salem. He
died in 1705. His daughter Hannah, born in 1646,
became the wife of Captain William Raymond, one of
the founders of the numerous family of that name.

Edward Bishop, son of the preceding, called, for
distinction, " husbandman," was born in 1648. He
married Sarah, daughter of William Wilds, of Ipswich.
He was a respectable person, and lived in the village
on an estate also occupied by " the sawyer." His
house was west of the avenue leading to Cherry Hill.
In 1703 he removed to Rehoboth.

Edward Bishop, the eldest of his sons, married
Susanna, daughter of John Putnam, and in 1713 removed to that part of Ipswich now Hamilton. Prior to
1695, these four Edward Bishops were all living ; and
the youngest had a wife and children. All will be
found connected with our story, the second and third
prominently. The fourth owed his safety, perhaps,
to the influential connections of his wife.

The first notice we have of Bray Wilkins is in the
Massachusetts colonial records, Sept. 6, 1638, when
he was authorized to set up a house and keep a ferry
at Neponset River, and have " a penny a person." On

the 5th of November, 1639, the General Court accepted a report made by William Hathorne and Richard Davenport, commissioners appointed for the purpose, and, in accordance therewith, laid out a farm for Richard Bellingham, who had been deputy-governor, was then an assistant, and afterwards governor, " on the head of Salem, to the north-west of the town ; there being in it a hill, and an Indian plantation, and a pond." This nice little farm included seven hundred acres, and " about one hundred or one hundred and fifty acres of meadow " beside. The next thing we hear about the matter is a petition to the General Court, May 22, 1661, of " Bray Wilkins and John Gingle, humbly desiring that the farm called by the name of Will's Hill, which this Court granted to the worshipful Richard Bellingham, Esq., and they purchased of him, may be laid to, and appointed to belong to, Salem ; being nigh its lands, and the petitioners' of its society." The Court granted the request. It seems that, about a year before, on the 9th of March, " Bray Wilkins, husbandman, and John Gingle, tailor, both of Lynn," had bought the Bellingham farm for two hundred and fifty pounds, of which they paid at the time twenty-five pounds, and mortgaged it back for the residue. The twenty-five pounds was paid as follows : twenty-four pounds in a ton of bar-iron, and one pound in money. Wilkins had, some time before, removed from Neponset, and perhaps had been working in one of the iron-manufactories then in operation at Lynn. When the balance of his wages over his

SALEM VILLAGE. 145

expenses enabled him, with the aid of Gingle, to raise
a ton of iron and scrape together twenty shillings, they
entered upon their bold undertaking. He had not a
dollar in his pocket; but he had what was better than
dollars, — industrious habits, a resolute will, a strong
constitution, an iron frame, and six stout sons. After
a while, he took into the work, in addition to his own
effective family force, two trusty kinsmen, Aaron Way
and William Ireland, conveying to them good farms
out of his seven hundred acres. He enlarged his
farm, from time to time, by new purchases, so as to
more than make up for what he sold to Way and
Ireland. In 1676 the mortgage was fully discharged.
He and his sons bought out the heirs of Gingle, and
the work was done. They held, free from debt, in one
tract, a territory about two miles in length on the
Reading line. Each member of the family had a
house, barns, orchards, gardens, meadows, upland, and
woodland; and the homestead of the old patriarch was
in the midst of them, the enterprise of his laborious
life crowned with complete success. The innumerable
family of the name, scattered all over the country,
has largely, if not wholly, been derived from this
source. Bray Wilkins, and the members of his household in all its branches, were always on hand at
parish meetings in Salem Village. Over a distance,
as their route must have been, of five miles, they
came, in all seasons and all weathers, by the roughest
roads, and, in the earlier period, where there were no
roads at all, through the woods, fording streams, to

meeting on the Lord's Day. He continued vigorous, hale, and active to the last; and died, as he truly characterizes himself in his will, " an ancient," Jan. 1, 1702, at the age of ninety-two.

This was the way in which the large grants made to wealthy and eminent persons, governors, deputy-governors, and assistants, came into the possession and under the productive labor of a yeomanry who made good their title to the soil by the force of their characters and the strength of their muscles. One of the terms of Wilkins's purchase was, that, if he found and wrought minerals on the land, he was to pay to Bellingham or his heirs a royalty of ten pounds per annum. Believing that the best mine to be found in land is the crops that can be raised from it, he never tried to find any other.

Bray Wilkins will appear to have shared in the witchcraft delusion, and been very unhappily connected with it; but he lived to behold its termination, and to participate in the restoration of reason. The minister of the parish at the time of his death, the Rev. Joseph Green, kept a diary which has been preserved. He thus speaks of the old man : " He lived to a good old age, and saw his children's children, and their children, and peace upon our little Israel."

It is rather curious to notice such indications as the mineral clause in Wilkins's deed affords of the prevalent expectation, at the beginning of settlements in this region, that valuable minerals would be found in it. What makes it worthy of particular inquiry is, that they were found and wrought for some time, but that no one thinks of looking after them now. Simon Bradstreet, Daniel Dennison, and John Putnam put up and carried on together, upon a large scale, iron-works, in 1674, at Rowley Village, now Boxford. Samuel and Nathan Leonard were employed to construct them, and carried them on by contract. These iron-works were long regarded as a promising enterprise and valuable investment. The Leonards were probably of the same family that, at Raynham and the neighborhood, engaged in this business to a great extent, and for a long period, making it a source of wealth and the foundation of eminent families. We know that the business was carried on extensively in Lynn, and that Governor Endicott was quite sure that he had found copper on his Orchard Farm. Who knows but that modern science and more searching methods of detection may yet discover the hidden treasures of which the fathers caught a glimpse, and their enterprises be revived and conducted with permanent energy and success ?

In 1669, Joseph Houlton testified, that, when he was about twenty years of age, in 1641, he was " a servant to Richard Ingersoll," and worked on his land at Ingersoll's Point. About the year 1652, he married Sarah, daughter of Richard Ingersoll, and widow of William Haynes. By her he had five sons and two daughters, who lived to maturity. He gave to each of them a farm ; and their houses were in his near neighborhood. The sons were respectable and substantial

citizens, and persons of just views and amiable sentiments. The father was one of the honored heads of
the village, and lived to a good old age. He died
May 30, 1705. From him, it is probable, all of the
name in this country have sprung. It will be for ever
preserved in the public annals and on the geographical
face of the country. Samuel Houlton, great-grandson
of the original Joseph, was a representative of Massachusetts for ten years in the old Congress of the Con-
federation, for a time presiding over its deliberations.
He was also a member of the first Congress under the
Constitution, and subsequently, for a very long period,
Judge of Probate for the county of Essex. He was
a true patriot and wise legislator; enjoyed to an
extraordinary degree the confidence and love of the
people; had a commanding person and a noble and
venerable aspect; and was always conspicuous by the
dignity and courtesy of his manners. He was a
physician by profession; but his whole life was spent
in the public service. He was in both branches of the
Legislature of the State, also in the Executive Council.
He was major of the Essex regiment at the opening of
the Revolution; was a member of the Committee
of Safety, and of every convention for the framing of
the Government; and, for more than thirty years,
a judge of the Court of Common Pleas. He died,
where he was born and had his home for the greater
part of his life, in Salem Village, Jan. 2, 1816, in the
seventy-eighth year of his age.

In 1724 a petition was presented to the Legislature,

commencing as follows: " Whereas Salem is a most
ancient town of Massachusetts Province, and very
much straitened for land," the petitioners pray for
a grant in the western part of the province. The petition was allowed on condition that one lot be reserved
for the first settled minister, one for the ministry, and
one for a school. Each grantee was required to give
a bond of twenty-five pounds to be on the spot; have a
house of seven feet stud and eighteen square at least,
seven acres of English hay ready to be mowed, and help
to build a meeting-house and settle a minister, within
five years. A grandson of Joseph Houlton, of the
same name, led the company that emigrated to the assigned location. The first result was the town of New
Salem, in Franklin County, incorporated in 1753;
named in honor of the old town from which their leading founder had come. But the people were not satisfied with having merely a school. They must have
an academy. They went to work with a will, and an
academy was established and incorporated in 1795.
This was the second result. The academy did not
flourish to an extent to suit their views, and they
beset the Legislature to grant them a township of land
in the woods of Maine to enable them to endow it.
They carried their point, and in 1797 obtained the
grant. The effort had been great, and great was
the rejoicing at its successful issue. But, as bad luck
would have it, just at that time land could not be sold
at any price. The grant became worthless; and deep
and bitter was the disappointment of the people of

New Salem. The doom of the academy seemed to be
settled, and its days numbered and finished. But
there were men in New Salem who were determined
that the academy should be saved. They met in
consultation, and, under the lead of still another
Joseph Houlton, of the same descent, fixed their purpose. They sold or mortgaged their farms, which
more than half a century of labor had rendered productive, and which every association and every sentiment rendered dear to them. With the money thus
raised they bought the granted tract, paying a good
price for it. The preservation and endowment of the
academy were thus secured; but all benefit from it
to themselves or their descendants was wholly relinquished. It was the only way in which the academy
could be saved. Some must make the sacrifice, and
they made it. They packed up bag and baggage; sold
off all they could not carry; gathered their families
together; bid farewell to the scenes of their birth and
childhood, the homes of their life, and the fruits of
their labor; and started in wagons and carts on the
journey to Boston. Their location was hundreds of
miles distant, far down in the eastern wilderness, and
inaccessible from the extremes of settlement at that
time on the Penobscot. As the only alternative, they
embarked in a coasting-vessel; went down the Bay of
Fundy to St. John, N.B.; took a river-sloop up to
Fredericton, — a hundred miles; got up the river as
they could, in barges or canoes, eighty miles further
to Woodstock; and there, turning to the left, struck

into the forest, until they reached their location. The third result of this emigration, in successive generations and stages, from Salem Farms, is to be seen to-day in a handsome and flourishing village, interspersed and surrounded with well-cultivated fields, — the shire town of the county of Aroostook, in the State of Maine ; which bears the name of the leader of this disinterested, self-sacrificing, and noble company. Three times was it the lot of this one family to encounter and conquer the difficulties, endure and triumph over the privations, and carry through the herculean labors, of subduing a rugged wilderness, and bringing it into the domain of civilization, — at Salem Village, New Salem, and Houlton. It would be difficult to find, in all our history, a story that more strikingly than this illustrates the elements of the glory and strength of New England, — zeal for education, — enterprise invigorated by difficulties, — and prowess equal to all emergencies.

John Burton came early to Salem by way of Barbadoes. He combined the pursuits of a farmer and a tanner. He was a sturdy old Englishman, who, while probably holding the theological sentiments that prevailed in his day, abhorred the spirit of persecution, and was unwilling to live where it was allowed to bear sway. He does not appear to have been a Quaker, but sympathized with all who suffered wrong. In 1658, he went off in their company to Rhode Island, sharing their banishment. But his conscience would not let him rest in voluntary flight. He came

back in 1661, to bear his testimony against oppression.
He was brought before the Court, as an abettor and
shelterer of Quakers. He told the justices that they
were robbers and destroyers of the widows and father-
less, that their priests divined for money, and that
their worship was not the worship of God. They
commanded him to keep silent. He commanded them
to keep silent. They thought it best to bring the col-
loquy to a close by ordering him to the stocks. They
finally concluded, upon the whole, to let him alone;
and he remained here the rest of his life. His descendants are through a daughter (who married William Osborne) and his son Isaac. They are numerous, under both names. Isaac was an active and
respectable citizen of the village, and a farmer of enterprise and energy. He carried on, under a lease,
Governor Endicott's farm of over five hundred acres
on Ipswich River, and had lands of his own. In subsequent generations, this family branched off in various directions to Connecticut, Vermont, and elsewhere.
One detachment of them went to Wilton, N.H., where
the family still remains on the original homestead.
The late Warren Burton, who was born in Wilton, —
a graduate of Harvard College in the class of 1821,
and well known for his invaluable services in the
cause of education, philanthropy, and letters, — was a
direct descendant of John Burton, and as true to the
rights of conscience as the old tanner, who bearded
the lion of persecution in the day of his utmost wrath,
and in his very den.

Henry Herrick, who, as has been stated, purchased the Cherry-Hill farm of Alford, was the fifth son of Sir William Herrick, of Beau Manor Park, in the parish of Loughborough, in the county of Leicester, England. He came first to Virginia, and then to Salem. He was accompanied to America by another emigrant from Loughborough, named Cleaveland. Herrick became a member of the First Church at Salem in 1629, and his wife Edith about the same time. Their fifth son, Joseph, baptized Aug. 6, 1645, owned and occupied Cherry Hill in 1692. He married Sarah, daughter of Richard Leach, Feb. 7, 1667. He was a man of great firmness and dignity of character, and, in addition to the care and management of his large farm, was engaged in foreign commerce. As he bore the title of Governor, he had probably been at some time in command of a military post or district, or perhaps of a West-India colony. His descendants are numerous, and have occupied distinguished stations, often exhibiting a transmitted military stamp. Joseph Herrick was in the Narragansett fight. It illustrates the state of things at that time, that this eminent citizen, a large landholder, engaged in prosperous mercantile affairs, and who had been abroad, was, in 1692, when forty-seven years of age, a corporal in the village company. He was the acting constable of the place, and, as such, concerned in the early proceedings connected with the withcraft prosecutions. For a while he was under the influence of the delusion ; but his strong and enlightened mind soon led him out of it. He was one of

the petitioners in behalf of an accused person, when
intercession, by any for any, was highly dangerous;
and he was a leader in the party that rose against
the fanaticism, and vindicated the characters of its
victims. He inherited a repugnance to oppression,
and sympathy for the persecuted. His father and
mother appear, by a record of Court, to have been
fined "for aiding and comforting an excommunicated
person, contrary to order."

William Nichols, in 1651, bought two hundred acres,
which had been granted to Henry Bartholomew, partly
in the village, but mostly beyond the "six-mile extent," and consequently set off to Topsfield. He had
several other lots of land. He distributed nearly all
his real estate, during his lifetime, to his son John;
his adopted son, Isaac Burton; his daughters, the wives
of Thomas Wilkins and Thomas Cave; and his grand-
daughter, the wife of Humphrey Case. His only son
John had several sons, and from them the name has
been widely dispersed. In a deposition dated May 14,
1694, William Nichols declares himself "aged upwards
of one hundred years." As his will was offered for
Probate Feb. 24, 1696, he must have been one hundred
and two years of age at his death.

William Cantlebury was a large landholder, having
purchased three-quarters of the Corwin grant. He
died June 1, 1663. His name died with him, as he
had no male issue. His property went to his daughters, who were represented, in 1692, under the names
of Small, Sibley, and Buxton. The Flints, Popes,

Uptons, Princes, Phillipses, Needhams, and Walcotts, had valuable farms, and appear, from the records and documents, to have been respectable, energetic, and intelligent people. Daniel Andrew was one of the strong men of the village; had been a deputy to the General Court, and acted a prominent part before and after the witchcraft convulsion. But the great family of the village — greater in numbers and in aggregate wealth than any other, and eminently conspicuous on both sides in the witchcraft proceedings — remains to be mentioned.

John Putnam had a grant of one hundred acres, Jan. 20, 1641. With his wife Priscilla, he came from Buckinghamshire, England, and was probably about fifty years of age on his arrival in this country. He was a man of great energy and industry, and acquired a large estate. He died in 1662, leaving three sons, — Thomas, born in 1616; Nathaniel, in 1620; and John, in 1628. For a more convenient classification, I shall, in speaking of this family, refer, not to the original John at all, but to the sons as its three heads.

Thomas, the eldest, inherited a double share of his father's lands. He was of age when he came to America, and had received a good education. He appears to have settled, in the first instance, in Lynn, where for several years he acted as a magistrate, holding local courts, by appointment of the General Court. Upon removing to Salem, he was chosen, as the town-records show, to the office of constable. This was considered at that time as quite a distinguished position, carrying

with it a high authority, covering the whole executive local administration. Thomas Putnam was
the first clerk of Salem Village, and acted prominently in military, ecclesiastical, and municipal affairs.
He seems to have been a person of a quieter temperament than his younger brothers, and led a somewhat
less stirring life. Possessing a large property by inheritance, he was not quite so active in increasing it;
but, enjoying the society and friendship of the leading
men, lived a more retired life. At the same time,
he was always ready to serve the community if
called for, as he often was, when occasion arose
for the aid of his superior intelligence and personal
influence. He married first, while in Lynn, Ann,
daughter of Edward Holyoke, great-grandfather of the
President of Harvard College of that name whose
son, the venerable centenarian, Dr. Edward Augustus
Holyoke, is remembered as a true Christian philosopher by the generation still lingering on the
stage. Having lost his wife on the 1st of September, 1665, he married, on the 14th of November,
1666, Mary, widow of Nathaniel Veren; coming,
through her, into possession of property in Jamaica
and Barbadoes, in which places Veren had resided,
more or less, in the prosecution of commercial
business. His homestead, as shown on the map,
was occupied by his widow in 1692, and, after
her death, by her son Joseph, the father of General
Israel Putnam. He had also a town residence
on the north side of Essex Street, extending back to

the North River. Its front on Essex Street embraced
the western part of the grounds now occupied by the
North Church, and extended to a point beyond the
head of Cambridge Street. He left the eastern half of
this property to his son Thomas, and the western half
to his son Joseph. To his son Edward he left another
estate in the town, on the western side of St. Peter's
Street, to the north of Federal Street.

Thomas Putnam died on the 5th of May, 1686. He
left large estates in the village to each of his children,
and a valuable piece of meadow land, of fifteen acres,
to a faithful servant.

Nathaniel Putnam married Elizabeth, daughter of
Richard Hutchinson, and, besides what he received
from his father, came, through his wife, into possession
of seventy-five acres. On that tract he built his house
and passed his life. The property has remained unin-
terruptedly in his family. One of them, the late
Judge Samuel Putnam, of the Supreme Court of Massachusetts, enjoyed it as a country residence, and it is
still held by his children. Nathaniel Putnam was a
deputy to the General Court, and constantly connected
with all the interests of the community. He had great
business activity and ability, and was a person of extraordinary powers of mind, of great energy and skill
in the management of affairs, and of singular sagacity,
acumen, and quickness of perception. He died July
23, 1700, leaving a numerous family and a large estate.

John Putnam had the same indefatigable activity as

Nathaniel. He was often deputy to the General Court, and accumulated a very great landed property. He married Rebecca Prince, step-daughter of John Gedney, and died on the 7th of April, 1710. He was buried with military honors. He left a large family of sons and daughters. We shall often meet him in our narrative, and gather the materials, as we go along, to form an opinion of his character. The earliest rate-list in the parish record book is for 1681. At that time the three brothers were all living; the aggregate sum assessed upon ninety-four names was two hundred pounds. The rate of Thomas was £10. 6s. 3d.; that of Nathaniel, £9. 10s.; that of John, £8. No other person paid as much as either of them.

These brothers, as well as many others of the large landholders in the village, adopted the practice of giving to their sons and sons-in-law, outright, by deed, good farms, as soon as they became heads of families; so that, as the fathers advanced in life, their own estates were gradually diminished; and, when unable any longer to take an active part in managing their lands, they divided up their whole remaining real estate, making careful contracts with their children for an adequate maintenance, to the extent of their personal wants and comfort. Joseph Houlton did this: so did the widow Margery Scruggs, old William Nichols, Francis Nurse, and many others. In his last years, John Putnam was on the rate-list for five shillings only, while all his sons and daughters were assessed severally in large sums. In this way they had the satisfaction of making their children independent, and of seeing them take their places among the heads of the community.

Where this practice was followed, there were few quarrels in families over the graves of parents, and controversies seldom arose about the provisions of wills. In some cases no wills were needed to be made. It is apparent, that, in many respects, this was a wise and good practice. It was, moreover, a strictly just one. As the sons were growing to an adult age, they added, by their labors, to the value of lands, — inserted a property into them that was truly their own ; and their title was duly recognized. In a new country, land has but little value in itself; the value is imparted by the labor that clears it and prepares it to yield its products. In 1686, Nathaniel Putnam testified that for more than forty years he had lived in the village, and that in the early part of that time unimproved land brought only a shilling an acre, while a cow was worth five pounds. In 1672, the rate of taxation on unimproved land was a half penny per acre, and, for land on which labor had been expended, a penny per acre. In 1685 it was taxed at the rates of three shillings for a hundred acres of wild land, and one penny an acre for " land within fence." The relative value of improved land constantly increased with the length of time it had been under culture. It may be said that labor added two-thirds to the value of land, and that he who by the sweat of his brow added those two-thirds, to that extent owned the land. An industrious young man went out into his father's woods, cut down the trees, cleared the ground, fenced it in, and prepared it for cultivation. All that was thus added to its value was his creation, and he its rightful owner. The right was recognized, and full possession given him, by deed, as soon as he had opened a farm, and built a house, and brought a wife into it.

The effect of this was to anchor a family, from generation to generation, fast to its ancestral acres. It strengthened the ties that bound them to their native fields. Its moral effect was beyond calculation. When a young man was thus enabled to start in life on an independent footing, it made a man of him while he was young. It invested him with the dignity of a citizen by making him feel his share of responsibility for the security and welfare of society. It gave scope for enterprise, and inspiration to industry, at home. It led to early marriages, under circumstances that justified them. Joseph Putnam, the youngest son of Thomas, at the age of twenty years and seven months, took as his bride Elizabeth, daughter of Israel Porter, and grand-daughter of William Hathorne, when she was sixteen years and six months old. We shall see what a valuable citizen he became; and she was worthy of him. A large and noble family of children grew up to honor them, one of the youngest of whom was Israel Putnam, of illustrious Revolutionary fame.

Though there were descendants of this family in every company of emigrants that went forth from

Salem Village, in all directions, in every generation, to Yarmouth Nova Scotia, New Brunswick, Maine, and all parts of the New England, Middle, Western, and Pacific States, there is about as large a proportionate representation of the name within the precincts of Salem Village to-day, as there ever was. Fifty Putnams are at present voters in Danvers, on a list of eight hundred names, — one-sixteenth of the whole number. The rate-schedule of 1712 shows almost precisely the same proportion.

Edward Putnam, whom we shall meet again, was baptized July 4, 1654. After serving as deacon of the church from its organization, a period of forty years, he resigned on account of advancing age; and in 1733, as he was entering on his eightieth year, gave this account of his family: "From the three brothers proceeded twelve males; from these twelve males, forty males; and from these forty males, eighty-two males: there were none of the name of Putnam in New England but those from this family." With respect to their situation in life, he remarks: "I can say with the Psalmist, I have been young, and now am old; yet I have not seen the righteous forsaken, nor their seed begging bread except of God, who provides for all. For God hath given to the generation of my fathers a generous portion, neither poverty nor riches." When the infirmities of age prevented his longer partaking in the worship of the Lord's Day, this good old man relinquished his residence near the church, and removed to his original homestead, in the neighborhood of his children, which had then been included in the new town of Middleton. His will is dated March 11, 1731. It was offered in Probate, April 11, 1748. After making every reasonable deduction, in view of his share of responsibility for the earlier proceedings in the witchcraft prosecutions, we may participate in the affection and veneration with which this amiable and gentle-hearted man was regarded by his contemporaries.

The provisions of his will contain items which so strikingly illustrate his character, and give us such an insight of the domestic life of the times, that a few of them will be presented. According to the prevalent custom, he had given good farms to his several children when they became heads of families. In his will, he distributes the residue of his real estate among them with carefulness and an equal hand, describing the metes and bounds of the various tracts with great minuteness, so as to prevent all questions of controversy among them. He gives legacies in money to his daughters, ten pounds each; and, to his grand-daughters, five pounds each. To one of his five sons, he gives his "cross-cut saw." This was used to saw large logs crosswise, having two handles worked by two persons, and distinguished from the "pit saw," which was used to saw logs lengthwise. All his other tools were to be divided among his sons, to one of whom he also gives his cane; to another, his "Great Bible;" to another, "Mr. Jeremiah Burroughs's Works;" to another, "Mr. Flavel's Works;" and, to the other, his

" girdle and sword." To one of them he gives his desk, and " that box wherein are so many writings ; " to another, his " share in the iron-works ; " and to another, his share " in the great timber chain." This, with other evidence, shows that there was a boom, and arrangements on a large scale for the lumbering business, at that time, on Ipswich River. The provisions for his wife were very considerate, exact, and minute, so as to prevent all possibility of there being any difficulty in reference to her rights, or of her ever suffering want or neglect. He gives to her, absolutely and for her own disposal, the residue of his books and all his " movable estate " in the house and out of it, including all " cattle, sheep, swine," the whole stock of the homestead farm, agricultural implements, and carriages. He makes it the duty of one of his sons to furnish her with all the " firewood " she may want, with ten bushels of corn-meal, two bushels of English meal, four bushels of ground malt, four barrels of good cider, — he to find the barrels — as many apples " as she shall see cause," and nine or ten score weight of good pork, annually : he was to " keep for her two cows, winter and summer," and generally to provide all " things needful." The will specifies, apartment by apartment, from cellar to garret, one-half of the house, to be for her accommodation, use, and exclusive control, and half of the garden. The sons were to pay, in specified proportions, all his funeral charges. One of the sons was to pay her forthwith four pounds in money ; and they were severally to deliver to her annually, in proportions expressly stated, ten pounds for pocket money. When the relative value of money at that time is considered, and the other particulars above named taken into account, it will be allowed that he was faithful and wise in caring for the wife of his youth and the companion of his long life. There is no better criterion of the good sense and good feeling of a person than his last will and testament. The result of a quite extensive examination is a conviction that the application of this test to the early inhabitants of Salem Village is most creditable to them, particularly in the tender but judicious and effectual manner in which the rights, comfort, independence, and security of their wives were provided for.

In the third generation, the three Putnam families began to give their sons to the general service of the country in conspicuous public stations, and in the professional walks of life. Their names appear on the page of history and in the catalogues of colleges. Major-General Israel Putnam was a grandson of the first Thomas. On the 14th of May, 1718, Archelaus, a grandson of John, and son of James, died at Cambridge, while an undergraduate. Benjamin, a son of Nathaniel, in his will, presented for Probate, April 25, 1715, says, "I give my son Daniel one hundred and fifty pounds for his learning." Daniel lived and died in the ministry, at North Reading. His name heads the list of more than thirty — all, it is probable, of this family — in the last Triennial Catalogue of Harvard University.

The brightest name in the annals of Salem Village, though frequently referred to, has not yet been presented for your contemplation. I shall hold it up and keep it in your view by a somewhat detailed description, not only because it is necessary to a full understanding of our subject, but because it is good to gaze upon a life of virtue; to pause while beholding a portrait beaming with beneficence, and radiant with all excellent, beautiful, and attractive affections.

Nathaniel Ingersoll was about eleven years old at the death of his father. His mother married John Knights, of Newbury, who became the head of her household, and continued to carry on the Townsend Bishop farm for several years. Governor Endicott, the friend and neighbor of Richard Ingersoll, took Nathaniel, while still a lad, into his family. In a deposition made in Court, June 24, 1701, Nathaniel Ingersoll says, "I went to live with Governor Endicott as his servant four years, on 'the Orchard Farm." At that time, the term "servant" had no derogatory sense connected with it. It merely implied the relations between an employer and the employed, without the least tint of the feeling which we associate with the condition of servility. Here was a youth, who, by his father's will, was the owner of a valuable estate of seventy-five acres in the immediate neighborhood, voluntarily seeking the privilege of entering the service of his father's friend, because he thereby would be better qualified, when old enough, to enter upon his own estate. Governor Endicott's political duties were not then regarded as requiring him to live in Boston; and his usual residence was at the Orchard Farm, where he was making improvements and conducting agricultural operations upon so large a scale that it was the best school of instruction anywhere to be found for a young person intending to make that his pursuit in life. Young John Putnam, as has been stated, was there for the same purpose, under similar circumstances.

Having built a house and barn, and provided the necessary stock and materials, Nathaniel Ingersoll went upon his farm when about nineteen years of age. Soon after, probably, he married Hannah Collins of Lynn, who, during their long lives, proved a worthy helpmeet. His house was on a larger scale than was usual at that time. One of its rooms is spoken of as very large; and the uses to which his establishment was put, from time to time, prove that it must have had capacious apartments. Its site is shown on the map. The road from Salem to Andover passed it, not at an angle as now, but by a curve. The present parsonage of Danvers Centre stands on the lot. But Ingersoll's house was a little in the rear of the site occupied by the present parsonage. It faced south. In front was an open space, or lawn, called Ingersoll's Common. Here he lived nearly seventy years. During that long period, his doors were ever open to hospitality and benevolence. His house was the centre of good neighborhood and of all movements for the public welfare. His latch-string was always out for friend or stranger. In a military sense, and every other sense, it was the head-quarters of the village. On his land, a few rods to the north-east, stood the block-house where watch was kept against Indian attacks. There a sentinel was posted day and night, under his supervision. The spot was central to the several farming settlements; and all meetings of every kind took place there. To accommodate the public, he was licensed to keep a victualling-house; also to sell beer and cider by the quart "on the Lord's Day." This last provision was for the benefit of those who came great distances to meeting, and had to find refreshment somewhere between the services. To meet the occasions arising out of this business, he probably had a separate building. Indeed, the evidence, in the language used in reference to it, is quite decisive that there was an "ordinary," distinct from the dwelling-house. The location was thought to render such an establishment necessary, and his character secured its orderly maintenance.

Travellers through the country stopped at "Nathaniel Ingersoll's corner." The earliest path or roadway to and from the eastern settlements went by it. Here Increase and Cotton Mather, and all magistrates and ministers, were entertained. Here the wants of the poor and unfortunate were made known, and all men came for counsel and advice. From the first, even when he had not reached the age of maturity, he commanded to a singular extent the confidence and respect of all men. The influence of his bearing and character,

thus early established, was never lost or abated, or
disturbed for a moment during his long life. He was
the umpire to settle all differences, but never made an
enemy by his decisions. Although of moderate estate,
compared with some of his neighbors, they all treated
him with a deference greater than they sometimes
paid to each other. It was his lot to be mixed
up with innumerable controversies, to be in the very
centre of the most vehement and frightful social convulsions, and to act decisively in some of them; but
it is most marvellous to witness how uniform and universal was the consideration in which he was held.
These statements are justified abundantly by evidence
in records and documents.

When village business was to be transacted, or
consultation of any kind had, the house of Deacon
Ingersoll was designated, as a matter of course, for
the place of meeting. Whether it was an ecclesiastical or a military gathering, a prayer-meeting or a
train-band drill, it was there. Before they had a
meeting-house, it cannot be doubted, they met for
worship in his large room. We find it recorded, that,
after the meeting-house was built, if from the bitterness of the weather, or any other cause, it was too
uncomfortable to remain in, they would adjourn to
Deacon Ingersoll's. Such a free use of a particular
person's premises sometimes engenders a familiarity
that runs into license, and is apt to breed contempt.
Not so at all in his case. There was a native-born
dignity, an honest manliness and pervading integrity

about him, that were appreciated by all persons at all times. When wrong was meditated, his admonition was received with respectful consideration; when it had been committed, his rebuke awakened no resentment. The fact, that he was acknowledged and felt by all to be a perfectly just man, is apparent through the whole course of his action in all the affairs of life. His uprightness, freedom from unworthy prejudice, and clear and transparent conscientiousness, appear in all documents, depositions, and records that proceeded from him. He was often called to give evidence in land causes and other trials at law; and his testimony is always straightforward, fair, and lucid. You can tell from the style, temper, or tone of other witnesses, which side of the controversy they espoused, but not from his. In the great and protracted conflict in the courts, relating to the Townsend Bishop farm, he and all his most intimate connections and relatives were parties of adverse interest; but Zerubabel Endicott paid homage, and left it on record, to the truthfulness and uprightness of the testimony and the fairness of the course of Nathaniel Ingersoll. We shall meet other illustrations to the same effect in the course of our narrative.

Although it is anticipating the course of events, it may be well to trace the outlines of the life of this man to its distant close. Partaking of the general views of his age, he participated in the proceedings that led to the witchcraft prosecutions. He believed in what was regarded as decisive evidence against the

accused, and acted accordingly. But no one ever felt
that there was any vindictiveness in his course.

He lived to see the storm that desolated his beloved
village pass away, and to enjoy the restoration of
reason, peace, and good-will among a people who had
so long been torn by strife, and subjected to untold
horrors, — horrors that have never yet been fully described, and which I despair of being able adequately
to depict. He did all that a good and true man could
do to eradicate the causes of the mischief. He participated in the exercises of a day of Thanksgiving,
set apart for the purpose, in 1700, to express the devout and contrite gratitude of the people to a merciful
God for deliverance from the errors and passions that
had overwhelmed them with such awful judgments.
The removal of Mr. Parris having been effected,
Joseph Green was settled near the close of the year
1697. He was a wise and prudent man. By kind,
cautious, and well-timed measures, he gradually succeeded in extracting every root of bitterness, healing
all the breaches, and restoring harmony to a long-
distracted people. In this work, Deacon Ingersoll and
his good associate, Edward Putnam, aided him to the
utmost. When, by their united counsels and labors,
the difficult work was about accomplished, Mr. Green
was taken to his reward, in 1715. Greatly was he
lamented; but Nathaniel Ingersoll had realized all his
best wishes at last. The prayers he had poured forth
for fifty years had been answered. He had seen the
completed service of a pastor who had fulfilled his

highest estimate of what a Christian minister should be. He lived to witness and share in the warm and unanimous welcome of Peter Clark to a useful, honored, happy ministry which lasted more than half a century. The ordination of Mr. Clark, which took place on the 8th of June, 1717, was made the occasion of demonstrating the complete re-establishment of social harmony and Christian love throughout that entire community. The storms of strife had commenced with the settlement of the first minister, more than forty years before : they had increased in violence, until, at the witchcraft delusion, they swept in a tornado every thing to ruin. The clouds had been slowly dispersed, and the angry waves smoothed down, by Mr. Green's benignant ministry. The long, and yet unbroken, " era of good feeling " was fully inaugurated. It was a day of great rejoicing. Old men and matrons, young men and maidens, met together in happy union. Tradition says that they carried their grateful festivities to the highest point allowable by the proprieties of that period. Having witnessed this scene, and beheld the church and village of his affections start on a new and sure career of peace and prosperity, the Good Parishioner folded his mantle and departed from sight. He died in 1719, in his eighty-fifth year. He was truly the " Man of Ross." The celebrated portrait, which poetry has drawn under this name, was from an actual example in real life, not more shining than his. He left no issue ; but his brothers were the founders of a family

widely diffused, many members of which have, in
every subsequent age, contributed to the honor of the
name. Innumerable branches have spread out from
the same stock under other names. The children of
the late Dr. Nathaniel Bowditch, through both father
and mother, have descended from a brother of Nathaniel Ingersoll.

Citations and extracts from documents on file will
justify all I have said of this man.

His wife was a spirit kindred to his own. Their
only child, a daughter, died when quite young.
Their hearts demanded an object on which to exercise
parental affection, and to give opportunity for benevolent care, within their own household; and they induced their neighbor, Joseph Hutchinson, who had
several sons, to give one of them to be theirs by adop-
tion. When this child had grown to manhood, a deed
was recorded in the Essex Registry, Oct. 2, 1691, of
which this is the purport : —

"Benjamin Hutchinson, being an infant when he was
given to us by his parents, we have brought him up as our
own child ; and he, the said Benjamin, living with us as an
obedient son, until he came of one and twenty years of age,
he then marrying from us, I, the said Nathaniel Ingersoll, and
Hannah, my wife, on these considerations, do, upon the marriage of our adopted son, Benjamin Hutchinson, give and
bequeath to him, his heirs and assigns for ever, this deed
of gift of ten acres of upland, and also three acres of
meadow," &c.

When Mr. Parris was settled, it occurred to Deacon

Ingersoll, that it would be very convenient for him to have a certain piece of ground between the parsonage land and the Andover road; and he gave him a deed, from which the following is an extract. It is dated Jan. 2, 1689.

"To all Christian people to whom this present writing shall come, Nathaniel Ingersoll, of Salem Village, in the county of Essex, sendeth greeting. Know ye, that the said Nathaniel Ingersoll, husbandman, and Hannah, his wife, for and in consideration of the love, respect, and honor which they justly bear unto the public worship of the true and only God, and therefore for the encouragement of their well-beloved pastor, the Rev. Samuel Parris, who hath lately taken that office amongst them, and also for and in consideration of a very small sum of money to them in hand paid, with which they do acknowledge themselves fully contented and satisfied, do grant to said Samuel Parris and Elizabeth, his wife, for life, and then to the children of said Samuel and Elizabeth Parris, four and a half acres of land, adjoining upon the home field of the said Nathaniel Ingersoll; the three acres on the south alienated by gift, and the remainder by sale."

There was a fine young orchard on the land.

Joseph Houlton had conveyed to the parish a lot for the use of the ministry, attached to the parsonage house. A question having arisen in consequence of a lost deed, or some other imagined defect in the Houlton title, whether the land originally belonged to him or to Nathaniel Ingersoll, the latter disposed of it at once by an instrument recorded in the Essex Registry, of which the following is the substance: —

"Nathaniel Ingersoll to the Trustees of Salem Village Ministry land, for divers good causes and considerations me thereunto moving, but more especially for the true love and desire I have to the peace and welfare of Salem Village wherein I dwell, I hereby release, &c., all my right and title to five acres described in my brother Houlton's deed of sale," &c.

In the same Registry, the following extract is found, in a deed dated Jan. 28, 1708: —

"For the desire I have that children may be educated in Salem Village, I freely give four poles square of land to Rev. Joseph Green, to have and to hold the same, not for his own particular use, but for the setting a schoolhouse upon, and the encouragement of a school in this place."

The Essex Registry has a deed dated Jan. 6, 1714, of which the following is the substance: —

"For the good affection that I bear unto Deacon Edward Putnam, and the desire that I have of his comfortable attendance upon the public worship of God, I have freely given unto him, the said Deacon Edward Putnam, of Salem aforesaid, for him and his heirs for ever, a piece of land, bounded northerly upon the land of Joseph Green, next to his orchard gate, westerly on the highway, and southerly and easterly on my land."

Deacon Putnam was, at this time, sixty years of age. His homestead was at some distance; and it was often difficult for him to get to meeting. Ingersoll had always enjoyed the convenience of having only a few rods to go to the place of worship; and he desired to have his beloved colleague enjoy the same privilege. Besides, he longed to have him near. The proffer was probably accepted. We find that church-meetings were held at the house of Deacon Putnam, which would not probably so often have been the case, had he remained on his farm; and we know that there were two dwelling-houses, some time afterwards, on the Ingersoll lot. It was a pleasant arrangement: the two deacons and the minister being thus brought close together, and reaching each other through Ingersoll's garden and the minister's orchard. Of the personal friendship, attachment, and genial affection between the two good old deacons, the foregoing extract is a pleasing illustration.

Nathaniel Ingersoll's property was never very large; and, as he had enjoyed the luxury, all his life long, of benevolence and beneficence, there was no great amount to be left after suitably providing for his wife. But there was enough to enable him to express the family affection to which he was always true, and to give a parting assurance of his devotion to the church and people of the village. By his will, certain legacies were required to be paid by the residuary legatee and final heir within a reasonable time specified in the document. It bears date July 8, 1709, and was offered for Probate, Feb. 17, 1719. It begins thus: —

" In the name of God, Amen. I, Nathaniel Ingersoll, of Salem, in the county of Essex, in the Province of Massachutetts Bay, in New England, being through God's mercy in good health of body and of perfect memory, but not knowing how soon my great change may come, do make this my last will, in manner and form following: First, I give up my soul to God, in and through Jesus Christ my Redeemer, when he shall please to call for it, hoping for a glorious resurrection, in and through his merits; and my body to decent burial, at the discretion of my executors; and, as for the worldly estate God hath been pleased to give me, I dispose of it in the manner following," &c.

He gives a small sum of money, varying from thirty shillings to four pounds, to each and every nephew and niece then living, twenty-two in number. He provides for an annuity of twenty shillings a year for a sister, the only remaining member of his own immediate family, to be paid into the hands of the daughter who took care of her. Not being able to leave a large amount to any, he preferred to express his love for all. There were two items in the will which may be specially preserved from oblivion.

"I give to the church in Salem Village the sum of fifty shillings in money, for the more adorning the Lord's Table, to be laid out in some silver cup, at the discretion of the Pastor, Deacons, and my overseers." — "After my wife's decease, I give to Benjamin (my adopted son) who was very dutiful to me, while he lived with me, and helpful to me since he has gone from me, all the remaining part of my whole estate, both real and personal, — excepting a small parcel of land of about two acres, that lyeth between M[rs.] Walcots and George Wyotts by the highway, which I give to the inhabitants of Salem Village, for a training place for ever."

The bonds required of the executors by the Probate Court were to the amount of two hundred pounds only, showing that his movable or personal estate was a very moderate one. There is a feature in the will, which is, I think, worthy of being mentioned, as evincing the excellent judgment and practical wisdom of this man.

" I give to Hannah, my well-beloved wife, the use and improvement of my whole estate during her natural life : and my will is, that, if my wife should marry again, he that she so marrieth, before she marry, shall give sufficient security to my overseers not to make strip or waste upon any of my estate ; and, if he do not become so bound, I give one-half of my whole estate to Benjamin Hutchinson, at the time of my wife's marriage."

He did not cut her off entirely, as is sometimes attempted to be done, in the event of a second marriage, but secured her and the estate against suffering in case she took that step. He adopted an effectual method to prevent any one from seeking to marry her for the purpose of getting the benefit of her whole income and a comfortable establishment upon his property without providing for its preservation ; and, if she should be so improvident as to marry again without having his conditions complied with, he took care that she should not thereby expose to injury or loss more than one-half of his estate. Ingenuity is much exercised in making wills, particularly in reference to the rights, interests, and security of wives. It is worthy of consideration, whether, all things considered, Nathaniel

Ingersoll's plan is not about as skilful and just as any
that has been devised.

We shall meet this man again in the course of our
story. I trust to your good feeling in vindication of
the space I have given to his biography ; being strongly
impressed with a conviction, that you will agree with
me, — taking into view the influence he constantly
exerted, his steadfast integrity and honor, his personal
dignity and public spirit, — that the life of this citizen
of a retired rural community, this plain " husband
man," is itself a monument to his memory more truly
glorious than many which have been reared to perpetuate the names of men whom the world has called great.
The " training place " has been carefully preserved.
Occupying a central point, by the side of the principal
street, this pretty lawn is a fitting memorial of the
Father of the village. In its proper character, as a
training-field, it is invested with an interest not elsewhere surpassed, if equalled. Within its enclosure
the elements of the military art have been imparted to
a greater number of persons distinguished in their
day, and who have left an imperishable glory behind
them as the defenders of the country, a brave yeo-
manry in arms, than on any other spot. It was
probably used as a training field at the first settlement
of the village. From the slaughter of Bloody Brook,
the storming of the Narragansett Fort, and all the
early Indian wars; from the Heights of Abraham,
Lake George, Lexington, Bunker Hill, Brandywine,
Pea Ridge, and a hundred other battle-fields, a lustre

is reflected back upon this village parade-ground. It is associated with all the military traditions of the country, down to the late Rebellion. Lothrop, Davenport, Gardners, Dodges, Raymonds, Putnams, Porters, Hutchinsons, Herricks, Flints, and others, who here taught or learned the manual and drill, are names inscribed on the rolls of history for deeds of heroism and prowess.

There was the usual diversity and variety of character among the people of the village. John Procter originally lived in Ipswich, where he, as well as his father before him, had a farm of considerable value. In 1666, or about that time, he removed to Salem, and carried on the Downing farm, which had before been leased to the Flints. After a while, Procter purchased a part of it. If a conclusion can be drawn from the prevalent type of his posterity of our day, he was a man of herculean frame. There is, I think, a tradition to this effect. At any rate, his character was of that stamp. He had great native force and energy. He was bold in his spirit and in his language, — an upright man, no doubt, as the whole tone of the memorials of him indicate, but free and imprudent in speech, impulsive in feeling, and sometimes rash in action. He was liable from this cause, as we shall see, to get into contention and give offence. There was Jeremiah Watts, a representative of a class of men existing in every community where the intellect is stimulated and idiosyncrasies allowed to develop themselves. By occupation he was a dish-turner, but by temperament an enthu-

siast, a zealot, and an agitator. He was not satisfied
with things as they were, nor willing to give time an
opportunity to improve them. He took hold of the
horns of the altar with daring hands. He denounced
the Church and the world, — undertook to overturn
every thing, and to put all on a new foundation. He
entered on a crusade against what he called " pulpit
preaching," whereby particular persons, called ministers, " may deliver what they please, and none must
object; and this we must pay largely for; our bread
must be taken out of our mouths, to maintain the
beast's mark; and be wholly deprived of our Christian privileges. This is the time of Antichrist's reign,
and he must reign this time: now are the witnesses
slain, and the leaders in churches are these slayers.
But I see plainly that it is a vain thing to debate about
these things with our fellow-brethren; for they are all
for lording it, and trampling under foot." This man
imagined that he " was singled out alone to give his
testimony for Christ, discovering Antichrist's marks."
" If any," he cried out, " will be faithful for Christ,
they must witness against Antichrist, which is self-
love, and lovers of pleasure more than lovers of God.
The witnesses are now slain, but shortly they will rise
again," &c. He tried to get up " private Christian
meetings," to run an opposition to " pulpit preaching."
After going about from house to house, declaiming in
this style, denouncing all who would not fall in with
his notions and act with him, and not succeeding in
overthrowing things in general, he hit upon a new ex-

pedient. As his neighbors had wit enough to let him alone, and did not suffer themselves to be tempted to resort to the civil power to make him keep quiet, he did it himself. He instituted proceedings against the ministers and churches, on the charge, that, by taking the rule into their own hands, they were supplanting the magistrates and usurping the civil power. This was not in itself a bad move; but the Court wisely declined to engage in the proceedings. They neither prosecuted the case nor him, but let the whole go by. They adhered severely to the do-nothing policy. What a world of mischief would have been avoided, if all courts, everywhere, at all times, had shown an equal wisdom! Watts was allowed to vex the village, torment the minister, and perplex those who listened to him by the ingenuity and ability with which he urged his views. He continued his brawling declamations until he was tired; but, not being noticed by ministers or magistrates, no great harm was done, and he probably subsided into a quiet and respectable citizen.

The prominent place Giles Corey is to occupy in the scene before us renders an account of him particularly necessary. It is not easy to describe him. He was a very singular person. His manner of life and general bearing and conversation were so disregardful, in many particulars, of the conventional proprieties of his day, that it is not safe to receive implicitly the statements made by his contemporaries. By his peculiarities of some sort, he got a bad name. In the Book of Records of the First Church in Salem, where his public profession of religion is recorded, he is spoken of as a man of eighty years of age, and of a " scandalous life," but who made a confession of his sins satisfactory to that body. It cannot be denied that he was regarded in this light by some; but there is no reason to believe, that, in referring to the sinfulness of his past life, the old man meant more than was usually understood by such language on such occasions. He was often charged with criminal acts; but in every instance the charge was proved to be either wholly unfounded or greatly exaggerated. He had a good many contentions and rough passages; but they were the natural consequences, when a bold and strong man was put upon the defensive, or drawn to the offensive, by the habit of inconsiderate aspersion into which some of his neighbors had been led, and the bad repute put upon him by scandal-mongers. He was evidently an industrious, hard-working man. He was a person of some means, a holder of considerable property in lands and other forms. Deeds are often found on record from and to him. He owned meadows near Ipswich River. His homestead, during the last thirty years of his life, was a farm of more than a hundred acres of very valuable land, which has been in the possession of the family, now owning it, for a hundred years. The present proprietor, Mr. Benjamin Taylor, some twenty years ago, ploughed up the site of Corey's dwelling-house; the vestiges of the cellar being then quite visible. It was near the crossing of the Salem and Lowell, and Georgetown and Boston Railroads, about three hundred feet to the west of the crossing, and close to the track of the former road, on its south side. The spot is surrounded by beautiful fields; and their aspect shows that it must have been, in all respects, an eligible estate. What is now known as "the Curtis Field" is a part of Corey's farm.

Giles Corey lived previously, for some time, in the town of Salem. He sold his house there in 1659. The contract with a carpenter for building his farm-house is preserved. It was stipulated to be erected "where he shall appoint." While the carpenter was getting out the materials, he selected and bought the farm, on which he lived ever afterwards. The house was to be "twenty feet in length, fifteen in breadth, and eight feet stud." Nothing strikes us more, as strange and unaccountable, than the small size of houses in those days. One would have thought, that, where wood was so plenty and near at hand, and land of no account, they would have built larger houses. In a letter, dated Nov. 16, 1646, from Governor Winthrop to his son John, of Connecticut, he gives an account " of a tempest (than which I never observed a greater);" and mentions that the roof of " Lady Moody's house, at Salem," with all of the chimney above it, was blown off in two parts, and " carried six or eight rods. Ten persons lay under it, and knew not of it till they arose in the morning." The house had a flat roof, was of one story, and nine feet in height! Lady Deborah Moody was a person of high position, a connection of Sir Henry Vane, and a

woman of property. She bought Mr. Humphreys'
great plantation. But, like Townsend Bishop, she was
dealt with, and compelled to quit the colony, on account of her doubts about infant baptism. Winthrop
calls her a "wise and anciently religious woman."
She went to Long Island, where her influence was so
important, that Governor Stuyvesant consulted her in
his administration, and conceded to her the nomina-
tion of magistrates. It seems very strange that such
a lady should have had a house only nine feet high.
The early houses were built either as temporary struc-
tures or with a view to enlargement. Perhaps Lady
Moody intended to add a story to hers. They were
low-studded for warmth. The farm-houses generally
were designed to be increased in length, when convenience required. The chimney was very large,
placed at one end, and so constructed, that, on the
extension of the building, fire-places could be opened
into it on the new end. A building of twenty feet
was prepared to become one of forty feet in width or
length, as the case might be; and then the chimney
would be in the middle of it.

As has been intimated, Corey was in bad repute.
Either he was a lawless man, or much misunderstood.
I am inclined to the latter opinion. He belonged to
that class of persons, instances of which we occasionally meet, who care little about the opinions or the
talk of others. On one occasion, he was going into
town with a cartload of wood. He met Anthony
Needham, in company with John Procter whose house

he had just passed. Procter accosted him thus : " How now, Giles, wilt thou never leave thy old trade? Thou hast got some of my wood here upon thy cart." Corey answered, " True, I did take two or three sticks to lay behind the cart to ease the oxen, because they bore too hard." This shows the free way in which Procter bantered with Corey, and the slight account the latter made of it. But the thing before long got to be too serious to be trifled with. It became the fashion to charge all sorts of offences against Corey ; and, whatever any one lost or mislaid, he was considered as having abstracted it. The gossip against him was quite unrestrained, and created a bitter and angry feeling in the neighborhood. In the winter of 1676, a man named Goodell, who had been working on Corey's farm, was carried home to his friends by Corey's wife, in a feeble state of health, and died soon after. It was whispered about, and before long openly asserted, that he had come to his death in consequence of having been violently beaten by Corey, who was accordingly arrested and brought to trial for killing the man. There was a great excitement against him. He probably had punished the man severely for some alleged misconduct; and it was charged that the castigation had been so unmerciful and excessive as to have broken down his constitution and caused his death. There was conflicting evidence going to show that the man had been beaten, for some misconduct, after he had returned to his family. It was a circumstance in favor of Corey, that his wife had taken the invalid to his home; and there was no evidence of any ill feeling between her and the sick man during a stop they made at Procter's house on their way. The death, too, it was supposed by some, might have resulted from ordinary disease, and not from whipping, either at Corey's or at home. The result was, that, notwithstanding the prejudice against Corey, he was discharged on paying a fine; showing that the Court did not consider it a very serious offence. We shall hear of this affair again.

In the year 1678, there was a suit at law between Corey and a man named John Gloyd, a laborer on his farm, on a question of wages. The case was, by agreement of the parties, passed out of court into the hands of arbitrators mutually chosen. John Procter was one of the arbitrators, and, as it would seem, chosen as the friend of Gloyd: Nathaniel Putnam and Edmund Bridges were the others; one of them chosen by Corey, and the other mutually agreed upon. They brought in their award. Its precise character is not stated; but the circumstances indicate that it was favorable to Gloyd. The conduct of Corey on this occasion shows, that, though a rough man perhaps, and liable, from his peculiar ways, to be harshly spoken of, he had, after all, a generous, forgiving, and genial nature. Nathaniel Putnam and Edmund Bridges state, that, when they brought in their award, " it was greatly to the satisfaction of the parties concerned; and Giles Corey did manifest as much satisfaction, and gave as many thanks to every one of us, as

ever we heard; and Goodman Corey did manifest, to
our observation, as much satisfaction to John Procter
as he did to the rest of the arbitrators." Captain
Moore, being by when the award was brought in, says,
"I did see and take notice of the abundance of love
manifested from Corey to Procter, and from Procter to
Corey: for they drank wine together; and Procter
paid for part, and Corey for part."

This remarkable overflow of affection between these
two men is rendered interesting, not merely by the
collisions into which, before and after, their impulsive
and imprudent natures brought them, but by the
part they were destined to enact in an impending
tragedy, which was to bring them to a fearful end in
a manner and on a scene that will arrest the notice of
all ages, and attest to their strong characters and
heroic spirit. The passage has a unique interest,
and is worthy of a painter.

It happened unfortunately, that, a few days after
the loving embraces of these hardy men, Procter's
house took fire. According to their habit, some of the
neighbors at once started the idea, that Corey had set
fire to it because of the award of the arbitrators, of
whom Procter was one. Under the excitement of the
conflagration, with his usual rashness, and forgetting
the pledges of reconciliation that had just passed
between them, Procter fell in with the accusation,
and Corey was brought to trial. It appeared, in evidence, that John Phelps and Thomas Fuller, who lived
on the western borders of the village, near Ipswich

River, coming along the road towards Procter's Corner about two hours before daylight, on the way probably to Salem market, saw his roof on fire, gave the alarm, and stopped to help put it out. Thomas Gould and Thomas Flint thought it must be the work of an incendiary, or of " an evil hand," as they expressed it, from the place where it took and the hour when it occurred. On the other hand, it was testified by James Poland and Caleb and Jane Moore, that they heard John Procter say that his boy carried a lamp and set the fire by accident. This was said by him, probably before the idea of Corey's agency in the matter had been put into his head. The prisoner proved an *alibi* by the most conclusive evidence, which is so curious, as giving an insight of a farmer's life at that time, and of Corey's domestic condition, that it may well be inserted.

Abraham Walcot testifies, that, " Tuesday night last was a week, I lodged at Giles Corey's house, which night John Procter's house was damaged by fire ; and Giles Corey went to bed before nine o'clock, and rose about sunrise again, and could not have gone out of the house but I should have heard him ; and it must have been impossible that he should have gone to Procter's house that night ; for he cannot in a long time go afoot, and, for his horse-kind, they were all in the woods. And further testifieth, that said Corey came home very weary from work, and went to bed the rather." His wife testified that he was in bed from nine o'clock until sunrise.

John Parker, one of Corey's four sons-in-law, testified as follows: "I being at work with my father, Goodman Corey, the day Goodman Procter's house was on fire. I going home with my father the night before, he complained that he was very weary, and said he would go to bed. I did, on our way going, ask him whether or no he would eat his supper: my father answered me again, no, he could not eat any thing that night; and so went to bed, and so I left him abed. And, the next morning, my father came to me about sun-rising, and asked me to go with Abraham Walcot to fetch a load of hay; and my father said he would try whether or not he could cart up a load of peas. I do also testify that he had no horse-kind near at home at that time."

John Gloyd, the hired man, with whom he had the lawsuit that had been settled a day or two before by arbitrators, testified, in corroboration of Parker, and to show that the latter could not have had any thing to do with the fire, that he slept in the same room with said Parker that night, and that he came to bed between nine and ten o'clock in the evening, and never rose until the break of day. Gloyd's wife testified to the same effect. There turned out to be no evidence against Corey whatever, but abundant proof of his innocence. The hard-working, " weary " old man was triumphantly acquitted. He thought, however, from this high-handed and utterly groundless attempt to wrong and ruin him, and from calumnious general statements that had been made against him in the course of the trial, that it was time to put a stop to the malignant and mischievous slanders which had been current in the neighborhood. He instituted prosecutions of Procter and others for defamation, and recovered against them all. After this, we hear no more of him until he experienced religion and was received into the First Church. Whether he and Procter became reconciled again is not known. Probably they did; for they seem to have had points of attraction, and each of them traits of kind-heartedness and generosity, under a rather rough exterior. The manner in which they bore themselves in their last hours is a matter of history, and stamps them both with true manliness.

The incidents which have now been related, and the peculiar traits of this man, are perhaps sufficient to account for the fact, that he was spoken of as a person of " a scandalous " life. He had afforded food for scandal; and it is not surprising, that, in a rural community, where but few topics for talk occur beyond the village boundaries, all should have participated, more or less, in criticising his ways, and that the various difficulties into which he had been drawn, and the charges against him, should have made him the object of much prejudice. His wife Martha was also a noticeable character. She was a professor of religion, a member of the village church, and found her chief happiness in attendance upon public worship and in private devotions. Much of her time — indeed, all that she could rescue from the labors of the household

— was spent in prayer. She was a woman of spirit and pluck, as we shall see.

Another notability of the village was Bridget Bishop. In 1666 — then the widow Wasselbe — she was married to Thomas Oliver. After his death, she became the wife of Edward Bishop, who is spoken of as a "sawyer." This term did not describe the same occupation then to which it is almost wholly applied now. Firewood, in those days, was not, as a general thing, sawed, but chopped. The sawyer got out boards and joists, beams, and timber of all kinds, from logs; and before mills were constructed, or where they were not conveniently accessible, it was an indispensable employment, and held a high rank among the departments of useful industry. It was in constant requisition in shipyards. It was a manly form of labor, requiring a considerable outlay of apparatus, and developing finely the whole muscular organization. The implement employed, beside the ordinary tools, such as wedges, beetles, the broad-axe, chains, and crowbar, was a strong steel cutting-plate, of great breadth, with large teeth, highly polished and thoroughly wrought, some eight or ten feet in length, with a double handle, crossing the plate at each end at a right angle. It was worked by two men, and called a "pit-saw," because sometimes the man at the lower handle stood in a deep pit, dug for the purpose, and called a "saw-pit." But, among the early settlers, the usual method was to make a frame of strong timbers. The log to be sawed was raised by slings, or slid up an inclined plane, and

placed upon cross-beams. Above it, a scaffolding
was made on which one man stood ; the other stood
on the ground below. They each held the saw by
both hands, and worked in unison. The log was
pushed along by handspikes as they reached the cross-
timbers, and wedges were used to keep the cleft open,
that the saw might work free. So important was this
business considered, that, from time to time, the General Court regulated by law the rates of pay to the
sawyer. If a farmer had suitable woodlands, he provided in many cases a saw-frame or saw-pit of his
own, got out his logs, and worked them into boards or
square timber for sale. This was a profitable business.

Edward Bishop had resided, for some seven years
previous to the witchcraft delusion, within the limits
of Salem, near the Beverly line. His wife Bridget
was a singular character, not easily described. She
kept a house of refreshment for travellers, and a
shovel-board for the entertainment of her guests, and
generally seems to have countenanced amusements
and gayeties to an extent that exposed her to some
scandal. She is described as wearing " a black cap
and a black hat, and a red paragon bodice," bordered
and looped with different colors. This would appear
to have been rather a showy costume for the times.
Her freedom from the austerity of Puritan manners,
and disregard of conventional decorum in her conversation and conduct, brought her into disrepute ; and
the tongue of gossip was generally loosened against
her. She was charged with witchcraft, and actually

brought to trial on the charge, in 1680, but was acquitted ; the popular mind not being quite ripe for such proceedings as took place twelve years afterwards. She still continued to brave public sentiment, lived on in the same free and easy style, paying no regard to the scowls of the sanctimonious or the foolish tittle-tattle of the superstitious. She kept her house of entertainment, shovel-board, and other appurtenances. Sometimes, however, she resented the calumnies circulated about her being a witch, in a manner that made it to be felt that it was best to let her alone. A man called one day at the house of Samuel Shattuck, where there was a sick child. He was a stranger to the inmates of the family, and evidently had come to the place to make trouble for Bridget Bishop. He pretended great pity for the child, and said, among other things, in an oracular way, " We are all born, some to one thing, and some to another." The mother asked him what he thought her poor, suffering child was born to. He replied, " He is born to be bewitched, and is bewitched : you have a neighbor, that lives not far off, who is a witch." The good woman does not appear to have entertained any suspicion of the kind ; but the man insisted on the truth of what he had affirmed. He succeeded in exciting her feelings on the subject, and, by vague insinuations and general descriptions of the witch, led her mind to fix upon Bridget Bishop. He said he should go and see her, and that he could bring her out as the afflicter of her child. She consented to let another of her boys go with him, and show the way. They proceeded to the house, and knocked at the door. Bridget opened it, and asked what he would have: he said a pot of cider. There was something in the manner of the man which satisfied her that he had come with mischievous intent. She ordered him off, seized a spade that happened to be near, drove him out of her porch, and chased him from her premises. When he and the boy got back, they bore marks of the bad luck of the adventure. Such things had perhaps happened before, and it was found that whoever provoked her resentment was very likely to come off second best from the encounter; yet Bridget was a member of Mr. Hale's Church in Beverly, and retained her standing in full fellowship there. It must have been thought, by the pastor and members of that church, that no charge seriously affecting her moral or Christian character was justly imputable to her.

The traveller of to-day, in passing over Crane-river Bridge, approaching the present village of "The Plains," near the eastern end of the Townsend Bishop or Nurse farm, will notice a roadway by the side of the bridge descending through the brook and going up to rejoin the main road on the other side. Such turnouts are frequent by the side of bridges over small streams. They are refreshing and useful, cooling the feet and cleansing the fetlocks of horses, and washing the wheels of carriages. One afternoon, Edward Bishop, with his wife behind him on a pillion, was riding home from Salem. Two women, mounted in

the same way, joined them ; and they chatted together
pleasantly as their horses ambled along. When they
came to the bridge, Bishop, probably merely for the fun
of the thing, dashed down into the brook, instead of
going over the bridge, to the great consternation and
against the vehement remonstrances of his wife, who
berated him soundly for his reckless disregard of her
safety. They got through without accident; and the
four jogged on together until the Bishops turned up
to their house, and the other two kept on to their home
in Beverly. But all the way from the bridge, until
they parted company, Bishop was finding great fault
with his wife, saying that he should not have been
sorry if any mishap had occurred. She did not say
much after her first fright and resentment were over ;
but he kept on talking very freely about her, and using
some pretty hard language. This affair, which perhaps is not without a parallel in the occasional experiences of married life, was, with other things of an
equally trivial and irrelevant character, brought to
bear fatally against her at her trial on the charge of
witchcraft, between seven and eight years afterward.

I can find no evidence against the moral character
of this woman. One person, at least, who participated
largely in getting up accusations against her, acknowledged, in a death-bed repentance, the wrong she had
done. Mr. Hale, the minister of the Beverly congregation, states, in a deposition, that a certain woman,
" being in full communion in our church, came to me
to desire that Goodwife Bishop, her neighbor, wife of

Edward Bishop, Jr., might not be permitted to receive
the Lord's Supper in our church till she had given her
satisfaction for some offences that were against her;
namely, because the said Bishop did entertain people
in her house at unseasonable hours in the night, to
keep drinking and playing at shovel-board, whereby
discord did arise in other families, and young people
were in danger to be corrupted; that she knew these
things, and had once gone into the house, and,
finding some at shovel-board, had taken the pieces
they played with and thrown them into the fire, and
had reproved the said Bishop for promoting such dis-
orders, but received no satisfaction from her about
it." According to Mr. Hale's statement, the night
after this complaint was brought to him, the woman
was found to be distracted. "She continuing some
time distracted, we sought the Lord by fasting and
prayer." After a while, the woman recovered her
senses, and, as Mr. Hale says he understood, expressed
a suspicion " that she had been bewitched by Bishop's
wife." He declares that he did not, at the time, countenance the idea, "hoping better of Goody Bishop."
He says further, that he "inquired of Margaret
King, who kept at or near the house," what she had
observed concerning the woman who had been distracted. " She told me that she was much given to
reading and searching the prophecies of Scripture."
At length the woman appeared to have entirely recovered, went to Goody Bishop, gave satisfaction for what
she had said and done against her, and they became

friends again. Mr. Hale goes on to say, " I was oft praying with and counselling of her before her death." She earnestly desired that " Edward Bishop might be sent for, that she might make friends with him. I asked her if she had wronged Edward Bishop. She said, not that she knew of, unless it were in taking his shovel-board pieces, when people were at play with them, and throwing them into the fire ; and, if she did evil in it, she was very sorry for it, and desired he would be friends with her, or forgive her. This was the very day before she died." That night her distemper returned, and, in a paroxysm of insanity, she destroyed herself.

It is evident, from his own account, that Mr. Hale did not then fall in with, or countenance at all, any unfavorable impressions against Bridget Bishop ; and that the poor diseased woman, when entirely free from her malady, repented bitterly of what she had done and said of Goodman Bishop and his wife, and heartily desired their forgiveness. So far as the facts stated by Mr. Hale of his own knowledge go, they prove that Bridget Bishop was the victim of gross misrepresentation. Five years afterwards, as we shall see, Mr. Hale gave a very different version of the affair, and one which it is extremely difficult to reconcile with his own former deliberate convictions at the time when the circumstances occurred.

As it is my object to bring before you every thing that may help to explain the particular occurrences embraced in the account I am to give of the witchcraft prosecutions, two other persons must be mentioned before concluding this branch of my subject, — George Jacobs, Sr., and his son George Jacobs, Jr. They each had given offence to some persons, and suffered that sort of notoriety which led to the selection of victims, although both were persons of respectability. The father owned and had lived for about a half-century on a farm in North Fields, on the banks of Endicott River, a little to the eastward of the bridge at the iron-foundery. He was a person of good estate and an estimable man; but it was his misfortune to have an impulsive nature and quick passions. In June, 1677, he was prosecuted and fined for striking a man who had incensed him. George Jacobs, Jr., his only son, at a court held Nov. 7, 1674, was prosecuted, "found blamable, and ordered to pay costs of court." His offence and defence are embraced in his deposition on the occasion.

"GEORGE JACOBS'S ANSWER TO NATHANIEL PUTNAM'S COMPLAINT. — That I did follow some horses in our enclosure on the Royal Side, where they were trespassing upon us; that the end of my following them was to take them; but, rather than they would be taken, they took the water, and I did follow them no further; but straightway they turned ashore, and I did run to take them as they came out of the water, but could not: and I can truly take my oath that since that time I did never follow any horses or mares; and I hope my own oath will clear me."

The result of his attempt to drive off the horses was, that several valuable animals were drowned.

Their owner, Nathaniel Putnam, brought an action; but he could not recover damages. The horses were evidently trespassing, and the Court did not seem to regard Jacobs's conduct as a heinous matter. It is not to be supposed, that Nathaniel Putnam harbored sentiments of revenge or resentment for eighteen years, or had any hand in prosecuting Jacobs in 1692. There is every indication that he did not sympathize in the violent passions which raged on that occasion, although he was much under the power of the delusion. But the affair of drowning the horses was probably for a long time a topic of gossip, and may have given to the author of the catastrophe a notoriety which nearly cost him his life.

The account that has been given of the elements of the population of the Salem Farms or Village, shows that, while there were the usual varieties entering into the composition of all communities, it is wholly inadmissible to suppose that the witchcraft delusion took place there because it was the scene of greater ignorance or stupidity or barbarism than prevailed elsewhere. This will be made more apparent still by some general views of the state of society and manners. The people of a remote age are in general only regarded as they are seen through prominent occurrences and public movements. These constitute the ordinary materials of history. Dynasties, reigns of kings, armies, legislative proceedings, large ecclesiastical synods, dogmatic creeds, and the like, are, as a general thing, about all we know of the past. Portraits of individuals appear here and there; but, separated from the ordinary life of the times, they cannot be fairly or fully appreciated. The public life of the past is but the outline, or, more strictly speaking, the mere skeleton, of humanity. To fill up the outline, to clothe the skeleton with elastic nerves and warm flesh, and quicken it with a vital circulation, we must get at the domestic, social, familiar, and ordinary experience of individuals and private persons; we must obtain a view of the popular customs and the daily routine of life. In this way only can history fulfil its office in making˟ the past present.

The people of the early colonial settlements had a private and interior life, as much as we have now, and the people of all ages and countries have had. It is common to regard them in no other light than as a severe, sombre, and pleasure-abhorring generation. It was not so with them altogether. They had the same nature that we have. It was not all gloom and severity. They had their recreations, amusements, gayeties, and frolics. Youth was as buoyant with hope and gladness, love as warm and tender, mirth as natural to innocence, wit as sprightly, then as now. There was as much poetry and romance: the merry laugh enlivened the newly opened fields, and rang through the bordering woods as loud, jocund, and unrestrained as in these older and more crowded settlements. It is true that their theology was austere, and their polity, in Church and State, stern; but, in their modes of life, there were some features which gave peculiar opportunity to exercise and gratify a love of social excitement of a pleasurable kind. Let me mention some of the customs having a tendency in this direction, that prevailed in the early settlements of New England.

Whenever a young man had made his clearing in the forest, got out the frame of his house, and selected a helpmeet to dwell with him in it, there was " a 'raising." On an appointed day, the neighbors far and near assembled; all together put their shoulders to the work; and, before the shadows of night enveloped the scene, the house was up, and covered from sill to ridgepole. The same was done if the house of a neighbor had been destroyed by fire. In this case, often the timbers, joists, and boards were contributed as well as the labor. These were made the occasions of general merriment, in which all ages and both sexes participated. Then there were the "huskings." After the barns were filled with hay and grain, and the corn was ripe, at " harvest home," gatherings would be seen on the bright autumnal afternoons of successive days, in the neighborhood of the different farmhouses. The sheaves would be taken from the shocks and brought up from the fields, the golden leaves and milky tassels stripped from the full ear, and the crib filled to the brim. These were scenes of unalloyed enjoyment and unrestrained gayety.

At that time were prevalent, in rural neighborhoods, other recreations promotive of social hilarity to the

highest degree. As a wintry evening drew on, the
wide, deep fireplace — equalling in width nearly the
whole of one side of the room, and so deep that
benches were permanently attached to the jambs, on
which two or more could comfortably sit — was duly
prepared. A huge log, of a diameter equal to that
of "the mast of some great admiral," six feet perhaps in length, was worked in by handspikes to its
place as the "back-log;" a smaller one, as "back-
stick," placed over it; the great andirons duly adjusted, and the wood piled on artistically — for there
was an art in building a wood-fire. The kindlings
were placed on top of the whole; never by an experienced hand below. More than the light of day,
from dazzling chandeliers or the magic tongues of
flaming gas-burners, blazes through the halls of modern luxury and splendor; but the lights and shadows
from a glowing, old-fashioned, New-England country
fireplace created a scene as enlivening, exhilarating,
and genial as has ever been witnessed, and cannot be surpassed. Assembled neighbors in a single
evening accomplished what would have been the work
of a family for months. The corn and the nuts were
all shelled; the young birch was stripped down in
thin strands, and brooms enough made for a year's
service in house and barn; and various other useful
offices rendered. The sound of busy hands and nim-
ble fingers was lost in commingling happy voices.
Fun and jest, joy and love, ruled the hour. The whole
affair was followed by " Blind-man's Buff" or some

other sport. After the "old folks" had considerately retired, who knows but that the sons and daughters of Puritans sometimes wound up with a dance? There were sleigh-rides, and the woods rang with the happy laugh and jingling bells. The vehicles used on these occasions were, prior to 1700, more properly called "sleds." Our modern "sleigh" had not then been introduced. As the spring came on, logs would be hollowed or scooped out and placed near the feet of sugar maples, a slanting incision made a foot or two above them in the trunks of the trees, a slip of shingle inserted, and the delicious sap would trickle down into the troughs. When the proper time came, tents or booths made of evergreen boughs would be erected in the woods, great kettles hung over blazing fires, and a whole neighborhood camp out for several days and nights, until the work was accomplished, and the flavory syrup or solid cakes of sugar brought out.

These were some of the recreations of the country people in the early settlements of New England; continuing, perhaps, in frontier towns to this day. They constituted forms of enjoyment which cannot exist in cities or older communities; and possessed a charm, in the memory of all who ever participated in them, greater, far greater, than society in any later stage can possess.

The principal method of travelling in those days was on horseback. It afforded many special opportunities for social enjoyment. Women as well as men were trained to it. The people of the village were all at home in the saddle. The daughters of Joseph Putnam, sisters of Israel, were celebrated as equestrians. Tradition relates adventurous feats of theirs in this line, equal to that which constitutes a part of the history of their famous brother. There were, perhaps, several games of skill or chance practised more or less, even in those days, in this neighborhood. The only one that seems to have been openly allowed, of which we have any evidence, was shovel-board. This game, now supposed to be out of use, is referred to by Shakespeare, and was quite common in England as well as in this country. A board about two and a half feet wide and twenty feet long was placed three feet above the floor, somewhat like a billiard-table, though not with so wide a surface, precisely level and perfectly smooth, covered with a sprinkling of fine sand. It was provided with weights or balls, called " pieces," flattened on one end. The game consisted in shoving them as far as possible, without going over the end. A trough surrounded the table to catch the pieces if they fell. Richard Grant White, from whom this account of the game has been derived, says that " it required great accuracy of eye, and steadiness of hand, much more than ten-pins." He states that, when a boy, he saw it played by " brawny " men, in Brooklyn, N.Y., and that the pieces then used were of brass. It is probable that the " pieces " used on Bridget Bishop's shovel-board were made of some heavy wood, as they were thrown into the fire for the purpose of destroying them. The fact that a game like this was suffered to be openly played in Salem Village is quite remarkable, and shows that some license was left for such amusements.

The records and files of the local courts show, that, notwithstanding the austere gravity and strictness of manners and morals usually ascribed to our New-England ancestors, occasional irregularities occurred in the early settlements, which would be considered high misdemeanors in our day. The following deposition was given " on oath before the Court," Feb. 26,1651. Edward Norris was the son of the minister of the First Church; had been for more than ten years, and continued to be for twenty years after, schoolmaster of the town; and, by his character as well as office, commanded the highest respect. John Kitchen, in 1655, was chosen " searcher and sealer of leather." Giles Corey had not yet purchased his farm, but lived on his town-lot, extending from Essex Street, near its western extremity, to the North River. They were severally persons of good estate.

" THE TESTIMONY OF GILES COREY. — Mr. Edward Norris and I were going towards the brickkiln: John Kitchen, going with us, fell a nipping and pinching of us. And, when we came back again, John Kitchen struck up Mr. Edward Norris his heels and mine, and fell upon me, and catched me by the throat, and held me so long till he had almost stopped my breath. And I said unto John Kitchen, 'This is not good jesting.' And John Kitchen replied, 'This is nothing: I do owe you more than this of old: this is not half of that which you shall have afterwards.' After this, he went into his house, and he took stinking water and threw upon us, and took me and thrust me out of doors, and I went my ways. And John Kitchen followed me half-way up the lane, or thereabouts. Perceiving him to follow me, I went to go over the rails. He took me again, and threw me down off the rails, and fell a beating of me until I was all bloody. And, Thomas Bishop being present, I desired him to bear witness of what he saw. Upon my words, he let me rise. As soon as I was up, he fell a beating of me again.

"Testified on oath before the Court, 26th Feb., 1651.

"HENRY BARTHOLOMEW, *Clerk*."

This was indeed an extraordinary outburst of lawless violence, and gives a singular insight of the state of society. Such an occurrence in our day would create astonishment. The organized power of the community to suppress vicious and rude passions was probably never brought to bear with greater rigidness than in our Puritan villages; but it did not fully accomplish its end. Behind and beneath the solemn and formal exterior, there was, after all, perhaps as much irregularity of life as now. The nature of man had not been subdued. The people had their quarrels and fights, and their frolics and merriments, in defiance of the restraints of authority. Violations of local and general laws were not infrequent; and flowed, as ever since, from intemperance, in as large a measure. Kitchen, in this instance, acted as if under the influence of liquor. His behavior, in tripping up the heels and throwing dirty water upon the person of the school-

master of the town, the dignity of whose social position is indicated by the title of " Mr. ; " and in giving
to Corey such a persistent and gratuitous pommelling,
— bears the aspect of a drunken delirium. The latter
seems not to have supposed, for some time, that he was
in earnest, but to have looked upon his conduct as
rough play, which was carried rather too far. Poor
Corey was often getting before the town Court as accused or accuser. He was, to the end, the victim of
ill-usage, either given or taken. Though not a bad-
natured man, he was almost always in trouble. The
tenor of his long life was as eccentric and unruly as
the manner of his death was strange and horrible.

There was what may be called an institution in the
rural parishes of the early times, still existing to some
extent perhaps in country places, which must not be
omitted in an enumeration of controlling influences.
The people lived on farms, at some distance from each
other, and almost all at great distances from the meeting-house. Local and parental authority, church discipline, public opinion, enforced attendance upon the
regular religious services. Fashion, habit, and choice
concurred in bringing all to meeting on the Lord's
Day. It was impossible for many to return home
during the intermission between the services of the
forenoon and afternoon. The effect was, that the whole
community were thrown and kept together every week
for several hours, during which they could not avoid
social intercourse. It was a more effective institution
than the town-meeting; for it occurred oftener, and

included women and children. In pleasant weather, they would perhaps gather together in knots at eligible places, or stroll off in companies to the shades of the neighboring woods. In bad weather, they would remain in the meeting-house, or congregate at Deacon Ingersoll's ordinary, or in the great rooms of his dwelling-house. As a whole, this practice must have produced important results upon the character of the people. In the absence of newspapers, or of much intercourse with remote places, the day was made the occasion for hearing and telling all the news. It provided for the circulation of ideas, good and bad. It widened the sphere of influence of the wiser and better sort, and gave opportunity for mischievous people to do much harm. It was a sort of central bazaar, open every week, where all the varieties of local gossip could be interchanged and circulated far and wide. Of the aggregate character of the effects thus produced, I do not propose to strike the balance. It was undoubtedly an effective instrumentality in moulding the population of the country, developing the elements of society, quickening and rendering more vigorous the action of the people in masses, and elucidating the phenomena of their history. It answers my purpose, at present, to suggest, that, if any popular delusion or fanaticism arose, the means of giving it a rapid diffusion, and of intensifying its power, were in this way provided.

In the early settlement of the country, the pursuit of game in the forests, rivers, and lakes, was necessary as a means of subsistence, and has always been im-

portant in that view. A war against beasts and birds
of prey was also required to be incessantly kept up.
The methods adopted for these ends were various and
ingenious, often requiring courage and skill, and in
most instances conducted in companies. Deer and
moose were sometimes caged by surrounding them, or
trapped; but the gun was chiefly relied upon in their
pursuit. There were various methods for catching the
smaller animals. One of the sports of boyhood was to
spring the rabbits or hares. A sapling, or young tree,
was bent down and fastened to a stick slid into notches
cut in trees, on each side of the path of the animal.
The rabbit is wont to race through the woods at great
speed, and along established tracks, which, particularly
after snow has fallen, are clearly traceable. To the
cross-stick, thus placed above the path, one end of a
strong horse-hair was tied. The other end was in
a slip-knot, with a noose just large enough, and hanging at the height, to receive the head of the rabbit.
Not seeing the noose, and rushing along the path, the
rabbit would jerk the cross-stick out of the notches.
The tree would bound back to its original upright direction, and the rabbit remain swinging aloft, until, at
the break of day, the boys would rejoice in the success
of their stratagem. Pigeons in clouds frequented the
country in their seasons, and acres upon acres of the
forests bowed beneath their weight. They were taken
by nets, dozens at a time, or brought down in great
numbers by shot-guns. The marshalled hosts of wild
geese made their noisy flights over the land in the

spring and fall, traversing a space spanning the continent north and south. They were brought down by
the gun, on the wing, or surprised while resting in
their long route or stopped by storms, around secluded
ponds or swamps. Ducks and other aquatic birds were
abundant on the rivers and marshes, and pursued in
canoes along the bays and seashores. Salt-water fish
were within reach in the neighboring ocean; while an
unfailing supply of fresh-water fish was yielded by Wenham Lake, Wilkins's Pond, and the running streams.

The bear was a formidable prowler around the settlements, killing young cattle, making havoc in the
sheepfold, and depredating upon the barn and farm
yard. He was a dangerous antagonist, of immense
strength in his arms and claws. Sometimes he was
reached effectually by the gun, but the trap was mainly
relied upon to secure him. His skin made him a valu-
ble prize, and he supplied other beneficial uses. The
earliest and rudest method of trapping a bear was as
follows : A place was selected in the woods, where two
large fallen and mouldering trees were side by side
within two or three feet of each other. The space
between them would be roofed over by throwing
branches and boughs across them, and closed up at
one end. The other end would be left open. A gun
was placed inside, heavily loaded, the muzzle towards
the open end ; to the trigger a cord was fastened running along by the barrel of the gun, passing over a
cross-bar, and hanging down directly before the muzzle, baited with a piece of fresh meat. The bear,

ranging in the woods at night, would be attracted by
the smell of meat, and come snuffing around. At the
open end, he would see the bait, rush in, seize it
between his jaws, pull the cord, discharge the gun,
and his head and breast be torn to pieces. The men
engaged in the enterprise would remain awake in some
neighboring house, waiting and listening, with the ex-
tremest interest, for the report of the gun to announce
their success. At the break of day, they would gather
to the spot, and participate in the profit of the capture.
After a while, iron or steel traps were introduced.
They would be skilfully baited and set, and fastened to
a tree by a chain. The whole was covered over with
light soil and leaves. The bear would make for the
bait. The weight of his paw would spring the trap.
The iron-teeth would hold him fast till the morning.
In his suffering and exasperation, it would require
considerable effort to despatch him. In catching bears,
as well as foxes, much skill and art were needed.
They were each very wary and cautious; and, where
iron was used in the traps, some scent was necessary
to disguise the smell of the metal. All appearance of
having been disturbed had to be removed from the
ground. Trapping became quite a science, and was a
pursuit of much importance.

Wolves were perhaps the most destructive of the
beasts of prey. Although not so large or strong as
bears, they were far more fierce and rapacious. Bears
could be tamed, but wolves not. Bears were not dangerous, unless provoked, or suffering from hunger, or

alarmed for the safety of their young. It was thought
that kind treatment would awaken strong attachment
in them, but wolves were always snarling and ferocious.
They roamed mostly in packs, and would kill sheep,
lambs, and poultry long after hunger was appeased.
The farmers regarded them as their great enemy. A
long and deep trench would be dug, lined with slippery logs, from which the bark had been taken, standing upright, and touching each other. The trench was
covered by a slight framework, upon which leaves and
dirt were scattered, to make the surface appear like
the surrounding territory. Some savory bait would be
placed over it. The wolves, rushing on, would break-
through. Not being able to ascend the sides, they
would be found alive, the next morning, at the bottom.
These were called " wolf-pits." It was no easy matter
to dispose of or despatch the furious animals, and the
wolf-pits were often the scenes of much excitement.
There was another class of animals, — divided into different species, mostly according to their size, — smaller
but fiercer than wolves, of extraordinary strength and
activity, called wild-cats, catamounts, or loup-cerviers,
pronounced by the farmers lucifees. These were only
taken by the gun. It was considered a useful public
service, and no inconsiderable feat, to kill them.

Some of the laborious employments, at that time,
were especially promotive of social influence ; for instance, the making and mending highways. This was
secured by a tax, annually levied in town-meeting.
The work was placed under the care and direction of

surveyors, annually chosen. A small part of this tax, however, was paid in money. Most of it was " worked out." At convenient seasons, when there was a respite from the ordinary farm work, the men of a neighborhood would come together, in greater or less numbers, at a designated time and place, with their oxen and implements. Working in unison, they would work merrily and with energy ; and, as the tough roots and deeply bedded rocks gave way to the pickaxe, crowbar, and chain, and rough places became smooth, the wilderness would echo back their voices of gratulation, and a spirit of animating rivalry stimulate their toils. Many other operations were carried on, such as getting up hay from the salt-marshes and building stone-walls, by neighbors working in companies.

Particular circumstances in the history of the population of Salem Village contributed to keep up a condition of general intelligence, which served, to some degree, as a substitute for an organized system of education. Indeed, any thing like regular schools was rendered impossible by the then-existing circumstances. Clearings had made a very inconsiderable encroachment on the wilderness. There were here and there farmhouses, with deep forests between. It was long before easily traversable roads could be made. A schoolhouse placed permanently on any particular spot would be within the reach of but very few. Farmers most competent to the work, who had enjoyed the advantages of some degree of education, and could manage to set apart any time for the purpose, were, in some instances, prevailed upon to receive such children as were within reaching distance as pupils in their own houses, to be instructed by them at stated times and for a limited period. Daniel Andrew rendered this service occasionally. At one period, we find them practising the plan of a movable school and schoolmaster. He would be stationed in the houses of particular persons, with whom the arrangement could be made, a month at a time, in the different quarters of the village, from Will's Hill to Bass River. Of course, there was a great lack of elementary education. For a considerable time, it was reduced to a very low point; and there were heads of families, — men who had good farms, and possessed the confidence and respect of their neighbors, — who appear not to have been able to write.

It is difficult, however, to come to a definite estimate on this subject, as the singular fact is discovered, that some persons, who could write, occasionally preferred to " make their mark." Ann Putnam, in executing her will, made her mark; but her confession, with her own proper written signature, is spread out in the Church-book. Francis Nurse very frequently used his peculiar mark, representing, perhaps, some implement of his original mechanical trade; but, on other occasions, he wrote out his name in a good, round hand. The same was the case with Bray Wilkins. We can hardly reach any decisive conclusions as to the intelligence or education of the people of that day from their handwriting, or construction of sentences, much

less from their spelling. Their forms of speech were
very different from ours in many respects. What, at
first view, we might be apt to call errors of ignorance,
were perhaps conformity to good usage at the time.
Their use of verbs is different from ours, particularly
in the subjunctive mood, and in conjugation generally.
They did not follow our rule in reference to number.
When the nominative was a plural noun, or several
nouns, they often employ the connected verb in the
singular number, and *vice versâ*. They were inclined
to make construction conform to the sense, rather than
to the letter. It is not certain that their usage, in this
particular, is wholly indefensible. Cicero, in his fifth
oration against Verres, couples *rem* with *futurum*.
This was looked upon by some editors as an error,
and they altered the text accordingly; but Aulus
Gelius, in his "Attic Nights," maintains that it is
the true reading, and, in view of the sense of the passage, a legitimate and elegant use of language. He
cites instances, in Latin and Greek authors of the highest standard, of a similar usage.

Nothing, or scarcely any thing, can be inferred from
spelling. It was wholly unsettled among the best-
educated men, and in the practice of the same person.
In Winthrop's "Journal," he spells the name of his
distinguished friend — the governor of both Massachusetts and Connecticut — sometimes Haynes, and
sometimes Haines. The *r* is generally dropped from
his own signature, or, if not intentionally dropped, is
quite lost in one or the other of the contiguous let-

ters. It is a curious circumstance, that the name "Winthrop" is spelled differently by our governor, his wife, and his son, the governor of Connecticut; each varying from either of the other two. George Burroughs, a graduate of Harvard College, wrote his own name sometimes with, and sometimes without, the *s*. In our General-court records, the name of the first Captain Davenport is spelled in at least four different ways. The Putnams sometimes wrote their name Putman. The name of the Nurses was often written Nourse, and sometimes Nurs.

Unable to come to any reliable conclusions in reference to the general intelligence of the people of Salem Village from their orthography, etymology, syntax, or chirography, compared with their contemporaries, I can only say, that, in examining the records and papers which have come down to us, the wonder to me is that they expressed themselves so well. I do not hesitate to say, that, in the various controversies in which they were involved, prior to and immediately after the witchcraft delusion, there is a pervading appearance of uncommon appreciation of the questions at issue, and substantial evidence that there was a solid substratum of good sense among them.

Their manners appear to have been remarkably courteous and respectful, showing the effect still remaining upon their style of intercourse and personal bearing, of the society and example of the great number of eminent, enlightened, and accomplished men and families that had resided or mingled with them during all

the early period of their history. In their deportment
to each other, there was that sort of decorum which
indicates good breeding. They paid honor to gray
hairs, and assigned to age the first rank in seating the
congregation, — a matter to which, before the introduction of pews as a particular property, they gave the
greatest consideration. The " seating" was to continue for a year ; and a committee of persons who
would command the greatest confidence was regularly
appointed to report on the delicate and difficult subject. Their report, signed by them severally, was entered in full in the parish record-book. The invariable
rule was, first, age ; then, office ; last, rates. The chief
seats were given to old men and women of respectable characters, without regard to their circumstances
in life or position in society. Then came the families
of the minister and deacons, the parish committee and
clerk, the constable of the village, magistrates, and
military officers. These were preferred, because all
offices were then honorable, and held, if they were
called to them, by the principal people. Last came
rates, — that is, property. The richest man in the
parish, if not holding office, or old enough to be
counted among the aged, would take his place with
the residue of the congregation. The manner in
which parents were spoken of on all occasions is quite
observable, not only in written documents, but ordinary conversation, — always with tender respectfulness.
In almost all cases, the expressions used are " my honored father " or " my honored mother," and this by per-

sons in the humblest and most inferior positions in life. The terms " Goodman " and " Goodwife" were applied to the heads of families. The latter word was abbreviated to " Goody," but not at all, as our dictionaries have it, as a " low term of civility." It was applied to the most honored matrons, such as the wife of Deacon Ingersoll. It was a term of respect; conveying, perhaps, an affectionate sentiment, but not in the slightest degree disrespectful, derogatory, or belittling. Surely no better terms were ever used to characterize a worthy person. " Goodman " comprehends all that can be ascribed to a citizen of mature years in the way of commendation ; and the whole catalogue of pretentious titles ever given by flatterers or courtiers to a married lady cannot, all combined, convey a higher encomium than the term " Goodwife." How much more expressive, courteous to the persons to whom they are applied, and consistent with the self-respect of the person using them, than " Mr." and " Mrs." ! A more than questionable taste and a foolish pride have led us to adopt these terms because they were originally applicable to the gentry or to magistrates, and to abandon the good old words which had a meaning truly polite to others, and not degrading to ourselves !

A patriarchal authority and dignity was recognized in families. The oldest member was often called, by way of distinction, " Landlord," merely on account of his seniority, without reference particularly to the extent of his domain or the value of his acres. After

the death of Thomas Putnam, in 1686, his brother
Nathaniel had the title; after him, the surviving
brother, Captain John; after him, it fell to the next
generation, and Benjamin, a son of Nathaniel, became " Landlord Putnam." It was so with other
families.

The liberal and judicious policy, before described,
of giving estates to children on their marriage, with
the maintenance of parental authority in the household, produced the desired effect upon the character
of the people. It was almost a matter of course, that,
on reaching mature years, young men and women
would own the covenant, and become members of the
church. The general tone of society was undoubtedly
favorable to the moral and religious welfare of the
younger portion of the community. Some exceptions
occurred, but few in number. One case, however, in
which there was a flagrant violation of filial duty, may
not be omitted in this connection; for it belongs to
the public history of the country.

John Porter, Jr., the eldest son of the founder of
that most respectable family, about thirty years of
age, appears to have been a very wicked and incor-
rigible person. His abusive treatment of his parents
reached a point where it became necessary, in the last
resort, to appeal to the protection of the law. After
various proceedings, he was finally sentenced to stand
on the ladder of the gallows with a rope around his
neck for an hour; to be severely whipped; committed
to the House of Correction; kept closely at work on

prison diet, not to be released until so ordered by the Court of Assistants or the General Court; and to pay " a fine to the country of two hundred pounds." It is stated, that, if the mother of the culprit " had not been overmoved by her tender affections to forbear appearing against him, the Court must necessarily have proceeded with him as a capital offender, according to our law being grounded upon and expressed in the Word of God, in Deut. xxi. 18 to 21. See Capital Laws, p. 9, § 14." Some time afterward, the General Court, upon his petition, granted him a release from imprisonment, on condition of his immediate departure from this jurisdiction; first giving a bond of two hundred pounds not to return without leave of the General Court or Court of Assistants.

In 1664, four commissioners, Colonel Richard Nichols, Sir Robert Carr, George Cartwright, and Samuel Maverick, Esqs., were sent over by Charles II. " to hear and determine complaints and appeals in all causes, as well military as criminal and civil." There had always been a powerful influence at work in the English Court adverse to New England. It had been thus far successfully baffled by the admirable diplomacy of the colonial government and agents. All conflicts of authority had been prevented from coming to a head by a skilful policy of " protracting and avoiding." But the restoration of the Stuarts boded no good to the liberties of the colonies; and the arrival of these commissioners with their sweeping authority was regarded as designed to deal the long-deferred fatal blow at chartered rights. They began with a high hand. The General Court did not quail before them, but stood ready to take advantage of the first false step of the commissioners ; and they did not have long to wait.

Porter had taken refuge in Rhode Island. When the commissioners visited that colony, he appealed to them for redress against the Massachusetts General Court. They were inconsiderate enough to espouse his cause, and issued a proclamation giving him protection to return to Boston to have his case tried before them. The General Court at once took issue with them, and changed their attitude from the defensive to the offensive ; denounced their proceedings ; spread upon the official records a full account, in the plainest language, of Porter's outrages upon his parents, exhibiting it in details that could not but shock every sentiment of humanity and decency ; holding up the commissioners as the abettors and protectors of criminality of the deepest dye ; and planting themselves fair and square against them on the merits of Porter's case. The commissioners tried to explain and extricate themselves ; but they could not escape from the toils in which, through rashness, they had become entangled. The General Court made a public declaration charging the commissioners with " obstructing the sentence of justice passed against that notorious offender," and with sheltering and countenancing " his rebellion against his natural parents ; " with violating a court of justice, discharging a whole

country "from their oaths whereby they had sworn
obedience to His Majesty's authority according to the
Constitution of his Royal Charter;" and with attempt-
ing to overthrow the rights of the colony under the
charter by bringing in a military force to overawe and
suppress the civil authorities. They denounced them
as guilty of a perversion of their trust, and as having
committed a breach upon the dignity of the crown, by
pursuing a course "derogatory to His Majesty's authority here established," and "repugnant to His
Majesty's princely and gracious intention in betrusting
them with such a commission." The Court held the
vantage-ground, and the commissioners were unable
to dislodge them. The end of the matter was, that
the power of the commissioners was completely broken
down. They ingloriously gave up the contest, and
went home to England.

The instance of John Porter, Jr., to which such
extraordinary publicity and prominence were given by
the circumstances now related, does not bear against
what I have said of the general prevalence, in the
rural community of Salem Village, of parental authority and filial duty, as he was early withdrawn from it
to pursuits that led him into totally different spheres
of life. He had been engaged in trade, and exposed
to vicious influences in foreign ports. In voyages to
"Barbadoes, and so for England, he had prodigally
wasted and riotously expended about four hundred
pounds." Besides this, he had run himself, by his
vicious courses, into debts which his father had to pay

in order to release him from prison abroad. He came back the desperate character described by the General Court. His punishment was severe, but absolutely necessary, in the judgment of the whole community, for the safety of his parents and the preservation of domestic and public order.

Although living in humble dwellings on plain fare, working with their hands for daily bread, clad in rude garments, and practising a frugal economy, there was a certain style of things about the people I am describing unlike what is ordinarily associated with our ideas of them. The men wore swords or rapiers as a part of their daily apparel. Their wives had domestic servants. Every farmer had his hired laborers, and many of them had slaves. The relation of servitude, however, differed from that on Southern plantations in many respects. The slaves, without any formal manumission, easily obtained their freedom, and often became landholders. The courteous decorum acquired from the example of the eminent men among the first planters long continued to mark the manners of this people ; and its vestiges remain to the present day. It strikingly appeared in the latter half of the last and the earlier period of this century in the persons of Judge Samuel Houlton, Colonel Israel Hutchinson, General Moses Porter, and the late Judge Samuel Putnam.

The wise forethought of the company in London, at the outset of its operations, in providing for all that was needful to the establishment and welfare of the colony, has already been described. It was most strikingly illustrated in the careful selection of the first emigrants. Men were sought out who were experienced and skilful in the various mechanic arts. In the early population of Salem Farms, every species of handicraft was represented. When the number was less than a hundred householders, there were weavers, spinners, potters, joiners, housewrights, wheelwrights, brickmakers and masons, blacksmiths, coopers, painters, tailors, cordwainers, glovers, tanners, millers, maltsters, skinners, sawyers, tray-makers, and dish-turners. Every absolute want was provided for. These trades and callings were carried on in connection with agricultural employments, and their continuance kept carefully in view by the heads of the principal families. John Putnam not only gave large farms to each of his sons, but he trained them severally to some mechanical art. One was a weaver, another a bricklayer, &c. The farmer was also a mechanic, and every description of useful labor held in equal honor.

Another marked feature of this people was their military spirit. They were kept in a state of universal and thorough organization to protect themselves from Indian hostilities, or to respond, on any occasion, at a moment's warning, to the call of the country. The sentinel at the watch-house was ever on the alert. Authority was early obtained from the General Court to form a foot company. All adults of every description, including men much beyond middle life, — every

one, in fact, who could carry a musket, belonged to it.
Its officers were the fathers of the village. Every
title of rank, from corporal to captain, once obtained,
was worn ever after through life. Jonathan Walcot,
a citizen of the highest respectability, who had married as a second wife Deliverance a daughter of
Thomas Putnam, and was one of the deacons of the
parish, was its captain. Nathaniel Ingersoll, the other
deacon, is spoken of from time to time as corporal,
then sergeant, and finally lieutenant. He served with
that commission till late in life, and was always,
after attaining that rank, known as either Lieutenant or Deacon Ingersoll. The eldest son of Thomas
Putnam, a leading member of the church, a man of
large property, and the clerk of the parish, was one
of the sergeants, always known as such. In our narrative, with which he will be found in most unfortunate connection, I shall speak of him by that title. It
will distinguish him from his father. This " company " had frequent drills, probably from the first, in
the field left by will afterwards for that purpose by
Nathaniel Ingersoll. Often, no doubt, it paraded
on the open grounds around the meeting-house, or in
the fields of Joseph Hutchinson after the harvest had
been gathered. It marched and countermarched along
the neighboring roads. It was almost as much thought
of as the " church," officered by the same persons, and
composed of the same men. It was a common practice, at the close of a parade, before " breaking line,"
for the captain to give notices of prayer, church,

or parish meetings. Such men as Richard Leach, Thomas Fuller, and Nathaniel Putnam, esteemed it an honor to bear titles in this company; and held them ever after through life with pride, whether corporal, sergeant, lieutenant, or captain.

A company of troopers was early formed, made up from the village and neighboring settlements. In the colonial records, under date of Oct. 8, 1662, we find the following: "Mr. George Corwin for captain, Mr. Thomas Putnam for lieutenant, Mr. Walter Price for cornet, being presented to this Court as so chosen by the troopers of Salem, Lynn, &c., the Court allows and approves thereof." The inventory of Captain Corwin, before cited, indicates the stylish uniform he wore as captain of the troopers. Each of the officers was a wealthy man; and it cannot be doubted that a parade of the company was a dashing affair. The lapse of time having thinned their ranks and removed their officers, a vigorous and successful attempt was made in October, 1678, to revive the company. Thirty-six men, belonging, as they say, "to the reserve of Salem old troop," and very desirous "of being serviceable to God and the country," petition the General Court to re-organize them as a troop of horse, and to issue the necessary commissions. They request the appointment of William Brown, Jr., as captain, and Corporal John Putnam as lieutenant. The petition was granted, and the commissions issued. Among the signers of this petition are Anthony Needham, Peter and Ezekiel Cheever, Thomas Flint,

Thomas and Benjamin Wilkins, Thomas and Jacob Fuller, John Procter, William Osborne, Thomas Putnam, Jr., and others of the Farms. The officers named were men of property and energy; and the company of troopers was kept up ever afterwards, until all danger from Indians or other foes had passed away.

It is very observable how the military spirit with which this rural community was so early imbued has descended through all generations. Israel Putnam, the famous Revolutionary hero, a son of Joseph who was a younger brother of Sergeant Thomas and Deacon Edward Putnam, was born in the village. His brother David, much older than himself, who flourished in the period anterior to the Revolution, was a celebrated cavalry officer. Colonel Timothy Pickering used to mention, among the recollections of his boyhood, that David Putnam " rode the best horse in the province." General Rufus Putnam, a grandson of Deacon Edward, was a distinguished brigadier in the army of the Revolution. There are few officers of that army whose names are more honored than his by encomiums from the pen of Washington : and praise from him was praise indeed, for it was, like all his other judgments, the result of careful and discriminating observation. In a letter to the President of Congress, dated " At camp above Trenton Falls, Dec. 20, 1776," he speaks of the fact, that, owing to a neglect on the part of the Government to place the Engineer Department upon a proper footing, " Colo nel Putnam, who was at the head of it, has quitted, and taken a regiment in the State of Massachusetts." He expresses the opinion, that Putnam's qualifications as a military engineer were superior to those of any other man within his knowledge, far superior to those of the foreign officers whom he had seen. In a letter to the same, dated "Pompton Plains," July 12, 1777, speaking of General Schuyler's army, he says, "Colonel Putnam, I imagine, will be with him before this, as his regiment is a part of Nixon's Brigade, who will answer every purpose he can possibly have for an engineer at this crisis." The high opinion of Washington took effect in his promotion as brigadier-general. At the end of the war, he returned to civil life, but was soon called back and re-commissioned as brigadier-general. Washington felt the need of him. In a letter to General Knox, Secretary of War, dated Aug. 13, 1792, he says, "General Putnam merits thanks, in my opinion, for his plan, and the sentiments he has delivered on what he conceives to be a proper mode of carrying on the war against the hostile nations of Indians; and I wish he would continue to furnish them without reserve in future." During Washington's administration of the government under the Constitution, Rufus Putnam held the office of Surveyor-General of the United States. In addition to his military reputation, he will be for ever memorable as the first settler of Marietta, and founder of the State of Ohio.

Israel Hutchinson was born in 1727. In 1757 he

was one of a scouting-party under the command of his neighbor, Captain Israel Herrick, that penetrated through the wilderness in Maine in perilous Indian warfare. He fought at Ticonderoga and Lake George, and was with Wolfe when he scaled the Heights of Abraham. On the morning of the 19th of April, 1775, he led a company of minute-men, who met and fought the British in their bloody retreat from Lexington. He was prominently concerned during the siege of Boston ; and, on its evacuation, took command at Fort Hill. He was afterwards in command at Forts Lee and Washington. Throughout the war, he, like both the Putnams, had the confidence of his commander-in-chief. For twenty-one years, he was elected to one or the other branch of the Legislature, or to the Council. He was distinguished for the courtesy of his manners and the dignity of his address. Colonel Enoch Putnam was also at the battle of Lexington, and served with honor through the Revolutionary War, as did also Captain Jeremiah Putnam, both of them descendants of John. Captain Samuel Flint was among the bravest of the brave at Lexington, exciting universal admiration by his intrepidity ; and fell at the head of his company at Stillwater, Oct. 7, 1777.

Intelligence of the marching of the British towards Lexington, on the 19th of April, 1775, reached the lower part of Danvers about nine o'clock that morning. With a rapidity that is perfectly marvellous, when we consider the distances from each other over which the inhabitants were scattered, five companies, fully organized and equipped, — each of them containing men of the village, — rushed to the field in time to meet the retreating enemy at West Cambridge. It was a rally and a march without precedent, and never yet surpassed. The day was extremely sultry for the season ; and the distance traversed by many of the men from the village, before they got into that fight, could not have been less than twenty miles. Seven belonging to Danvers companies were killed, and others wounded. A larger offering was made that day at the baptismal sacrifice to American liberty by Danvers than by any other town except Lexington ; and no town represented in the scene was more remote. Of the men who fell on this occasion, the following appear to have been of the village : Samuel Cook, Benjamin Daland, and Perley Putnam, — the last a descendant of John. Their bodies were brought home, and buried with appropriate honors ; two companies from Salem, and military detachments from Newburyport, Amesbury, and Salisbury participating in the ceremonies, and giving the soldier's tribute to their glory, by volleys over their closing graves.

Moses Porter, when eighteen years of age, attracted attention by his heroic courage and indomitable pluck at Bunker Hill. He was in an artillery company, and would not quit his gun when almost every other man had fallen. His country never allowed him to quit it afterwards. From that day, he bore a commission in the army of the United States. He was retained on every peace establishment, always in the artillery, and at the head of that arm of the service for a great length of time, and until the day of his death. He was in the battle of Brandywine, and wounded in a subsequent fight on the banks of the Delaware. He was with Wayne in his campaign against the Western Indians, and won his share of the glory that crowned it in the final bloody and decisive conflict. He was at the head of the artillery when the war of 1812 took place, in active service on the Niagara frontier, and on the 10th of September, 1813, brevetted " for distinguished services." He commanded at Norfolk, in Virginia, in 1814, and received great credit for the ability and vigilance with which he held that most vital point of the coast defence. At successive periods after the war, he was at the head of each of the geographical military divisions of the country. He died at Cambridge, Mass., in 1822, while in command of the Eastern Department, near the scene of his youthful glory, forty-seven years before. No man who fought at Bunker Hill remained so long a soldier of the United States. No man had so extended a record, and it was bright with honor from the beginning to the end. His pre-eminent reputation, as a disciplinarian and artillerist of the highest class, was uniformly maintained. He added to the sterner qualities required by professional duty a polished urbanity of manners, and a dignified and commanding aspect and bearing. His ashes rest beneath the sod of his ancestral acres in Salem Village.

When the great war for the suppression of the Southern Rebellion came on, and the life of the Union was at stake, the same old spirit was found unabated. A descendant of the family of Raymonds, emulating the example of his ancestors, rallied his company to the front. At the end of the war, Lieutenant-Colonel John W. Raymond brought back, in command, the remnant of his veteran regiment, with its tattered banners; two of his predecessors in that commission having fallen in battle. The youthful patriot, William Lowell Putnam, who fell at Ball's Bluff on the 21st of October, 1861, was a direct descendant of Nathaniel Putnam. It is an interesting circumstance, that the names of men who trained in the foot company and with the troopers on the fields and roads about the village meeting-house two hundred years ago have re-appeared in the persons of their descendants, in the highest lines of service and with unsurpassed distinction, in the three great wars of America, — Major-General Israel, and Brigadier-General Rufus, Putnam, in the War of the Revolution; Brigadier-General Moses Porter, in the War of 1812; and Major-General Granville M. Dodge, in the War of the Rebellion. The last-named is a descendant of a hero of the Narragansett fight, and was born and educated in Salem Village.

Several lawsuits, particularly in land cases, have been referred to. They indicate, perhaps, to some extent the ingredients that aggravated the terrible scenes we are preparing to contemplate. They served to keep up the general intelligence of the community through a period necessarily destitute of such means of information as we enjoy. Attendance upon courts of law, serving on juries, having to give testimony at trials, are indeed in themselves no unimportant part in the education of a people. Principles and questions of great moment are forced upon general attention, and become topics of discussion in places of gathering and at private firesides. Of this material of intelligence, the people of the village had their full share. It was their fate to have their minds, and more or less their passions, stirred up by special local controversies thrust upon them. As a religious society, they had difficult points of disagreement with the mother-church, and the town of Salem. While they were supporting a minister and trying to build a meeting-house for themselves, attempts were made to tax them to support the minister and build a new meeting-house in the town. There was a natural reluctance to part with them, and it was long before an arrangement could be made. The great distance of many of the farmers from the town prevented their exercising what they deemed their rightful influence in municipal affairs. They felt, that, in many respects, their interests were not identical, and in some absolutely at variance. These topics were much discussed, and with considerable feeling at times on both sides. The papers which remain relating to the subject show that the farmers understood it in all its bearings, and maintained their cause with clearness of perception and forcibleness of argument and expression. At one time, they were very desirous to be set off as a distinct town, but this could not be allowed; and, finally, a sort of compromise was effected. A partial separation — a semi-municipality — was agreed upon. Salem Village was the result.

In 1670, a petition, with twenty signers, was presented to the town to be set off as a parish, and be allowed to provide a minister for themselves. In March, 1672, the town granted the request; and, in October following, the General Court approved of the project, and gave it legal effect. The line agreed upon by the town and the village is substantially defined by the vote of the former, which was as follows: " All farmers that now are, or hereafter shall be, willing to join together for providing a minister among themselves, whose habitations are above Ipswich Highway, from the horse bridge to the wooden bridge, at the hither end of Mr. Endicott's Plain, and from thence on a west line, shall have liberty to have a minister by themselves; and when they shall provide and pay him in a maintenance, that then they shall be discharged from their part of Salem ministers' maintenance," &c. The " horse bridge " was across Bass River. The " wooden bridge " was at the head of Cow-House or Endicott River. Ipswich highway runs along from one of these points to the other. The south line, beyond the wooden bridge, is seen on the map. All to the north of this line, and of Ipswich highway between the bridges, to the bounds of Beverly and Wenham on the east; Topsfield, Rowley Village, — since Boxford, and Andover on the north; and Reading and Lynn on the west, — was the Village. Middleton, incorporated afterwards, absorbed a large part of its western portion; but, at the time of the witchcraft delusion, the Village was bounded as above described, and as in the map. There was a specific arrangement fixing the point of time when the farmers were to become exempt from all charges in aid of the mother-church; that is, as soon as they had provided for the support of a minister and the erection of a meeting-house of their own. It was further stipulated, that the villagers should not form a church until a minister was ordained; and that they should not settle a minister permanently without the approval of the old church, and its consent to proceed to an ordination. This latter restriction was perhaps the cause of all the subsequent troubles.

Owing, as has been stated in another connection, to erroneous notions about the topography of the country; the incompetency perhaps, in some cases, of surveyors; and the want of due care in the General Court and the towns to have boundaries clearly defined, — uncertainties and conflicting claims arose in various portions of the colony, but nowhere to a greater extent than here. The village became involved in controversies about boundaries with each one of its neighbors; producing, at times, much exasperation. The documents drawn forth on these questions, as they appear in the record-book of the village, are written with ability, and show that there were men among them who knew how to express and enforce their views. The plain, lucid, well-considered style of Nathaniel Ingersoll's depositions on the court-files, in numerous cases, render it not improbable that his pen was put in requisition. Sergeant Thomas Putnam, the parish recorder, as he was sometimes entitled, was a good writer. His chirography, although not handsome, is singularly uniform, full, open, and clear, so easily legible that it is a refreshment to meet with it; and his sentences are well-constructed, simple, condensed, and to the purpose. His words do their office in conveying his meaning. No public body ever had a better clerk. Somehow or other, he and others, brought up in the woods, had contrived to acquire considerable efficiency in the use of the pen. Perhaps, a few who, like him, had parents able to afford it, had been sent to Ipswich or Charlestown to enjoy the privilege of what Cotton Mather calls " the Cheverian education."

The southern boundary of the village was intended to run due west from the Ipswich road to Lynn, and was accordingly spoken of as " on a west line." As originally established, it was defined by an enumeration of a variety of objects such as trees of different kinds and sizes, as running through the lands of John Felton, Nathaniel Putnam, and Anthony Needham, to " a dry stump standing at the corner of Widow Pope's cow-pen, leaving her house and the saw-mill within the farmer's range," and so on to " the top of the hill by the highway side near Berry Pond." From the changeable conditions of some of the objects, and a diversity of methods adopted by surveyors, — many

of them being unacquainted with, or making no allowance for, the variation of the compass, — controversies
arose with the mother-town : and some proprietors,
like the Gardners, were left in doubt how the line
affected them; and there was, in consequence, much
disquietude The line was not accurately run until
1700.

It is observable, that the " saw-mill " is still in
operation on the same spot. The " cow-pen," then on
the south side of the mill, was, more than a century
ago, removed to the north side, where it has remained
ever since. This estate has interesting reminiscences.
It was an original grant in January, 1640, to Edward
Norris, at the time of his settlement as pastor of the
First Church in Salem. He sold to Eleanor Trussler
in 1654. It then went into the possession of Henry
Phelps, who sold to Joseph Pope in 1664. His widow,
Gertrude, owned it in 1672. In 1793, Eleazer Pope
sold to Nathaniel Ropes, son of Judge Ropes, of
Salem. His heirs sold it back to the Phelpses ; and it
is now in the possession of the Rev. Willard Spaulding,
of Salem. Originally given as an ordination present
to a minister of the old town, it has, after the lapse
of two hundred and twenty-six years, come round into
the hands of another. The house in which the Popes
lived one hundred and twenty-nine years, and the
families that succeeded them for above half a century
more, — a venerable and picturesque specimen of the
rural architecture, in its best form, of the earliest
times,— has, within the last ten years, given place to a

new one on the same spot. In that old house, besides
unnumbered and unknown instances of the same sort,
Israel Putnam conducted his courtship; and there, on
the 19th of July, 1739, he was married to Hannah,
daughter of Joseph Pope.

Contests for what they deemed their rights with the
old church and the border towns and their own town,
as in the case just mentioned, undoubtedly produced a
bad effect upon the temper of the people, by occasional expenses that consumed their substance, and
incidents that sowed the seeds of personal animosities;
preparing the way for that dreadful convulsion which
was near at hand. At the very time when the witchcraft frenzy broke out, they were in the crisis of an
exasperating conflict with Topsfield, occasioned by a
wrong done them by the General Court. This requires to be explained, as it can be, by a collation of
facts of record.

On the 3d of March, 1636, the General Court passed
an order that the bounds of Salem, Ipswich, and Newbury, should extend six miles into the country. It
was afterwards defined to mean that "the six-mile
extent," as it was called, should be measured from the
meeting-houses of the respective towns. On the 5th
of November, 1639, the General Court passed an order
in these words: " Whereas the inhabitants of Salem
have agreed to plant a village near the river that runs
to Ipswich, it is ordered that all the land near their
bounds between Salem and the said river, not belonging to any other town or person by any former grant,

shall belong to the said village." On the strength of
this order, the farmers in that part of Salem pushed
settlements out beyond the "six-mile extent," over
the ground thus pledged to them; cleared off the forests, built houses, brought the land under culture,
erected bridges, made roads, and fulfilled their part of
the contract by preparing to establish their village.
Four years after the General Court had thus pledged
to "inhabitants of Salem" the privileges of a village
organization on the lands between "Salem and the
said river," they authorized some inhabitants of Ipswich, who had gone there, to establish the village on
the territory, independent of the Salem men. This
was an unjustifiable and flagrant violation of the
stipulated agreement on the part of the General
Court; because it appears by their own records, that
Salem farmers had promptly fulfilled the condition on
their part by going directly upon the ground, and getting farms under way there before 1643. This careless and indefensible procedure by the General Court
was the cause of interminable trouble and strife on
the tract between Salem bounds and the river, introduced the elements of discord, and gave a color of
legal justification to a conflict of authority between
Salem and Ipswich men. It sowed the seeds of animosities which aggravated the scenes that occurred in
Salem Village in 1692. In 1658, the General Court
passed an order creating the town of Topsfield, including the larger part of these lands within its limits.
No heed was paid to the remonstrances, against these

proceedings, of the Salem farmers, who found themselves, without their consent, permanently bereft of the benefit that had been promised them, cut off from all connection with the town of Salem, to which they originally belonged, and put in the outskirts of another town. It was a clear case of wrong, and ought to have been rectified. But public bodies are more reluctant even than individuals to acknowledge themselves in fault. The people of Salem Village joined in earnest protests against the acts of the General Court. The old town of Salem declared by a public vote, that they had always regarded the lands in controversy as belonging to the village which, under the plighted faith of the General Court, their inhabitants had been forming. But it was all in vain. Neither remedy nor reparation could be obtained. The struggle against this injustice lasted until some time after the witchcraft occurrences had terminated, and was finally brought to a close by an order of the Court, that the people on the territory might maintain parish relations with Salem Village or with Topsfield, at their individual option. Entire satisfaction was never realized until, in 1728, they were incorporated, in accordance with their petition, into a township, under the name of Middleton, with parts of Topsfield, Boxford, and Andover added. During a period of half a century, this grievance remained unadjusted. The proceedings on the part of the village in its public action, as shown in the records, were conducted with skill, ability, and firmness. But the collisions that occurred between particular parties were violent and bitter. Salem settlers were called to pay parish and town rates to Topsfield, but refused to do it. Constables and tax-collectors were defied. Topsfield went so far as to claim not only unoccupied lands, but lands within fence, with houses on them, and families within them, and orchards and growing fields around them, as part of its " commons ; " and it disputed the titles given by Salem. Of course, the question went, in various forms, into the county courts ; but sometimes, there is reason to believe, it came to a rougher arbitrament, in the depths of the woods, between man and man.

John Putnam had gone out and settled lands between the " six-mile extent " of Salem and Ipswich River. Some of his sons had gone with him. They had two dwelling-houses, cultivated meadows, orchards, &c. Isaac Burton says, that, one day, when near John Nichols's house, he heard a tree fall in the woods ; and that he went to see who was chopping there. It seems that Jacob Towne and John How, Topsfield men, had come in defiance of John Putnam, and cut down a tree before his face. As they were two to one, Putnam had to swallow the insult ; but he was not the man to let it rest so. He went out shortly after, accompanied by an adequate force of sons and nephews, and proceeded to fell the trees. The sound of the axes reached the ears of the Topsfield men ; and Isaac Easty, Sr., John Easty, John Towne, and Joseph Towne, Jr., undertook to put a stop to the operation. On reaching the spot, they

warned Putnam against cutting timber. He replied,
" The timber now and here cut down has been felled
by me and my orders ; " and he proceeded to say, " I
will keep cutting and carrying away from this land
until next March." They asked him, " What, by
violence ? " He answered, " Aye, by violence. You
may sue me : you know where I dwell ; " and, turning to his company, he said, " Fall on." The Putnams were evidently the stronger party ; and the
Topsfield men, counting forces, concluded, in their
turn, that discretion, at that time, was the better
part of valor. Such scenes occurred on the disputed
ground for a whole generation. It is not wonderful
that all sorts of animosities were kindled. The fact
will be borne in mind, that Isaac Easty and son, with
John Towne and son, constituted the Topsfield force
on this occasion.

It cannot be doubted, that these controversies with
the surrounding towns, the mother-church, and the
General Court itself, gradually engendered a very
bad state of feeling. The people were deeply impressed with a conviction that they had been wronged
all around and all the way through. They felt that
the whole world was against them ; and when, by a
train of mischievous influences, hell itself seemed to
be let loose upon them, it is not strange that they were
driven to distraction.

We come, at last, to that chapter in the history of
Salem Village which will lead us directly to the witchcraft delusion. Its religious organization was some-

what peculiar; and, although instituted by a particular arrangement made by the General Court, was, in one or two features, a complete departure from the ecclesiastical polity elsewhere rigidly enforced. It was a congregation forbidden, for the time being, to have a church. It was a society for religious worship, administered, not by professors of religion or by persons regarded at all in a religious light, but by householders. The people of the village liked it, perhaps, all the better for this; and they took hold of it with a will. Joseph Houlton gave to the parish five and a half acres of land, in the centre of the village, for the use of the minister. A parsonage-house was built, " forty-two feet in length, twenty feet broad, thirteen-feet stud, four chimneys, and no gable-ends." It was the custom to have a leanto attached to their houses, generally on the northern side; and one was finally added to the parsonage. There was a garden within the enclosure. Joseph Hutchinson gave an acre out of his broad meadow as a site for the meeting-house and it was erected; " thirty-four feet in length, twenty-eight feet broad, and sixteen feet between joints." Two end galleries were added, and a " canopy " placed over the pulpit. The mother-church, having about the same time built a new meeting-house, voted to give " the farmers their old pulpit and deacons' seats," which were brought up and duly installed. In the course of these proceedings, some slight differences arose among them about matters of detail, but not more than is usual in such cases. In order

to despatch at once all that may be required to be said
about the meeting-houses of the village, it may be
allowable here to mention, that the original building
did not survive the century. In 1700, partly because
the growth of the society began to require it, but
mainly, no doubt, to escape from the painful associations which had become connected with it, a new
meeting-house was built on another site. The old one
was dismantled of all its removable parts, and the site
reverted to Joseph Hutchinson. It is supposed that he
removed the frame to the other side of the road, and
converted it into a barn; and that it was used as such
until, in the memory of old persons now living, it
mouldered, crumbled into powder-post, and sunk to
the ground. It stood, after being converted into a
barn, on the south side of the road, nearly in front of
Joseph Hutchinson's homestead. Hutchinson's dwelling-house was probably some distance further down in
the field, where the remains of an old cellar are still
to be seen. Nathaniel Ingersoll gave the land for the
new meeting-house. The records contain the vote,
that it "shall stand upon Watch-House Hill, before
Deacon Ingersoll's door." The meeting-houses of the
society have stood there ever since. At that time, it
was an elevated spot, probably covered with the original forest; for the work of clearing, levelling, and
preparing it for occupancy was so considerable as to
require a special provision. The labor and expense
of the operation were put on that portion of the

congregation brought nearer to the meeting-house by the change of the site.

In urging their petition to be set off as an independent parish, distinct from the First Church in Salem, the people of the village declared, that, if they could not have a ministry established among them, they would soon " become worse than the heathen around them." Little did they foresee the immediate, long-continued, and terrible effects that were to follow the boon thus prayed for. The establishment of the ministry among them was not merely an opening of Pandora's box : it was emptying and shaking it over their heads. It led them to a condition of bitterness and violence, of confusion and convulsion, of horror and misery, of cruelty and outrage, worse than heathen ever experienced or savages inflicted.

James Bayley of Newbury, born Sept. 12, 1650, a graduate of Harvard College in the class of 1669, was employed to preach at the village. In October, 1671, he transferred his relations from the church in Newbury to the First Church in Salem. It seems that several persons of considerable influence in the village were dissatisfied with the manner in which he had been brought forward, and became prejudiced against him. The disaffection was not removed, but suffered to take deep root in their minds. The parish soon became the scene of one of those violent and heated dissensions to which religious societies are sometimes liable. The unhappy strife was aggravated from day to day, until it spread alienation and acrimony

throughout the village. A majority of the people
were all along in favor of Bayley; but the minority were implacable. His engagement to preach was
renewed from year to year. At length, the controversy
waxed so warm that some definite action became
necessary. On the 10th of March, 1679, both parties
applied to the mother-church for advice. A paper
was presented by his opponents, with sixteen, and
another from his friends, with thirty-nine signers.
There was still another, also in his favor, signed by
ten persons living near, but not within the village line.
Although the number of his opponents was so much
less than of his friends, they included persons, such
as Nathaniel Putnam and Bray Wilkins, of large estates and families, and much general influence; and it
is evident that the First Church was not inclined
wholly to disregard them. The record of that church
says, "There was much agitation on both sides, and
divers things were spoken of by the brethren; but the
business being long, and many of the brethren gone,
we could not make a church act of advice in the case;
therefore it was left to another time." At a meeting
on the 22d of April, the Salem Church advised the
minority "to submit to the generality for the present;
but, when a church should be formed there, "then
they might choose him or any other." This advice
does not appear to have satisfied either party; and the
quarrel went on with renewed vehemence on both
sides. At length, it reached such a pitch that it
became necessary to carry it up to the General

Court. The whole affair was investigated by that body, and all the papers that had passed in relation to it were adduced. They are quite voluminous, and on file in the office of the Secretary of State, in Boston. These interesting and curious documents illustrate the energy of action of both parties; and give, it is probable, the best picture anywhere to be found of a first-rate parish controversy of the olden times.

The General Court came down upon the case with a strong hand. They decided in favor of Bayley, whom they pronounced " orthodox, and competently able, and of a blameless and self-denying conversation;" and they " do order, that Mr. Bayley be continued and settled the minister of that place, and that he be allowed sixty pounds per annum for his maintenance, one-third part thereof in money, the other two-thirds in provisions of all sorts such as a family needs, at equal prices, and fuel for his family's occasions; this sum to be paid by the inhabitants of that place." This was thirteen pounds a year more than Bayley's friends had ever voted for him. To make the matter sure, the General Court required the parish to choose three or five men among themselves to apportion every man's share of the tax to secure the sixty pounds: and, if any difficulty should occur in getting men among themselves to perform this duty, they appointed to act, in that event, Mr. Batter, Captain Jonathan Corwin, and Captain Price, of the old parish of Salem, to make the rate; and gave

ample power to the constable of the village or the
marshal of the county, to enforce the collection of it,
by distress and attachment, if any should neglect
or refuse to pay the sum assessed upon him.   To
make it still more certain that Mr. Bayley should get
his money, they ordered " that all the rate is to be
paid in for the use of the ministry unto two persons
chosen by the householders to supply the place of
deacons for the time, who are to reckon with the
people, and to deliver the same to the said minister or
to his order."   The arrangement as to the agency of
deacons was " to continue until the Court shall take
further order, or that there be a church of Christ
orderly gathered and approved in that place."   This
procedure of the Court was a pretty high-handed
stretch of power even for those days ; and giving the
appointment of officers, with the title and character of
deacons to mere householders, and where there was no
church or organized body of professed believers, was
in absolute conflict with the whole tenor and spirit of
the ecclesiastical system then in force and rigidly
maintained elsewhere throughout the colony.   The
Court seems itself to have been alarmed at the extent
to which it had gone in forcing Mr. Bayley upon the
people of Salem Village, and fell back, in conclusion,
upon the following proviso : " This order shall continue for one year only from the last of September
last past."   The date of the order was the 15th of
October, 1679.   It had less than a year to run.   In
fact, the order, after all, before it comes to the end, is

diluted into a mere recommendation of Mr. Bayley. " In the mean while, all parties," it is hoped, will " endeavor an agreement in him or some other meet person for a minister among them ; " but the General Court takes care to wind up by demanding " five pounds for hearing the case, the whole number of villagers equally to bear their proportion thereof."

While the power thus incautiously conceded to householders was duly noted, the apparently formidable action of the Court did not in the least alarm the opposition, or in the slightest degree abate their zeal. The householders continued, as before, to manage all affairs relating to the ministry in general meetings of the inhabitants. They proceeded at once to elect their two deacons. " Corporal Nathaniel Ingersoll " was one of them ; and he continued to hold the office, in parish and in church, for forty years.

As no attention was paid to the order of the General Court, so far as it attempted to fasten Mr. Bayley upon the parish ; as the church in Salem would not take the responsibility of recommending his ordination in the face of such an opposition ; and as it was out of the question to think of reconciling or reducing it, Mr. Bayley concluded to retire from the conflict and quit the field; and his ministry in the village came to an end. As evidence that the heat of this protracted controversy had not consumed all just and considerate sentiments in the minds of the people, I present the substance of a deed found in the Essex Registry. It will be noticed, that the most conspicuous of Mr. Bayley's opponents, Nathaniel Putnam, is one of the parties to the instrument.

"Thomas Putnam, Sr., Nathaniel Putnam, Sr., Thomas Fuller, Sr., John Putnam, Sr., and Joseph Hutchinson, Sr. Deed of gift to Mr. James Bayley. Whereas, Mr. James Bayley, minister of the gospel, now resident of Salem Village, hath been in the exercise of his gifts by preaching amongst us several years, having had a call thereunto by the inhabitants of the place ; and at the said Mr. Bayley's first coming amongst us, we above-named put the said Bayley in possession of a suitable accommodation of land and meadow, for his more comfortable subsistence amongst us. But the providence of God having so ordered it, that the said Mr. Bayley doth not continue amongst us in the work of the ministry, yet, considering the premises, and as a testimony of our good affection to the said Mr. Bayley, and as full satisfaction of all demands of us or any of us, of land relating to the premises, do by these presents fully grant, &c., to said Bayley " twenty-eight acres of upland, and thirteen acres of meadow in all. The several lots are described in the deed, and constitute a very valuable property. The instrument bears date May 6, 1680. Mr. Bayley's residence is indicated on the map. The land on which it stood belonged to the part contributed by Nathaniel Putnam, with some acres in front of it contributed by Joseph Hutchinson. He continued to own and occasionally occupy his property in the village for some years after the witchcraft transactions. He left the ministry, and prepared himself for the profession of medicine, which he practised in Roxbury. He died on the 17th of January, 1707.

It is not very easy to ascertain from the parish records, or from the mass of papers in the State-house files, the precise grounds of the obstinate controversy in reference to him. It is evident that it began in consequence of some alleged irregularity in the proceedings that led to his first engagement to preach at the village. There are intimations, that, in the tone and style of his preaching, he did not quite come up to the mark required by some. The objection does not seem to have been against his talents or learning, but, rather, that he did not take hold with sufficient vehemence, or handle with sufficient zeal and warmth, points then engrossing attention. One or two expressions in the papers which proceeded from his opponents seem to hint that he had not the degree of strictness or severity in his aspect or ways thought necessary in a minister. Papers in the files of the County Court bring to light, perhaps, precisely the shape in which the charges against him had currency. On the 4th of April, 1679, complaint was made by Thomas and John Putnam, Srs., Daniel Andrew, and Nathaniel Ingersoll, against Henry Kenny " for slandering our minister, Mr. Bayley, by reporting that he doth not perform family duties in his family." This was an expression then in use for " family prayers." One young woman testified as follows : " Being at Mr. Bayley's house three weeks together, I never heard Mr. Bayley read a chapter, nor expound on any part of the Scripture, which was a great grief to me." On the other hand, three men and one woman depose thus: "Having, for a year, some more, some less, since Mr. Bayley's coming to Salem Farms, lived at his house, we testify to our knowledge, that he hath continually performed family duties, morning and evening, unless sickness or some other unavoidable providence hath prevented." Two of the above witnesses depose more specifically as follows: "We testify, — one of us being a boarder at Mr. Bayley's house, at times, for two or three years, and the other having lived there about a year and a quarter, — that Mr. Bayley did not only constantly perform family prayers twice a day, except some unusual providence at any time prevented, but also did sometimes read the Scriptures and other profitable books, and also repeat his own sermons in his family that he preached upon the Lord's Days; always endeavoring to keep good order in his family, carrying himself exemplarily therein." The evidence against Bayley was afterwards found to be unworthy of credit, and was wholly overborne at the time by unimpeachable testimony in his favor. The conclusion seems to be safe, from all the papers and proceedings, that Mr. Bayley was, as the General Court had pronounced him, "of a blameless conversation." A letter from him to his people, relating to the disaffection of some, and expressing a willingness to relinquish his position, if the interests of the society would thereby be promoted, is among the papers. It is creditable to his understanding, temper, and character.

The opposition to Mr. Bayley laid the train for all the disastrous and terrible scenes that followed. His wife was Mary Carr, of Salisbury. Her family, besides land in that town, owned the large island in the Merrimack, just above Newburyport, called still by their name, and occupied by their descendants to this day. Mrs. Bayley brought with her to the village a younger sister, Ann, who, when scarcely sixteen years of age, — on the 25th of November, 1678, — married Sergeant Thomas Putnam. The Carrs were evidently well-educated young women; and there is every indication that Ann was possessed of qualities which gave her much influence in private circles. Her husband was the eldest son of the richest man in the village, had the most powerful and extensive connections, was a member of the company of troopers, had been in the Narragansett fight, and, as his records show, was a well-educated person. Marriage with him brought his wife into the centre of the great Putnam family; and, her sister Bayley being the wife of the minister, a powerful combination was secured to his support. The opposition so obstinately made to his settlement, appearing to his friends, as it does to us, so unreasonable, if not perverse, engendered a very bitter resentment, which spread from house to house. Every thing served to aggravate it. The disregard, by the opposition, of the advice of the old church to agree to his ordination, and of the strong endorsement of him by the General Court; and the failure of either of those bodies to take the responsibility of proceeding to his ordination, — made the dissatisfaction and disappointment of his friends intense. His connection by marriage with such a wide-spread influence, and the harmony and happiness of social life, made his settlement so very desirable that his friends could not account for the resistance made to it. His amiable character, which had been shown to be proof against slander; and his domestic bereavements in the loss of his wife and three children, — made him dear to his friends. More than three to one earnestly, persistently, from year to year, begged that he might be ordained; but what was regarded as an unworthy faction was permitted to succeed in preventing it. All these things sunk deep into the heart of the wife of Sergeant Thomas Putnam. She was a woman of an excitable temperament, and, by her talents, zeal, and personal qualities, wrought all within her influence into the highest state of exasperation. This must be borne in mind when we reach the details of our story. It is the key to all that followed.

The friends of Bayley, while they yielded to his determination to withdraw from his disagreeable position, never relinquished the hope to get him back, but renewed a struggle to that end, whenever a vacancy occurred in the village ministry. With that object in view, they were unwise and unjust enough to cherish aversion to every one who succeeded him, and thus kept alive the fatal elements of division. But it is due to him to say, that he does not appear to have been at all responsible for the course of his friends. Although retaining his property in the village, and often residing there, there is no indication that he had a hand in subsequent proceedings, or was in the slightest degree connected with the troubles that afterwards arose. Arts were used to inveigle him into the witchcraft prosecucutions: his resentments, if he had any, were invoked; but in vain. He resisted attempts, which were made with more effect upon one of his successors, to rouse his passions against parties accused. He kept himself free from the whole affair. His name nowhere appears as complainant, witness, or actor in any shape. He was, so far as the evidence goes, a peaceable, prudent, kind, and good man; and if the people of Salem Village had been wise enough, or been permitted, to settle him, the world might never have known that such a place existed.

George Burroughs, in November, 1680, was engaged to preach at Salem Village. He is supposed to have been born in Scituate; but his origin is as uncertain as his history was sad, and his end tragical. He was a graduate of Harvard College in the class of 1670. What little is known of him shows that he was a man of ability and integrity. Papers on file in the State House prove, that, in the district of Maine, where he lived and preached before and after his settlement at the village, he was regarded with confidence by his neighbors, and looked up to as a friend and counsellor. Certain incidents are related, which prove that he was self-denying, generous, and public-spirited, laboring in humility and with zeal in the midst of great privations, sharing the exposures of his people to Indian violence, and experiencing all the sufferings of an unprotected outpost. In 1676, while preaching at Casco, — now Portland, — the entire settlement was broken up by an Indian assault. Thirty-two of the inhabitants were killed or carried into captivity. Mr. Burroughs escaped to an island in the bay, from which he was rescued by timely aid from the mainland. He wrote an account of the catastrophe, communicated by Brian Pendleton to the Governor and Council at Boston. In 1683 he was again at Casco; and, again driven off by the Indians in 1690, transferred his labors to Wells. A grant of one hundred and fifty acres of land was made to him, included in the site of the present city of Portland. As population began to thicken near the spot, the town applied to him to relinquish a part of it, other lands to be given him in exchange. In their account of the transaction, they state, that, in answer to their application, Mr. Burroughs said they were welcome to it; that he freely gave it back, "not desiring any land anywhere else, nor any thing else in consideration thereof."

In a vote passed at a meeting of Salem Village parish, Feb. 10, 1681, it was agreed that Mr. Burroughs should receive £93. 6s. 8d. per annum for three years, and £60 per annum afterwards. I suppose that he had no money or property of any kind. The parsonage was out of repair; and the larger sum for the first three years, amounting to £100, in three instalments, was to be given him as an outfit in housekeeping. Immediately upon coming to the village to reside, he encountered the hostility of those persons who, as the special friends of Mr. Bayley, allowed their prejudices to be concentrated upon his innocent successor. The unhappy animosities arising from this source entirely demoralized the Society, and, besides making it otherwise very uncomfortable to a minister, led to a neglect and derangement of all financial affairs. In September, 1681, Mr. Burroughs's wife died, and he had to run in debt for her funeral expenses. Rates were not collected, and his salary was in arrears. In making the contract with the parish, he had taken care to add, at the end of the articles, these words, "All is to be understood so long as I have gospel encouragement." It is not improbable that there was a lack of sympathy between him and the ministers in this part of the country. He concluded that no benefit would accrue from calling a council to put things into order; and, as he was in despair of remedying the evils that had become fastened upon the village, he concluded to give up the idea of getting a settlement of his accounts, abandoned his claims altogether, and removed from the village.

At the April term of Court in Ipswich, 1683, a committee of the parish petitioned for relief, stating that Mr. Burroughs had left them, and that they had been without services in their meeting-house for four sabbaths. They pray the Court, that "they be pleased to write to Mr. Burroughs, requiring him to attend an orderly hearing and clearing up the case," and " to come to account" with them. The Court accordingly directed a meeting of the inhabitants to be held, and wrote to Mr. Burroughs to attend it. When the day came, the Court sent a letter to be read at the meeting, directing the parties to " reckon," and settle their accounts. What transpired at this curious meeting is best given by presenting the documents on file in a case that went into Court. They show the proceedings that interrupted the " reckoning " at the meeting in a most extraordinary manner : —

[COUNTY COURT, June, 1683. — Lieutenant John Putnam *versus* Mr. George Burroughs. Action of debt for two gallons of Canary wine, and cloth, &c., bought of Mr. Gedney on John Putnam's account, for the funeral of Mrs. Burroughs.]

" *Deposition.*

" We, whose names are underwritten, testify and say, that at a public meeting of the people of Salem Farms, April 24, 1683, we heard a letter read, which letter was sent from the Court. After the said letter was read, Mr. Burroughs came in. After the said Burroughs had been a while in, he asked ' whether they took up with the advice of the Court, given in the letter, or whether they rejected it.' The moderator made answer, ' Yes, we take up with it ; ' and not a man contradicted it to any of our hearing. After this was passed, was a discourse of settling accounts between the said Burroughs and the inhabitants, and issuing things in peace, and parting in love, as they came together in love. Further, we say that the second, third, and fourth days of the following week were agreed upon by Mr. Burroughs and

the people to be the days for every man to come in and to
reckon with the said Burroughs; and so they adjourned the
meeting to the last of the aforesaid three days, in the afternoon, then to make up the whole account in public.

"We further testify and say, that, May the second, 1683,
Mr. Burroughs and the inhabitants met at the meeting-
house to make up accounts in public, according to their
agreement the meeting before; and, just as the said Burroughs began to give in his accounts, the marshal came in,
and, after a while, went up to John Putnam, Sr., and whispered to him, and said Putnam said to him, 'You know
what you have to do: do your office.' Then the marshal
came to Mr. Burroughs, and said, 'Sir, I have a writing to
read to you.' Then he read the attachment, and demanded
goods. Mr. Burroughs answered, 'that he had no goods to
show, and that he was now reckoning with the inhabitants,
for we know not yet who is in debt, but there was his body.'
As we were ready to go out of the meeting-house, Mr. Burroughs said, 'Well, what will you do with me?' Then
the marshal went to John Putnam, Sr., and said to him,
'What shall I do?' The said Putnam replied, 'You know
your business.' And then the said Putnam went to his
brother, Thomas Putnam, and pulled him by the coat; and
they went out of the house together, and presently came in
again. Then said John Putnam, 'Marshal, take your
prisoner, and have him up to the ordinary, — that is a public house, — and secure him till the morning.'

(Signed)   "NATHANIEL INGERSOLL, aged about fifty.
SAMUEL SIBLEY, aged about twenty-four.

"To the first of these, I, John Putnam, Jr., testify, being
at the meeting."

The above document illustrates the general position of the Putnam family through all the troubles of the Salem Village parish. Thomas and John were the heads of two of its branches, and participated in the proceedings against Burroughs. Nathaniel generally was on the other side in the course of the various controversies which finally culminated in the witchcraft delusion. His son, John Putnam, Jr., on this occasion, was a witness friendly to Mr. Burroughs. Nathaniel Ingersoll does not appear to have been a partisan on either side. His sympathies, generally, were with the friends of Bayley; but, on this occasion, his sense of justice led him to take the lead in behalf of Burroughs. Other depositions are as follows: —

"The Testimony of Thomas Haynes, aged thirty-two years or thereabouts. — Testifieth and saith, that, at a meeting of the inhabitants of Salem Farms, May the second, 1683, after the marshal had read John Putnam's attachment to Mr. Burroughs, then Mr. Burroughs asked Putnam ' what money it was he attached him for.' John Putnam answered, ' For five pounds and odd money at Shippen's at Boston, and for thirteen shillings at his father Gedney's, and for twenty-four shillings at Mrs. Darby's;' that then Nathaniel Ingersoll stood up, and said, ' Lieutenant, I wonder that you attach Mr. Burroughs for the money at Darby's and your father Gedney's, when, to my knowledge, you and Mr. Burroughs have reckoned and balanced accounts two or three times since, as you say, it was due, and you never made any mention of it when you reckoned with Mr. Burroughs.' John Putnam answered, ' It is true, and I own it.'

Samuel Sibley, aged twenty-four years or thereabouts, testifieth to all above written."

"THE TESTIMONY OF NATHANIEL INGERSOLL, *aged*, *&c.* — Testifieth, that I heard Mr. Burroughs ask Lieutenant John Putnam to give him a bill to Mr. Shippen. The said Putnam asked the said Burroughs how much he would take up at Mr. Shippen's. Mr. Burroughs said it might be five pounds; but, after the said Burroughs had considered a little, he said to the said Putnam, ' It may be it might come to more : ' therefore he would have him give him a bill to the value of five or six pounds, — when Putnam answered, it was all one to him. Then the said Putnam went and writ it, and read it to Mr. Burroughs, and said to him that it should go for part of the £33. 6s. 8d. for which he had given a bill to him in behalf of the inhabitants. I, Hannah Ingersoll, aged forty-six years or thereabouts, testify the same."

It seems by the foregoing, that Mr. Burroughs had presented a bill, of the amount just mentioned, to John Putnam, who, as chairman of the committee the preceding year, represented the inhabitants; and it was deliberately and formally agreed, that the sum borrowed of Putnam by Burroughs should "go for part of it." The records of the parish show, that, on the 24th of May, — three weeks after this meeting "for reckoning," — a vote was passed to raise, by a rate, "fifteen pounds for Mr. Burroughs for the last quarter of a year he preached with us." At a meeting in December of the same year, a rate was ordered, to pay the debts of the parish, amounting to £52. 1s. 1d. On the 22d of the ensuing February, the parish voted to raise "fifteen pounds for Mr. Burroughs."

The record of a meeting in April, 1684, contains an order, left on the book, with Mr. Burroughs's proper signature, authorizing Lieutenant Thomas Putnam to receive of the committee "what is due to me from the inhabitants of Salem Farms." Thus it is evident, that, at the very day when the ruthless proceedings above described took place, a considerable balance was due to Mr. Burroughs, after all claims from all quarters had been "reckoned." The return of the marshal, made to the Court, was as follows: —

"I have attached the body of George Burroughs he tendered to me, — for he said he had no pay, — and taken bonds to the value of fourteen pounds money, and read this to him.

Per me, HENRY SKERRY, *Marshal.*"

The bond is as follows. I give the names of the signers. The persons who interposed to rescue a persecuted man from unjust imprisonment deserve to be held in honored remembrance.

"We whose names are underwritten do bind ourselves jointly and severally to Henry Skerry, Marshal of Salem, our heirs, executors, and administrators, in the sum of fourteen pounds money, that George Burroughs shall appear at the next court at Salem, to answer to Lieutenant John Putnam, according to the summons of this attachment, and to abide the order of the court therein, and not to depart without license; as witness our hands this 2d of May, 1683.

"GEORGE BURROUGHS.   SAMUEL SIBLEY.
NATHANIEL INGERSOLL.   WILLIAM SIBLEY.
JOHN BUXTON.   WILLIAM IRELAND, JR."
THOMAS HAYNES.

The case was withdrawn, and Burroughs was glad to get away. He preferred the Indians at Casco Bay to the people here. When we consider, that a committee of the parish petitioned the Court to have such a meeting of the inhabitants; that it was held, by an order of Court, in compliance with said petition; that Burroughs came back to the village to attend it; that the meeting agreed, in answer to an inquiry from him to that effect, to conform to the order of the Court in making it the occasion of a full and final "reckoning" between them; that they spent two days and a half in bringing in and sifting all claims on either side; and that, when, at the time agreed upon, — the afternoon of the third day, — the whole body of the inhabitants had come together to ratify and give effect to the "reckoning," the marshal came in with a writ, and, evidently in violation of his feelings, was forced by John Putnam to arrest Burroughs, thereby breaking up the proceedings asked for by the parish and ordered by the Court, for a debt which he did not owe, — it must be allowed, that it was one of the most audacious and abominable outrages ever committed.

The scene presented in these documents is perhaps as vivid, and brings the actual life before us as strikingly, as any thing that has come down to us from that day. We can see, as though we were looking in at the door, the spectacle presented in the old meeting-house: the farmers gathered from their remote and widely scattered plantations, some possibly coming in travelling family-vehicles, — although it is quite uncertain whether there were any at that time among the farmers; some in companies on farm-carts; many on foot; but the greater number on horseback, in their picturesque costume of homespun or moose-skin, with cowl-shaped hoods, or hats with a brim, narrow in front, but broad and slouching behind, hanging over the shoulders. Every man was belted and sworded. They did not wear weapons merely for show. There was half a score of men in that assembly who were in the Narragansett fight; and some bore on their persons scars from that bloody scene of desperate heroism. Every man, it is probable, had come to the meeting with his firelock on his shoulder, to defend himself and companions against Indians lurking in the thick woods through which they had to pass. Their countenances bespoke the passions to which they had been wrought up by their fierce parish quarrels, — rugged, severe, and earnest. We can see the grim bearing of the cavalry lieutenant, John Putnam, and of his elder brother and predecessor in commission. Marshal Skerry, with his badges of office, is reluctant to execute its functions upon a persecuted and penniless minister; but, in accordance with the stern demands of the inexorable prosecutors, is faithful still to his painful duty. The minister is the central object in the picture, — a small, dark-complexioned man, the amazed but calm and patient victim of an animosity in which he had no part, and for which he was in no wise responsible. The unresisting dignity of his bearing is quite observable. " We are now reckoning; we know not yet who is in debt. I have no pay ; but here is my body." Perhaps, in that unconspicuous frame, and through that humble garb, the sinewy nerves and muscles of steel, the compact and concentrated forces, that were the marvel of his times, and finally cost him his life, were apparent in his movements and attitudes. It may be, that the sufferings and exposures of his previous life had left upon his swarthy features a stamp of care and melancholy, foreshadowing the greater wrongs and trials in store for him. But the chief figure in the group is the just man who rose and rebuked the harsh and reprehensible procedure of the powerful landholder, neighbor and friend though he was. The manner in which the arbitrary trooper bowed to the rebuke, if it does not mitigate our resentment of his conduct, illustrates the extraordinary influence of Nathaniel Ingersoll's character, and demonstrates the deference in which all men held him.

There are in this affair other points worthy of notice, as showing the effects of their bitter feuds in rendering them insensible to every appeal of charity or humanity. Their minds had become so soured, and their sense of what was right so impaired, that they neglected and refused to fulfil their most ordinary obligations to each other, and to themselves as a society. Rates were not collected, and contracts were not complied with. The minister and his family were left without the necessaries of life. They were compelled to borrow even their clothing, articles of which constituted a part of the debt for which he was arrested in such a public and unfeeling manner. A young woman testifies that she lived with Mr. Burroughs about two years, and says: "My mistress did tell me that she had some serge of John Putnam's wife, to make Mary a coat; and also some fustian of his wife, to make my mistress a pair of sleeves." The principal items in the account were for articles required at the death of his wife, by the usages of that day on funeral occasions. Surely it was an outrage upon human nature to spring a suit at law and have a writ served on him, and take him as a prisoner, on such an occasion, under such circumstances, on an alleged debt incurred by such a bereavement, when poverty and necessity had left him no alternative. The whole procedure receives the stamp, not only of cruelty, but of infamy, from the fact, which Nathaniel Ingersoll compelled Putnam to acknowledge before the whole congregation, that the account had been settled and the debt paid long before.

John Putnam, although a hard and stern man, had many traits of dignity and respectability in his character. That he could have done this thing, in this way, proves the extent to which prejudice and passion may carry one, particularly where party spirit consumes individual reason and conscience. At this point it is well to consider a piece of testimony brought against Burroughs nine years afterwards. There was no propriety or sense in giving it when it was adduced. It was, in truth, an outrage to have introduced such testimony in a case where Burroughs was on trial for witchcraft; and it was allowed, only to prejudice and mislead the minds of a jury and of the public. But it is proper to be taken into view, in forming a just estimate, with an impartial aim, of his general character. The document is found in a promiscuous bundle of witchcraft papers.

" THE DEPOSITION OF JOHN PUTNAM AND REBECCA HIS WIFE. — Testifieth and saith, that, in the year 1680, Mr. Burroughs lived in our house nine months. There being a great difference betwixt said Burroughs and his wife, the difference was so great that they did desire us, the deponents, to come into their room to hear their difference. The controversy that was betwixt them was, that the aforesaid Burroughs did require his wife to give him a written covenant, under her hand and seal, that she would never reveal his secrets. Our answer was, that they had once made a covenant we did conceive did bind each other to keep their lawful secrets. And further saith, that, all the time that said Burroughs did live at our house, he was a very harsh and sharp man to his wife; notwithstanding, to our observation, she was a very good and dutiful wife to him."

The first observation that occurs in examining this piece of testimony is, that the answer made by Putnam and his wife was excellent, and, like every thing from him, shows that he was a man of strong common sense, and had a forcible and effectual way of expressing himself. The next thing to be considered is, that Mr. Burroughs probably discovered, soon after coming to the village, into what a hornets' nest he had got, —

every one tattling about and backbiting each other.
His innocent and unsuspicious wife may have indulged
a little in what is considered the amiable proclivity of
her sex, and have let fall, in tea-table talk, what cavil-
lers and mischief-makers were on hand to take up;
and he may have found it both necessary and difficult
to teach her caution and reserve. He saw, more
perhaps than she did, the danger of getting involved
in the personal acrimonies with which the whole community was poisoned. Her unguarded carelessness
might get herself and him into trouble, and vitally
impair their happiness and his usefulness. The only
other point to be remarked upon is the general charge
against Mr. Burroughs's temper and disposition. It
may be that he became so disgusted with the state of
things as to have shown some acerbity in his manners,
but such a supposition is not in harmony with what
little is known of him from other sources; and John
Putnam's conduct at the meeting described proves
that his mind was fully perverted, and bereft as it
were of all moral rectitude of judgment, in reference
to Mr. Burroughs. We must part with Mr. Burroughs
for the present. We shall meet him again, where the
powers of malignity will be more shamelessly let loose
upon him, and prevail to his destruction.

He was succeeded in the ministry at Salem Village
by a character of a totally different class. Deodat
Lawson is first heard of in this country, according to
Mr. Savage, at Martha's Vineyard in 1671. He took
the freeman's oath at Boston in 1680, and continued

to have his residence there. It was not until after much negotiation and considerable importunity, that he was prevailed upon to enter into an engagement to preach at the Village. He began his ministry early in 1684, as appears by the parish record of a meeting Feb. 22, 1684: "Voted that Joseph Herrick, Jonathan Putnam, and Goodman Cloyse are desired to take care for to get a boat for the removing of Mr. Lawson's goods." Votes, about this time, were passed to repair the parsonage, and the fences around the ministry land; thus putting things in readiness to receive him. It does not appear that he became particularly entangled in the conflicts which had so long disturbed the Village, although, while the mother-church signified its readiness to approve of his ordination, and some movement was made in the Village to that end, it was found impossible to bring the hostile parties sufficiently into co-operation to allow of any thing being definitely accomplished. Fortunately for Mr. Lawson, the spirit of strife found other objects upon which to expend its energies for the time being. Some persons brought forward complaints, that the records of the parish had not been correctly kept (this was before Sergeant Thomas Putnam had been charged with that trust); that votes which had passed in "Mr. Bayley's days" and in "Mr. Burroughs's days" had not been truly recorded, or recorded at all; and that what had never been passed had been entered as votes. A great agitation arose on this subject, and many meetings were held. Some demanded that the spurious votes should be expunged; others, that the omitted votes should be inserted. Then there was an excited disputation about the ministry lands, and the validity or sufficiency of their title to them. Joseph Houlton had given them; but he had nothing to do with raising the question, and did all he could to suppress it. Some person had discovered that William Haynes, to whom Houlton had succeeded by the right of his wife, had omitted to get his deed of purchase recorded, and the original could not be found. Disputes also arose about the use of the grounds around the meeting-house. These, added to the conflicts with the "Topsfield men," and matters not fully adjusted with the town of Salem, created and kept up a violent fermentation, in which all were miscellaneously involved. In the midst of this confusion, the matter of ordaining Mr. Lawson was put into the warrant for a meeting to be held on the 10th of December, 1686. But it was found impossible to recall the people from their divisions, and no favorable action could be had.

At length, all attempts to settle their difficulties among themselves were abandoned; and they called for help from outside. At a legally warned meeting on the 17th of January, 1687, the inhabitants made choice of "Captain John Putnam" (he had been promoted in the military line since the affair in the meeting-house with Mr. Burroughs), "Lieutenant Jonathan Walcot, Ensign Thomas Flint, and Corporal Joseph Herrick, for to transact with Joseph Hutchinson, Job Swinnerton, Joseph Porter, and Daniel Andrew about their grievances relating to the public affairs of this place; and, if they cannot agree among themselves, that then they shall refer their differences to the Honored Major Gedney and John Hathorne, Esqs., and to the reverend elders of the Salem Church, for a full determination of those differences." Of course, it was impossible to settle the matter among themselves, and the referees were called in. William Brown, Jr., Esq., was added to them. They were all of the old town, and men of the highest consideration. Their judgment in the case is a well-drawn and interesting document, and shows the view which near neighbors took of the distractions in the village. The following passage will exhibit the purport and spirit of it: —

" *Loving Brethren, Friends and Neighbors,* — Upon serious consideration of, and mature deliberation upon, what hath been offered to us about your calling and transacting in order to the settling and ordaining the Rev. Mr. Deodat Lawson, and the grievances offered by some to obstruct and impede that proceeding, our sense of the matter is this, — first, that the affair of calling and transacting in order to the settling and ordaining the Reverend Mr. Lawson hath not been so inoffensively managed as might have been, — at least, not in all the parts and passages of it; second, that the grievances offered by some amongst you are not in themselves of sufficient weight to obstruct so great a work, and that they have not been improved so peaceably and orderly as Christian prudence and self-denial doth direct; third, to our grief, we observe such uncharitable expressions and uncomely reflections tossed to and fro as look like the effects of settled prejudice and resolved animosity, though we are much rather willing to account them the product of weakness than wilfulness: however, we must needs say, that, come whence they will, they have a tendency to make such a gap as we fear, if not timely prevented, will let out peace and order, and let in confusion and every evil work."

They then proceed to give some good advice to "prevent contention and trouble for the future, that it may not devour for ever, and that, if the Lord please, you may be happier henceforth than to make one another miserable; and not make your place uncomfortable to your present, and undesirable to any other, minister, and the ministry itself in a great measure unprofitable: and that you may not bring impositions on yourselves by convincing all about you that you cannot, or will not, use your liberty as becomes the gospel." Their advice is, "that you desist, at present, from urging the ordination of the Rev. Mr. Lawson, till your spirits are better quieted and composed." They give some judicious suggestions about various matters that had been the occasion of difficulty among them, especially to help them get their records put into good shape, and kept so for the future; and wind up in the following excellent, and in some of the clauses rather emphatic and pithy, expressions: —

"Finally, we think peace cheap, if it may be procured by complying with the aforementioned particulars, which are few, fair, and easy; and that they will hardly pass for lovers of peace, truth, ministry, and order, in the day of the Lord, that shall so lean to their own understanding and will that they shall refuse such easy methods for the obtaining of them. And, if peace and agreement amongst you be once comfortably obtained, we advise you with all convenient speed to go on with your intended ordination; and so we shall follow our advice with our prayers. But, if our advice be rejected, we wish you better, and hearts to follow it; and only add, if you will unreasonably trouble yourselves, we pray you not any further to trouble us. We leave all to the blessing of God, the wonderful Counsellor, and your own serious consideration: praying you to read and consider the whole, and then act as God shall direct you. Farewell."

[Salem, Feb. 14, 1687. Signed by the five referees, — John Higginson and Nicholas Noyes (the elders of the old church), and the three gentlemen before named.]

At a meeting of the inhabitants of the Village on the 18th of February, it was voted that " we do accept of and embrace the advice of the honored and reverend gentlemen of Salem, sent to us under their hands, and order that it shall be entered on our book of records." But they took care further to vote, that they accepted it " in general, and not in parts." In accordance with the advice of the referees, they brought up, considered anew, and put to question, every entry in their past records about the genuineness and validity of which any division of opinion existed. Some entries that had been complained of and given offence as incorrect were voted out, and others were confirmed by being adopted on a new vote. A new book of records was prepared, to conform to these decisions, which, having been submitted for examination to leading persons, appointed for the purpose at a legal meeting representing both parties, and approved by them, was adopted and sanctioned at a subsequent meeting also called for the purpose.

In accordance with the same advice "that the old book of records be kept in being," it was ordered by the meeting to leave the votes that had, by the foregoing proceedings, been rendered null and void, to "lie in the old book of records as they are." From the new book of records we learn that "some votes are left out that passed in Mr. Bayley's days, and some that passed in Mr. Burroughs's days," particularly all the votes but one that passed at a meeting held on the fifth day of June, 1683, the very time that Mr. Burroughs was under bonds in the action of debt brought by John Putnam. The new record specifies some few, but not all, of the votes that were rescinded because it was adjudged that they had not rightfully passed, or been correctly stated. Unfortunately, the old book, after all, has not been "kept in being;" and much that would have exhibited more fully and clearly the unhappy early history of the parish is for ever lost. If the records that have been suffered to remain present the picture I have endeavored faithfully to draw, how much darker might have been its shades had we been permitted to behold what the parties concerned concurred in thinking too bad to be left to view!

The attempt to expunge records is always indefensible, besides being in itself irrational and absurd. It may cover up the details of wrong and folly; but it leaves an unlimited range to the most unfriendly conjecture. We are compelled to imagine what we ought to be allowed to know; and, in many particulars, our fancies may be worse than the facts. But later times, and public bodies of greater pretensions than " the inhabitants of Salem Village," have attempted, and succeeded in perpetrating, this outrage upon history. In trying to conceal their errors, men have sometimes destroyed the means of their vindication. This may be the case with the story that is to be told of " Salem Witchcraft." It has been the case in reference to wider fields of history. The Parliamentary journals and other public records of the period of the Commonwealth and the Protectorate were suppressed by the infatuated stupidity of the Government of the Restoration. They foolishly imagined that they were hiding the shame, while they were obscuring the glory, of their country. Every Englishman, every intelligent man, now knows, that, during that very period, all that has made England great was done. The seeds of her naval and maritime prosperity were planted : and she was pushed at once by wise measures of policy, internal and external; by legislation developing her resources and invigorating the power of her people; by a decisive and comprehensive diplomacy that commanded the respect of foreign courts, and secured to her a controlling influence upon the traffic of the world; by developments of her military genius under the greatest of all the great generals of modern times; and by naval achievements that snatched into her hands the balancing trident of the seas, — to the place she still holds (how much longer she may hold it remains to be seen) as the leading power of the world. If she has to relinquish that position, it will only be to a power that is true to the spirit, and is not ashamed of the name, of a republic. The nation that fully develops the policy which pervaded the records of the English Commonwealth will be the leader of the world. The suppression of those records has not suppressed the spirit of popular liberty, or the progress of mankind in the path of reform, freedom, equal rights, and a true civilization. It has only cast a shadow, which can never wholly be dispelled, over what otherwise would have been the brightest page in the annals of a great people. We depend for our knowledge of the steps by which England then made a most wonderful stride to prosperity and power, not upon official and authoritative records, but upon the desultory and sometimes merely gossiping memoirs of particular persons, and such other miscellaneous materials as can be picked up. The only consequence of an attempt to extinguish the memory of republicans, radicals, reformers, and regicides has been, that the history of England's true glory can never be adequately written.

The referees used the following language touching the point of the ordination of Mr. Lawson: "If more than a mere major part should not consent to it, we should be loath to advise our brethren to proceed." This, in connection with the other sentence I have quoted from their communication recommending them " to desist at present" from urging it, was fatal to the immediate movement in his favor; and, not seeing any prospect of their "spirits becoming better quieted and composed," and weary of the attempt to bring them to any comfortable degree of unanimity, Mr. Lawson threw up his connection with them, and removed back to Boston. We shall meet him again; but it is well to despatch at this point what is to be said of his character and history.

It is evident that Deodat Lawson had received the best education of his day. It is not easy to account for his not having left a more distinguished mark in Old or New England. He had much learning and great talents. Of his power in getting up pulpit performances in the highest style of eloquence, of which that period afforded remarkable specimens, I shall have occasion to speak. Among his other attainments, he was, what cannot be said of learned and professional men generally now any more than then, an admirable penman. The village parish adopted the practice at the beginning, when paying the salaries of its ministers from time to time, instead of taking receipts on detached and loose pieces of paper, of having them write them out in their own hand on the pages of the record-book, with their signatures. It is a luxury, in looking over the old volume, to come upon the receipts of Deodat Lawson, in his plain, round hand.

A specimen is given among the autographs. His chirography is easy, free, graceful, clear, and clean. It unites with wonderful taste the highest degrees of simplicity and ornament. Each style is used, and both are blended, as occasion required. During his ministry, the trouble about the old record-book occurred. The first four pages of the new book are in his handwriting. The ink has somewhat faded; the paper has become discolored, and, around the margins and at the bottom of the leaves, lamentably worn and broken. The first page exhibits Lawson's penmanship in its various styles. It is artistically executed in several sizes of letters, appropriate to the position of the clauses and the import and weight of the matter. In each there is an elegant combination of ornament and simplicity. His chirography was often had in requisition; and papers, evidently from his pen, are on file in various cases, occurring in court at the time, in which his friends were interested.

The first four ministers of the village parish were excellent penmen. Bayley's hand is more like the modern style than the rest. Burroughs's is as legible as print, uniform in its character, open and upright. The specimen among the autographs is from the record referred to at the top of page 262. As it was written at the bottom of a page in the record-book, where there was hardly sufficient room, it had to be in a slanting line. I give it just as it there appears. Parris wrote three different hands, all perfectly easy to read. The larger kind was used when signing his

Townsend Bishop

Thomas [illegible]

Thomas Putnam cler:

Em: Downinge

Lucie Downinge

Simon Bradstreet
13. Ap̃ 1692.

James Bayley.

George Burroughs

p̄ me, Deodat Lawson

Sam: Parris

Nathaniel Ingersoll

name to important papers, or in brief entries of record. The specimen I give is from a receipt in the parish-book, which Thomas Putnam, as clerk, made oath in court, that Parris wrote and signed in his presence. His notes of examinations of persons charged with witchcraft by the committing magistrate, many of which are preserved, are in his smallest hand, very minute, but always legible. In his church-records he uses sometimes a medium hand, and sometimes the smallest. The autographs of Townsend Bishop and Thomas Putnam show the handwriting that seems to have prevailed among well-educated people in England at the time of the first settlement of this country. There was often a profusion of flourishes that obscured the letters. The initial capitals were quite complicated and very curious. The signature of Thomas Putnam, Jr., exhibits his excellent handwriting.

I have adduced these facts and given these illustrations to show, that, in this branch of education, — the value and desirableness of which cannot be overrated, — it is at least an open question, whether we have much ground to boast of being in advance of the first generations of our ancestors in America. The early ministers of the Salem Village parish certainly compare, in this particular, favorably with ministers and professional men, and recording officers generally in public bodies of all kinds, in later times.

Sergeant Thomas Putnam did not act as clerk of the parish from April, 1687, to April, 1694. A few entries are made by his hand ; but the record, very

meagre and fragmentary, is for the most part made
by others. This is much to be regretted, as the
interval covers the very period of our history. His
time, probably, was taken up, and his mind wholly
engrossed, by an unhappy family difficulty, in which,
during that period, he was involved. Thomas Putnam Sr. died, as has been stated, in 1686. It was
thought, by the children of his first wife, that the
influence of the second wife had been unduly exercised
over him, in his last years, so as to induce him to
make a will giving to her, and her only child by him,
Joseph, a very unfair proportion of his estate. It was
felt by them to be so unjust that they attempted to
break the will. The management of the case was con-
fided to Sergeant Thomas Putnam, as the eldest son of
the family ; and the affair, it may be supposed, absorbed
his thoughts to such a degree as to render it necessary
for him to abandon his services as clerk of the parish.
The attempt to set aside the will failed. The circumstances connected with the subject disturbed very seriously — perhaps permanently — the happiness of the
whole family, and may have contributed to create
the morbid excitement which afterwards was so fear-
fully displayed by the wife of the younger Thomas.

While Mr. Lawson was at the village, he lost his
wife and daughter. In 1690, he was again married, to
Deborah Allen. He was settled afterwards over the
Second Society in Scituate, — it is singular that our
local histories do not tell us when, but that we get all
we know on the point from a sentence written by the

pen on a leaf of one of the two folio volumes of John
Quick's " Synodicon in Gallia Reformata," in the possession of a gentleman in this country, Henry M.
Dexter, who says it is evidently Quick's autograph.
It is in these words : " For my reverend and dear
brother, Mr. Lawson, minister of the gospel, and pastor of the church of Scituate, in the province of Massachusetts in New England ; from the publisher, John
Quick, *honoris et amoris ergo*, Aug. 6, 1693." In 1696,
Mr. Lawson went over to England, merely for a short
visit, as his people supposed. They heard from him
no more. He never asked a dismission, or communicated with them in any way. In 1698, an ecclesiastical council declared them free to settle another
minister, which they did in due time. He was, no
doubt, alive and in London when, in 1704, his famous
Salem Village sermon was reprinted there. But this
is the last glimpse we have of him. An inscrutable
mystery covers the rest of his history. His manner of leaving the Scituate parish shows him to have
been an eccentric person, leaves an unfavorable impression of his character, and is as inexplicable as
the only other reference to him that has thus far
been found. Calamy, in his " Continuation of the
Account of Ejected Ministers," published in 1727, has
a notice of Thomas Lawson, whom he describes as
minister of Denton in the county of Norfolk, educated at Katherine Hall in Cambridge, and afterwards
chosen " to a fellowship in St. John's. He was a man
of parts, but had no good utterance. He was the

father of the unhappy Mr. Deodat Lawson, who came hither from New England." With all his abilities, learning, and eloquence, he disappears, after the republication of his Salem Village sermon in London, in the dark, impenetrable cloud of this expression, " the unhappy Mr. Deodat Lawson." Of the melancholy fate implied in the language of Calamy, I have not been able to obtain the slightest information.

The troubles that covered the whole period, since the beginning of Mr. Bayley's ministry, had led to the neglect and derangement of the entire organization of the Village, and resulted in the loss of what little opportunities for education might otherwise have been provided. So great was this evil regarded, that the old town felt it necessary to interpose; and we find it voted Jan. 24, 1682, that " Lieutenant John Putnam is desired, and is hereby empowered, to take care that the law relating to the catechising of children and youth be duly attended at the Village." He is also " desired to have a diligent care that all the families do carefully and constantly attend the due education of their children and youth according to law." We cannot but feel that the man who was ready to fight the " Topsfield men " in the woods — who, when they asked him, " What, by violence ? " answered, with axe in hand, " Ay, by violence," and who figured in the manner described in the scene with Mr. Burroughs — was a singular person to intrust with the charge of " catechising the children and youth." But those were queer times, and he was a queer character. He

had always been a church-member ; and, to the day of
his death, church and prayer meetings were more frequently held at his house than in any other. He was
a rough man, but he was no hypocrite. He was in
the front of every encounter ; but he was tolerant, too,
of difference of opinion. When, at one time, the contests of the Village were at their height, and two committees were raised representing the two conflicting
parties, he was at the head of one, and his eldest son
(Jonathan) of the other. Their opposition does not
seem to have alienated them. While I have found it
necessary to hold him up, in some of his actions, for
condemnation, there were many good points about
him ; although he was not the sort of man that would
be likely, in our times, to be selected to execute the
functions of a Sunday-school teacher.

During all this period, there was a variety of minor
controversies among themselves, causing greater or
less disturbance. Joseph Hutchinson, who had given
a site out of his homestead-grounds for the meeting-
house, had no patience with their perpetual wrang-
lings. He fenced up his lands around the meeting-
house lot, leaving them an entrance on the end towards the road. They went to court about it, and
he was called to account by the usual process of law.
The plain, gruff old farmer, who seems all along to
have been a man of strong sense and decided character, filed an answer, which is unsurpassed for blunt-
ness of expression. It has no language of ceremony,
but goes to the point at once. It has a general inter-

est as showing, to how late a period the inhabitants of
this neighborhood were exposed to Indian attacks, and
what means of defence were resorted to by the Village
worshippers. The document manifests the contempt
in which he held the complainants, and it was all the
satisfaction they got.

" Joseph Hutchinson his answer is as followeth : —

"First, as to the covenant they spoke of, I conceive it is
neither known of by me nor them, as will appear by records
from the farmer's book.

" Second, I conceive they have no cause to complain of
me for fencing in my own land; for I am sure I fenced in
none of theirs. I wish they would not pull down my fences.
I am loath to complain, though I have just cause.

" Third, for blocking up the meeting-house, it was they
did it, and not I, in the time of the Indian wars; and
they made Salem pay for it. I wish they would bring me
my rocks they took to do it with ; for I want them to make
fence with.

" Thus, hoping this honored Court will see that there was
no just cause to complain against me, and their cause will
appear unjust in that they would in an unjust way take
away my land, I trust I shall have relief; so I rest, your
Honor's servant,   JOSEPH HUTCHINSON."

[Nov. 27, 1686.]

The next minister of Salem Village brought matters
to a crisis. Samuel Parris is stated to have been a
son of Thomas Parris, of London, and was born in
1653. He was, for a time, a member of Harvard College, but did not finish the academic course, being

drawn to a commercial life. He was engaged in the West-India business, and probably lived at Barbadoes. After a while, he abandoned commerce, and prepared himself for the ministry. There was at this time, and long subsequently, a very particular mercantile connection between Salem and Barbadoes. The former husband of the wife of Thomas Putnam, Sr., — Nathaniel Veren, — as has been stated, had property in that island, and was more or less acquainted with its people. Perhaps it was through this channel that the thoughts of the people of the Village were turned towards Mr. Parris. From a deposition made by him a few years afterwards in a suit at law between him and his parishioners, we learn some interesting facts relating to the negotiations that led to his settlement.

It appears from his statement that a committee, consisting of " Captain John Putnam, Mr. Joshua Rea, Sr., and Francis Nurse," was appointed, on the 15th of November, 1688, to treat with him " about taking ministerial office." On the 25th of November, " after the services in the afternoon, the audience was stayed, and, by a general vote, requested Mr. Parris to take office." He hung back for a while, and exercised the skill and adroitness acquired in his mercantile life in making as sharp a bargain as he could.

At that time, there appeared to be a degree of harmony among the people, such as they had never known before. There was a disposition on all sides to come together, and avail themselves of the occasion of settling a new minister, to bury their past animosities, and forget their grievances; and there is every reason to believe, if Mr. Parris had promptly closed with their terms, he might have enjoyed a peaceful ministry, and a happy oblivion have covered for ever his name and the history of the village. But he withheld response to the call. The people were impatient, and felt that the golden opportunity might be lost, and the old feuds revive. On the 10th of December, another committee was raised, consisting of Lieutenant Nathaniel Putnam, Sergeant Fuller, Mr. Joshua Rea, Sr., and Sergeant Ingersoll, as " messengers, to know whether Mr. Parris would accept of office." His answer was, " the work was weighty; they should know in due time." They were thus kept in suspense during the whole winter, getting no reply from him. On the 29th of April, 1689, " Deacons Nathaniel Ingersoll and Edward Putnam, Daniel Rea, Thomas Fuller, Jr., and John Tarbell, came to Mr. Parris from the meeting-house," where there had been a general meeting of the inhabitants, and said, " Being the aged men had had the matter of Mr. Parris's settlement so long in hand, and effected nothing, they were desirous to try what the younger could do." Deacon Ingersoll was about fifty-five years of age; but his spirit and character kept him in sympathy with the progressive impulses of younger men. Deacon Putnam was thirty-four years of age. Daniel Rea was the son of Joshua; Thomas Fuller, Jr., the son of Sergeant Fuller; and John Tarbell, the son-in-law of Francis Nurse.

This is the first appearance, I believe, in our history, of that notorious and most pretentious personage who has figured so largely in all our affairs ever since, " Young America." The sequel shows, that, in this instance at least, no benefit arose from discarding the caution and experience of years. The "younger men" were determined to "go ahead." They said they were desirous of a speedy answer. Finding them in a temper to " finish the thing up," at any rate, and seeing that they were ambitious to get the credit of " effecting something," and, for that end, predisposed to come to his terms, he disclosed them. They had offered him a salary of sixty pounds per annum,— one third in money, the rest in provisions, at certain specified rates. He agreed to accept the call on the foregoing terms, with certain additional conditions thus described by himself: " First, when money shall be more plenteous, the money part to be paid me shall accordingly be increased. Second, though corn or like provisions should arise to a higher price than you have set, yet, for my own family use, I shall have what is needful at the price now stated, and so if it fall lower. Third, the whole sixty pounds to be only from our inhabitants that are dwelling in our bounds, proportionable to what lands they have within the same. Fourth, no provision to be brought in without first asking whether needed, and myself to make choice of what, unless the person is unable to pay in any sort but one. Fifth, firewood to be given in yearly, freely. Sixth, two men to be chosen yearly to see that due payments be made.

Seventh, contributions each sabbath in papers; and only such as are in papers, and dwelling within our bounds, to be accounted a part of the sixty pounds. Eighth, as God shall please to bless the place so as to be able to rise higher than the sixty pounds, that then a proportionable increase be made. If God shall please, for our sins, to diminish the substance of said place, I will endeavor accordingly to bear such losses, by proportionable abatements of such as shall reasonably desire it."

A contribution-box was either handed around by the deacons, before the congregation was dismissed, or attached permanently near the porch or door. Rate-payers would inclose their money in papers, with their names, and drop them in. When the box was opened, the sums inclosed would be entered to their credit on the rate-schedule. There was always a considerable number of stated worshippers in the congregation who lived without the bounds of the village, and often transient visitors or strangers happened to be at meeting. It was a point that had not been determined, whether moneys collected from the above descriptions of persons should go into the general treasury of the parish, to be used in meeting their contract to pay the minister's salary, or be kept as a separate surplus.

The terms, as thus described by Mr. Parris, show that he had profited by his experience in trade, and knew how to make a shrewd bargain. It was quite certain that a farming community in a new country, with fields continually reclaimed from the wilderness and added to culture, would increase in substance : if so, his annual stipend would increase. If the place should decline, he was to abate the tax of individuals, if desired by them personally, so far as he should judge their petition to that effect reasonable. If " strangers' money," or contributions from " outsiders," were not to go to make up his sixty pounds, it was quite probable that it would come into his pocket as an extra allowance, or perquisite.

He says that the committee accepted these terms, and agreed to them, expressing their belief that the people also would. No record appears on the parish-books of the appointment of this committee of the " younger men," or of the action of the society on their report, or of any report having been made at that time. In the mean while, Mr. Parris continued to preach and act as the minister of the society until his ordination, near the close of the year. There was a meeting on the 21st of May ; but the record consists of but a single entry, — the appointment of a committee " as overseers for the year ensuing, to take care of our meeting-house and other public charges, and to make return according to law." The next entry is of a general meeting of the inhabitants, on the 18th of June, 1689. The choice of the regular standing· committee for the year is recorded. Immediately following this entry, are these words : —

" At the same meeting, — the 18th of June, 1689, — it was agreed and voted by general concurrence, that, for Mr. Parris, his encouragement and settlement in the work of the ministry amongst us, we will give him sixty six pounds for his yearly salary, — one-third paid in money, the other two-third parts for provisions, &c.; and Mr. Parris to find himself firewood, and Mr. Parris to keep the ministry-house in good repair; and that Mr. Parris shall also have the use of the ministry-pasture, and the inhabitants to keep the fence in repair; and that we will keep up our contributions, and our inhabitants to put their money in papers, and this to continue so long as Mr. Parris continues in the work of the ministry amongst us, and all productions to be good and merchantable. And, if it please God to bless the inhabitants, we shall be willing to give more; and to expect, that if God shall diminish the estates of the people, that then Mr. Parris do abate of his salary according to proportion."

Comparing this record with the account given by Mr. Parris of the eight conditions upon which he agreed, in conference with the committee of the "younger" sort, on the 29th of April, to accept the call of the parish, the difference is not very essential. The matter of firewood was arranged, according to his account, by mutual agreement, they to add six pounds to his salary, and he to find his own wood. The rates of "the inhabitants" were to be paid "in papers." The only point of difference, touching this matter, is that the record is silent about contributions by outsiders and strangers; whereas he says it was agreed, on the 29th of April, that they should not go towards making up his salary. The idea of his salary rising with the growth and sinking with the decline of the society is expressed in the record substantially as it is by him, only it is made exact; and, in case of a decline in the means of the people, a corresponding decline is to be in the aggregate of his salary, and not by abatements made by him in individual cases. The variations are nearly, if not quite, all unimportant in their nature, and such as a regard to mutual convenience would suggest. Yet there was something in the above record which highly exasperated Mr. Parris.

In his deposition he states, that, at a meeting held on the 17th of May, of which there is no record in the parish book, he was sent for and was present. He says that there was "much agitation" at the meeting. He says that objection was made by the people to two of his "eight" conditions, the fifth and seventh. But there is nothing in the record of the 18th of June in conflict with what he says was finally agreed upon, except the disposition that should be made of "strangers' money." The question then recurs, What was the cause of the "much agitation" at that meeting? What was it in the language of that record which always so excited Mr. Parris's wrath?

I am inclined to think that the offensive words were those which require "Mr. Parris to keep the ministry house in good repair," and that he "shall also have the use of the ministry pasture;" and this was not objectionable as involving any expense upon him, but solely because the language employed precluded the supposition that the parish had countenanced the idea of ever conveying the parsonage and parsonage lands to him in his own right and absolutely. This was an object which he evidently had in view from the first, and to which he clung to the last. It is to be feared, that some of the members of the "Young-America" committee, in their heedless and inconsiderate eagerness to "effect" something, to settle Mr. Parris forthwith, and thereby prove how much more competent they were than "the aged men" to transact a weighty business, had encouraged Mr. Parris to think that his favorite object could be accomplished. Upon a little inquiry, however, they discovered that it could not be done; but that the house and land were secured by the original deeds of conveyance, and by irreversible agreements and conditions, to the use of the ministry, for the time being and for ever. So far as the committee or any of its members had favored this idea in their conference with Mr. Parris, they had taken a position from which they had to retreat. They had compromised themselves and the parish. For this reason, perhaps, they made no report; and no mention of their agency appears on the records. How far Deacon Ingersoll was misled by his younger associates on this occasion, I know not; but he was not a man to break a promise if he could keep it, no matter how much to his own loss. He recognized his responsibility as chairman of the unfortunate committee, and retrieved the mistake they had made, by giving to Mr. Parris, by deed, a lot of land adjoining the parsonage property, and in value equal to the whole of it. The date of that conveyance, immediately after Mr. Parris's ordination, corroborates

the conjecture that it was made to compensate Mr.
Parris for the failure of his expectation to get possession
of the ministry property. It ought to have been received
by him as an equivalent, and have soothed his angry
disappointment; but it did not. He had indulged the
belief, that he had effected a bargain with the parish, at
his settlement, which had made him the owner, in fee
simple, of the parish property; and when he found that
the record of the terms of his settlement, in the parish-
book, absolutely precluded that idea, his exasperation
was great, and no reparation Deacon Ingersoll or any
one else could make was suffered to appease it. The
following deposition, made in court some years afterwards, gives an account of a scene in the meeting-
house after Parris's ordination: —

"IPSWICH COURT, 1697. — Parris *versus* Inhabitants of Salem
Village.

" We the undersigned testify and say, that, a considerable
time after Mr. Parris his ordination, there was a meeting of
the inhabitants of Salem Village at the usual place of meeting; and the occasion of the meeting was concerning Mr.
Parris, and several persons were at that meeting, that had
not, before this meeting, joined with the people in calling
or agreeing with Mr. Parris; and the said persons desired
that those things that concerned Mr. Parris and the people
might be read, and accordingly it was. And the entry, that
some call a salary, being read, there arose a difference
among the people, the occasion of which was finding an
entry in the book of the Village records, relating to Mr.
Parris his maintenance, which was dated the 18th of June,

1689; and, the entry being read to the people, some replied that they believed that Mr. Parris would not comply with that entry; whereupon one said it was best to send for Mr. Parris to resolve the question. Accordingly, he was sent for. He coming to the people, this entry of the 18th of June, 1689, was read to Mr. Parris. His answer was as follows: 'He never heard or knew any thing of it, neither could or would he take up with it, or any part of it;' and further he said, 'They were knaves and cheaters that entered it.' And Lieutenant Nathaniel Putnam, being moderator of that meeting, replied to Mr. Parris, and said, 'Sir, then there is only proposals on both sides, and no agreement between you and the people.' And Mr. Parris answered and said, 'No more, there is not; for I am free from the people, and the people free from me:' and so the meeting broke up. And we further testify, that there hath not been any agreement made with Mr. Parris, that we knew of or ever heard of, — never since.

" Joseph Porter.
Daniel Andrew.
Joseph Putnam.

" Sworn in Court, at Ipswich, April 13, 1697, by all three.
Attest, Stephen Sewall, *Clerk*."

The answer which Mr. Parris made to Nathaniel Putnam's inquiry probably settled the question in the suit then pending, and led to the final release of the parish from him. It is hard to find any point of difference between his own account of the conditions he himself made, and the record of the parish-book, of sufficient importance to account for the storm of passion into which the reading of the latter drove him, except in the language which I have suggested as the probable occasion of his wrath. Unfortunately for him, there is evidence quite corroborative of this suggestion.

The parish-book has the following record : —

"At a general meeting of the inhabitants of Salem Village, Oct. 10, 1689, it was agreed and voted, that the vote, in our book of record of 1681, that lays, as some say, an entailment upon our ministry house and land, is hereby made void and of no effect ; one man only dissenting.

"It was voted and agreed by a general concurrence, that we will give to Mr. Parris our ministry house and barn, and two acres of land next adjoining to the house ; and that Mr. Parris take office amongst us, and live and die in the work of the ministry among us ; and, if Mr. Parris or his heirs do sell the house and land, that the people may have the first refusal of it, by giving as much as other men will. A committee was chosen to lay out the land, and make a conveyance of the house and land, and to make the conveyance in the name and in the behalf of the inhabitants unto Mr. Parris and his heirs."

The record of these votes is not signed by the clerk, and there is no evidence that the meeting was legally warned. It does not appear in whose custody the book then was. But, however the entry got in, it proves that Parris's friends were determined to gratify his all but insane purpose to get possession of what he ought to have known it was impossible for the parish to give, or for him or his heirs to hold. It was indeed a miserable commencement of his ministry, to introduce such a strife with a people who really seem to have had an earnest desire to receive him with united hearts, and make his settlement and ministry the harbinger of a better day. But he alienated many of them, at the very start, by his sharp practice in negotiating about the pecuniary details of his agreement with the parish. When, after all their care to prevent it, it became known that somehow or other a vote had got upon the records, conveying to him outright their ministerial property, there was great indignation; and a determined effort was made to recover what they declared to be " a fraudulent conveying-away " of the property of the society.

A more violent conflict than any before was let loose upon that devoted people. The old passions were rekindled. Men ranged themselves as the friends and opponents of Mr. Parris in bitter antagonism. Rates were not collected; the meeting-house went into dilapidation; complaints were made to the County Court; orders were issued to collect rates, but they were disregarded; and all was confusion, disorder, and contention.

A church was organized in connection with the village parish, and Mr. Parris ordained on Monday, Nov. 19, 1689. The covenant adopted was the " confession of faith owned and consented unto by the elders and messengers of the churches assembled at Boston, New England, May 12, 1680." In the library of the Connecticut Historical Society, there is a manuscript volume of sermons and abstracts of sermons preached by Mr. Parris between November, 1689, and May, 1694. It begins with his ordination sermon, which has this prefix: "My poor and weak ordination sermon, at the embodying of a church at Salem Village on the 19th of the ninth month, 1689, the Rev. Mr. Nicholas Noyes embodying of us; who also ordained my most unworthy self pastor, and, together with the Rev. Mr. Samuel Phillips and the Rev. Mr. John Hale, imposed hands, — the same Mr. Phillips giving me the right hand of fellowship with beautiful loveliness and humility." The text is from Josh. v. 9: "And the Lord said unto Joshua, This day have I rolled away the reproach of Egypt from off you."

The first entry in the church-records, after the covenant and the names of the members, is the following: "Nov. 24, 1689. — Sab: day. Brother Nathaniel Ingersoll chosen, by a general vote of the brethren, to officiate in the place of a deacon for a time."

Mr. Parris commenced his administration by showing that he meant to exercise the disciplinary powers intrusted to him, as pastor of a church, with a high hand, and without much regard to persons or circumstances. Ezekiel Cheever had been a member of the mother-church in Salem twenty years before, was one of the founders of the parish church, and appears to have been a worthy and amiable person, occupying and owning the farm of his uncle, Captain Lothrop. On the sudden illness of a member of his family, being "in distress for a horse," none of his own being available at the time, he rushed, in his hurry and alarm, to the stable of a neighbor, took one of his horses, " without leave or asking of it," and rode, post haste, for a doctor. One would have thought that an affair of this sort, in such an exigency, might have been left to neighborly explanation or adjustment. But Mr. Parris regarded it as giving a good opportunity for an exercise of power that would strike the terrors of discipline home upon the whole community. About five or six weeks after the occurrence, Cheever was dealt with in the manner thus described by Mr. Parris, in his church-record, dated " Sab : 30 March, 1690." He was " called forth to give satisfaction to the offended church, as also the last sabbath he was called forth for the same purpose; but then he failed in giving satisfaction, by reason of somewhat mincing in the latter part of his confession, which, in the former, he had more ingenuously acknowledged : but this day, the church received satisfaction, as was testified by their holding-up of their hands ; and, after the whole, a word of caution by the pastor was dropped upon the offender in particular, and upon us all in general."

Mr. Parris was evidently inclined to magnify the importance of the church, and to get it into such a state of subserviency to his authority, that he could wield it effectually as a weapon in his fight with the congregation. With this view, he endeavored to render the action of the church as dignified and imposing as possible; to enlarge and expand its ceremonial proceedings, and make it the theatre for the exercise of his authority as its head and ruler. This feature of his policy was so strikingly illustrated in the course he took in reference to the deacons, that I must present it as recorded by him in the church-book. It is worth preserving as a curiosity in ecclesiastical administration.

Nathaniel Ingersoll had been a professor of religion almost as long as Mr. Parris had lived. He was eminently a Christian man, of acknowledged piety, and beloved and revered by all. He had been the patron, benefactor, and guardian of the parish and all its interests from its formation. He had long held the title of deacon, and exercised the functions of that office so far as they could be exercised previous to the organization of a church. He had been the almoner of the charities of the people, and their adviser and religious friend in all things. He was approaching the boundaries of advanced years, and already recognized among the fathers of the community. It would have seemed no more than what all might have expected, to have had him recognized as a deacon of the church, in full standing, at the first. It was, no doubt, what all did expect. But no: he must be put upon probation. He was chosen deacon "for the present" in November, 1689. Mr. Parris kept the matter of confirmation hanging in his own hands for a year and a half. The appointment of the other deacon was kept suspended for a full year. On the 30th of November, 1690, there is the following entry: —

" This evening, after the public service was over, the
church was, by the pastor, desired to stay, and then by him
Brother Edward Putnam was propounded as a meet person
for to be chosen as another deacon. The issue whereof was,
that, it being now an excessive cold day, some did propose
that another season might be pitched upon for discourse
thereof. Whereupon the pastor mentioned the next fourth
day, at two of the clock, at the pastor's house, for further
discourse thereof; to which the church agreed by not dissenting."

The record of the proceedings on the " next fourth
day " is as follows : —

" 3 December, 1690. — This afternoon, at a church meeting appointed the last sabbath, Brother Edward Putnam was
again propounded to the church for choice to office in the place
of a deacon to join with, and be assistant to, Brother Ingersoll in the service, and in order to said Putnam's ordination
in the office, upon his well approving himself therein.
Some proposed that two might be nominated to the church,
out of which the church to choose one. But arguments
satisfactory were produced against that way. Some also
moved for a choice by papers ; but that way also was disapproved by the arguments of the pastor and some others.
In fine, the pastor put it to vote (there appearing not the least
exception from any, unless a modest and humble exception
of the person himself, once and again), and it was carried
in the affirmative by a universal vote, *nemine non suffra-
gante*.

" Afterwards, the pastor addressed himself to the elected
brother, and, in the name of the church, desired his answer,
who replied to this purpose : —

' Seeing, sir, you say the voice of God's people is the voice of God, desiring your prayers and the prayers of the church for divine assistance therein, I do accept of the call.' "

When we consider that Edward Putnam was, at Mr. Parris's ordination more than a year before, and had been for some time previous to that event, Ingersoll's associate deacon, and that there probably never was any other person spoken or thought of than these two for deacons, it is evident that it was Mr. Parris's policy to make a great matter of the affair, and produce a general feeling of the weighty importance of church action in the premises. But this was only the beginning of the long-drawn ceremonial solemnities by which the occasion was magnified.

" Sab: day, 7 December, 1690. — After the evening public service was over, several things needful were transacted; viz.: —

" 1. The pastor acquainted those of the church that were ignorant of it, that Brother Edward Putnam was chosen deacon the last church meeting.

" 2. He also generally admonished those of the brethren that were absent at that time, of their disorderliness therein, telling them that such, the apostle bids, should be noted or marked (2 Thess. iii. 6–16) ; that is, with a church mark, — a mark in a disciplinary way ; and therefore begged amendment for the future in that point and to that purpose.

" 3. He propounded whether they so far were satisfied in Brother Ingersoll's service as to call him to settlement in the deaconship by ordination, or had aught against it. But no brother made personal exception. Therefore, it being put to vote, it was carried in the affirmative by a plurality, if not universality.

"4. The Lord's Table, not being provided for with aught else but two pewter tankards, the pastor propounded and desired that the next sacrament-day, which is to be the 21st instant, there be a more open and liberal contribution by the communicants, that so the deacons may have wherewith to furnish the said table decently ; which was consented to."

The last clause, " which was consented to," is in a smaller hand than the rest of the record. It was written by Mr. Parris, but apparently some time afterwards, and with fainter ink. There is reason to suppose that nothing was accomplished at that time in the way of getting rid of the " pewter tankards." The farmers were too hard pressed by taxes imposed by the province, and by the weight of local assessments, to listen to fanciful appeals. They probably continued for some time, and perhaps until after receiving Deacon Ingersoll's legacy, in 1720, to get along as they were. They did not believe, that, in order to approach the presence, and partake of the memorials, of the Saviour, it was necessary to bring vessels of silver or gold. In their circumstances, gathered in their humble rustic edifice for worship, they did not feel that, in the sight of the Lord, costly furniture would add to the adornment of his table.

Nearly six months after Putnam's election, Mr.

Parris brought up the matter again at a meeting of the church, on the 31st of May, 1691, and made a speech relating to it, which he entered on the records thus : —

"The pastor spoke to the brethren to this purpose, viz. : —

"BRETHREN, — The ordination of Brother Ingersoll has already been voted a good while since, and I thought to have consummated the affair a good time since, but have been put by, by diversity of occurrents ; and, seeing it is so long since, I think it needless to make two works of one, and therefore intend the ordination of Brother Putnam together with Brother Ingersoll in the deaconship, if you continue in the same mind as when you elected him : therefore, if you are so, let a vote manifest it. Voted by all, or at least the most. I observed none that voted not."

At last the mighty work was accomplished. Deacon Ingersoll had been on probation for eighteen months from the date of his election, which took place five days after Mr. Parris's ordination. His final induction to office was observed with great formality, and in the presence of the whole congregation. Mr. Parris enters the order of performances in the church records as follows : —

"Sab : 28 June, 1691. — After the afternoon sermon upon 1 Tim. iii. 8, 9, 10, 11, 12, 13, as the brethren had renewed their call of Brother Ingersoll to the office of a deacon, and he himself had declared his acceptance, the pastor proceeded to ordain him, using the form following :

"BELOVED BROTHER, God having called you to the office

of a deacon by the choice of the brethren and your own acceptance, and that call being now to be consummated according to the primitive pattern, 6 Acts 6, by prayer and imposition of hands, —

"We do, therefore, by this solemnity, declare your investiture into that office, solemnly charging you in the name of our Lord Jesus Christ, the King of his Church, who walks in the midst of his golden candlesticks, with eyes as of a flame of fire, exactly observing the demeanor of all in his house, both officers and members, that you labor so to carry it, as to evidence you are sanctified by grace, qualified for this work, and to grow in those qualifications; behaving of yourself gravely, sincerely, temperately, with due care for the government of your own house, holding the mystery of the faith in a pure conscience; that as they in this office are called 'helps,' so you be helpful in your place and capacity, doing what is your part for the promoting of the work of Christ here. We do charge you, that, whatever you do in this office, you do it faithfully, giving with simplicity, showing mercy with cheerfulness. Look on it, brother, as matter of care, and likewise of encouragement, that both the office itself and also your being set up in it is of God, who, being waited upon, will be with you, and accept you therein, assisting you to use the office of a deacon well, so as that you may be blameless, purchasing to yourself a good degree and great boldness in the faith.

"NOTE. — That Brother Putnam was not yet willing to be ordained, but desired further considering time, between him and I and Brother Ingersoll, in private discourse the week before the ordination above said."

"Brother Putnam" probably partook of the general

wonder what all this appearance of difficulty and delay, under the peculiar circumstances of the case, meant; and being, as the record truly says, a modest and humble man, he naturally shrank from the formidable ceremoniousness and pretentious parade with which Mr. Parris surrounded the transaction. At any rate, he hesitated long before he was willing to encounter it. It is probable that he positively refused to have his induction to the office heralded with such solemn pomp. There is no mention of his public ordination, which Mr. Parris would not have omitted to record, had any such scene occurred. All we know is that he was recognized as deacon forthwith, and held the office for forty years.

The disposition of Mr. Parris to make use of his office, as the head of the church, to multiply occasions for the exercise of his influence, and to gain control over the minds of the brethren, is apparent throughout his records. He raised objections in order to show how he could remove them, and started difficulties about matters which had not before been brought into question. In the beginning of his ministry, he manifested this propensity. At a church meeting at John Putnam's house, Feb. 20, 1690, less than three months after his ordination, he threw open the whole question of baptism for discussion among the brethren. There is no reason to suppose that their attention had been drawn to it before. He propounded the question to the plain, practical husbandmen, " Who are the proper subjects of baptism ? " He laid down the true doctrine, as he regarded it, in this answer, " Covenant-professing believers and their infant seed." He put the answer to vote, and none voted against it. He then proceeded with another question, " How far may we account such seed infant seed, and so to be baptized ? " Here he had got beyond their depth, and, as some of them thought, his own too ; for there was only a " major vote " in favor of his answer : " two or three, I think not four, dissented." There was some danger of getting into divisions by introducing such questions ; but he managed to avoid it, so far as his church was concerned. He worked them up to the highest confidence in his learning and wisdom, and gained complete ascendency over them. He aggrandized their sense of importance, and accomplished his object in securing their support in his controversies with his congregation. The brethren, after a while, became his devoted body-guard, and the church a fortress of defence and assault. There is reason, however, to believe, that the points he raised on the subject of baptism led to perplexities, in some minds, which long continued to disturb them. While showing off his learning, and displaying his capacity to dispose of the deep questions of theology, he let fall seeds of division and doubt that ripened into contention in subsequent generations. The only ripple on the surface of the Village Church during its long record of peace, since the close of his disastrous ministry, was occasioned by differing opinions on this subject. It required all the wisdom of his successors to quiet them. From time to time, formulas had

to be constructed, half-way covenants of varying expressions to be framed, to meet and dispose of the difficulties thus gratuitously raised by him.

The following passages from his record-book show
how he made much of a matter which any other pastor
would have quietly arranged without calling for the
intervention of church or congregation: they are also
interesting as a picture of the times: —

"Sab: 9 Aug. 1691. — After all public worship was
over, and the church stayed on purpose, I proposed to the
church whether they were free to admit to baptism, upon
occasion, such as were not at present free to come up to
full communion. I told them there was a young woman, by
name Han: Wilkins, the daughter of our Brother Thomas
Wilkins, who much desired to be baptized, but yet did not
dare to come to the Lord's Supper. If they had nothing
against it, I should take their silence for consent, and in due
time acquaint them with what she had offered me to my
satisfaction, and proceed accordingly."

No answer was made *pro* or *con*, and so the church
was dismissed.

"Sab: 23 Aug. 1691. — Hannah Wilkins, aged about
twenty-one years, was called forth, and her relation read in the
full assembly, and then it was propounded to the church, that,
if they had just exceptions, or, on the other hand, had any
thing farther to encourage, they had opportunity and liberty
to speak. None said any thing but Brother Bray Wilkins
(Han: grandfather), who said, that, for all he knew, such
a relation as had been given and a conversation suitable

(as he judged hers to be) was enough to enjoy full communion. None else saying any thing, it was put to vote whether they were so well satisfied as to receive this young woman into membership, and therefore initiate her therein by baptism. It was voted fully. Whereupon the covenant was given to her as if she had entered into full communion. And the pastor told her, in the name of the church, that we would expect and wait for her rising higher, and therefore advised her to attend all means conscientiously for that end.

"After all, I pronounced her a member of this church, and then baptized her.

"28 August, 1691. — This day, Sister Hannah Wilkins aforesaid came to me, and spake to this like effect, following: —

"Before I was baptized (you know, sir), I was desirous of communion at the Lord's Table, but not yet; I was afraid of going so far: but since my baptism I find my desires growing to the Lord's Table, and I am afraid to turn my back upon that ordinance, or to refuse to partake thereof. And that which moves me now to desire full communion, which I was afraid of before, is that of Thomas, 20 John 26, &c., where he, being absent from the disciples, though but once, lost a sight of Christ, and got more hardness of heart, or increase of unbelief. And also those words of Ananias to Paul after his conversion, 22 Acts 16, 'And now why tarriest thou? Arise,' &c. So I am afraid of tarrying. The present time is only mine. And God having, beyond my deserts, graciously opened a door, I look upon it my duty to make present improvement of it.

"Sab: and Sacrament Day, 30 Aug. 1691. — Sister Han: Wilkins's motion (before the celebration of the

Lord's Supper was begun) was mentioned or propounded to the church, and what she said to me (before hinted) read to them, and then their vote was called for, to answer her desire if they saw good; whereupon the church voted in the affirmative plentifully."

The foregoing passages illustrate Mr. Parris's propensity to magnify the operations of the church, and to bring its movements as conspicuously and as often as possible before the eyes of the people. It is evident that the humble and timid scruples of this interesting and intelligent young woman might have been met and removed by personal conference with her pastor. As her old grandfather seemed to think, there was no difficulty in the case whatever. The reflections of a few days made the path plain before her. But Mr. Parris paraded the matter on three sabbaths before the church, and on one of them at least before the congregation. He called her to come forth, and stand out in the presence of the " full assembly." As the result of the ordeal, she owned the covenant; the church voted her in, as to full communion; and the pastor pronounced her a member of the church, and baptized her as such. Her sensible conversation with him the next Friday was evidently intended for the satisfaction of him and others, as explaining her appearance at the next communion. But another opportunity was offered to make a display of the case, and he could not resist the temptation. He desired to create an impression by reading what she had said to him in his study, before the church, if not before the whole congregation.

To give a show of propriety in bringing it forward again, he felt that some action must be had upon it; hence the vote. Accordingly, Hannah Wilkins appears by the record to have been twice, on two successive Lord's Days, voted " plentifully " into the Salem Village Church, when there was no occasion for such an extraordinary repetition, as everybody from the first welcomed her into it with the cordial confidence she merited. I have spread out this proceeding to your view, not altogether from its intrinsic interest, but because, perhaps, it affords the key to interpret the course of this ill-starred man in his wrangles with his congregation, and his terrible prominency in the awful scenes of the witchcraft delusion. He seemed to have had a love of excitement that was irrepressible, an all but insane passion for getting up a scene. When we come to the details of our story, it will be for a charitable judgment to determine whether this trait of his nature may not be regarded as the cause of all the woes in which he involved others and became involved himself.

The church records are, in one respect, in singular contrast with the parish records. The latter are often silent in reference to matters of interest at the time, which might without impropriety have been entered in them. They are confined strictly to votes and proceedings in legal meetings, or what purport to have been meetings legally called ; and we look in vain for comments or notices relating to outside matters. Except when kept by Sergeant Thomas Putnam, they are defective and imperfect. The church records, while made by Mr. Parris, are full of side remarks, and touches of criticism concerning whatever was going on. This makes them particularly interesting and valuable now. They are composed in their author's clear, natural, and sprightly style; and, although for the most part in an exceedingly small hand, are legible with perfect ease, and give us a transcript, not only of the formal doings of the church, but of the writer's mind and feelings about matters and things in general. We gather from them by far the greater part of all we know relating to his quarrel with his congregation.

This subject constantly engrossed his thoughts. He was continually introducing, at church meetings, complaints against the conduct of the parish committee, and enlarging upon the wrongs he was suffering at their hands. He took occasion on Lecture days, if not in ordinary discourses on the Lord's Day, to give all possible circulation and publicity to his grievances. The effect of this was, instead of bringing his people into subjection and carrying his points against them, to aggravate their alienation. His manner of dealing with the difficulties of the situation into which they had been brought was harsh and exasperating, and utterly injudicious, imprudent, and mischievous in all its bearings, producing a condition of things truly scandalous. His notions and methods, acquired in his mercantile life; his haggling with the people about the terms of his salary; and his general manner and tone, particularly so far as they had been formed by residence

in West-India slave Islands,— were thoroughly distasteful, and entirely repugnant, to the feelings, notions,
ideas, and spirit of the farmers of Salem Village. At
their meetings, they showed a continually increasing
strength of opposition to him, and were careful to
appoint committees who could not be brought under
his influence, and would stand firm against all outside
pressure.

It is quite apparent, that Mr. Parris employed his
church, and the ministerial offices generally, as engines
to operate against his opponents ; and sometimes rather
unscrupulously, as a collocation of dates and entries
shows. A meeting of the parish was warned to be
held Oct. 16, 1691. It was important to bring his
machinery to bear upon the feelings of the people, so
as to strengthen the hands of his friends at that meeting. The following entry is in the church-book, dated
8th October, 1691: " Being my Lecture-day, after public service was ended, I was so bare of firewood, that I
was forced publicly to desire the inhabitants to take
care that I might be provided for ; telling them, that,
had it not been for Mr. Corwin (who had bought wood,
being then at my house), I should hardly have any to
burn." According to his own account, as we have
seen, it had been arranged, by mutual agreement, that
he was to provide his own firewood, six pounds per
annum having been added to his salary for that purpose. He selected that item as one of the necessaries
of which he was in want, probably because, as the win
ter was approaching, it would be the best point on

which to appeal to the public sympathies, and get up a clamor against his opponents.

The parish meeting was duly held on the 16th of October. Mr. Parris's speech, at the preceding Lecture-day, about " firewood," was found not to have produced the desired effect. The majority against him was as strong as ever. A committee made up of his opponents was elected. A motion to instruct them to make a rate was rejected, and a warrant ordered to be forth-with issued for a special meeting of the inhabitants, to examine into all the circumstances connected with the settlement of Mr. Parris, and to ascertain whether the meetings which had acted therein were legally called, and by what means the right and title of the parish to its ministry house and lands had been brought into question. This was pressing matters to an issue. Mr. Parris saw it, and determined to meet it in advance. He resorted to his church, as usual, to execute his plan, as the following entries on the record-book show : —

" 1 Nov. 1691. — The pastor desired the brethren to meet at my house, on to-morrow, an hour and half before sundown.

" 2 Nov. 1691. — After sunset, about seventeen of the brethren met; to whom, after prayer, I spoke to this effect : Brethren, I have not much to trouble you with now ; but you know what committee, the last town-meeting here, were chosen ; and what they have done, or intend to do ; it may be better than I. But, you see, I have hardly any wood to burn. I need say no more, but leave the matter to your serious and godly consideration.

"In fine, after some discourse to and fro, the church voted that Captain Putnam and the two deacons should go, as messengers from the church, to the committee, to desire them to make a rate for the minister, and to take care of necessary supplies for him; and that said messengers should make their return to the church the next tenth day, an hour before sunset, at the minister's house, where they would expect it.

"10 Nov. 1691. — The messengers abovesaid came with their return, as appointed; which was, that the committee did not see good to take notice of their message, without they had some letter to show under the church's and pastor's hand. But, at this last church meeting, besides the three messengers, but three other brethren did appear, — namely, Brother Thomas Putnam, Thomas Wilkins, and Peter Prescot, — which slight and neglect of other brethren did not a little trouble me, as I expressed myself. But I told these brethren I expected the church should be more mindful of me than other people, and their way was plain before them, &c.

"Sab: 15 Nov. 1691. — The church were desired to meet at Brother Nathaniel Putnam's, the next 18th instant, at twelve o'clock, to spend some time in prayer, and seeking God's presence with us, the next Lord's Day, at his table, as has been usual with us, some time before the sacrament.

"18 Nov. 1691. — After some time spent, as above said, at this church meeting, the pastor desired the brethren to stay, forasmuch as he had somewhat to offer to them, which was to this purpose; viz.: Brethren, several church meetings have been occasionally warned, and sometimes the appearance of the brethren is but small to what it might be expected, and particularly the case mentioned 10th instant. I told them I did not desire to warn meetings unnecessarily, and, therefore, when I did, I prayed them they would regularly attend them.

"Furthermore, I told them I had scarce wood enough to burn till the morrow, and prayed that some care might be taken. In fine, after discourses passed, these following votes were made unanimously, namely : —

"1. That it was needful that complaint should be made to the next honored County Court, to sit at Salem, the next third day of the week, against the neglects of the present committee.

"2. That the said complaint should be drawn up, which was immediately done by one of the brethren, and consented to.

"3. That our brethren, Nathaniel Putnam, Thomas Putnam, and Thomas Wilkins, should sign said complaint in behalf of the church.

"4. Last, That our brethren, Captain John Putnam and the two deacons, should be improved to present the said complaint to the said Court.

"In the mean time, the pastor desired the brethren that care might be taken that he might not be destitute of wood."

The record proceeds to give several other votes, the object of which was to arrange the details of the manner in which the business was to be put into court. There we leave it for the present, and there it remained for nearly seven years. Mr. Parris probably got the start of his opponents, in being first to invoke the law. This is what he meant when he told his church " that their way was plain before them." If extraordinary and unforeseen circumstances had not intervened, the case would more speedily have been disposed of, and we cannot doubt what would have been its issue. Whatever might be the bias or preju- dice of the courts, or however they might have at- tempted to enforce their first decisions, there can be no question, that, in such a contest, the people would have finally prevailed. The committee were men com- petent to carry the parish through. A religious society, with such feelings between them and their minister, after all that had happened, and the just grounds given them of dissatisfaction and resentment, could not always, or long, have been kept under such an infliction.

In the immediately preceding entries, there are some points that illustrate the policy on which Mr. Parris acted, and exhibit the skill and vigilance of his man- agement. The motive that led him to harp so con- stantly upon " firewood " is obvious. It was to create a sympathy in his behalf, and bring opprobrium upon his opponents. But it cannot stand the test of scru- tiny : for it had been expressly agreed, as I have said, that he should find his own fuel ; and it cannot be sup- posed that his friends, if he then had any real ones, surrounded, as they were, with forests of their own, within sight of the parsonage, would have allowed him to suffer from this cause. There is indication that the " brethren of the church " were getting luke-warm, as their non-attendance at important meetings led Mr. Parris to fear. At any rate, he felt it neces-sary to administer some rather significant rebukes to them. The meeting for prayer, preparatory to the en-suing communion service, was very adroitly converted into a business consultation to inaugurate a lawsuit. But the most characteristic thing, in this part of the church-book, is a marginal entry, against the first paragraph of the record of the 2d November, 1691. It is in these words : —

" The town-meeting, about or at 16th October last. Jos : Porter, Jos : Hutchinson, Jos : Putnam, Dan : Andrew, Francis Nurse."

These were the committee appointed at the meeting. Their names, thus abbreviated, are given, and not a syllable added. But the manner, the then state of things, and their relation to the controversy, give a deep import and intense bitterness to this entry. He knew the men, and in their names read the hand-writing on the wall.

But a turn was soon given to the current that was bearing Mr. Parris down. A power was evoked — whether he raised it designedly, or whether it merely happened to appear on the scene, we cannot certainly say ; but it came into action just at the nick of time — which instantly reversed the position of the parties, and clothed him with a terrible strength, enabling him to crush his opponents beneath his feet. In a few short

months, he was the arbiter of life and death of all the
people of the village and the country. "Jos: Porter
and Jos: Hutchinson" escaped. The power of destruction broke down before it became strong enough
to reach them perhaps. "Jos: Putnam" was kept for
six months in the constant peril of his life. During all
that time, he and his family were armed, and kept
watch. "Dan: Andrew" saved himself from the
gallows by flight to a foreign land. The unutterable
woes brought upon the family of "Francis Nurse" remain to be related.

The witchcraft delusion at Salem Village, in 1692,
has attracted universal attention, constitutes a permanent chapter in the world's history, and demands a full
exposition, and, if possible, a true solution. Being
convinced that it cannot be correctly interpreted without a thorough knowledge of the people among whom
it appeared, I have felt it indispensable, before opening
its scenes to view, or treating the subject of demonology, of which it was an outgrowth, in the first place
to prepare myself, and those who accompany me in its
examination and discussion, to fully comprehend it, by
traversing the ground over which we have now passed.
By a thorough history of Salem Village from its origin
to the period of our story, by calling its founders and
their children and successors into life before you by
personal, private, domestic, and local details, gleaned
from old records and documents, I have tried to place
you at the standpoint from which the entire occurrence
can be intelligibly contemplated. We can in no other

way get a true view of a passage of history than by
looking at the men who acted in it, as they really were.
We must understand their characters, enter into their
life, see with their eyes, feel with their hearts, and
be enveloped, as it were, with their associations, sentiments, beliefs, and principles of action. In this way
only can we bring the past into our presence, comprehend its elements, fathom its depths, read its meaning,
or receive its lessons.

I am confident you will agree with me, that it was
not because the people of Salem Village were more
ignorant, stupid, or weak-minded than the people of
other places, that the delusion made its appearance or
held its sway among them. This is a vital point to the
just consideration of the subject. I do not mean
justice to them so much as to ourselves and all who
wish to understand, and be benefited by understanding, the subject. There never was a community composed originally of better materials, or better trained
in all good usages. Although the generations subsequent to the first had not enjoyed, to any considerable
extent, the advantages of education, the circumstances
of their experience had kept their faculties in the fullest exercise. They were an energetic and intelligent
people. Their moral condition, social intercourse,
manners, and personal bearing, were excellent. The
lesson of the catastrophe impending over them, at the
point to which we have arrived, can only be truly
and fully received, for the warning of all coming time,
by having correct views on this point. The delusion

that brought ruin upon them was not the result of any essential inferiority in their moral or intellectual condition. What we call their ignorance was the received philosophy and wisdom of the day, accepted generally by the great scholars of that and previous ages, preached from the pulpits, taught in the universities, recognized in law and in medicine as well as theology, and carried out in the proceedings of public tribunals and legislative assemblies.

The history of the planting, settlement, and progress of Salem Village, to 1692, has now been given. We know, so far as existing materials within reach enable us to know, what sort of a population occupied the place at the date of our story. Their descent, breeding, and experiences have been related. They were, at least, equal in intelligence to any of the people of their day. They were strenuous in action, trained to earnestness and zeal, accustomed to become deeply engaged in whatever interested them, and to take strong hold of the ideas and sentiments they received. It becomes necessary, therefore, in the next place, to ascertain what their ideas were in reference to witchcraft, diabolical agency, and supernaturalism generally. I shall proceed accordingly to give the condition of opinion, at that time, on the subject of demonology.

PART SECOND.

PART SECOND

WITCHCRAFT.

DEMONOLOGY, as a general term, may be employed, for convenience, to include a whole class of ideas — which, under different names and a vast variety of conceptions, have come through all ages, and prevailed among all races of mankind — relating to the supposed agency of supernatural, invisible, and spiritual beings in terrestrial affairs. As necessarily applicable to evil spirits, particularly to the arch-enemy and supreme adversary of God and man under the name of Satan or the Devil, the term does not appear to have been used in ancient times. Professed communications with supernatural beings were not originally stamped with a diabolical character, but, like some alleged to be had in our day, were regarded as innocent, and even creditable. Men sought to hold intercourse with spirits belonging to the unseen world, as some persons do now; assuming that they were worthy of confidence, and that responses from them were valuable and desirable. This was the case under the reign of classical mythology, and of heathen superstition in general. Those individuals who were supposed to be conversant with demons were looked upon by the credulous multitude as a highly privileged class; and they arrogated the credit of being raised to a higher sphere of knowledge than the rest of mankind.

It is one of the most remarkable peculiarities of the Hebrew polity, that it denounced such pretended communications as criminal, and subjected the practice to the highest penalties. It was assumed to be dangerous; the welfare of individuals and of society requiring that such pretensions and practices should be abandoned. The observation and experience of mankind have justified this view. In the first ages of Christianity, it was believed that the Divine Being alone was to be sought in prayer for light and guidance by the human soul. Gradually, as the dark ages began to settle upon Christendom, the doctrine of the Devil as the head and ruler of a world of demons, and as able to hold communications with mortals, to interfere in their affairs, and to exercise more or less control over the laws and phenomena of nature, began to become prevalent. It was believed that human beings could enter into alliance with the Prince of the power of the air; become his confederates; join in a league with him and wicked spirits subordinate to him, in undermining the Gospel and overthrowing the Church; and conspire and co-operate in rebellion against God. This, of course, was regarded as the most flagrant of crimes, and constituted the real character of the sin denominated " witchcraft."

As the fullest, most memorable, and, by the notice it has ever since attracted throughout the world, the pre-eminent instance and demonstration of this supposed iniquity was in the crisis that took place in Salem Village in 1692, it justly claims a place in history. The community in which it occurred has been fully described, in its moral, social, and intellectual condition, so far as the materials I have been enabled to obtain have rendered possible. It has, I believe, been made to appear, that, in their training, experience, and traits of character, they were well adapted to give full effect to any excitement, or earnest action of any kind, that could be got up among them, — a people of great energy, courage, and resolution, well prepared to carry out to its natural and legitimate results any movement, and follow established convictions fearlessly to logical conclusions. The experiment of bringing supernaturalism to operate in human affairs, to become a ground of action in society, and to interfere in the relations of life and the dealings of men with each other, was as well tried upon this people as it ever could or can be anywhere.

All that remains to be brought to view, before entering upon the details of the narrative, is to give a just and adequate idea of the form and shape in which the general subject of supernaturalism, in its aspect as demonology, lay in the minds of men here at that time. To do this, I must give a sketch, as condensed and brief as I can make it, of the formation and progress of opinions and notions touching the subject, until they reached their full demonstration and final explosion, in this neighborhood, at Salem Village, near the close of the seventeenth century.

No person who looks around him on the scene in which he is placed, reflects upon the infinite wonders of creation, and meditates upon the equal wonders of his own mind, can be at a loss respecting the sources and causes of superstition. Let him transport himself back to the condition of a primitive and unlettered people, before whom the world appears in all its original and sublime mystery. Science has not lifted to their eyes the curtain behind which the secret operations of nature are carried on. They observe the tides rise and fall, but know not the attractive law that regulates their movements; they contemplate the procession of the seasons, without any conception of the principles and causes that determine and produce their changes; they witness the storm as it rises in its wrath; they listen with awe to the thunder-peal, and gaze with startling terror upon the lightning as it flashes from within the bosom of the black cloud, and are utterly ignorant to what power to attribute the dreadful phenomena; they look upward to the face of the sky, and see the myriad starry hosts that glitter there, and all is to them a mighty maze of dazzling confusion. It is for their fancy to explain, interpret, and fill up the brilliant and magnificent scene.

The imagination was the faculty the exercise of which was chiefly called for in such a state as this. Before science had traced the operations and unfolded the secrets of nature, man was living in a world full of marvel and mystery. His curiosity was attracted to every object within the reach of his senses; and, in the absence of knowledge, it was imagination alone that could make answer to its inquiries. It is natural to suppose that he would be led to attribute all the movements and operations of the external world which did not appear to be occasioned by the exercise of his own power, or the power of any other animal, to the agency of supernatural beings. We may also conclude, that his belief would not be likely to fix upon the notion of a single overruling Being. Although revelation and science have disclosed to us a beautiful and entire unity and harmony in the creation, the phenomena of the external world would probably impress the unenlightened and unphilosophic observer with the belief that there was a diversity in the powers which caused them. He would imagine the agency of a being of an amiable and beneficent spirit in the bright sunshine, the fresh breeze, and the mild moonlight; and his fancy would suggest to his fears, that a dark, severe, and terrible being was in the ascendant during a day overshadowed by frowning clouds, or a night black with the storm and torn by the tempest.

By the aid of such reflections as these, we are easily conducted to a satisfactory and sufficient explanation of the origin of the mythology and fabulous superstitions of all ancient and primitive nations. From this the progress is plain, obvious, and immediate to the pretensions of magicians, diviners, sorcerers, conjurers, oracles, soothsayers, augurs, and the whole catalogue of those persons who professed to hold intercourse with higher and spiritual powers. There are several classes into which they may be divided.

There were those who, to acquire an influence over the people, pretended to possess the confidence, and enjoy the friendship and counsel, of some one or more deities. Such was Numa, the early lawgiver of the Roman State. In order to induce the people to adopt the regulations, institutions, and religious rites he proposed, he made them believe that he had access to a divinity, and received all his plans and ideas as a communication from on high.

Persons who, in consequence of their superior acquirements, were enabled to excel others in any pursuit, or who could foresee and avail themselves of events in the natural world, were liable, without any intention to deceive, to be classed under some of these denominations. For instance, a Roman farmer, Furius Cresinus, surpassed all his neighbors in the skill and success with which he managed his agricultural affairs. He was accordingly accused of using magic arts in the operations of his farm. So far were his neighbors carried by their feelings of envy and jealousy, that they explained the fact of his being able to derive more produce from a small lot of land than they could from large ones, by charging him with attracting and drawing off the productions of their fields into his own by the employment of certain mysterious charms. For his defence, as we are informed by Pliny, he produced his strong and well-constructed ploughs, his light and convenient spades, and his sun-burnt daughters, and pointing to them exclaimed: "Here are my charms; this is my magic; these only are the witchcraft I have used." Zoroaster, the great philosopher and astronomer of the ancient East, was charged with divination and magic, merely, it is probable, because he possessed uncommon acquirements.

There were persons who had acquired an extraordinary amount of natural knowledge, and, for the sake of being regarded with wonder and awe by the people, pretended to obtain their superior endowments from supernatural beings. They affected the name and character of sorcerers, diviners, and soothsayers. It is easy to conceive of the early existence and the great influence of such impostors. Patient observation, and often mere accident, would suggest discoveries of the existence and operation of natural causes in producing phenomena before ascribed to superhuman agency. The knowledge thus acquired would be cautiously concealed, and cunningly used, to create astonishment and win admiration. Its fortunate possessors were enabled to secure the confidence, obedience, and even reverence, of the benighted and deceived people.

Every one, indeed, who could discover a secret of

nature, and keep it secret, was able to impose himself on the world as being allied with supernatural powers. Hence arose the whole host of diviners, astrologers, soothsayers, and oracles. After having once acquired possession of the credulous faith of the people, they could impose upon them almost without limit.

Those who pretended to hold this kind of intercourse with divinity became, as a natural consequence, the priests of the nation, constituted a distinct and regular profession, and perpetuated their body by the admission of new members, to whom they explained their arts, and communicated their knowledge. While they were continually discovering and applying the secret principles and laws of nature, and the people were kept in utter ignorance and darkness, it is no wonder that they reached a great and unparalleled degree of power over the mass of the population. In this manner we account for the origin, and trace the history, of the Chaldean priests in Assyria, the Bramins of India, the Magi of Persia, the Oracles of Greece, the Augurs of Italy, the Druids of Britain, and the Pow-wows, Prophets, or " Medicins," as they sometimes called them, among our Indians.

It is probable that the witches mentioned in the Scriptures were of this description. Neither in sacred nor profane ancient history do we find what was understood in the days of our ancestors by witchcraft, which meant a formal and actual compact with the great Prince of evil beings. The sorcery of antiquity consisted in pretending to possess certain mysterious charms, and to do by their means, or by the co-operation of superhuman spirits, without any reference to their character as evil or good beings, what transcends the action of mere natural powers.

The witch of Endor, for instance, was a conjurer and necromancer, rather than a witch. By referring to the 28th chapter of 1 Samuel, where the interview between her and Saul is related, you will find no ground for the opinion that the being from whom she pretended to receive her mysterious power was Satan. Saul, as the ruler of a people who were under the special government, and enjoyed the peculiar protection of the true God, had forbidden, under the sanction of the highest penalties, the exercise of the arts of divination and sorcery within his jurisdiction. Some time after this, the unfortunate monarch was overtaken by trouble and distress. His enemies had risen up, and were gathered in fearful strength around him. His "heart greatly trembled," a dark and gloomy presentiment came over his spirit, and his bosom was convulsed by an agony of solicitude. He turned toward his God for light and strength. He applied for relief to the priests of the altar, and to the prophets of the Most High; but his prayers were unanswered, and his efforts vain. In his sorrow and apprehension, he appealed to a woman who was reputed to have supernatural powers, and to hold communion with spiritual beings; thus violating his own law, and departing from duty and fidelity to his God. He begged her to recall Samuel to life, that he might be comforted and instructed by him. She pretended to comply with his request; but, before she could commence her usual mysterious operations, Samuel arose! and the forlorn, wretched, and heart-broken king listened to his tremendous doom, as it was uttered by the spirit of the departed prophet.

I have alluded particularly to the witch of Endor, because she will serve to illustrate the sorcery or divination of antiquity. She was probably possessed of some secret knowledge of natural properties; was skilful in the use of her arts and pretended charms; had, perhaps, the peculiar powers of a ventriloquist; and, by successful imposture, had acquired an uncommon degree of notoriety, and the entire confidence of the public. She professed to be in alliance with supernatural beings, and, by their assistance, to raise the dead.

This passage has afforded a topic for a great deal of discussion among interpreters. It seems to me, on the face of the narrative, to suggest the following view of the transaction: The woman was an impostor. When she summoned the spirit of Samuel, instead of the results of her magic lantern, or of whatever contrivances she may have had, by the immediate agency of the Almighty the spirit of Samuel really rose, to the consternation and horror of the pretended necromancer. The writer appears to have indicated this as the proper interpretation of the scene, by saying, " that, when the woman saw Samuel, she cried with a loud voice;" thus giving evidence of alarm and surprise totally different from the deportment of such pretenders on such occasions: they used rather to exhibit joy at the success of their arts, and a proud composure and dignified complacency in the control they were believed to exercise over the spirits that appeared to have obeyed their call. Sir Walter Scott took this view of the transaction. His opinion, it is true, would be considered more important in any other department than that of biblical interpretation: on all questions, however, connected with the spiritual world of fancy and with its history, he must be allowed to speak, if not with the authority, at least with the tone of a master. This wonderful author, in the infinite profusion and variety of his productions, published a volume upon Demonology and Witchcraft: it is, of course, entertaining and instructive to all who are curious to know the capacity and to appreciate the operations of the human imagination.

It will be regarded by intelligent and judicious persons as a circumstance of importance in reference to the view now given of the transaction in which the witch of Endor acts the leading part, that Hugh Farmer, beyond all question the most learned, discreet, and profound writer on such subjects, is inclined to throw the weight of his authority in its favor. His ample and elaborate discussion of the question is to be seen in his work on Miracles, chap. iv. sec. 2.

Among the heathen nations of antiquity, the art of divination consisted, to a great degree, in the magical

use of mysterious charms. Many plants were considered as possessed of wonderful virtues, and there was
scarcely a limit to the supposed power of those persons
who knew how to use and apply them skilfully. Virgil,
in his eighth eclogue, thus speaks of this species of
sorcery : —

> " These herbs did Mœris give to me
>   And poisons pluckt at Pontus ;
> For there they grow and multiplie
>   And do not so amongst us :
> With these she made herselfe become
>   A wolfe, and hid hir in the wood ;
> She fetcht up souls out of their toome,
>   Removing corne from where it stood."

In the fourth Æneid, the lovesick Tyrian queen is
thus made to describe the magic which was then believed to be practised : —

> " Rejoice," she said : " instructed from above,
> My lover I shall gain, or lose my love ;
> Nigh rising Atlas, next the falling sun
> Long tracts of Ethiopian climates run :
> There a Massylian priestess I have found,
> Honored for age, for magic arts renowned :
> The Hesperian temple was her trusted care ;
> 'Twas she supplied the wakeful dragon's fare ;
> She, poppy-seeds in honey taught to steep,
> Reclaimed his rage, and soothed him into sleep ;
> She watched the golden fruit. Her charms unbind
> The chains of love, or fix them on the mind ;
> She stops the torrent, leaves the channel dry,
> Repels the stars, and backward bears the sky.
> The yawning earth rebellows to her call,
> Pale ghosts ascend, and mountain ashes fall."

Tibullus, in the second elegy of his first book, gives the following account of the powers ascribed to a magician : —

> " She plucks each star out of his throne,
>   And turneth back the raging waves ;
> With charms she makes the earth to cone,
>   And raiseth souls out of their graves ;
> She burns men's bones as with a fire,
>   And pulleth down the lights of Heaven,
> And makes it snow at her desire
>   E'en in the midst of summer season."

These views continued to hold undisturbed dominion over the people during a long succession of centuries. As the twilight of the dark ages began to settle upon Christendom, superstition, that night-blooming plant, extended itself rapidly, and in all directions, over the surface of the world. While every thing else drooped and withered, it struck deeper its roots, spread wider its branches, and brought forth more abundantly its fruit. The unnumbered fables of Greek and Roman mythology, the arts of augury and divination, the visions of oriental romance, the fanciful and attenuated theories of the later philosophy, the abstract and spiritual doctrines of Platonism, and all the grosser and wilder conceptions of the northern conquerors of the Roman Empire, became mingled together in the faith of the inhabitants of the European kingdoms. From this multifarious combination, the infinitely diversified popular superstitions of the modern nations have sprung.

We first begin to trace the clear outlines of the doctrine of witchcraft not far from the commencement of the Christian era. It presupposes the belief of the Devil. I shall not enter upon the question, whether the Scriptures, properly interpreted, require the belief of the existence of such a being. Directing our attention solely to profane sources of information, we discover the heathen origin of the belief of the existence of the Devil in the ancient systems of oriental philosophy. Early observers of nature in the East were led to the conclusion, that the world was a divided empire, ruled by the alternate or simultaneous energy of two great antagonist principles or beings, one perfectly good, and the other perfectly bad. It was for a long time, and perhaps is at this day, a prevalent faith among Christians, that the Bible teaches a similar doctrine; that it presents, to our adoration and obedience, a being of infinite perfections in the Deity; and to our abhorrence and our fears, a being infinitely wicked, and of great power, in the Devil.

It is obvious, that, when the entire enginery of supernaturalism was organized in adaptation to the idea of the Devil, and demonology became synonymous with diabolism, the credulity and superstition of mankind would give a wide extension to that form of belief. It soon occupied a large space in the theories of religion and the fancies of the people, and got to be a leading element in the life of society. It made its impress on the forms of speech, and many of the phrases to which it gave rise still remain in familiar use. It figured in the rituals of religion, in the paraphernalia of public shows, and in fireside tales. It afforded leading characters to the drama in the miracle plays and the moral plays, as they were called, at successive periods. It offered a ready weapon to satire, and also to defamation. Gerbert, a native of France, who was elevated to the pontificate about the close of the tenth century, under the name of Sylvester II., is eulogized by Mosheim as the first great restorer of science and literature. He was a person of an extensive and sublime genius, of wonderful attainments in learning, particularly mathematics, geometry, and arithmetic. He broke the profound sleep of the dark ages, and awakened the torpid intellect of the European nations. His efforts in this direction roused the apprehensions and resentment of the monks; and they circulated, after Gerbert's death, and made the ignorant masses believe the story, that he had obtained his rapid promotion in the Church by the practice of the black art, which he disguised under the show of learning; that he secured the Archbishopric of Ravenna by bribery and corruption; and that, finally, he made a bargain with Satan, promising him his soul after death, on condition that he (Satan) should put forth his great influence over the cardinals in such a manner as would secure his election to the throne of St. Peter. The arrangement was carried into successful operation. Sylvester, the monks averred, consulted the Devil through the medium of a brazen head during his whole reign, and enjoyed his faithful friendship and unwavering patronage. But, when His Holiness came to die, he endeavored to defraud Satan of his rightful claim to his soul, by repenting, and acknowledging his sin. This illustrates the way in which the popular idea of the Devil was used to awaken ridicule and gratify malignity.

The natural and ultimate effect of the diffusion of Christianity was to overthrow, or rather to revolutionize, the whole system of incantation and sorcery.

In heathen countries, as in the East at present and with those among us who profess to hold communications with spirits, no reproach or sentiment of disapprobation, as has already been observed, was necessarily connected with the arts of divination ; for the supernatural beings with whom intercourse was alleged to be had were not, with a few exceptions, regarded as evil beings. The persons who were thought to be skilful in their use were, on the contrary, held in great esteem, and looked upon with reverence. Magicians and philosophers were convertible and synonymous terms. Learned and scientific men were induced to encourage, and turn to their own advantage, the popular credulity that ascribed their extraordinary skill to their connection with spiritual and divine beings. At length, however, they found themselves placed in a very uncomfortable predicament by the prevalence of the new theology. It was exceedingly difficult to dispel the delusion, and correct the error they had previously found it for their interest to perpetuate in the minds of the community. They could not convince them that their knowledge was acquired from natural sources, or their operations conducted solely by the aid of natural causes and laws. The people would not surrender the belief, that the results of scientific experiments, and the accuracy of predictions of physical phenomena, were secured by the assistance of supernatural beings.

As the doctrines of the gospel gradually undermined the popular belief in other spiritual beings inferior to the Deity, and were at the same time supposed to teach the existence and extensively diffused energy of an almost infinite and omnipotent agent of evil, it was exceedingly natural, nay, it necessarily followed, that the credulity and superstition which had led to the supposition of an alliance between philosophers and spiritual beings should settle down into a full conviction that the Devil was the being with whom they were thus confederated. The consequence was that they were charged with witchcraft, and many fell victims to the general prejudice and abhorrence occasioned by the imputation. The influence of this state of things was soon seen: it was one of the most effectual causes of the rapid diffusion of knowledge in modern times. Philosophers and men of science became as anxious to explain and publish their discoveries as they had been in former ages to conceal and cover them with mystery. The following instances will be sufficient to illustrate the correctness of these views.

In the thirteenth century, Roger Bacon was charged with witchcraft on account of his discoveries in optics, chemistry, and astronomy; and, although he did what he could to circulate and explain his own acquirements, he could not escape a papal denunciation, and two long and painful imprisonments. In 1305, Arnold de Villa Nova, a learned physician and philosopher, was burned at Padua, by order of inquisitors, on the charge of witchcraft. He was eighty years of age. Ten years afterwards, Peter Apon, also of Padua, who had made extraordinary progress in knowledge, was accused of the same crime, and condemned to death, but expired previous to the time appointed for his execution.

I will now present a brief sketch of the most noticeable facts relating to the subject in Europe and Great Britain previous to the close of the seventeenth century. Some writers have computed that thirty thousand persons were executed for this supposed crime, within one hundred and fifty years. It will of course be in my power to mention only a few instances.

In 1484, Pope Innocent the Eighth issued a bull encouraging and requiring the arrest and punishment of persons suspected of witchcraft. From this moment, the prosecutions became frequent and the victims numerous in every country. The very next year, forty-one aged females were consigned to the flames in one nation; and, not long after, a hundred were burned by one inquisition in the devoted valleys of Piedmont; forty-eight were burned in Ravensburg in five years; and, in the year 1515, five hundred were burned at Geneva in three months! One writer de-

clares that " almost an infinite number " were burned
for witchcraft in France, — a thousand in a single
diocese! These sanguinary and horrible transactions
were promoted and sanctioned by theological hatred
and rancor. It was soon perceived that there was no
kind of difficulty in clearing the Church of heretics
by hanging or burning them all as witches! The imputation of witchcraft could be fixed upon any one
with the greatest facility. In the earlier part of the
fifteenth century, the Earl of Bedford, having taken
the celebrated Joan of Arc prisoner, put her to death
on this charge. She had been almost adored by the
people rescued by her romantic valor, and was universally known among them by the venerable title of
" Holy Maid of God ; " but no difficulty was experienced in procuring evidence enough to lead her to the
stake as a servant and confederate of Satan! Luther
was just beginning his attack upon the papal power,
and he was instantly accused of being in confederacy
with the Devil.

In 1534, Elizabeth Barton, " the Maid of Kent,"
was executed for witchcraft in England, together with
seven men who had been confederate with her. In
1541 the Earl of Hungerford was beheaded for in-
quiring of a witch how long Henry VIII. would live.
In 1549 it was made the duty of bishops, by Archbishop Cranmer's articles of visitation, to inquire of
their clergy, whether " they know of any that use
charms, sorcery, enchantments, witchcraft, soothsay-
ing, or any like craft invented by the Devil." In 1563

the King of Sweden carried four witches with him, as
a part of his armament, to aid him in his wars with
the Danes. In 1576, seventeen or eighteen were condemned in Essex, in England. A single judge or in-
quisitor, Remigius, condemned and burned nine hundred within fifteen years, from 1580 to 1595, in the
single district of Lorraine ; and as many more fled out
of the country ; whole villages were depopulated, and
fifteen persons destroyed themselves rather than submit to the torture which, under the administration
of this successor of Draco and rival of Jeffries, was
the first step taken in the trial of an accused person.
The application of the rack and other instruments of
torment, in the examination of prisoners, was recommended by him in a work on witchcraft. He observes
that " scarcely any one was known to be brought to
repentance and confession but by these means " !

The most eminent persons of the sixteenth century
were believers in the popular superstition respecting
the existence of compacts between Satan and human
beings, and in the notions associated with it. The excellent Melancthon was an interpreter of dreams and
caster of nativities. Luther was a strenuous supporter of the doctrine of witchcraft, and seems to have
seriously believed that he had had frequent interviews
with the arch-enemy himself, and had disputed with
him on points of theology, face to face. In his " Table-
Talk," he gives the following account of his intimacy
with the Devil: speaking of his confinement in the
Castle of Wartburg, he says, " Among other things

they brought me hazel-nuts, which I put into a box, and sometimes I used to crack and eat of them. In the night-times, my gentleman, the Devil, came and got the nuts out of the box, and cracked them against one of the bedposts, making a very great noise and rumbling about my bed; but I regarded him nothing at all: when afterwards I began to slumber, then he kept such a racket and rumbling upon the chamber stairs, as if many empty barrels and hogsheads had been tumbled down." Kepler, whose name is immortalized by being associated with the laws he discovered that regulate the orbits of the heavenly bodies, was a zealous advocate of astrology; and his great predecessor and master, the Prince of Astronomers, as he is called, Tycho Brahe, kept an idiot in his presence, fed him from his own table, with his own hand, and listened to his incoherent, unmeaning, and fatuous expressions as to a revelation from the spiritual world.

The following is the language addressed to Queen Elizabeth by Bishop Jewell. He was one of the most learned persons of his age, and is to this day regarded as the mighty champion of the Church of England, and of the cause of the Reformation in Great Britain. He was the terrible foe of Roman-Catholic superstition. "It may please Your Grace," says he, "to understand that witches and sorcerers within these four last years are marvellously increased within Your Grace's realm; Your Grace's subjects pine away even unto the death; their color fadeth, their flesh rotteth, their speech is benumbed, their senses are bereft. I

pray God," continues the courtly preacher, " they
never practise further than upon the subject." The
petition of the polite prelate appears to have been
answered. The virgin queen resisted inexorably the
arts of all charmers, and is thought never to have
been bewitched in her life.

It is probable that Spenser, in his " Faërie Queen,"
has described with accuracy the witch of the sixteenth
century in the following beautiful lines : —

> " There, in a gloomy hollow glen, she found
> A little cottage built of sticks and weedes,
> In homely wise, and wald with sods around,
> In which a witch did dwell in loathly weedes
> And wilful want, all careless of her needes ;
> So choosing solitarie to abide
> Far from all neighbors, that her devilish deedes
> And hellish arts from people she might hide,
> And hurt far off unknowne whomever she envide."

So prone were some to indulge in the contemplation of the agency of the Devil and his myrmidons, that
they strained, violated, and perverted the language of
Scripture to make it speak of them. Thus they insisted that the word " Philistines " meant confederates
and subjects of the Devil, and accordingly interpreted
the expression, " I will deliver you into the hands of
the Philistines," thus, " I will deliver you into the
hands of demons."

I cannot describe the extent to which the superstition we are reviewing was carried about the close of
the sixteenth century in stronger language than the
following, from a candid and learned French Roman-

Catholic historian: "So great folly," says he, "did then oppress the miserable world, that Christians believed greater absurdities than could ever be imposed upon the heathens."

We have now arrived at the commencement of the seventeenth century, within which the prosecutions for witchcraft took place in Salem. To show the opinions of the clergy of the English Church at this time, I will quote the following curious canon, made by the convocation in 1603 : —

"That no minister or ministers, without license and direction of the bishop, under his hand and seal obtained, attempt, upon any pretence whatsoever, either of possession or obsession, by fasting and prayer, to cast out any devil or devils, under pain of the imputation of imposture or cozenage, and deposition from the ministry." In the same year, licenses were actually granted, as required above, by the Bishop of Chester ; and several ministers were duly authorized by him to cast out devils !

During this whole century, there were trials and executions for witchcraft in all civilized countries. More than two hundred were hanged in England, thousands were burned in Scotland, and still larger numbers in various parts of Europe.

Edward Fairfax, the poet, was one of the most accomplished men in England. He is celebrated as the translator of Tasso's "Jerusalem Delivered," in allusion to which work Collins thus speaks of him : —

" How have I sate, while piped the pensive wind,
  To hear thy harp, by British Fairfax strung,
Prevailing poet, whose undoubting mind
  Believed the magic wonders that he sung."

This same Fairfax prosecuted six of his neighbors
for bewitching his children. The trials took place
about the time the first pilgrims came to America.

In 1634, Urbain Grandier, a very learned and eminent French minister, rendered himself odious to the
bigoted nuns of Loudun, by his moderation towards
heretics. Secretly instigated, as has been supposed, by
Cardinal Richelieu, against whom he had written a
satire, they pretended to be bewitched by him, and procured his prosecution : he was tortured upon the rack
until he swooned, and then was burned at the stake.
In 1640, Dr. Lamb, of London, was murdered in the
streets of that city by the mob, on suspicion of witchcraft. Several were hanged in England, only a few
years before the proceedings commenced in Salem.
Some were tried by water ordeal, and drowned in the
process, in Suffolk, Essex, Cambridgeshire, and North-
amptonshire, at the very time the executions were
going on here ; and a considerable number of capital
punishments took place in various parts of Great Britain, some years after the prosecution had ceased in
America.

The trials and executions in England and Scotland
were attended by circumstances as painful, as barbarous, and in all respects as disgraceful, as those. occurring in Salem. Every species of torture seems to

have been resorted to : the principles of reason, justice, and humanity were set at defiance, and the whole body of the people kept in a state of the most fierce excitement against the sufferers. Indeed, there is nothing more distressing in the contemplation of these sanguinary proceedings than the spirit of deliberate and unmitigated cruelty with which they were conducted. No symptoms of pity, compassion, or sympathy, appear to have been manifested by the judges or the community. The following account of the expenses attending the execution of two persons convicted of witchcraft in Scotland, shows in what a cool, business-like style the affair was managed : —

" For ten loads of coal, to burn them £3 6 8
For a tar barrel 0 14 0
For towes 0 6 0
For hurden to be jumps for them 3 10 0
For making of them 0 8 0
For one to go to Finmouth for the Laird to sit
    upon their assize as judge 0 6 0
For the executioner for his pains 8 14 0
For his expenses here . . . . 0 16 4 "

The brutalizing effects of capital punishments are clearly seen in these, as in all other instances. They gradually impart a feeling of indifference to the value of human life, or to the idea of cutting it off by the hand of violence, to all who become accustomed to the spectacle. In various ways they exercise influences upon the tone and temper of society, which cannot but be regarded with regret by the citizen, the legislator, the moralist, the philanthropist, and the Christian.

Sinclair, in his work called " Satan's Invisible World Discovered," gives the following affecting declaration made by one of the confessing witches, as she was on her way to the stake : —

" Now all you that see me this day know that I am now to die as a witch by my own confession ; and I free all men, especially the ministers and magistrates, of the guilt of my blood; I take it wholly upon myself, my blood be upon my own head : and, as I must make answer to the God of heaven presently, I declare I am as free of witchcraft as any child ; but, being delated by a malicious woman, and put in prison under the name of a witch, disowned by my husband and friends, and seeing no ground of hope of my coming out of prison, or ever coming in credit again, through the temptation of the Devil, I made up that confession on purpose to destroy my own life, being weary of it, and choosing rather to die than live."

Sir George Mackenzie says that he went to examine some women who had confessed, and that one of them, who was a silly creature, told him, " under secresie," " that she had not confessed because she was guilty, but, being a poor creature, who wrought for her meat, and being defamed for a witch, she knew she would starve, for no person thereafter would either give her meat or lodging, and that all men would beat her, and hound dogs at her, and that therefore she desired to be out of the world." Whereupon she wept most bitterly, and, upon her knees, called God to witness to what she said.

A wretch, named Matthew Hopkins, rendered himself infamously conspicuous in the prosecutions for witchcraft that took place in the counties of Essex, Sussex, Norfolk, and Huntingdon, in England, in the years 1645 and 1646. The title he assumed indicates the part he acted: it was "Witch-finder-general." He travelled from place to place; his expenses were paid; and he required, in addition, regular fees for the discovery of a witch. Besides pricking the body to find the witch-mark, he compelled the wretched and decrepit victims of his cruel practices to sit in a painful posture, on an elevated stool, with their limbs crossed; and, if they persevered in refusing to confess, he would prolong their torture, in some cases, to more than twenty-four hours. He would prevent their going to sleep, and drag them about barefoot over the rough ground, thus overcoming them with extreme weariness and pain: but his favorite method was to tie the thumb of the right hand close to the great toe of the left foot, and draw them through a river or pond; if they floated, as they would be likely to do, while their heavier limbs were thus sustained and upborne by the rope, it was considered as conclusive proof of their guilt. This monster was encouraged and sanctioned by the government; and he procured the death, in one year and in one county, of more than three times as many as suffered in Salem during the whole delusion. He and his exploits are referred to in the following lines, from that storehouse of good sense and keen wit, Butler's "Hudibras:" —

> "Hath not this present Parliament
> A leiger to the Devil sent,
> Fully empowered to treat about
> Finding revolted witches out?
> And has he not within a year
> Hanged threescore of them in one shire?"

The infatuated people looked upon this Hopkins with admiration and astonishment, and could only account for his success by the supposition, which, we are told, was generally entertained, that he had stolen the memorandum-book in which Satan had recorded the names of all the persons in England who were in league with him!

The most melancholy circumstance connected with the history of this creature is, that Richard Baxter and Edmund Calamy — names dear and venerable in the estimation of all virtuous and pious men — were deceived and deluded by him: they countenanced his conduct, followed him in his movements, and aided him in his proceedings.

At length, however, some gentlemen, shocked at the cruelty and suspicious of the integrity of Hopkins, seized him, tied his thumbs and toes together, threw him into a pond, and dragged him about to their hearts' content. They were fully satisfied with the result of the experiment. It was found that he did not sink. He stood condemned on his own principles; and thus the country was rescued from the power of the malicious impostor.

Among the persons whose death Hopkins procured, was a venerable, gray-headed clergyman, named Lewis. He was of the Church of England, had been the minister of a congregation for more than half a century, and was over eighty years of age. His infirm frame was subjected to the customary tests, even to the trial by water ordeal: he was compelled to walk almost incessantly for several days and nights, until, in the exhaustion of his nature, he yielded assent to a confession that was adduced against him in Court; which, however, he disowned and denied there and at all times, from the moment of release from the torments, by which it had been extorted, to his last breath. As he was about to die the death of a felon, he knew that the rites of sepulture, according to the forms of his denomination, would be denied to his remains. The aged sufferer, it is related, read his own funeral service while on the scaffold. Solemn, sublime, and affecting as are passages of this portion of the ritual of the Church, surely it was never performed under circumstances so well suited to impress with awe and tenderness as when uttered by the calumniated, oppressed, and dying old man. Baxter had been tried for sedition, on the ground that one of his publications contained a reflection upon Episcopacy, and was imprisoned for two years. It is a striking and melancholy illustration of the moral infirmity of human nature, that the author of the " Saints' Everlasting Rest," and the "Call to the Unconverted," permitted such a vengeful feeling against the Establishment to enter his breast, that he took pleasure, and almost exulted, in relating the fate of this innocent and aged clergyman, whom he denominates, in derision, a "Reading Parson."

Baxter's writings are pervaded by his belief in all sorts of supernatural things. In the "Saints' Everlasting Rest," he declares his conviction of the reality and authenticity of stories of ghosts, apparitions, haunted houses, &c. He placed full faith in a tale, current among the people of his day, of the "dispossession of the Devil out of many persons together in a room in Lancashire, at the prayer of some godly ministers." In his "Dying Thoughts," he says, "I have had many convincing proofs of witches, the contracts they have made with devils, and the power which they have received from them;" and he seems to have credited the most absurd fables ever invented on the subject by ignorance, folly, or fraud.

The case to which he refers, as one of the "dispossession of devils," may be found in a tract published in London in 1697, entitled, "The Surey Demoniac; or, an Account of Satan's strange and dreadful actings, in and about the body of Richard Dugdale, of Surey, near Whalley, in Lancashire. And how he was dispossessed by God's blessing on the Fastings and Prayers of divers Ministers and People. The matter of fact attested by the oaths of several creditable persons, before some of his Majestie's Justices of the Peace in the said county." The "London Monthly Repository" (vol. v., 1810) describes the affair as follows: "These dreadful actings of Satan continued above a year; during which there was a desperate struggle between him and nine ministers of the gospel, who had undertaken to cast him out, and, for that purpose, successively relieved each other in their daily combats with him: while Satan tried all his arts to baffle their attempts, insulting them with scoffs and raillery, puzzling them sometimes with Greek and Latin, and threatening them with the effects of his vengeance, till he was finally vanquished and put to flight by the persevering prayers and fastings of the said ministers."

No name in English history is regarded with more respect and admiration, by wise and virtuous men, than that of Sir Matthew Hale. His character was almost venerated by our ancestors; and it has been thought that it was the influence of his authority, more than any thing else, that prevailed upon them to pursue the course they adopted in the prosecutions at Salem. This great and good man presided, as Lord Chief Baron, at the trial of two females, — Amy Dunny and Rose Cullender, — at Bury St. Edmunds, in Suffolk, in the year 1664. They were convicted and executed.

Baxter relates the following circumstance as having occurred at this trial: "A godly minister, yet living, sitting by to see one of the girls (who appeared as a witness against the prisoners) in her fits, suddenly felt a force pull one of the hooks from his breeches; and, while he looked with wonder at what was become of it, the tormented girl vomited it up out of her mouth."

To give an idea of the nature of the testimony upon which the principal stress was laid by the government, I will extract the following passages from the report of the trial : " Robert Sherringham testified that the axle-tree of his cart, happening, in passing, to break some part of Rose Cullender's house, in her anger at it, she vehemently threatened him his horses should suffer for it ; and, within a short time, all his four horses died ; after which he sustained many other losses, in the sudden dying of his cattle. He was also taken with a lameness in his limbs, and so far vexed with lice of an extraordinary number and bigness, that no art could hinder the swarming of them, till he burned up two suits of apparel." — " Margaret Arnold testified that Amy Dunny afflicted her children : they (the children), she said, would see mice running round the house, and, when they caught them and threw them into the fire, they would screech out like rats." — " A thing like a bee flew at the face of the younger child ; the child fell into a fit, and at last vomited up a two-penny nail, with a broad head, affirming that the bee brought this nail, and forced it into her mouth." — " She one day caught an invisible mouse, and, throwing it into the fire, it flashed like to gunpowder. None besides the child saw the mouse, but every one saw the flash ! "

In this instance we perceive the influence of prejudice in perverting evidence. The circumstance that the mouse was invisible to all eyes but those of the child ought to have satisfied the Court and jury that she was either under the power of a delusion or practising an imposture. But, as they were predisposed to find something supernatural in the transaction, their minds seized upon the pretended invisibility of the mouse as conclusive proof of diabolical agency.

Many persons who were present expressed the opinion, that the issue of the trial would have been favorable to the prisoners, had it not been for the following circumstance: Sir Thomas Browne, a physician, philosopher, and scholar of unrivalled celebrity at that time, happened to be upon the spot; and it was the universal wish that he should be called to the stand, and his opinion be obtained on the general subject of witchcraft. An enthusiastic contemporary admirer of Sir Thomas Browne thus describes him: "The horizon of his understanding was much larger than the hemisphere of the world: all that was visible in the heavens he comprehended so well, that few that are under them knew so much; and of the earth he had such a minute and exact geographical knowledge as if he had been by Divine Providence ordained surveyor-general of the whole terrestrial globe and its products, minerals, plants, and animals." His memory is stated to have been inferior only to that of Seneca or Scaliger; and he was reputed master of seven languages. Dr. Johnson, who has written his biography, sums up his character in the following terms: "But it is not on the praises of others, but on his

own writings, that he is to depend for the esteem of
posterity, of which he will not easily be deprived,
while learning shall have any reverence among men :
for there is no science in which he does not discover
some skill ; and scarce any kind of knowledge, profane
or sacred, abstruse or elegant, which he does not
appear to have cultivated with success."

Sir Thomas Browne was considered by those of his
own generation to have made great advances beyond
the wisdom of his age. He claimed the character of
a reformer, and gave to his principal publication the
title of an " Enquiry into Vulgar Errors." So bold
and free were his speculations, that he was looked
upon invidiously by many as a daring innovator, and
did not escape the denunciatory imputation of heresy.
Nothing could be more unjust, however, than this
latter charge. He was a most ardent and zealous
believer in the doctrines of the Established Church.
He declares " that he assumes the honorable style of
a Christian," not because " it is the religion of his
country," but because, " having in his riper years and
confirmed judgment seen and examined all, he finds
himself obliged, by the principles of grace and the
law of his own reason, to embrace no other name but
this." He exults and " blesses himself, that he lived
not in the days of miracles, when faith had been
thrust upon him, but enjoys that greater blessing pronounced to all that believed, and saw not : " nay, he
goes so far as to say, that they only had the advantage " of a bold and noble faith, who lived before the

coming of the Saviour, and, upon obscure prophecies and mystical types, could raise a belief." The fact that such a man was accused of infidelity is an affecting proof of the injustice that is sometimes done by the judgment of contemporaries.

This prodigy of learning and philosophy went into Court, took the stand, and declared his opinion in favor of the reality of witchcraft, entered into a particular discussion of the subject before the jury, threw the whole weight of his great name into the wavering scales of justice, and the poor women were convicted. The authority of Sir Thomas Browne, added to the other evidence, perplexed Sir Matthew Hale. A reporter of the trial says, " that it made this great and good man doubtful; but he was in such fears, and proceeded with such caution, that he would not so much as sum up the evidence, but left it to the jury with prayers, ' that the great God of heaven would direct their hearts in that weighty matter.' "

The result of this important trial established decisively the interpretation of English law; and the printed report of it was used as an authoritative text-book in the Court at Salem.

The celebrated Robert Boyle flourished in the latter half of the seventeenth century. He is allowed by all to have done much towards the introduction of an improved philosophy, and the promotion of experimental science. But he could not entirely shake off the superstition of his age.

A small city in Burgundy, called Mascon, was

famous in the annals of witchcraft. In a work called
" The Theatre of God's Judgments," published, in
London, by Thomas Beard in 1612, there is the following passage : " It was a very lamentable spectacle
that chanced to the Governor of Mascon, a magician,
whom the Devil snatched up in dinner-while, and
hoisted aloft, carrying him three times about the towr
of Mascon, in the presence of many beholders, to whom
he cried in this manner, ' Help, help, my friends ! ' so
that the whole town stood amazed thereat; yea, and
the remembrance of this strange accident sticketh at
this day fast in the minds of all the inhabitants of
this country." A malicious and bigoted monk, who
discharged the office of chief legend-maker to the
Benedictine Abbey, in the vicinity of Mascon, fabri-
cated this ridiculous story for the purpose of bringing
the Governor into disrepute. An account of another
diabolical visitation, suggested, it is probable, by the
one just described, was issued from the press, under
the title of " The Devil of Mascon," during the lifetime
of Boyle, who gave his sanction to the work, promoted its version into English, and, as late as 1678,
publicly declared his belief of the supernatural transaction it related.

The subject of demonology, in all its forms and
phases, embracing witchcraft, held a more commanding place throughout Europe, in the literature of the
centuries immediately preceding the eighteenth, than
any other. Works of the highest pretension, elaborate,
learned, voluminous, and exhausting, were published,

by the authority of governments and universities, to expound it. It was regarded as occupying the most eminent department of jurisprudence, as well as of science and theology.

Raphael De La Torre and Adam Tanner published treatises establishing the right and duty of ecclesiastical tribunals to punish all who practised or dealt with the arts of demonology. In 1484, Sprenger came out with his famous book, "Malleus Maleficarum;" or, the "Hammer of Witches." Paul Layman, in 1629, issued an elaborate work on "Judicial Processes against Sorcerers and Witches." The following is the title of a bulky volume of some seven hundred pages: "Demonology, or Natural Magic or demoniacal, lawful and unlawful, also open or secret, by the intervention and invocation of a Demon," published in 1612. It consists of four books, treating of the crime of witchcraft, and its punishment in the ordinary tribunals and the Inquisitorial office. Its author was Don Francisco Torreblanca Villalpando, of Cordova, Advocate Royal in the courts of Grenada. It was republished in 1623, by command of Philip III. of Spain, on the recommendation of the Fiscal General, and with the sanction of the Royal Council and the Holy Inquisition. This work may be considered as establishing and defining the doctrines, in reference to witchcraft, prevailing in all Catholic countries. It was indorsed by royal, judicial, academical, and ecclesiastical approval; is replete with extraordinary erudition, arranged in the most scientific form, em-

bracing in a methodical classification all the minutest
details of the subject, and codifying it into a complete
system of law. There was no particular in all the
proceedings and all the doctrines brought out at the
trials in Salem, which did not find ample justification and support in this work of Catholic, imperial,
and European authority.

But perhaps the writer of the greatest influence on
this subject in England and America, during the whole
of the seventeenth century, was William Perkins, " the
learned, pious, and painful preacher of God's Word, at
St. Andrew's, in Cambridge," where he died, in 1602,
aged forty-four years. He was quite a voluminous
author; and many of his works were translated into
French, Dutch, Italian, and Spanish. Fuller, in " The
Holy State," selects him as the impersonation of the
qualities requisite to " the Faithful Minister." In his
glowing eulogium upon his learning and talents, he
says : —

" He would pronounce the word *damne* with such an em-
phasis as left a doleful echo in his auditors' ears a good while
after. And, when catechist of Christ's College, in expound-
ing the Commandments, applied them so home, — able almost to make his hearers' hearts fall down, and hairs to stand
upright. But, in his older age, he altered his voice, and
remitted much of his former rigidness, often professing that
to preach mercy was that proper office of the ministers of the
gospel." — " Our Perkins brought the schools into the pulpit,
and, unshelling their controversies out of their hard school-
terms, made thereof plain and wholesome meat for his peo-

ple ; for he had a capacious head, with angles winding, and roomy enough to lodge all controversial intricacies." — " He had a rare felicity in speedy reading of books ; so that, as it were, riding post through an author, he took strict notice of all passages. Perusing books so speedily, one would think he read nothing ; so accurately, one would think he read all."

An octavo volume, written by this great scholar and divine, was published at Cambridge in England, under the title, " Discourse of the Damned Art of Witchcraft." It went through several editions, and had a wide and permanent circulation.

This work, the character of which is sufficiently indicated in its emphatic title, was the great authority on the subject with our fathers ; and Mr. Parris had a copy of it in his possession when the proceedings in reference to witchcraft began at Salem Village.

John Gaule published an octavo volume in London, in 1646, entitled, " Select Cases of Conscience concerning Witches and Witchcraft." He is one of the most exact writers on the subject, and arranges witches in the following classes : " 1. The diviner, gypsy, or fortune-telling witch ; 2. The astrologian, star-gazing, planetary, prognosticating witch ; 3. The chanting, canting, or calculating witch, who works by signs and numbers ; 4. The venefical, or poisoning witch ; 5. The exorcist, or conjuring witch ; 6. The gastronomic witch ; 7. The magical, speculative, sciential, or arted witch ; 8. The necromancer."

Besides innumerable writers of this class, who spread out the scholastic learning on the subject, and presented it in a logical and theological form, there were others who treated it in a more popular style, and invested it with the charms of elegant literature. Henry Hallywell published an octavo in London, in 1681, in which, while the main doctrines of witchcraft as then almost universally received are enforced, an attempt was made to divest it of some of its most repulsive and terrible features. He gives the following account of the means by which a person may place himself beyond the reach of the power of witchcraft : —

" It is possible for the soul to arise to such a height, and become so divine, that no witchcraft or evil demons can have any power upon the body. When the bodily life is too far invigorated and awakened, and draws the intellect, the flower and summity of the soul, into a conspiration with it, then are we subject and obnoxious to magical assaults. For magic or sorcery, being founded only in this lower or mundane spirit, he that makes it his business to be freed and released from all its blandishments and flattering devocations, and endeavors wholly to withdraw himself from the love of corporeity and too near a sympathy with the frail flesh, he, by it, enkindles such a divine principle as lifts him above the fate of this inferior world, and adorns his mind with such an awful majesty that beats back all enchantments, and makes the infernal fiends tremble at his presence, hating those vigorous beams of light which are so contrary and repugnant to their dark natures."

The mind of this beautiful writer found encouragement and security in the midst of the diabolical spirits, with whom he believed the world to be infested, in the following views and speculations : —

" For there is a chain of government that runs down from God, the Supreme Monarch, whose bright and piercing eyes look through all that he has made, to the lowest degree of the creation ; and there are presidential angels of empires and kingdoms, and such as under them have the tutelage of private families ; and, lastly, every man's particular guardian genius.   Nor is the inanimate or material world left to blind chance or fortune ; but there are, likewise, mighty and potent spirits, to whom is committed the guidance and care of the fluctuating and uncertain motions of it, and by their ministry, fire and vapor, storms and tempests, snow and hail, heat and cold, are all kept within such bounds and limits as are most serviceable to the ends of Providence.   They take care of the variety of seasons, and superintend the tillage and fruits of the earth ; upon which account, Origen calls them *invisible* husbandmen.   So that, all affairs and things being under the inspection and government of these incorporeal beings, the power of the dark kingdom and its agents is under a strict confinement and restraint ; and they cannot bring a general mischief upon the world without a special permission of a superior Providence."

Spenser has the same imagery and sentiment : —

" How oft do they their silver bowers leave,
    To come to succor us, that succor want ?
  How oft do they with golden pinions cleave
  The flitting skies, like flying pursuivant,
  Against foul fiends to aid us militant ?
  They for us fight, they watch and duly ward,
  And their bright squadrons round about us plant,
  And all for love and nothing for reward :
  Oh ! why should heavenly God to man have such regard ? "

While there can be no doubt that the superstitious opinions we have been reviewing were diffused generally among the great body of the people of all ranks and conditions, it would be unjust to truth not to mention that there were some persons who looked upon them as empty fables and vain imaginations. Error has never yet made a complete and universal conquest. In the darkest ages and most benighted regions, it has been found impossible utterly to extinguish the light of reason. There always have been some in whose souls the torch of truth has been kept burning with vestal watchfulness : we can discern its glimmer here and there through the deepest night that has yet settled upon the earth. In the midst of the most extravagant superstition, there have been individuals who have disowned the popular belief, and considered it a mark of wisdom and true philosophy to discard the idle fancies and absurd schemes of faith that possessed the minds of the great mass of their contemporaries. This was the case with Horace, as appears from lines thus quite freely but effectively translated : —

> " These dreams and terrors magical,
> These miracles and witches,
> Night-walking spirites or Thessal bugs,
> Esteeme them not two rushes."

The intellect of Seneca also rose above the reach of the popular credulity with respect to the agency of supernatural beings and the efficacy of mysterious charms.

If we could but obtain access to the secret thoughts

of the wisest philosophers and of the men of genius of antiquity, we should probably find that many of them were superior to the superstitions of their times. Even in the thick darkness of the dark ages, there were minds too powerful to be kept in chains by error and delusion.

Henry Cornelius Agrippa, who was born in the latter part of the fifteenth century, was, perhaps, the greatest philosopher and scholar of his period. In early life, he was very much devoted to the science of magic, and was a strenuous supporter of demonology and witchcraft. In the course of his studies and meditations, he was led to a change of views on these subjects, and did all that he could to warn others from putting confidence in such vain, frivolous, and absurd superstitions as then possessed the world. The consequence was, that he was denounced and prosecuted as a conjurer, and charged with having written against magic and witchcraft, in order the more securely to shelter himself from the suspicion of practising them. As an instance of the calumnies that were heaped upon him, I would mention that Paulus Jovius asserted that " Cornelius Agrippa went always accompanied with an evil spirit in the similitude of a black dog ; " and that, when the time of his death drew near, " he took off the enchanted collar from the dog's neck, and sent him away with these terms, ' Get thee hence, thou cursed beast, which hast utterly destroyed me : ' neither was the dog ever seen after." Butler, in his " Hudibras," has not neglected to celebrate this remarkable connection between Satan and the man of learning: —

> " Agrippa kept a Stygian pug
> I' th' garb and habit of a dog,
> That was his tutor; and the cur
> Read to th' occult philosopher."

John Wierus wrote an elaborate, learned, and judicious book, in which he treated at large of magic, sorcery, and witchcraft, and did all that scholarship, talent, and philosophy could do to undermine and subvert the whole system of the prevailing popular superstition. But he fared no better than his predecessor, patron, and master, Agrippa; for, like him, he was accused of having attempted to persuade the world that there was no reality in supernatural charms and diabolical confederacies, in order that he might devote himself to them without suspicion or molestation, and was borne down by the bigotry and fanaticism of his times.

King James merely gave utterance to the general sentiment, and pronounced the verdict of popular opinion, in the following extract from the preface to his " Demonologie: " " Wierus, a German physician, sets out a public apologie for all these crafts-folkes, whereby, procuring for them impunitie, he plainly bewrays himself to have been of that profession."

In 1584, a quarto volume was published in London, the work of Reginald Scott, a learned English gentleman, whose title sufficiently indicates its import, " The Discovery of Witchcraft, wherein the lewde dealing of witches and witchmongers is notably detected; the knavery of conjurers, the impiety of inchanters, the folly of soothsayers, the impudent falsehood of cozeners, the infidelity of atheists, the pestilent practices of pythonists, the curiosities of figure-casters, the vanity of dreamers, the beggarly art of alcumstrie, the abomination of idolatrie, the horrible art of poisoning, the virtue and power of natural magic, and all the conveniencies of legerdemaine and juggling, are discovered, &c."

In 1599, Samuel Harsnett, Archbishop of York, wrote a work, published in London, to expose certain persons who pretended to have the power of casting out devils, and detecting their " deceitful trade." This writer was among the first to bring the power of bold satire and open denunciation to bear against the superstitions of demonology. He thus describes the motives and the methods of such impostors : —

" Out of these," saith he, " is shaped us the true idea of a witch, — an old, weather-beaten crone, having her chin and her knees meeting for age, walking like a bow, leaning on a staff; hollow-eyed, untoothed, furrowed on her face, having her limbs trembling with the palsy, going mumbling in the streets ; one that hath forgotten her Pater-noster, and yet hath a shrewd tongue to call a drab a drab. If she hath learned of an old wife, in a chimney-end, Pax, Max, Fax, for a spell, or can say Sir John Grantham's curse for the miller's eels, ' All ye that have stolen the miller's eels, Laudate dominum de cœlis : and all they that have consented thereto, Benedicamus domino :' why then, beware ! look about you, my neighbors. If any of you have a sheep sick of the giddies, or a hog of the mumps, or a horse of the staggers, or a knavish boy of the school, or an idle girl of the wheel, or a young drab of the sullens, and hath not fat enough for her porridge, or butter enough for her bread, and she hath a little help of the epilepsy or cramp, to teach her to roll her eyes, wry her mouth, gnash her teeth, startle with her body, hold her arms and hands stiff, &c. ; and then, when an old Mother Nobs hath by chance called her an idle young housewife, or bid the Devil scratch her, then no doubt but Mother Nobs is the witch, and the young girl is owl blasted, &c. They that have their brains baited and their fancies distempered with the imaginations and apprehensions of witches, conjurers, and fairies, and all that lymphatic chimera, I find to be mar-shalled in one of these five ranks : children, fools, women, cowards, sick or black melancholic discomposed wits."

In 1669, a work was published in London with the following title : "The Question of Witchcraft Debated; or, a Discourse against their Opinions that affirm Witches." It is a work of great merit, and would do honor to a scholar and logician of the present day. The author was John Wagstaffe, of Oxford University : he is described as a crooked, shrivelled, little man, of a most despicable appearance. This circumstance, to-gether with his writings against the popular belief in witchcraft, led his academical associates to accuse him, some of them in sport, but others with grave suspicion, of being a wizard. Wood, the historian of Oxford, says that " he died in a manner distracted, occasioned by a deep conceit of his own parts, and by a continual bibbing of strong and high-tasted liquors." But poor Wagstaffe was assailed by something more than private raillery and slander. His heretical sentiments exposed him to the battery of the host of writers who will always be found ready to advocate a prevailing opinion. But Wagstaffe was not left entirely alone to defend the cause of reason and truth. He had one most zealous advocate and ardent admirer in the author of a work on "The Doctrine of Devils," published in 1676. This writer sums up a panegyric upon Wagstaffe's performance, by pronouncing it "a judicious book, that contains more good reason, true religion, and right Christianity, than all those lumps and cartloads of luggage that hath been fardled up by all the faggeters of demonologistical winter-tales, and witchcraftical legendaries, since they first began to foul clean paper."

Dr. Balthasar Bekker, of Amsterdam, who was equally eminent in astronomy, philosophy, and theology, published in 1691 a learned and powerful work, called "The World Bewitched," in which he openly assailed the doctrines of witchcraft and of the Devil, and anticipated many of the views and arguments presented in Farmer's excellent publications. As a reward for his exertions to enlighten his fellow-creatures, he was turned out of the ministry, and assaulted by nearly all the writers of his age.

Dr. Bekker was one of the ablest and boldest writers of his day, and did much to advance the cause of natural science, scriptural interpretation, and the principles of enlightened Christianity. In 1680 he published an " Inquiry concerning Comets," rescuing them from the realm of superstition, placing them within the natural physical laws, and exploding the then-received opinion, that, in any way, they are the presages or forerunners of evil. His " Exposition on the Prophet Daniel " gives proof of his learning and judgment. His great merits were recognized by John Locke and Richard Bentley. In the preface to his " World Bewitched," he says, that it grieved him to see the great honors, powers, and miracles which are ascribed to the Devil. " It has come to that pass," to use his own language, " that men think it piety and godliness to ascribe a great many wonders to the Devil, and impiety and heresy, if a man will not believe that the Devil can do what a thousand persons say he does. It is now reckoned godliness, if a man who fears God fear also the Devil. If he be not afraid of the Devil, he passes for an atheist, who does not believe in God, because he cannot think that there are two gods, the one good, the other bad. But these, I think, with much more reason, may be called ditheists. For my part, if, on account of my opinion, they will give me a new name, let them call me a monotheist, a believer of but one God." The work struck down the whole system of demonology and witchcraft, by proving that there never was really such a thing as sorcery or possession, and that devils have no influence over human affairs or the persons of men. It is not surprising that it raised a great clamor. The wonder is that it did not cost him his life. It is probable that his protection was the confidence the people had in his character and learning. Attempts were made to diminish that confidence, and bring him into odium, by levelling against him every form of abuse. A medal was struck, and extensively circulated, representing the Devil, clothed like a minister or priest, riding on an ass. The device was so arranged as to excite ridicule and abhorrence, in the vulgar mind, against Bekker. But it was found impossible to turn the popular feeling, which had set in his favor; and his-persecutors and defamers were completely baffled. He was followed, soon after, by the learned Thomasius, whose writings against demonology produced a decided effect upon the convictions of the age.

While Bekker, and the other writers of his class, endeavored to overthrow the superstitious practices and fancies then prevalent respecting demonology and communications with spiritual beings, they so far acceded to the popular theology as to maintain the doctrine of the personality of the Devil. They believed in the existence of the arch-fiend, but denied his agency in human affairs. They held that he was kept confined " to bottomless perdition, there to dwell —

"In adamantine chains and penal fire."

Sir Robert Filmer, in 1680, published "An Advertisement to the jurymen of England, touching Witches," in which he criticised and condemned many of the opinions and methods then countenanced on the subject.

But Bekker, Thomasius, and Filmer appeared too late to operate upon the prevalent opinions of Europe or America prior to the witchcraft delusion of 1692. The productions of the other writers, in the same direction, to whom I have referred, probably had a very limited circulation, and made at the time but little impression. Error is seldom overthrown by mere reasoning. It yields only to the logic of events. No power of learning or wit could have rooted the witchcraft superstitions out of the minds of men. Nothing short of a demonstration of their deformities, follies, and horrors, such as here was held up to the view of the world, could have given their death-blow. This was the final cause of Salem Witchcraft, and makes it one of the great landmarks in the world's history.

A full and just view of the position and obligations of the persons who took part in the transactions at Salem requires a previous knowledge of the principles and the state of the law, as it was then in force and understood by the courts, and all concerned in judicial proceedings. Although the ancients did not regard pretended intercourse between magicians and enchanters and spiritual beings as necessarily or always criminal, we find that they enacted laws against the abuse of the power supposed to result from the connection. The old Roman code of the Twelve Tables contained the following prohibition : " That they should not bewitch the fruits of the earth, nor use any charms to draw their neighbor's corn into their own fields." There were several special edicts on the subject during the existence of the Roman State. In the early Christian councils, sorcery was frequently made the object of denunciation. At Laodicea, for instance, in the year 364, it was voted to excommunicate any clergymen who were magicians, enchanters, astrologers, or mathematicians! The Bull of Pope Innocent VIII., near the close of the fifteenth century, has already been mentioned.

Dr. Turner, in his history of the Anglo-Saxons, says that they had laws against sorcerers and witches, but that they did not punish them with death. There was an English statute against witchcraft, in the reign of Henry VIII., and another in that of Elizabeth.

Up to this time, however, the legislation of parliament on the subject was merciful and judicious: for it did not attach to the guilt of witchcraft the punishment of death, unless it had been used to destroy life; that is, unless it had become murder.

On the demise of Elizabeth, James of Scotland ascended the throne. His pedantic and eccentric character is well known. He had an early and decided inclination towards abstruse or mysterious speculations. Before he had reached his twentieth year, he undertook to accomplish what only the most sanguine and profound theologians have ever dared to attempt: he expounded the Book of Revelation. When he was about twenty-five years of age, he published a work on the "Doctrine of Devils and Witchcraft." Not long after, he succeeded to the British crown. It may easily be imagined that the subject of demonology

soon became a fashionable and prevailing topic of
conversation in the royal saloons and throughout the
nation. It served as a medium through which obse-
quious courtiers could convey their flattery to the
ears of their accomplished and learned sovereign. His
Majesty's book was reprinted and extensively circulated. It was of course praised and recommended
in all quarters.

The parliament, actuated by a base desire to com-
pliment the vain and superstitious king, enacted a
new and much more severe statute against witchcraft,
in the very first year of his reign. It was under this
law that so many persons here and in England were
deprived of their lives. The blood of hundreds of
innocent persons was thus unrighteously shed. It was
a fearful price which these servile lawgivers paid for
the favor of their prince.

But this was not the only mischief brought about
by courtly deference to the prejudices of King James.
It was under his direction that our present transla-
tion of the Scriptures was made. To please His
Royal Majesty, and to strengthen the arguments in
his work on demonology, the word "witch" was
used to represent expressions in the original Hebrew,
that conveyed an entirely different idea; and it was
freely inserted in the headings of the chapters.* A
person having "a familiar spirit" was a favorite description of a witch in the king's book. The trans-

---

* For a thorough discussion of the several Hebrew words that relate to Divination and Magic, see Wierus de Præstigiis, L. 2, c. 1.

lators, forgetful of their high and solemn function, endeavored to establish this definition by inserting it into their version. Accordingly, they introduced it in several places; in the eleventh verse of the eighteenth chapter of Deuteronomy, for instance, " a consulter with familiar spirits." There is no word in the Hebrew which corresponds with " familiar." And this is the important, the essential word in the definition. It conveys the idea of alliance, stated connection, confederacy, or compact, which is characteristic and distinctive of a witch. The expression in the original signifies " a consulter with spirits," — especially, as was the case with the " Witch of Endor," a consulter with departed spirits. It was a shocking perversion of the word of God, for the purpose of flattering a frail and mortal sovereign! King James lived to see and acknowledge the error of his early opinions, and he would gladly have counteracted their bad effect; but it is easier to make laws and translations than it is to alter and amend them.

While the law of the land required the capital punishment of witches, no blame ought to be attached to judges and jurors for discharging their respective duties in carrying it into execution. It will not do for us to assert, that they ought to have refused, let the consequences to themselves have been what they would, to sanction and give effect to such inhuman and unreasonable enactments. We cannot consistently take this ground; for there is nothing more certain than that, with their notions, our ancestors had at least as good reasons to advance in favor of punishing witch-craft with death, as we have for punishing any crime whatsoever in the same awful and summary manner. We appeal, in defence of our capital punishments, to the text of Moses, "Whoso sheddeth man's blood, bv man shall his blood be shed." The apologist of our fathers, for carrying into effect the law making witch-craft a capital offence, tells us in reply, in the first place, that this passage is not of the nature of a pre-cept, but merely of an admonition; that it does not enjoin any particular method of proceeding, but simply describes the natural consequences of cruel and con-tentious conduct; and that it amounts only to this: that quarrelsome, violent, and bloodthirsty persons will be apt to meet the same fate they bring upon others; that the duellist will be likely to fall in private combat, the ambitious conqueror to perish, and the warlike nation to be destroyed, on the field of battle. If this is not considered by us a sufficient and satisfactory answer, he advances to our own ground, points to the same text where we place our defence, and puts his finger on the following plain and authoritative pre-cept: "Thou shalt not suffer a witch to live." Indeed we must acknowledge, that the capital punishment of witches is as strongly supported and fortified by the Scriptures of the Old Testament — at least, as they appear in our present version — as the capital punish-ment of any crime whatever.

If we adopt another line of argument, and say that it is necessary to punish some particular crimes with death, in order to maintain the security of society, or hold up an impressive warning to others, here also we find that our opponent has full as much to offer in defence of our fathers as can be offered in our own defence. He describes to us the tremendous and infernal power which was universally believed by them to be possessed by a witch; a power which, as it was not derived from a natural source, could not easily be held in check by natural restraints: neither chains nor dungeons could bind it down or confine it. You might load the witch with irons, you might bury her in the lowest cell of a feudal prison, and still it was believed that she could send forth her imps or her spectre to ravage the fields, and blight the meadows, and throw the elements into confusion, and torture the bodies, and craze the minds, of any who might be the objects of her malice.

Shakspeare, in the description which he puts into the mouth of Macbeth of the supernatural energy of witchcraft, does not surpass, if he does justice to, the prevailing belief on the subject: —

> " I conjure you, by that which you profess,
> (Howe'er you came to know it) answer me, —
> Though you untie the winds, and let them fight
> Against the churches; though the yesty waves
> Confound and swallow navigation up;
> Though bladed corn be lodged, and trees blown down;
> Though castles topple on their warders' heads;
> Though palaces and pyramids do slope
> Their heads to their foundations; though the treasure
> Of nature's germins tumble all together,
> Even till destruction sicken, — answer me
> To what I ask you."

There was indeed an almost infinite power to do mischief associated with a disposition to do it. No human strength could strip the witch of these mighty energies while she lived; nothing but death could destroy them. There was, as our ancestors considered, incontestable evidence, that she had put them forth to the injury, loss, and perhaps death, of others.

Can it be wondered at, that, under such circumstances, the law connecting capital punishment with the guilt of witchcraft was resorted to as the only means to protect society, and warn others from entering into the dark, wicked, and malignant compact?

It is not probable that even King James's Parliament would have been willing to go to the length of Selden in his "Table-Talk," who takes this ground in defence of the capital punishment of witches. "The law against witches does not prove there be any, but it punishes the malice of those people that use such means to take away men's lives. If one should profess, that, by turning his hat thrice and crying 'Buzz,' he could take away a man's life (though in truth he could do no such thing), yet this were a just law made by the State, that whoever should turn his hat thrice and cry 'Buzz,' with an intention to take away a man's life, shall be put to death."

There are other considerations that deserve to be weighed before a final judgment should be made up respecting the conduct of our fathers in the witchcraft delusion. Among these is the condition of physical science in their day. But little knowledge of the laws of nature was possessed, and that little was confined to a few. The world was still, to the mass of the people, almost as full of mystery in its physical departments as it was to its first inhabitants. Politics, poetry, rhetoric, ethics, and history had been cultivated to a great extent in previous ages; but the philosophy of the natural and material world was almost unknown. Astronomy, chemistry, optics, pneumatics, and even geography, were involved in the general darkness and error. Some of our most important sciences, such as electricity, date their origin from a later period.

This remarkable tardiness in the progress of physical science for some time after the era of the revival of learning is to be accounted for by referring to the erroneous methods of reasoning and observation then prevalent in the world. A false logic was adopted in the schools of learning and philosophy. The great instrument for the discovery and investigation of truth was the syllogism, the most absurd contrivance of the human mind; an argumentative process whose conclusion is contained in the premises; a method of proof, in the first step of which the matter to be proved is taken for granted.* In a word, the whole system of philosophy was made up of hypotheses, and

* The syllogism was originally designed to serve as a *method of determining the arrangement and classification of truth already shown;* and, when employed for this purpose, was of great value and excellence. It was its perverted application to the *discovery* of truth which rendered utterly worthless so large a part of the learning and philosophy of the

the only foundation of science was laid in conjecture. The imagination, called necessarily into extraordinary action, in the absence of scientific certainty, was still further exercised in vain attempts to discover, unassisted by observation and experiment, the elements and first principles of nature. It had reached a monstrous growth about the time to which we are referring. Indeed it may be said, that all the intellectual productions of modern times, from the seventeenth century back to the dark ages, were works of imagination. The bulkiest and most voluminous writings that proceeded from the cloisters or the universities, even the metaphysical disquisitions of the Nominalists and Realists, and the boundless subtleties of the contending schools of the "Divine Doctors," Thomas Aquinas and Duns Scotus, fall under this description. Dull, dreary, unintelligible, and interminable as they are, they are still in reality works of fancy. They are the offspring, almost exclusively, of the imaginative faculty. It ought not to create surprise, to find that this faculty predominated in the minds and characters of our ancestors, and developed itself to an extent beyond our conception, when we reflect that it was almost the only one called into exercise, and that it was the leading element of every branch of literature and philosophy.

middle ages. The reader will perceive, that it is to the syllogism, as thus misapplied and misunderstood by the schoolmen, not as designed and used by Aristotle, that the remarks in the text are intended to apply.

It is true, that, in the earlier part of the seventeenth century, Lord Bacon made his sublime discoveries in the department of physical science. By disclosing the true method of investigation and reasoning on such subjects, he may be said to have found, or rather to have invented, the key that unlocked the hitherto unopened halls of nature. He introduced man to the secret chambers of the universe, and placed in his hand the thread by which he has been conducted to the magnificent results of modern science, and will undoubtedly be led on to results still more magnificent in times to come. But it was not for human nature to pass in a moment from darkness to light. The transition was slow and gradual: a long twilight intervened before the sun shed its clear and full radiance upon the world.

The great discoverer himself refused to admit, or was unable to discern, some of the truths his system had revealed. Bacon was numbered among the opponents of the Copernican or true system of astronomy to the day of his death; so also was Sir Thomas Browne, the great philosopher already described, and who flourished during the latter half of the same century. Indeed, it may be said, that, at the time of the witchcraft delusion, the ancient empire of darkness which had oppressed and crushed the world of science had hardly been shaken. The great and triumphant progress of modern discovery had scarcely begun.

I shall now proceed to illustrate these views of the state of science in the world at that time by presenting a few instances. The slightest examination of the accounts which remain of occurrences deemed supernatural by our ancestors will satisfy any one that they were brought about by causes entirely natural, although unknown to them. For instance, the following circumstances are related by the Rev. James Pierpont, pastor of a church in New Haven, in a letter to Cotton Mather, and published by him in his " Magnalia : " * —

In the year 1646, a new ship, containing a valuable cargo, and having several distinguished persons on board as passengers, put to sea from New Haven in the month of January, bound to England. The vessels that came over the ensuing spring brought no tidings of her arrival in the mother-country. The pious colonists were earnest and instant in their prayers that intelligence might be received of the missing vessel. In the month of June, 1648, "a great thunder-storm arose out of the north-west ; after which (the hemisphere being serene), about an hour before sunset, a ship of like dimensions with the aforesaid, with her canvas and colors abroad (although

* The manner in which Dr. Mather brings forward this affair shows how loose and inaccurate he was in his description of events. It also illustrates the tendency of the times to exaggerate, or to paint in the highest colors, whatever was susceptible of being represented as miraculous. There is no reason, however, to doubt that the facts took place substantially as described in the text. The reader is referred, on this as on all points connected with our early history, to Mr. Savage's instructive, elaborate, and entertaining edition of Winthrop's " New England."

the wind was northerly), appeared in the air, coming up from the harbor's mouth, which lies southward from the town, — seemingly with her sails filled under a fresh gale, holding her course north, and continuing under observation, sailing against the wind for the space of half an hour." The phantom-ship was borne along, until, to the excited imaginations of the spectators, she seemed to have approached so near that they could throw a stone into her. Her main-topmast then disappeared, then her mizzen-topmast; then her masts were entirely carried away; and, finally, her hull fell off, and vanished from sight, — leaving a dull and smoke-colored cloud, which soon dissolved, and the whole atmosphere became clear. All affirmed that the airy vision was a precise copy and image of the missing vessel, and that it was sent to announce and describe her fate. They considered it the spectre of the lost ship; and the Rev. Mr. Davenport declared in public, "that God had condescended, for the quieting their afflicted spirits, this extraordinary account of his sovereign disposal of those for whom so many fervent prayers were made continually."

The results of modern science enable us to explain the mysterious appearance. It is probable that some Dutch vessel, proceeding slowly, quietly, and unconsciously on her voyage from Amsterdam to the New Netherlands, happened at the time to be passing through the Sound. At the moment the apparition was seen in the sky, she was so near, that her reflected image was painted or delineated, to the eyes of the observers, on the clouds, by laws of optics now generally well known, before her actual outlines could be discerned by them on the horizon. As the sun sunk behind the western hills, and his rays were gradually withdrawn, the visionary ship slowly disappeared; and the approach of night effectually concealed the vessel as she continued her course along the Sound.

The optical illusions that present themselves on the sea-shore, by which distant objects are raised to view, the opposite capes and islands made to loom up, lifted above the line of the apparent circumference of the earth, and thrown into every variety of shape which the imagination can conceive, are among the most beautiful phenomena of nature; and they impress the mind with the idea of enchantment and mystery, more perhaps than any others: but they have received a complete solution from modern discovery.

It should be observed, that the optical principles which explain these phenomena have recently afforded a foundation for the science, or rather art, of nauscopy; and there are persons in some places, — in the Isle of France, as I have been told, — whose calling and profession is to ascertain and predict the approach of vessels, by their reflection in the atmosphere and on the clouds, long before they are visible to the eye, or through the glass.

The following opinion prevailed at the time of our narrative. The discoveries in electricity, itself a recent science, have rendered it impossible for us to contemplate it without ridicule. But it was the sober opinion of the age. "A great man has noted it," says a learned writer, "that thunders break oftener on churches than any other houses, because demons have a peculiar spite at houses that are set apart for the peculiar service of God."

Every thing that was strange or remarkable — every thing at all out of the usual course, every thing that was not clear and plain — was attributed to supernatural interposition. Indeed, our fathers lived, as they thought, continually in the midst of miracles ; and felt themselves surrounded, at all times, in all scenes, with innumerable invisible beings. The beautiful verse of Milton describes their faith : —

> "Millions of spiritual creatures walk the earth
> Unseen, both when we wake and when we sleep."

What was to him, however, a momentary vision of the imagination, was to them like a perpetual perception of the senses : it was a practical belief, an everyday common sentiment, an all-pervading feeling. But these supernatural beings very frequently were believed to have become visible to our superstitious ancestors. The instances, indeed, were not rare, of individuals having seen the Devil himself with their mortal eyes. They may well be brought to notice, as illustrating the ideas which then prevailed, and had an immediate, practical effect on the conduct of men, in reference to the power, presence, and action of the Devil in human affairs. This, in fact, is necessary, that we may understand the narrative we are preparing to contemplate of transactions based wholly on those ideas.

The following passage is extracted from a letter written to Increase Mather by the Rev. John Higginson : —

" The godly Mr. Sharp, who was ruling elder of the church of Salem almost thirty years after, related it of himself, that, being bred up to learning till he was eighteen years old, and then taken off, and put to be an apprentice to a draper in London, he yet notwithstanding continued a strong inclination and eager affection to books, with a curiosity of hearkening after and reading of the strangest and oddest books he could get, spending much of his time that way to the neglect of his business. At one time, there came a man into the shop, and brought a book with him, and said to him, ' Here is a book for you, keep this till I call for it again ; ' and so went away. Mr. Sharp, after his wonted bookish manner, was eagerly affected to look into that book, and read it, which he did : but, as he read in it, he was seized on by a strange kind of horror, both of body and mind, the hair of his head standing up ; and, finding these effects several times, he acquainted his master with it, who, observing the same effects, they concluded it was a conjuring book, and resolved to burn it, which they did. He that brought it in the shape of a man never coming to call for it, they concluded it was the Devil. He, taking this as a solemn warning from God to take heed what books he read, was much taken off from his former bookishness ; confining himself to reading the Bible, and other known good books of divinity, which were profitable to his soul."

Kircher relates the following anecdote, with a full belief of its truth : He had a friend who was zealously and perseveringly devoted to the study of alchemy. At one time, while he was intent upon his operations, a gentleman entered his laboratory, and kindly offered to assist him. In a few moments, a large mass of the purest gold was brought forth from the crucible. The gentleman then took his hat, and went out: before leaving the apartment, however, he wrote a recipe for making the precious article. The grateful and admiring mortal continued his operations, according to the directions of his visitor; but the charm was lost: he could not succeed, and was at last completely ruined by his costly and fruitless experiments. Both he and his friend Kircher were fully persuaded that the mysterious stranger-visitor was the Devil.

Baxter has recorded a curious interview between Satan and Mr. White, of Dorchester, assessor to the Westminster Assembly: —

" The Devil, in a light night, stood by his bedside. The assessor looked a while, whether he would say or do any thing, and then said, ' If thou hast nothing to do, I have; ' and so turned himself to sleep." Dr. Hibbert is of opinion, that the Rev. Mr. White treated his satanic majesty, on this occasion, with " a cool contempt, to which he had not often been accustomed."

Indeed, there is nothing more curious or instructive, in the history of that period, than the light which it sheds upon the influence of the belief of the personal existence and operations of the Devil, when that belief is carried out fully into its practical effects. The Christian doctrine had relapsed into a system almost identical with Manicheism. Wierus thus describes

Satan, as he was regarded in the prevalent theology: " He possesses great courage, incredible cunning, superhuman wisdom, the most acute penetration, consummate prudence, an incomparable skill in veiling the most pernicious artifices under a specious disguise, and a malicious and infinite hatred towards the human race, implacable and incurable." Milton merely responded to the popular sentiment in making Satan a character of lofty dignity, and in placing him on an elevation not " less than archangel ruined." Hallywell, in his work on witchcraft, declares that " that mighty angel of darkness is not foolishly nor idly to be scoffed at or blasphemed. The Devil," says he, " may properly be looked upon as a dignity, though his glory be pale and wan, and those once bright and orient colors faded and darkened in his robes ; and the Scriptures represent him as a prince, though it be of devils." Although our fathers cannot be charged with having regarded the Devil in this respectful and deferential light, it must be acknowledged that they gave him a conspicuous and distinguished — we might almost say a dignified — agency in the affairs of life and the government of the world: they were prone to confess, if not to revere, his presence, in all scenes and at all times. He occupied a wide space, not merely in their theology and philosophy, but in their daily and familiar thoughts.*

* It is much to be regretted, that Farmer, after having written with such admirable success upon the temptation, the demoniacs, miracles, and the worship of human spirits, did not live to accomplish his origi-

Cotton Mather, in one of his sermons, carries home this peculiar belief to the consciences of his hearers, in a manner that could not have failed to quicken and startle the most dull and drowsy among them.

"No place," says he, "that I know of, has got such a spell upon it as will always keep the Devil out. The meeting-house, wherein we assemble for the worship of God, is filled with many holy people and many holy concerns continually; but, if our eyes were so refined as the servant of the prophet had his of old, I suppose we should now see a throng of devils in this very place. The apostle has intimated that angels come in among us: there are angels, it seems, that hark how I preach, and how you hear, at this hour. And our own sad experience is enough to intimate that the devils are likewise rendezvousing here. It is reported in Job i. 5, 'When the sons of God came to present themselves before the Lord, Satan came also among them.' When we are in our church assemblies, oh, how many devils, do you imagine, crowd in among us! There is a devil that rocks one to sleep. There is a devil that makes another to be thinking of, he scarcely knows what himself. And there is a devil that makes another to be pleasing himself with wanton and wicked speculations. It is also possible, that we have our closets or our studies gloriously perfumed with devotions every day; but, alas! can we shut the Devil out of them? No: let us go where we will, we shall still find a devil nigh unto us. Only when we come to heaven, we shall be out of his reach for ever."

nal design, by giving the world a complete discussion and elucidation of the Scripture doctrine of the Devil.

It is very remarkable, that such a train of thought as this did not suggest to the mind of Dr. Mather the true doctrine of the Bible respecting the Devil. One would have supposed, that, in carrying out the mode of speaking of him as a person to this extent, it would have occurred to him, that it might be that the scriptural expressions of a similar kind were also mere personifications of moral and abstract ideas. In describing the inattention, irreverence, and unholy reflections of his hearers as the operations of the Devil, it is wonderful that his eyes were not opened to discern the import of our Saviour's interpretation of the Parable of the Tares, in which he declares, that he understands by the Devil whatever obstructs the growth of virtue and piety in the soul, the causes that efface good impressions and give a wrong inclination to the thoughts and affections, such as " the cares of this world " or " the deceitfulness of riches." By these are the tares planted, and by these is their growth promoted. " The enemy that sowed them is the Devil."

Satan was regarded as the foe and opposer of all improvement in knowledge and civilization. The same writer thus quaintly expresses this opinion : He " has hindered mankind, for many ages, from hitting those useful inventions which yet were so obvious and facile that it is everybody's wonder that they were not sooner hit upon. The bemisted world must jog on for thousands of years without the knowledge of the loadstone, till a Neapolitan stumbled upon it about three hundred years ago. Nor must the world be blessed with such a matchless engine of learning and virtue as that of printing, till about the middle of the fifteenth century. Nor could one old man, all over the face of the whole earth, have the benefit of such a little, though most needful, thing as a pair of spectacles, till a Dutchman, a little while ago, accommodated us. Indeed, as the Devil does begrudge us all manner of good, so he does annoy us with all manner of woe." In one of his sermons, Cotton Mather claimed for himself and his clerical brethren the honor of being particularly obnoxious to the malice of the Evil One. "The ministers of God," says he, "are more dogged by the Devil than other persons are."

Without a knowledge of this sentiment, the witchcraft delusion of our fathers cannot be understood. They were under an impression, that the Devil, having failed to prevent the progress of knowledge in Europe, had abandoned his efforts to obstruct it effectually there; had withdrawn into the American wilderness, intending here to make a final stand; and had resolved to retain an undiminished empire over the whole continent and his pagan allies, the native inhabitants. Our fathers accounted for the extraordinary descent and incursions of the Evil One among them, in 1692, on the supposition that it was a desperate effort to prevent them from bringing civilization and Christianity within his favorite retreat; and their souls were fired with the glorious thought, that, by carrying on the war with vigor against him and his confederates, the witches, they would become chosen and honored instruments in the hand of God for breaking down and abolishing the last stronghold on the earth of the kingdom of darkness.

That this opinion was not merely a conceit of their vanity, or an overweening estimate of their local importance, but a calm, deliberate conviction entertained by others as well as themselves, can be shown by abundant evidence from the literature of that period. I will quote a single illustration of the form in which this thought occupied their minds. The subject is worthy of being thoroughly appreciated, as it affords the key that opens to view the motives and sentiments which gave the mighty impetus to the witchcraft prosecution here in New England.

Joseph Mede, B.D., Fellow of Christ's College, in Cambridge, England, died in 1638, at the age of fifty-three years. He was perhaps, all things considered, the most profound scholar of his times. His writings give evidence of a brilliant genius and an enlightened spirit. They were held in the highest esteem by his contemporaries of all denominations, and in all parts of Europe. He was a Churchman; but had, to a remarkable degree, the confidence of nonconformists. He entertained, as will appear by what follows, in the boldest form, the then prevalent opinions concerning diabolical agency and influence; but, at the same time, was singularly free from some of the worst traits of superstition and bigotry. His intimacy with the learned Dr. William Ames, and the general tone and tendency of his writings, naturally made him an authority with Protestants, particularly the Pilgrims and Puritans of New England. His posthumous writings, published in 1652, are exceedingly interesting. They contain fragments found among his papers, brief discussions of points of criticism, philosophy, and theology, and a varied correspondence on such subjects with eminent men of his day. Among his principal correspondents was Dr. William Twiss, himself a person of much ingenious learning, and whom John Norton, as we are told by Cotton Mather, "loved and admired" above all men of that age. The following passages between them illustrate the point before us.

In a letter dated March 2, 1634, Twiss writes thus : —

"Now, I beseech you, let me know what your opinion is of our English plantations in the New World. Heretofore, I have wondered in my thoughts at the providence of God concerning that world; not discovered till this Old World of ours is almost at an end ; and then no footsteps found of the knowledge of the true God, much less of Christ ; and then considering our English plantations of late, and the opinion of many grave divines concerning the gospel's fleeting westward. Sometimes I have had such thoughts, Why may not *that* be the place of the *New Jerusalem?* But you have handsomely and fully cleared me from such odd conceits. But what, I pray? Shall our English there degenerate, and join themselves with Gog and Magog? We have heard lately divers ways, that our people there have no hope of the conversion of the natives. And, the very week after I received your last letter, I saw a letter, written from New

England, discoursing of an impossibility of subsisting there ; and seems to prefer the confession of God's truth in any condition here in Old England, rather than run over to enjoy their liberty there ; yea, and that the gospel is like to be more dear in New England than in Old. And, lastly, unless they be exceeding careful, and God wonderfully merciful, they are like to lose that life and zeal for God and his truth in New England which they enjoyed in Old ; as whereof they have already woful experience, and many there feel it to their smart."

Mr. Mede's answer was as follows : —

" Concerning our plantations in the American world, I wish them as well as anybody ; though I differ from them far, both in other things, and on the grounds they go upon. And though there be but little hope of the general conversion of those natives or any considerable part of that continent, yet I suppose it may be a work pleasing to Almighty God and our blessed Saviour to affront the Devil with the sound of the gospel and the cross of Christ, in those places where he had thought to have reigned securely, and out of the din thereof ; and, though we make no Christians there, yet to bring some thither to disturb and vex him, where he reigned without check.

" For that I may reveal my conceit further, though perhaps I cannot prove it, yet I think thus, — that those countries were first inhabited since our Saviour and his apostles' times, and not before ; yea, perhaps, some ages after, there being no signs or footsteps found among them, or any monuments of older habitation, as there is with us.

" That the Devil, being impatient of the sound of the gospel and cross of Christ, in every part of this Old World, so that he could in no place be quiet for it ; and foreseeing that he was like to lose all here ; so he thought to provide himself of a seed over which he might reign securely, and in a place *ubi nec Pelopidarum facta neque nomen audiret.* That, accordingly, he drew a colony out of some of those barbarous nations dwelling upon the Northern Ocean (whither the sound of Christ had not yet come), and promising them by some oracle to show them a country far better than their own (which he might soon do), pleasant and large, where never man yet inhabited ; he conducted them over those desert lands and islands (of which there are many in that sea) by the way of the north into America, which none would ever have gone, had they not first been assured there was a passage that way into a more desirable country. Namely, as when the world apostatized from the worship of the true God, God called Abraham out of Chaldee into the land of Canaan, of him to raise a seed to preserve a light unto his name : so the Devil, when he saw the world apostatizing from him, laid the foundations of a new kingdom, by deducting this colony from the north into America, where they have increased since into an innumerable multitude. And where did the Devil ever reign more abso lutely, and without control, since mankind first fell under his clutches ?

" And here it is to be noted, that the story of the Mexican kingdom (which was not founded above four hundred years before ours came thither) relates, out of their own memorials and traditions, that they came to that place from the *north*, whence their god, *Vitziliputzli*, led them, going in an ark before them : and, after divers years' travel and many stations (like enough after some generations), they came to the place which the sign he had given them at their first setting-forth pointed out; where they were to finish their travels, build themselves a *city*, and their god a *temple*, which is the place where Mexico was built. Now, if the Devil were God's ape in *this*, why might he not be likewise in bringing the first colony of men into that world out of ours? namely, by oracle, as God did Abraham out of Chaldee, whereto I before resembled it.

"But see the hand of Divine Providence. When the offspring of these *runagates* from the sound of Christ's gospel had now replenished that other world, and began to flourish in those two kingdoms of Peru and Mexico, Christ our Lord sends his mastives, the Spaniards, to hunt them out, and worry them; which they did in so hideous a manner, as the like thereunto scarce ever was done since the sons of Noah came out of the ark. What an affront to the Devil was this, where he had thought to have reigned securely, and been for ever concealed from the knowledge of the followers of Christ!

"Yet the Devil perhaps is *less grieved* for the loss of his servants by the *destroying* of them, than he would be to lose them by the *saving* of them; by which latter way, I doubt the Spaniards have despoiled him but of a few. What, then, if Christ our Lord will give him his *second affront* with better Christians, which may be more grievous to him than the former? And, if Christ shall set him up a light in this manner to dazzle and torment the Devil at his own home, I hope they (viz., the Americans) shall not so far degenerate (not all of them) as to come into that army of Gog and Magog against the kingdom of Christ, but be translated thither before the Devil be loosed; if not, presently after his tying up."

Dr. Twiss, in a reply to the above, dated April 6, 1635, thanks Mede for his letter, which he says he read " with recreation and delight ; " and, particularly in reference to the " peopling of the New World," he affirms that there is " more in this letter of yours than formerly I have been acquainted with. Your conceit thereabouts, if I have any judgment, is grave and ponderous."

This correspondence, while it serves as a specimen of the style of Mede, is a remarkable instance of the power of a sagacious intellect to penetrate through the darkness of theoretical and fanciful errors, and behold the truth that lies behind and beyond. The whole superstructure of the Devil, his oracles, and his schemes of policy and dominion, covers, in this brief familiar epistle, what is, I suppose, the theory most accredited at this day of the origin and traduction of the aboriginal races of America, proceeding from the nearest portions of the ancient continent on the North, and advancing down over the vast spaces towards Central and South America. The letter also foreshadows the decisive conflict which is here to be waged between the elements of freedom and slavery, between social and political systems that will rescue and exalt humanity, and those which depress and degrade it. In the phraseology of that age, it was to be determined whether — the Old World, in the language of Twiss, " being almost at an end " — a " light " should be " set up " here to usher in the " kingdom of Christ," or America also be for ever given over to the "army of Gog and Magog."

Our fathers were justified in feeling that this was the sense of their responsibility entertained by all learned men and true Christians in the Old World; and they were ready to meet and discharge it faithfully and manfully. They were told, and they believed, that it had fallen to their lot to be the champions of the cross of Christ against the power of the Devil. They felt, as I have said, that they were fighting him in his last stronghold, and they were determined to "tie him up" for ever.

This is the true and just explanation of their general policy of administration, in other matters, as well as in the witchcraft prosecutions.

The conclusion to which we are brought, by a review of the seventeenth century up to the period when the prosecutions took place here, is, that the witchcraft delusion pervaded the whole civilized world and every profession and department of society. It received the sanction of all the learned and distinguished English judges who flourished within the century, from Sir Edward Coke to Sir Matthew Hale. It was countenanced by the greatest philosophers and physicians, and was embraced by men of the highest genius and accomplishments, even by Lord Bacon himself. It was established by the convocation of bishops, and preached by the clergy. Dr. Henry More, of Christ's College, Cambridge, in addition to his admirable poetical and philosophical works, wrote volumes to defend it. It was considered as worthy of the study of the most cultivated and liberal minds to discover and distinguish "a true witch by proper trials and symptoms." The excellent Dr. Calamy has already been mentioned in this connection; and Richard Baxter wrote his work entitled "The Certainty of the World of Spirits," for the special purpose of confirming and diffusing the belief. He kept up a correspondence with Cotton Mather, and with his father, Increase Mather, through the medium of which he stimulated and encouraged them in their proceedings against supposed witches in Boston and elsewhere. The divines of that day seem to have persuaded themselves into the belief that the doctrines of demonology were essential to the gospel, and that the rejection of them was equivalent to infidelity. A writer in one of our modern journals, in speaking of the prosecutions for witchcraft, happily and justly observes, "It was truly hazardous to oppose those judicial murders. If any one ventured to do so, the Catholics burned him as a heretic, and the Protestants had a vehement longing to hang him for an atheist." The writings of Dr. More, of Baxter, Glanvil, Perkins, and others, had been circulating for a long time in New England before the trials began at Salem. It was such a review of the history of opinion as we have now made, which led Dr. Bentley to declare that "the agency of invisible beings, if not a part of every religion, is not contrary to any one. It may be found in all ages, and in the most remote countries. It is then no just subject for our admiration, that a

belief so alarming to our fears, so natural to our prejudices, and so easily abused by superstition, should
obtain among our fathers, when it had not been rejected in the ages of philosophy, letters, and even
revelation."

The works on demonology, the legal proceedings in
prosecutions, and the phraseology of the people, gave
more or less definite form to certain prominent points
which may be summarily noticed. Several terms and
expressions were employed to characterize persons
supposed to be conversant with supernatural and magic
art; such as diviner, enchanter, charmer, conjurer,
necromancer, fortune-teller, soothsayer, augur, and
sorcerer. These words are sometimes used as more
or less synonymous, although, strictly speaking, they
have meanings quite distinct. But none of them convey the idea attached to the name of witch. It was
sometimes especially used to signify a female, while
wizard was exclusively applied to a male. The distinction was not, however, often attempted to be made;
the former title being prevailingly applied to either
sex. A witch was regarded as a person who had made
an actual, deliberate, formal compact with Satan, by
which it was agreed that she should become his faithful subject, and do all in her power to aid him in
his rebellion against God and his warfare against the
gospel and church of Christ; and, in consideration of
such allegiance and service, Satan, on his part, agreed
to exercise his supernatural powers in her favor, and
communicate to her those powers, in a greater or less

degree, as she proved herself an efficient and devoted supporter of his cause. Thus, a witch was considered as a person who had transferred allegiance and worship from God to the Devil.

The existence of this compact was supposed to confer great additional power on the Devil, as well as on his new subject; for the doctrine seems to have prevailed, that, for him to act with effect upon men, the intervention, instrumentality, and co-operation of human beings was necessary; and almost unlimited potency was ascribed to the combined exertions of Satan and those persons in league with him. A witch was believed to have the power, through her compact with the Devil, of afflicting, distressing, and rending whomsoever she would. She could cause them to pine away, throw them into the most frightful convulsions, choke, bruise, pierce, and craze them, subjecting them to every description of pain, disease, and torture, and even to death itself. She was believed to possess the faculty of being present, in her shape or apparition, at a different place, at any distance whatever, from that which her actual body occupied. Indeed, an indefinite amount of supernatural ability, and a boundless freedom and variety of methods for its exercise, were supposed to result from the diabolical compact. Those upon whom she thus exercised her malignant and mysterious energies were said to be bewitched.

Beside these infernal powers, the alliance with Satan was believed to confer knowledge such as no other mortal possessed. The witch could perform the same wonders, in giving information of the things that belong to the invisible world, which is alleged in our day, by spirit-rappers, to be received through mediums. She could read inmost thoughts, suggest ideas to the minds of the absent, throw temptations in the path of those whom she desired to delude and destroy, bring up the spirits of the departed, and hear from them the secrets of their lives and of their deaths, and their experiences in the scenes of being on which they entered at their departure from this.

When we consider that these opinions were not merely prevalent among the common people, but sanctioned by learning and philosophy, science and jurisprudence ; that they possessed an authority, which but few ventured to question and had been firmly established by the convictions of centuries, — none can be surprised at the alarm it created, when the belief became current, that there were those in the community, and even in the churches, who had actually entered into this dark confederacy against God and heaven, religion and virtue ; and that individuals were beginning to suffer from their diabolical power. It cannot be considered strange, that men looked with more than common horror upon persons against whom what was regarded as overwhelming evidence was borne of having engaged in this conspiracy with all that was evil, and this treason against all that was good.

Elaborate works, scientific, philosophical, and judicial in their pretensions and reputation, — to some of which reference has been made, — defined and par-

ticularized the various forms of evidence by which
the crime of confederacy with Satan could be proved.

It was believed that the Devil affixed his mark to
the bodies of those in alliance with him, and that the
point where this mark was made became callous and
dead. The law provided, specifically, the means of
detecting and identifying this sign. It required that
the prisoner should be subjected to the scrutiny of
a jury of the same sex, who would make a minute
inspection of the body, shaving the head and handling
every part. They would pierce it with pins ; and if,
as might have been expected, particularly in aged persons, any spot could be found insensible to the torture,
or any excrescence, induration, or fixed discoloration,
it was looked upon as visible evidence and demonstration of guilt. A physician or " chirurgeon " was
required to be present at these examinations. In conducting them, there was liability to great roughness
and unfeeling recklessness of treatment; and the whole
procedure was barbarous and shocking to every just
and delicate sensibility. There is reason to believe,
that, in the trials here, there was more considerateness, humanity, and regard to a sense of decent
propriety, than in similar proceedings in other countries, so far as this branch of the investigation is
regarded.

Another accredited field of evidence, recognized in
the books and in legal proceedings, was as follows : It
was believed, that, when witches found it inconvenient
from any cause to execute their infernal designs upon

hurt

those whom they wished to afflict by going to them in
their natural human persons, they transformed themselves into the likeness of some animal, — a dog, hog,
cat, rat, mouse, or toad; birds — particularly yellow
birds — were often imagined to perform this service, as
representing witches or the Devil. They also had
imps under their control. These imps were generally
supposed to bear the resemblance of some small in-
sect, — such as a fly or a spider. The latter animal
was prevailingly considered as most likely to act in
this character. The accused person was closely
watched, in order that the spider imp might be seen
when it approached to obtain its nourishment, as it
was thought to do, from the witchmark on the body of
the culprit. Within the cells of a prison, spiders were,
of course, often seen. Whenever one made its appearance, the guard attacked it with all the zeal and vehemence with which it was natural and proper to assault
an agent of the Wicked One. If the spider was killed
in the encounter, it was considered as an innocent
animal, and all suspicion was removed from its character as the diabolical confederate of the prisoner;
but if it escaped into a crack or crevice of the apartment, as spiders often do when assailed, all doubt of
its guilty connection with the person accused of witchcraft was removed: it was set down as, beyond question or cavil, her veritable imp; and the evidence of
her confederacy with Satan was thenceforward regarded
as complete. The books of law and other learned
writings, as well as the practice of courts in the old

countries, recognized this doctrine of transformation
into the shapes of animals, and the employment of
Where judicial tribunals countenanced the
credulity in maintaining these ideas, there
purity for innocence, and no escape from
matter how clear and certain the evidence
an accused individual, at the time al-
sent from the specified place; no matter
how far distant, whether twenty or a thousand miles,
it availed him nothing; for it was charged that he was
present, and acted through his agent or imp. This
notion was further enlarged by the establishment of
the additional doctrine, that a witch could be present,
and act with demoniac power upon her victims, anywhere, at all times, and at any distance, without the
instrumental agency of any other animal or being, in
her spirit, spectre, or apparition. When the person
on trial was accused of having tortured or strangled
or pinched or bruised another, it did not break the
force of the accusation to bring hundreds of witnesses
to prove that he was, at the very time, in another
remote place or country; for it was alleged that he
was present in the spectral shape in which Satan enabled his spirit to be and to act any and every where at
once. It was impossible to disprove the charge, and
the last defence of innocence was swept away.

If any thing strange or remarkable could be discovered in the persons, histories, or deportment of accused
persons, the usage of the tribunals, and the books of
authority on the subject, allowed it to be brought in

evidence against them. If any thing they had fore-warned, or even conjectured, happened to come to pass, any careless speech had been verified by events, any extraordinary knowledge had been manifested, or any marvellous feats of strength or agility been dis-played, they were brought up with decisive and fatal effect.

A witch was believed to have the power of operating upon her victims, at any distance, by the instrumen-tality of puppets. She would procure or make an object like a doll, or a figure of some animal, — any little bunch of cloth or bundle of rags would answer the purpose. She would will the puppet to represent the person whom she proposed to torment or afflict; and then whatever she did to the puppet would be suffered by the party it represented at any distance, however remote. A pin stuck into the puppet would pierce the flesh of the person whom she wished to afflict, and produce the appropriate sensations of pain. So would a pinch, or a blow, or any kind of violence. When any one was arrested on the charge of witch-craft, a search was immediately made for puppets from garret to cellar; and if any thing could be found that might possibly be imagined to possess that char-acter, — any remnant of flannel or linen wrapped up, the foot of an old stocking, or a cushion of any kind, particularly if there were any pins in it, — it was con-sidered as weighty and quite decisive evidence against the accused party.

A writer, in a recent number of the " North-American Review," on the superstitions of the American Indians, makes the following statement:—

"The sorcerer, by charms, magic songs, magic feats, and the beating of his drum, had power over the spirits, and those occult influences inherent in animals and inanimate things. He could call to him the souls of his enemies. They appeared before him in the form of stones. He chopped and bruised them with his hatchet; blood and flesh issued forth; and the intended victim, however distant, languished and died. Like the sorcerer of the middle ages, he made images of those he wished to destroy, and, muttering incantations, punctured them with an awl; whereupon the persons represented sickened and pined away."

It was a received opinion, accredited and acted upon in courts, that a person in confederacy with the Evil One could not weep. Those accused of this crime, both in Europe and America, were, in many instances, of an age and condition which rendered it impossible for them, however innocent, to escape the effect of this test. A decrepit, emaciated person, shrivelled and desiccated by age, was placed at the bar : and if she could not weep on the spot; if, in consequence of her withered frame, her amazement and indignation at the false and malignant charges by which she was circumvented, her exhausted sensibility, her sullen despair, the hopeless horror of her situation, or, from what often was found to be the effect of the treatment such persons received, a high-toned consciousness of innocence, and a brave defiance and stern condemnation of her maligners and persecutors; if, from any cause, the fountain of tears was closed or dried up, — their failure to come forth at the bidding of her defamers was regarded as a sure and irrefragable proof of her guilt.

King James explains the circumstance, that witches could not weep, in rather a curious manner : —

"For as, in a secret murther, if the dead carkasse bee at any time thereafter handled by the murtherer it will gush out of bloud, as if the bloud were crying to the heaven for revenge of the murtherer, God having appointed that secret supernaturall signe for triall of that secret unnaturall crime ; so it appeares that God hath appointed (for a supernaturall signe of the monstrous impietie of witches), that the water shall refuse to receive them in her bosome that have shaken off them the sacred water of baptisme, and wilfully refused the benefite thereof: no, not so much as their eyes are able to shed teares (threaten and torture them as ye please), while first they repent (God not permitting them to dissemble their obstinacie in so horrible a crime), albeit the woman kind especially be able otherwise to shed teares at every light occasion when they will, — yea, although it were dissemblingly like the crocodiles."

Reginald Scott, in introducing a Romish form of adjuration, makes the following excellent remarks on the trial by tears : —

"But alas that teares should be thought sufficient to excuse or condemn in so great a cause, and so weightie a triall ! I am sure that the worst sort of the children of Israel wept bitterlie ; yea, if there were any witches at all in Israel, they wept. For it is written, that all the children

of Israel wept. Finallie, if there be any witches in hell, I
am sure they weepe; for there is weeping and wailing and
gnashing of teeth. But God knoweth many an honest
matron cannot sometimes in the heaviness of her heart shed
teares; the which oftentimes are more readie and common
with crafty queans and strumpets than with sober women.
For we read of two kinds of teares in a woman's eie; the
one of true greefe, and the other of deceipt. And it is written, that ' Dediscere flere fœminam est mendacium;' which
argueth that they lie, which saie that wicked women cannot
weepe. But let these tormentors take heed, that the teares
in this case which runne down the widowe's cheeks, with
their crie, spoken of by Jesus Sirach, be not heard above.
But, lo, what learned, godlie and lawful meanes these
Popish Inquisitors have invented for the triall of true or
false teares : —

' I conjure thee, by the amorous tears which Jesus Christ,
our Saviour, shed upon the crosse for the salvation of the
world; and by the most earnest and burning teares of his
mother, the most glorious Virgine Marie, sprinkled upon
his wounds late in the evening; and by all the teares which
everie saint and elect vessell of God hath poured out heere
in the world, and from whose eies he hath wiped awaie all
teares, — that, if thou be without fault, thou maist poure
downe teares aboundantlie; and, if thou be guiltie, that thou
weep in no wise. In the name of the Father, of the Sonne,
and of the Holie Ghost. Amen.'

" The more you conjure, the lesse she weepeth."

A distinction was made between black and white
witches. The former were those who had leagued
with Satan for the purpose of doing injury to others,

while the latter class was composed of such persons as
had resorted to the arts and charms of divination and
sorcery in order to protect themselves and others from
diabolical influence. They were both considered as
highly, if not equally, criminal. Fuller, in his "Profane State," thus speaks of them: "Better is it to lap
one's pottage like a dog, than to eat it mannerly, with
a spoon of the Devil's giving. Black witches hurt and
do mischief; but, in deeds of darkness, there is no
difference of colors. The white and the black are
both guilty alike in compounding with the Devil."
White witches pretended to extract their power from the
mysterious virtues of certain plants. The following
form of charmed words was used in plucking them: —

> "Hail to thee, holy herb,
>   Growing in the ground;
> On the Mount of Calvarie,
>   First wert thou found;
> Thou art good for many a grief,
>   And healest many a wound:
> In the name of sweet Jesu,
>   I lift thee from the ground."

Then there was the evidence of ocular fascination.
The accused and the accusers were brought into the
presence of the examining magistrate, and the supposed witch was ordered to look upon the afflicted
persons; instantly upon coming within the glance of
her eye, they would scream out, and fall down as in a
fit. It was thought that an invisible and impalpable
fluid darted from the eye of the witch, and penetrated
the brain of the bewitched. By bringing the witch so

near that she could touch the afflicted persons with her hand, the malignant fluid was attracted back into her hand, and the sufferers recovered their senses. It is singular to notice the curious resemblance between this opinion — the joint product of superstition and imposture — and the results to which modern science has led us in the discoveries of galvanism and animal electricity. The doctrine of fascination maintained its hold upon the public credulity for a long time, and gave occasion to the phrase, still in familiar use among us, of "looking upon a person with an evil eye." Its advocates claimed, in its defence, the authority of the Cartesian philosophy; but it cannot be considered, in an age of science and reason, as having any better support than the rural superstition of Virgil's simple shepherd, who thus complains of the condition of his emaciated flock : —

> "They look so thin,
> Their bones are barely covered with their skin.
> What magic has bewitched the woolly dams ?
> And what ill eyes beheld the tender lambs ? "

Witchcraft, in all ages and countries, was recognized as a reality, just as much as any of the facts of nature, or incidents to which mankind is liable. By the laws of all nations, Catholic and Protestant alike, in the old country and in the new, it was treated as a capital offence, and classed with murder and other highest crimes, although regarded as of a deeper dye and blacker character than them all. Indictments and trials of persons accused of it were not, therefore, considered as of any special interest, or as differing in any essential particulars from proceedings against any other description of offenders. There had been many such proceedings in the American colonies, — more, perhaps, than have come to our knowledge, — previous to 1692. They were not looked upon as sufficiently extraordinary to be transferred, from the oblivion sweeping like a perpetual deluge over the vast multitude of human experiences, to the ark of history, which rescues only a select few. The following are the principal facts of this class of which we have information : —

William Penn presided, in his judicial character, at the trial of two Swedish women for witchcraft; the grand jury, acting under instructions from him, having found bills against them. They were saved, not in consequence of any peculiar reluctance to proceed against them arising out of the nature of the alleged crime, but only from some technical defect in the indictment. If it had not been for this accidental circumstance, as the annalist of Philadelphia suggests, scenes similar to those subsequently occurring in Salem Village might have darkened the history of the Quakers, Swedes, Germans, and Dutch, who dwelt in the City of Brotherly Love and the adjacent colonies. There had been trials and executions for witchcraft in other parts of New England, and excitements had obtained more or less currency in reference to the assaults of the powers of darkness upon human affairs. These incidents prepared the way for the delusion in Salem, and provided elements to form its character. They must not, therefore, be wholly overlooked. But the memorials for their elucidation are very defective. Hutchinson's " History of Massachusetts " is, perhaps, the most valuable authority on the subject. He enjoyed an advantage over any other writer, before, since, or hereafter, so far as relates to the witchcraft proceedings in 1692; for he had access to all the records and documents connected with it, a great part of which have subsequently been lost or destroyed. His treatment of that particular topic is more satisfactory than can elsewhere be found. But of incidents of the sort that preceded it, his information appears to have been very slight and unreliable. It is a singular fact, that we know more of the history of the first century of New England than was known by the most enlightened persons of the intermediate century. There was no regular organized newspaper press, the commemorative age had not begun, and none seem to have been fully aware of the importance of putting events on record. The publication, but a few years since, of the colonial journals of the first half-century of Massachusetts; researches by innumerable hands among papers on file in public offices; the printing of town-histories, and the collections made by historical and genealogical societies, — have rescued from oblivion, and redeemed from error, many points of the greatest interest and importance.

Winthrop, in his "Journal," gives an account of the execution of Margaret Jones, of Charlestown, who had been tried and condemned by the Court of Assistants.

The charges against her were, that she had a malignant touch, so that many persons,— "men, women, and children,"— on coming in contact with her, were "taken with deafness, vomiting, or other violent pains or sickness;" that she practised physic, and her medicines, "being such things as (by her own confession) were harmless, as aniseed, liquors, &c., yet had extraordinary violent effects;" and that they found on her body, "upon a forced search," the witchmarks, particularly "a teat, as fresh if it had been newly sucked." Other ridiculous allegations were made against her. As for the effects of the touch, it is obvious that they could be easily simulated by evil-disposed persons. The whole substance of her offence seems to have been, that she was very successful in the use of simple prescriptions for the cure of diseases. Her practice was charged as "against the ordinary course, and beyond the apprehension of all physicians and surgeons." A bitter animosity was, accordingly, raised against her. She treated her accusers and defamers with indignant resentment. "Her behavior at her trial," says Winthrop, "was very intemperate, lying notoriously, and railing upon the jury and witnesses, &c.; and, in the like distemper, she died." We shall find that the bold assertion of innocence, and indignant denunciations of the persecutors and defamers who had destroyed their reputations and pursued them to the death, by persons tried and executed for witchcraft, in 1692, were regarded by some, as they were by Winthrop, as proofs of ill-temper and falsehood. The Governor closes his statement about Margaret Jones, by relating what he regarded as a demonstration of her guilt: "The same day and hour she was executed, there was a very great tempest at Connecticut, which blew down many trees, &c." The records of the General Court contain no express notice of this case. Perhaps it is referred to in the following paragraph, under date of May 13, 1648 : —

"This Court, being desirous that the same course which hath been taken in England for the discovery of witches, by watching, may also be taken here, with the witch now in question, and therefore do order that a strict watch be set about her every night, and that her husband be confined to a private room, and watched also."

Margaret Jones was executed in Boston on the 15th of June. Hutchinson refers to the statement made by Johnson, in the "Wonder-working Providence," that "more than one or two in Springfield, in 1645, were suspected of witchcraft; that much diligence was used, both for the finding them and for the Lord's assisting them against their witchery; yet have they, as is supposed, bewitched not a few persons, among whom two of the reverend elder's children." Johnson's loose and immethodical narrative covers the period from 1645 till toward the end of 1651; and Hutchinson was probably misled in supposing that the Springfield cases occurred as early as 1645. The Massachusetts colonial records, under the date of May 8, 1651, have this entry : —

" The Court, understanding that Mary Parsons, now in prison, accused for a witch, is likely, through weakness, to die before trial, if it be deferred, do order, that, on the morrow, by eight o'clock in the morning, she be brought before and tried by the General Court, the rather that Mr. Pinchon may be present to give his testimony in the case."

Mr. Pinchon was probably able to stay a few days longer. She was not brought to trial before the Court until the 13th, under which date is the following : —

" Mary Parsons, wife of Hugh Parsons, of Springfield, being committed to prison for suspicion of witchcraft, as also for murdering her own child, was this day called forth, and indicted for witchcraft. ' By the name of Mary Parsons, you are here, before the General Court, charged, in the name of this Commonwealth, that, not having the fear of God before your eyes nor in your heart, being seduced by the Devil, and yielding to his malicious motion, about the end of February last, at Springfield, to have familiarity, or consulted with, a familiar spirit, making a covenant with him ; and have used divers devilish practices by witchcraft, to the hurt of the persons of Martha and Rebecca Moxon, against the word of God and the laws of this jurisdiction, long since made and published.' To which indictment she pleaded ' Not guilty.' All evidences brought in against her being heard and examined, the Court found the evidences were not sufficient to prove her a witch, and therefore she was cleared in that respect.

" At the same time, she was indicted for murdering her child. ' By the name of Mary Parsons, you are here, before the General Court, charged, in the name of this Common-

wealth, that, not having the fear of God before your eyes
nor in your heart, being seduced by the Devil, and yielding
to his instigations and the wickedness of your own heart,
about the beginning of March last, in Springfield, in or near
your own house, did wilfully and most wickedly murder
your own child, against the word of God and the laws of
this jurisdiction, long since made and published.' To which
she acknowledged herself guilty.

"The Court, finding her guilty of murder by her own confession, &c., proceeded to judgment: 'You shall be carried
from this place to the place from whence you came, and
from thence to the place of execution, and there hang till
you be dead.'"

Under the same date — May 13 — is an order of
the Court appointing a day of humiliation "throughout our jurisdiction in all the churches," in consideration, among other things, of the extent to which
"Satan prevails amongst us in respect of witchcrafts."

The colonial records, under date of May 31, 1652,
recite the facts, that Hugh Parsons, of Springfield, had
been tried before the Court of Assistants — held at
Boston, May 12, 1652 — for witchcraft; that the case
was transferred to a "jury of trials," which found him
guilty. The magistrates not consenting to the verdict
of the jury, the case came legally to the General
Court, which body decided that "he was not legally
guilty of witchcraft, and so not to die by law."

When these citations are collated and examined, and
it is remembered that Mr. Moxon was the "reverend
elder" of the church at Springfield, it cannot be doubted

that the case of the Parsonses is that referred to by Johnson in the "Wonder-working Providence," and that Hutchinson was in error as to the date. We are left in doubt as to the fate of Mary Parsons. There is a marginal entry on the records, to the effect that she was reprieved to the 29th of May. Neither Johnson nor Hutchinson seem to have thought that the sentence was ever carried into effect. It clearly never ought to have been. The woman was in a weak and dying condition, her mind was probably broken down, — the victim of that peculiar kind of mania — partaking of the character of a religious fanaticism and perversion of ideas — that has often led to child-murder.

These instances show, that, at that time, the General Court exercised consideration and discrimination in the treatment of questions of this kind brought before it.

Hutchinson, on the authority of Hale, says that a woman at Dorchester, and another at Cambridge, were executed, not far from this time, for witchcraft; and that they asserted their innocence with their dying breath. He also says, that, in 1650, " a poor wretch, — Mary Oliver, — probably weary of her life from the general reputation of being a witch, after long examination, was brought to a confession of her guilt; but I do not find that she was executed."

In 1656, a very remarkable case occurred. William Hibbins was a merchant in Boston, and one of the most prominent and honored citizens of Massachusetts. He was admitted a freeman in 1640; was deputy in the

General Court in that and the following year; was elected an assistant for twelve successive years, — from 1643 to 1654; represented the Colony, for a time, as its agent in England, and received the thanks of the General Court for his valuable service there. No one appears to have had more influence, or to have enjoyed more honorable distinction, during his long legislative career. He died in 1654. Hutchinson says, in the text of his first and second volumes, that his widow was tried, condemned, and hanged as a witch in 1655, although he corrects the error in a note to the passage in the first volume. The following is the statement of the case in the Massachusetts colonial records, under the date of May 14, 1656: —

"The magistrates not receiving the verdict of the jury in Mrs. Hibbins her case, having been on trial for witchcraft, it came and fell, of course, to the General Court. Mrs. Ann Hibbins was called forth, appeared at the bar, the indictment against her was read; to which she answered, 'Not guilty,' and was willing to be tried by God and this Court. The evidence against her was read, the parties witnessing being present, her answers considered on; and the whole Court, being met together, by their vote, determined that Mrs. Ann Hibbins is guilty of witchcraft, according to the bill of indictment found against her by the jury of life and death. The Governor, in open Court, pronounced sentence accordingly; declaring she was to go from the bar to the place from whence she came, and from thence to the place of execution, and there to hang till she was dead.

"It is ordered, that warrant shall issue out from the secretary to the marshal general, for the execution of Mrs. Hib-

bins, on the fifth day next come fortnight, presently after the
lecture at Boston, being the 19th of June next ; the marshal
general taking with him a sufficient guard."

Mrs. Hibbins is stated to have been a sister of Richard Bellingham, at that very time deputy-governor,
and always regarded as one of the chief men in the
country. Strange to say, very little notice appears to
have been taken of this event, beyond the immediate
locality ; but what little has come down to us indicates that it was a case of outrageous folly and bar-
barity, justly reflecting infamy upon the community at
the time. Hutchinson, who wrote a hundred years
after the event, and evidently had no other foundation
for his opinion than vague conjectural tradition, gives
the following explanation of the proceedings against
her : " Losses, in the latter part of her husband's life,
had reduced his estate, and increased the natural crab-
bedness of his wife's temper, which made her turbulent
and quarrelsome, and brought her under church cen-
sures, and at length rendered her so odious to her
neighbors as to cause some of them to accuse her of
witchcraft."

While this is hardly worthy of being considered a
sufficient explanation of the matter,— it being beyond
belief, that, even at that time, a person could be condemned and executed merely on account of a " crabbed
temper,"— it is not consistent with the facts, as made
known to us from the record-offices. She could not
have been so reduced in circumstances as to produce
such extraordinary effects upon her character, for she

left a good estate. The truth is, that the tongue of
slander was let loose upon her, and the calumnies circulated by reckless gossip became so magnified and
exaggerated, and assumed such proportions, as enabled
her vilifiers to bring her under the censure of the
church, and that emboldened them to cry out against
her as a witch. Hutchinson expresses the opinion that
she was the victim of popular clamor. But that alone,
without some pretence or show of evidence, could not
have brought the General Court, in reversal of the
judgment of the magistrates, to condemn to death a
person of such a high social position.

The only clue we have to the kind of evidence bearing upon the charge of witchcraft that brought this
recently bereaved widow to so cruel and shameful
a death, is in a letter, written by a clergyman in
Jamaica to Increase Mather in 1684, in which he says,
" You may remember what I have sometimes told you
your famous Mr. Norton once said at his own table,
— before Mr. Wilson, the pastor, elder Penn, and myself and wife, &c., who had the honor to be his guests,
— that one of your magistrate's wives, as I remember,
was hanged for a witch only for having more wit than
her neighbors. It was his very expression ; she having, as he explained it, unhappily guessed that two of
her persecutors, whom she saw talking in the street,
were talking of her, which, proving true, cost her her
life, notwithstanding all he could do to the contrary, as
he himself told us." Nothing was more natural than
for her to suppose, knowing the parties, witnessing their

manner, considering their active co-operation in getting up the excitement against her, which was then the
all-engrossing topic, that they were talking about her.
But, in the blind infatuation of the time, it was considered proof positive of her being possessed, by the aid
of the Devil, of supernatural insight, — precisely as,
forty years afterwards, such evidence was brought to
bear, with telling effect, against George Burroughs. —
The body of this unfortunate lady was searched for
witchmarks, and her trunks and premises rummaged
for puppets.

It is quite evident that means were used to get up a
violent popular excitement against her, which became
so formidable as to silence every voice that dared to
speak in her favor.   Joshua Scottow, a citizen of great
respectability and a selectman, ventured to give evidence in her favor, counter, in its bearings, to some
testimony against her; and he was dealt with very
severely, and compelled to write an humble apology to
the Court, to disavow all friendly interest in Mrs. Hibbins, and to pray " that the sword of justice may be
drawn forth against all wickedness."   He says, " I am
cordially sorry that any thing from me, either by word
or writing, should give offence to the honored Court,
my dear brethren in the church, or any others."

Hutchinson states that there were, however, some
persons then in Boston, who denounced the proceedings against Mrs. Hibbins, and regarded her, not merely
as a persecuted woman, but as " a saint; " that a deep
feeling of resentment against her persecutors long

remained in their minds; and that they afterwards
" observed solemn marks of Providence set upon those
who were very forward to condemn her." It is evident that the Court of Magistrates were opposed to
her conviction, and that Mr. Norton did what he could
to save her. He was one of the four " great Johns,"
who were the first ministers of the church in Boston;
and it is remarkable, as showing the violence of the
people against her, that even his influence was of no
avail in her favor. But she had other friends, as
appears from her will, which, after all, is the only
source of reliable information we have respecting her
character. It is dated May 27, 1656, a few days after
she received the sentence of death. In it she names,
as overseers and administrators of her estate, " Captain Thomas Clarke, Lieutenant Edward Hutchinson,
Lieutenant William Hudson, Ensign Joshua Scottow,
and Cornet Peter Oliver." In a codicil, she says, " I
do earnestly desire my loving friends, Captain Johnson
and Mr. Edward Rawson, to be added to the rest of the
gentlemen mentioned as overseers of my will." It can
hardly be doubted, that these persons — and they were
all leading citizens — were known by her to be among
her friends.

The whole tone and manner of these instruments
give evidence, that she had a mind capable of rising
above the power of wrong, suffering, and death itself.
They show a spirit calm and serene. The disposition
of her property indicates good sense, good feeling, and
business faculties suitable to the occasion. In the

body of the will, there is not a word, a syllable, or a turn of expression, that refers to, or is in the slightest degree colored by, her peculiar situation. In the codicil, dated June 16, there is this sentence: "My desire is, that all my overseers would be pleased to show so much respect unto my dead corpse as to cause it to be decently interred, and, if it may be, near my late husband."

When married to Mr. Hibbins, she was a widow, named Moore. There were no children by her last marriage,— certainly none living at the time of her death. There were three sons by her former marriage,— John, Joseph, and Jonathan. These were all in England; but the youngest, hearing of her situation, embarked for America. When she wrote the codicil, — three days before her execution,— she added, at the end, having apparently just heard of his coming, "I give my son Jonathan twenty pounds, over and above what I have already given him, towards his pains and charge in coming to see me, which shall be first paid out of my estate." There is reason to cherish the belief that he reached her in the short interval between the date of the codicil and her death, from the tenor of the following postscript, written and signed on the morning of her execution: "My further mind and will is, out of my sense of the more than ordinary affection and pains of my son Jonathan in the times of my distress, I give him, as a further legacy, ten pounds." The will was proved in Court, July 2, 1656. The will and codicil speak of her "farms at Muddy River;" and of chests and a desk, in which were valuables of such importance that she took especial pains to intrust the keys of them to Edward Rawson, in a provision of the codicil. The estate was inventoried at £344. 14s., which was a considerable property in those days, as money was then valued.

Hutchinson mentions a case of witchcraft in Hartford, in 1662, where some women were accused, and, after being proceeded against until they were confounded and bewildered, one of them made the most preposterous confessions, which ought to have satisfied every one that her reason was overthrown; three of them were condemned, and one, certainly, — probably all, — executed. In 1669, he says that Susanna Martin, of Salisbury, — whom we shall meet again, — was bound over to the Court on the same charge, " but escaped at that time." Another case is mentioned by him as having occurred, in 1671, at Groton, in which the party confessed, and thereby avoided condemnation. In 1673, a case occurred at Hampton; but the jury, although, as they said, there was strong ground of suspicion, returned a verdict of " Not guilty ; " the evidence not being deemed quite sufficient. There were several other cases, about this time, in which some persons were severely handled in consequence of being reputed witches; and others suffered, as they imagined, " under an evil hand."

In this immediate neighborhood, there had been several attempts, previous to the delusion at Salem Village in 1692, to get up witchcraft prosecutions, but without much success. The people of this county had not become sufficiently infected with the fanaticism of the times to proceed to extremities.

In September, 1652, the following presentment was made by the grand jury : —

"We present John Bradstreet, of Rowley, for suspicion of having familiarity with the Devil. He said he read in a book of magic, and that he heard a voice asking him what work he had for him. He answered, ' Go make a bridge of sand over the sea ; go make a ladder of sand up to heaven, and go to God, and come down no more.'

"Witness hereof, FRANCIS PARAT and his wife, of Rowley.
"Witness, WILLIAM BARTHOLOMEW, of Ipswich."

On the 28th of that month, the jury at Ipswich, "upon examination of the case, found he had told a lie, which was a second, being convicted once before. The Court sets a fine of twenty shillings, or else to be whipped."

Bradstreet was probably in the habit of romancing, and it was wisely concluded not to take a more serious view of his offences.

In 1658, a singular case of this kind occurred in Essex County. The following papers relating to it illustrate the sentiments and forms of thought prevalent at that time, and give an insight of the state of society in some particulars : —

" *To the Honored Court to be holden at Ipswich, this twelfth month, '58 or '59.*

" HONORED GENTLEMEN, — Whereas divers of esteem with us, and as we hear in other places also, have for

some time suffered losses in their estates, and some affliction in their bodies also, — which, as they suppose, doth not
arise from any natural cause, or any neglect in themselves,
but rather from some ill-disposed person, — that, upon differences had betwixt themselves and one John Godfrey,
resident at Andover or elsewhere at his pleasure, we whose
names are underwritten do make bold to sue by way of re
quest to this honored court, that you, in your wisdom, will
be pleased, if you see cause for it, to call him in question,
and to hear, at present or at some after sessions, what may
be said in this respect.

> "JAMES DAVIS, Sr., in the behalf of his son EPHRAIM DAVIS.
> JOHN HASELDIN, and JANE his wife.
> ABRAHAM WHITAKER, for his ox and other things.
> EPHRAIM DAVIS, in the behalf of himself."

The petitioners mention in brief some instances
in confirmation of their complaint. There are several depositions. That of Charles Browne and wife
says : —

" About six or seven years since, in the meeting-house of
Rowley, being in the gallery in the first seat, there was one
in the second seat which he doth, to his best remembrance,
think and believe it was John Godfrey. This deponent did
see him, yawning, open his mouth ; and, while he so yawned,
this deponent did see a small teat under his tongue. And,
further, this deponent saith that John Godfrey was in this
deponent's house about three years since. Speaking about
the power of witches, he the said Godfrey spoke, that, if
witches were not kindly entertained, the Devil will appear
unto them, and ask them if they were grieved or vexed with
anybody, and ask them what he should do for them ; and, if

they would not give them beer or victuals, they might let all
the beer run out of the cellar; and, if they looked stead-
fastly upon any creature, it would die; and, if it were hard
to some witches to take away life, either of man or beast,
yet, when they once begin it, then it is easy to them."

The depositions in this case are presented as they
are in the originals on file, leaving in blank such
words or parts of words as have been worn off. They
are given in full.

"THE DEPOSITION OF ISABEL HOLDRED, who testifieth
that John Godfree came to the house of Henry Blazdall,
where her husband and herself were, and demanded a debt
of her husband, and said a warrant was out, and Goodman
Lord was suddenly to come. John Godfree asked if we would
not pay him. The deponent answered, 'Yes, to-night or to-
morrow, if we had it; for I believe we shall not . . . . we
are in thy debt.' John Godfree answered, 'That is a bitter
word;' . . . . said, 'I must begin, and must send Goodman
Lord.' The deponent answered, '. . . . when thou wilt. I
fear thee not, nor all the devils in hell!' And, further, this
deponent testifieth, that, two days after this, she was taken
with those strange fits, with which she was tormented a
fortnight together, night and day. And several apparitions
appeared to the deponent in the night. The first night, a
humble-bee, the next night a bear, appeared, which grinned
the teeth and shook the claw: 'Thou sayest thou art not
afraid. Thou thinkest Harry Blazdall's house will save
thee.' The deponent answered, 'I hope the Lord Jesus
Christ will save me.' The apparition then spake: 'Thou
sayst thou art not afraid of all the devils in hell; but I will

have thy heart's blood within a few hours ! ' The next was the apparition of a great snake, at which the deponent was exceedingly affrighted, and skipt to Nathan Gold, who was in the opposite chimney-corner, and caught hold of the hair of his head ; and her speech was taken away for the space of half an hour. The next night appeared a great horse ; and, Thomas Hayne being there, the deponent told him of it, and showed him where. The said Tho. Hayne took a stick, and struck at the place where the apparition was; and his stroke glanced by the side of it, and it went under the table. And he went to strike again ; then the apparition fled to the . . . . and made it shake, and went away. And, about a week after, the deponent . . . . son were at the door of Nathan Gold, and heard a rushing on the . . . . The deponent said to her son, ' Yonder is a beast.' He answered, ' 'Tis one of Goodman Cobbye's black oxen ;' and it came toward them, and came within . . . . yards of them. The deponent her heart began to ache, for it seemed to have great eyes ; and spoke to the boy, ' Let's go in.' But suddenly the ox beat her up against the wall, and struck her down ; and she was much hurt by it, not being able to rise up. But some others carried me into the house, all my face being bloody, being much bruised. The boy was much affrighted a long time after ; and, for the space of two hours, he was in a sweat that one might have washed hands on his hair. Further this deponent affirmeth, that she hath been often troubled with . . . . black cat sometimes appearing in the house, and sometimes in the night . . . . bed, and lay on her, and sometimes stroking her face. The cat seemed . . . . thrice as big as an ordinary cat."

" THOMAS HAYNE testifieth, that, being with Goodwife Holdridge, she told me that she saw a great horse, and showed me where it stood. I then took a stick, and struck on the place, but felt nothing; and I heard the door shake, and Good. H. said it was gone out at the door. Immediately after, she was taken with extremity of fear and pain, so that she presently fell into a sweat, and I thought she would swoon. She trembled and shook like a leaf.

"THOMAS HAYNE."

"NATHAN GOULD being with Goodwife Holgreg one night, there appeared a great snake, as she said, with open mouth; and she, being weak, — hardly able to go alone, — yet then ran and laid hold of Nathan Gould by the head, and could not speak for the space of half an hour.

"NATHAN GOULD."

"WILLIAM OSGOOD testifieth, that, in the yeare '40, in the month of August, — he being then building a barn for Mr. Spencer, — John Godfree being then Mr. Spencer's herdsman, he on an evening came to the frame, where divers men were at work, and said that he had gotten a new master against the time he had done keeping cows. The said William Osgood asked him who it was. He answered, he knew not. He again asked him where he dwelt. He answered, he knew not. He asked him what his name was. He answered, he knew not. He then said to him, 'How, then, wilt thou go to him when thy time is out?' He said, 'The man will come and fetch me then.' I asked him, 'Hast thou made an absolute bargain?' He answered that a covenant was made, and he had set his hand to it. He then asked of him whether he had not a counter covenant. Godfree answered, 'No.' W. O. said, 'What a mad fellow art thou to make a covenant in this manner!' He said, 'He's an honest man.' — 'How knowest thou?' said W. O. J. Godfree answered. 'He looks like one.' W. O. then

answered, 'I am persuaded thou hast made a covenant with
the Devil.' He then skipped about, and said, 'I profess, I
profess!' WILLIAM OSGOOD."

The proceedings against Godfrey were carried up to
other tribunals, as appears by a record of the County
Court at Salem, 28th of June, 1659: —

"John Godfrey stands bound in one hundred pound bond
to the treasurer of this county for his appearance at a General Court, or Court of Assistants, when he shall be legally
summonsed thereunto."

What action, if any, was had by either of these
high courts, I have found no information. But he
must have come off unscathed; for, soon after, he commenced actions in the County Court for defamation
against his accusers, with the following results: —

"John Godfery plt. agst. Will. Simonds & Sam.ll his
son dfts. in an action of slander that the said Sam.ll son to
Will. Simons, hath don him in his name, Charging him to
be a witch, the jury find for the plt. 2^d damage & cost of
Court 29$^{sh.}$, yet notwithstanding doe conceiue, that by the
testmonyes he is rendred suspicious."

"John Godfery plt. agst. Jonathan Singletary defendt.
in an action of Slander & Defamation for calling him
witch & said is this witch on this side Boston Gallows yet,
the attachm^t & other evidences were read, committed to the
Jury & are on file. The Jury found for the plt. a pub-
lique acknowledgmt, at Haverhill within a month that he
hath done the plt. wrong in his words or 10^{sh} damage &
costs of Court £2-16-0."

In the trial of the case between Godfrey and Singletary, the latter attempted to prove the truth of his
allegations against the former, by giving the following
piece of testimony, which, while it failed to convince
the jury, is worth preserving, from the inherent interest of some of its details : —

" Date the fourteenth the twelfth month, '62. — THE DE-
POSITION OF JONATHAN SINGLETARY, aged about 23, who
testifieth that I, being in the prison at Ipswich this night last
past between nine and ten of the clock at night, after the
bell had rung, I being set in a corner of the prison, upon
a sudden I heard a great noise as if many cats had been
climbing up the prison walls, and skipping into the house
at the windows, and jumping about the chamber; and a
noise as if boards' ends or stools had been thrown about,
and men walking in the chambers, and a crackling and
shaking as if the house would have fallen upon me. I seeing this, and considering what I knew by a young man that
kept at my house last Indian Harvest, and, upon some
difference with John Godfre, he was presently several nights
in a strange manner troubled, and complaining as he did, and
upon consideration of this and other things that I knew by
him, I was at present something affrighted ; yet considering
what I had lately heard made out by Mr. Mitchel at
Cambridge, that there is more good in God than there is
evil in sin, and that although God is the greatest good, and
sin the greatest evil, yet the first Being of evil cannot weane
the scales or overpower the first Being of good : so considering that the author of good was of greater power than the
author of evil, God was pleased of his goodness to keep me
from being out of measure frighted. So this noise above-

said held as I suppose about a quarter of an hour, and then ceased: and presently I heard the bolt of the door shoot or go back as perfectly, to my thinking, as I did the next morning when the keeper came to unlock it; and I could not see the door open, but I saw John Godfre stand within the door and said, 'Jonathan, Jonathan.' So I, looking on him, said, 'What have you to do with me?' He said, 'I come to see you: are you weary of your place yet?' I answered, 'I take no delight in being here, but I will be out as soon as I can.' He said, 'If you will pay me in corn, you shall come out.' I answered, 'No: if that had been my intent, I would have paid the marshal, and never have come hither.' He, knocking of his fist at me in a kind of a threatening way, said he would make me weary of my part, and so went away, I knew not how nor which way; and, as I was walking about in the prison, I tripped upon a stone with my heel, and took it up in my hand, thinking that if he came again I would strike at him. So, as I was walking about, he called at the window, 'Jonathan,' said he, 'if you will pay me corn, I will give you two years day, and we will come to an agreement;' I answered him saying, 'Why do you come dissembling and playing the Devil's part here? Your nature is nothing but envy and malice, which you will vent, though to your own loss; and you seek peace with no man.' — 'I do not dissemble,' said he: 'I will give you my hand upon it, I am in earnest.' So he put his hand in at the window, and I took hold of it with my left hand, and pulled him to me; and with the stone in my right hand I thought I struck him, and went to recover my hand to strike again, and his hand was gone, and I would have struck, but there was nothing to strike: and how he went away I know not; for I could neither feel when his hand went out of mine, nor see which way he went."

It can hardly be doubted, that Singletary's story was the result of the workings of an excited imagination, in wild and frightful dreams under the spasms of nightmare. We shall meet similar phenomena, when we come to the testimony in the trials of 1692.

Godfrey was a most eccentric character. He courted and challenged the imputation of witchcraft, and took delight in playing upon the credulity of his neighbors, enjoying the exhibition of their amazement, horror, and consternation. He was a person of much notoriety, had more lawsuits, it is probable, than any other man in the colony, and in one instance came under the criminal jurisdiction for familiarity with other than immaterial spirits; for we find, by the record of Sept. 25, 1666, that John Godfrey was "fined for being drunk."

I have allowed so much space to the foregoing documents, because they show the fancies which, fermenting in the public mind, and inflamed by the prevalent literature, theology, and philosophy, came to a head thirty years afterwards; and because they prove that in 1660 a conviction for witchcraft could not be obtained in this county. The evidence against none of the convicts in 1692, throwing out of view the statements and actings of the "afflicted children," was half so strong as that against Godfrey. Short work would have been made with him then.

There is one particularly interesting item in Singletary's deposition. It illustrates the value of good preaching. This young man, in his gloomy prison, and overwhelmed with the terrors of superstition, found consolation, courage, and strength in what he remembered of a sermon, to which he had happened to listen, from " Matchless Mitchel." It was indeed good doctrine ; and it is to be lamented that it was not carried out to its logical conclusions, and constantly enforced by the divines of that and subsequent times.

In November, 1669, there was a prosecution of " Goody Burt," a widow, concerning whom the most marvellous stories were told. The principal witness against her was Philip Reed, a physician, who on oath declared his belief that " no natural cause " could produce such effects as were wrought by Goody Burt upon persons whom she afflicted. Her range of operations seems to have been confined to Marblehead, Lynn, Salem, and the vicinity : as nothing more was ever heard of the case, another evidence is afforded, that an Essex jury, notwithstanding this positive opinion of a doctor, was not ready to convict on the charge of witchcraft. This same Philip Reed tried very hard to prosecute proceedings, eleven years afterwards, against Margaret Gifford as a witch. But she failed to appear, and no effort is recorded as having been made to apprehend her.

In 1673, Eunice Cole, of Hampton, was tried before a county court, at Salisbury, on the charge of witchcraft ; and she was committed to jail, in Boston, for further proceedings. She was subsequently indicted by the Grand Jury for the Massachusetts jurisdiction for "familiarity with the Devil." The Court of Assistants found that there was "just ground of vehement suspicion of her having had familiarity with the Devil," and got rid of the case by ordering her "to depart from and abide out of this jurisdiction."

At a County Court, held at Salem, Nov. 24, 1674, a case was brought up, of which the following is all we know: —

"Christopher Browne having reported that he had been treating or discoursing with one whom he apprehended to be the Devil, which came like a gentleman, in order to his binding himself to be a servant to him, upon his examination, his discourse seeming inconsistent with truth, &c., the Court, giving him good counsel and caution, for the present dismiss him."

It would have been well if the action of this Court had been followed as an authoritative precedent.

In the year 1679, the house of William Morse, of Newbury, was, for more than two months, infested in a most strange and vexatious manner. The affair was brought into court, where it played a conspicuous part, and was near reaching a tragical conclusion. The history of the proceedings in reference to it is very curious.

Mr. John Woodbridge, of Newbury, had been for some time an associate county judge, and was commissioned to administer oaths and join persons in marriage. The following is a record of what occurred before him, sitting as a magistrate, and as a commissioner to adjudicate in small, local causes, and hold examinations in matters that went to higher courts : —

" Dec. 3, 1679. — Caleb Powell, being complained of for suspicion of working with the Devil to the molesting of William Morse and his family, was by warrant directed to the constable brought in by him. The accusation and testimonies were read, and the complaint respited till the Monday following.

" Dec. 8, 1679. — Caleb Powell appeared according to order, and further testimony produced against him by William Morse, which being read and considered, it was determined that the said William Morse should prosecute the case against said Powell at the County Court to be held at Ipswich the last Tuesday in March ensuing ; and, in order hereunto, William Morse acknowledgeth himself indebted to the Treasurer of the County of Essex the full sum of twenty pounds. The condition of this obligation is, that the said William Morse shall prosecute his complaint against Caleb Powell at that Court.

Caleb Powell was delivered as a prisoner to the constable till he could find security of twenty pounds for the answering of the said complaint, or else he was to be carried to prison.   Jo : WOODBRIDGE, *Commissioner.*"

Powell was accordingly brought before the Court at Ipswich, March 30, 1680, under an indictment for witchcraft. Before giving the substance of the evidence adduced on this occasion, it will be well to mention the manner in which he got into the case as a principal. He was a mate of a vessel. While at home, between voyages, he happened to hear of the wonderful occurrences at Mr. Morse's house. His curiosity was awakened, and he was also actuated by feelings of commiseration for the family under the torments and terrors with which they were said to be afflicted. Determined to see what it all meant, and to put a stop to it if he could, he went to the house, and soon became satisfied that a roguish grandchild was the cause of all the trouble. He prevailed upon the old grandparents to let him take off the boy. Immediately upon his removal, the difficulty ceased.

New-England navigators, at that time and long afterwards, sailed almost wholly by the stars; and Powell probably had often related his own skill, which, as mate of a vessel, he would have been likely to acquire, in calculating his position, rate of sailing, and distances, on the boundless and trackless ocean, by his knowledge and observations of the heavenly bodies. He had said, perhaps, that, by gazing among the stars, he could, at any hour of the night, however long or far he had been tossed and driven on the ocean, tell exactly where his vessel was. Hence the charge of being an astrologist. Probably, like other sailors, Powell may have indulged in "long yarns" to the country people, of the wonders he had seen, "some in one country, and some in another." It is not unlikely, that, in foreign ports, he had witnessed exhibitions of necromancy and mesmerism, which, in various forms and under different names, have always been practised. Possibly he may have boasted to be a medium himself, a scholar and adept in the mystic art, able to read and divine "the workings of spirits." At any rate, when it became known, that, at a glance, he attributed to the boy the cause of the mischief, and that it ceased on his taking him away from the house, the opinion became settled that he was a wizard. He was arrested forthwith, and brought to trial, as has been stated, for witchcraft. His astronomy, astrology, and spiritualism brought him in peril of his life.

"THE TESTIMONY OF WILLIAM MORSE: which saith, together with his wife, aged both about sixty-five years: that, Thursday night, being the twenty-seventh day of November, we heard a great noise without, round the house, of knocking the boards of the house, and, as we conceived, throwing of stones against the house. Whereupon myself and wife looked out and saw nobody, and the boy all this time with us; but we had stones and sticks thrown at us, that we were forced to retire into the house again. Afterwards we went to bed, and the boy with us; and then the like noise was upon the roof of the house.

"2. The same night about midnight, the door being locked when we went to bed, we heard a great hog in the house grunt and make a noise, as we thought willing to get out; and, that we might not be disturbed in our sleep, I rose to let him out, and I found a hog in the house and the door unlocked: the door was firmly locked when we went to bed.

"3. The next morning, a stick of links hanging in the chimney, they were thrown out of their place, and we hanged them up again, and they were thrown down again, and some into the fire.

"4. The night following, I had a great awl lying in the window, the which awl we saw fall down out of the chimney into the ashes by the fire.

"5. After this, I bid the boy put the same awl into the cupboard, which we saw done, and the door shut to: this same awl came presently down the chimney again in our sight, and I took it up myself. Again, the same night, we saw a little Indian basket, that was in the loft before, come down the chimney again. And I took the same basket, and put a piece of brick into it, and the basket with the brick was gone, and came down again the third time with the brick in it, and went up again the fourth time, and came down again without the brick; and the brick came down again a little after.

"6. The next day, being Saturday, stones, sticks, and pieces of bricks came down, so that we could not quietly dress our breakfast; and sticks of fire also came down at the same time.

"7. That day in the afternoon, my thread four times taken away, and came down the chimney; again, my awl and gimlet, wanting, came down the chimney; again, my leather, taken away, came down the chimney; again, my nails, being in the cover of a firkin, taken away, came down the chimney. Again, the same night, the door being locked, a little before day, hearing a hog in the house, I rose, and saw the hog to be mine: I let him out.

"8. The next day being sabbath-day, many stones and sticks and pieces of bricks came down the chimney: on the Monday, Mr. Richardson and my brother being there, the frame of my cowhouse they saw very firm. I sent my boy out to scare the fowls from my hog's meat : he went to the cowhouse, and it fell down, my boy crying with the hurt of the fall. In the afternoon, the pots hanging over the fire did dash so vehemently one against the other, we set down one that they might not dash to pieces. I saw the andiron leap into the pot, and dance and leap out, and again leap in and dance and leap out again, and leap on a table and there abide, and my wife saw the andiron on the table : also I saw the pot turn itself over, and throw down all the water. Again, we saw a tray with wool leap up and down, and throw the wool out, and so many times, and saw nobody meddle with it. Again, a tub his hoop fly off of itself and the tub turn over, and nobody near it. Again, the woollen wheel turned upside down, and stood up on its end, and a spade set on it; Steph. Greenleafe saw it, and myself and my wife. Again, my rope-tools fell down upon the ground before my boy could take them, being sent for them; and the same thing of nails tumbled down from the loft into the ground, and nobody near. Again, my wife and boy making the bed, the chest did open and shut : the bed-clothes could not be made to lie on the bed, but fly off again.

" Again, Caleb Powell came in, and, being affected to see our trouble, did promise me and my wife, that, if we would be willing to let him keep the boy, we should see ourselves that we should be never disturbed while he was gone with him : he had the boy, and had been quiet ever since.

"THO. ROGERS and GEORGE HARDY, being at William Morse his house, affirm that the earth in the chimney-corner moved, and scattered on them; that Tho. Rogers was hit with somewhat, Hardy with an iron ladle as is supposed. Somewhat hit William Morse a great blow, but it was so swift that they could not certainly tell what it was ; but, looking down after they heard the noise, they saw a shoe. The boy was in the corner at the first, afterwards in the house.

"Mr. RICHARDSON on Saturday testifieth that a board flew against his chair, and he heard a noise in another room, which he supposed in all reason to be diabolical.

"JOHN DOLE saw a pine stick of candlewood to fall down, a stone, a firebrand; and these things he saw not what way they came, till they fell down by him.

"The same affirmed by John Tucker: the boy was in one corner, whom they saw and observed all the while, and saw no motion in him.

"ELIZABETH TITCOMB affirmeth that Powell said that he could find the witch by his learning, if he had another scholar with him: this she saith were his expressions, to the best of her memory.

"JO. TUCKER affirmeth that Powell said to him, he saw the boy throw the shoe while he was at prayer.

"JO. EMERSON affirmeth that Powell said he was brought up under Norwood; and it was judged by the people there, that Norwood studied the black art.

"A FURTHER TESTIMONY OF WILLIAM MORSE AND HIS WIFE. — We saw a keeler of bread turn over against me, and struck me, not any being near it, and so overturned. I saw a chair standing in the house, and not anybody near: it did often bow towards me, and so rise up again. My wife also being in the chamber, the chamber-door did violently fly together, not anybody being near it. My wife, going to make a bed, it did move to and fro, not anybody being near it. I also saw an iron wedge and spade was flying out of the chamber on my wife, and did not strike her. My wife going into the cellar, a drum, standing in the house, did roll over the door of the cellar; and, being taken up again, the door did violently fly down again. My barn-doors four times unpinned, I know not how. I, going to shut my barn-door, looking for the pin, — the boy being with me, as I did judge, — the pin, coming down out of the air, did fall down near to me. Again, Caleb Powell came in, as beforesaid, and, seeing our spirits very low by the sense of our great affliction, began to bemoan our condition, and said that he was troubled for our afflictions, and said that he had eyed this boy, and drawed near to us with great compassion: 'Poor old man, poor old woman! this boy is the occasion of your grief; for he hath done these things, and hath caused his good old grandmother to be counted a witch.' 'Then,' said I, 'how can all these things be done by him?' Said he, 'Although he may not have done all, yet most of them; for this boy is a young rogue, a vile rogue: I have watched him, and see him do things as to come up and down.' Caleb Powell also said he had understanding in astrology and astronomy, and knew the working of spirits, some in one country, and some in another; and, looking on the boy, said, 'You young rogue, to begin so soon. Goodman Morse, if you be willing to let me have this boy, I will undertake you shall be free from any trouble of this kind while he is with me.' I was very unwilling at the first, and my wife; but, by often urging me, till he told me whither, and what employment and company, he should go, I did consent to it, and this was before Jo. Badger came; and we have been freed from any trouble of this kind ever since that promise, made on Monday night last, to this time, being Friday in the afternoon. Then we heard a great noise in the other room, oftentimes, but, looking after it, could not see any thing; but, afterwards looking into the room, we saw a board hanged to the press. Then we, being by the fire, sitting in a chair, my chair often would not stand still, but ready to throw me backward oftentimes. Afterward, my cap almost taken off my head three times. Again, a great blow on my poll, and my cat did leap from me into the chimney corner. Presently after, this cat was thrown at my wife. We saw the cat to be ours : we put her out of the house, and shut the door. Presently, the cat was throwed into the house. We went to go to bed. Suddenly, — my wife being with me in bed, the lamp-light by our side, — my cat again throwed at us five times, jumping away presently into the floor ; and, one of those times, a red waistcoat throwed on the bed, and the cat wrapped up in it. Again, the lamp, standing by us on the chest, we said it should stand and burn out ; but presently was beaten down, and all the oil shed, and we left in the dark. Again, a great voice, a great while, very dreadful. Again, in the morning, a great stone, being six-pound weight, did remove from place to place, — we saw it, — two spoons throwed off the table, and presently the table throwed down. And, being minded to write, my inkhorn was hid from me, which I found, covered with a rag, and my pen quite gone. I made a new pen ; and, while I was writing, one ear of corn hit me in the face, and fire, sticks, and stones throwed at me, and my pen brought to me. While I was writing with my new pen, my inkhorn taken away : and, not knowing how to write any more, we looked under the table, and there found him ; and so I was able to write again. Again, my wife her hat taken from her head, sitting by the fire by me, the table almost thrown down. Again, my spectacles thrown from the table, and thrown almost into the fire by me, and my wife and the boy. Again, my book of all my accounts thrown into the fire, and had been burnt presently, if I had not taken it up. Again, boards taken off a tub, and set upright by themselves; and my paper, do what I could, hardly keep it while I was writing this relation, and things thrown at me while a-writing. Presently, before I could dry my writing, a mormouth hat rubbed along it; but I held so fast that it did blot but some of it. My wife and I, being much afraid that I should not preserve it for public use, did think best to lay it in the Bible, and it lay safe that night. Again, the next, I would lay it there again; but, in the morning, it was not there to be found, the bag hanged down empty; but, after, was found in a box alone. Again, while I was writing this morning, I was forced to forbear writing any more, I was so disturbed with so many things constantly thrown at me.

"This relation brought in Dec. 8.

" I, ANTHONY MORSE, occasionally being at my brother Morse's house, my brother showed me a piece of a brick which had several times come down the chimney. I sitting in the corner, I took the piece of brick in my hand. Within a little space of time, the piece of brick was gone from me, I knew not by what means. Quickly after, the piece of brick came down the chimney. Also, in the chimney-corner I saw a hammer on the ground: there being no person near the hammer, it was suddenly gone, by what means I know not. But, within a little space after, the hammer came down the chimney. And, within a little space of time after that, came a piece of wood down the chimney, about a foot long; and, within a little after that, came down a firebrand, the fire being out. This was about ten days ago.

" JOHN BADGER affirmeth, that, being at William Morse his house, and heard Caleb Powell say that he thought by astrology, and I think he said by astronomy too, with it, he could find out whether or no there were diabolical means used about the said Morse his trouble, and that the said Caleb said he thought to try to find it out.

"THE DEPOSITION OF MARY TUCKER, aged about twenty. — She remembered that Caleb Powell came into her house, and said to this purpose : That he, coming to William Morse his house, and the old man, being at prayer, he thought not fit to go in, but looked in at the window ; and he said he had broken the enchantment ; for he saw the boy play tricks while he was at prayer, and mentioned some, and, among the rest, that he saw him to fling the shoe at the said Morse's head.

"Taken on oath, March 29, 1680, before me,

"JO : WOODBRIDGE, *Commissioner.*

"Mary Richardson confirmed the truth of the above written testimony, on oath, at the same time."

There seem to have been several hearings before Commissioner Woodbridge. The boy had returned to his grandparents before the last deposition of William Morse, and his audacious operations were persisted in to the last. The final decision of the Court was as follows : —

"Upon the hearing the complaint brought to this Court against Caleb Powell for suspicion of working by the Devil to the molesting of the family of William Morse of Newbury, though this court cannot find any evident ground of proceeding further against the said Caleb Powell, yet we determine that he hath given such ground of suspicion of his so dealing that we cannot so acquit him, but that he justly deserves to bear his own share and the costs of the prosecution of the complaint.

"Referred to Mr. Woodbridge to examine and determine the charges."

The entry of this sentence, in the records of the County Court, is as follows; the clerk strangely mistaking the name of the party : —

"The Court held at Ipswich, the 30th of March, 1680.

"In the case of Abell Powell, though the Court do not see sufficient to charge further, yet find so much suspicion as that he pay the charges. The ordering of the charges left to Mr. Jo : Woodbridge."

The matter of Powell's connection with the affair being thus disposed of, and no one seeming to entertain his idea of the guilt of the boy, the next step was to fasten suspicion upon the good old grandmother; and a general outcry was raised against her. Her arrest and condemnation were clamored for. But the result of Powell's trial, and all preceding cases, showed that an Essex jury could not yet be relied on for a conviction in witchcraft cases; and it was resolved to institute proceedings in a more favorable quarter. The Grand Jury returned a bill of indictment against her to the Court of Assistants, sitting in Boston. This was the highest tribunal in the country, subject only to the General Court, and embracing the whole colony in its jurisdiction. The following is the substance of the record of the case : —

At a Court of Assistants, on adjournment, held at Boston, on the 20th of May, 1680.

The Grand Jury having presented Elizabeth Morse, wife of William Morse, she was tried and convicted of the crime of witchcraft. The Governor, on the 27th of May, "after the lecture," in the First Church of Boston, pronounced the sentence of death upon her. On the 1st of June, the Governor and Assistants voted to reprieve her "until the next session of the Court in Boston." At the said next session, the reprieval was still further continued. This seems to have produced much dissatisfaction, as is shown by the following extract from the records of the House of Deputies: —

"The Deputies, on perusal of the Acts of the Honored Court of Assistants, relating to the woman condemned for witchcraft, do not understand the reason why the sentence, given against her by said Court, is not executed: and the second reprieval seems to us beyond what the law will allow, and do therefore judge meet to declare ourselves against it, with reference to the concurrence of the honored magistrates hereto. WILLIAM TORREY, *Clerk.*"

The action of the magistrates, on this reference, is recorded as follows: —

"3d of November, 1680. — Not consented to by magistrates. EDWARD RAWSON, *Secretary.*"

The evidence against Mrs. Morse was frivolous to the last degree, without any of the force and effect given to support the prosecutions in Salem, twelve years afterwards, by the astounding confessions of the accused, and the splendid acting of the "afflicted children;" yet she was tried and condemned in Boston, and sentenced there on "Lecture-day." The representatives of the people, in the House of Deputies, cried out against her reprieve. She was saved by the courage and wisdom of Governor Bradstreet, subsequently a resident of Salem, where his ashes rest. He was living here, at the age of ninety years, during the witchcraft prosecutions in 1692; but, old as he was, he made known his entire disapprobation of them. It is safe to say, that, if he had not been superseded by the arrival of Sir William Phipps as governor under the new charter, they would never have taken place. Notwithstanding all this, — in spite of the remonstrances, at the time, of Brattle, and afterwards of Hutchinson, — Boston and other towns (earlier, if not equally, committed to such proceedings) have, by a sort of general conspiracy, joined the rest of the world in trying to throw and fasten the whole responsibility and disgrace of witchcraft prosecutions upon Salem.

Things continued in the condition just described, — Mrs. Morse in jail under sentence of death; that sentence suspended by reprieves from the Governor, from time to time, until the next year, when her husband, in her behalf and in her name, presented an earnest and touching petition "to the honored Governor, Deputy-governor, Magistrates, and Deputies now assembled in Court, May the 18th, 1681," that her case might be concluded, one way or another. After referring to her condemnation, and to her attestation of innocence, she says, "By the mercy of God, and the goodness of the honored Governor, I am reprieved." She begs the Court to "hearken to her cry, a poor prisoner." She places herself at the foot of the tribunal of the General Court: " I now stand humbly praying your justice in hearing my case, and to determine therein as the Lord shall direct. I do not understand law, nor do I know how to lay my case before you as I ought; for want of which I humbly beg of your honors that my request may not be rejected." The House of Deputies, on the 24th of May, voted to give her a new trial. But the magistrates refused to concur in the vote; and so the matter stood, for how long a time there are, I believe, no means of knowing. Finally, however, she was released from prison, and allowed to return to her own house. This we learn from a publication made by Mr. Hale, of Beverly, in 1697. It seems, that, after getting her out of prison and restored to her home, to use Mr. Hale's words, " her husband, who was esteemed a sincere and understanding Christian by those that knew him, desired some neighbor ministers, of whom I was one, to discourse his wife, which we did ; and her discourse was very Christian, and still pleaded her innocence as to that which was laid to her charge." From Mr. Hale's language, it may be inferred that she had not been pardoned or discharged, but still lay under sentence of death, after her removal to her own house : for he and his brethren did not " esteem it prudence to pass any definite sentence upon one under her circumstances ; " but they ventured to say that they were " inclined to the more charitable side." Mr. Hale states, that, " in her last sickness, she was in much trouble and darkness of spirit, which occasioned a judicious friend to examine her strictly, whether she had been guilty of witchcraft; but she said *no*, but the ground of her trouble was some impatient and passionate speeches and actions of hers while in prison, upon the account of her suffering wrongfully, whereby she had provoked the Lord by putting contempt upon his Word. And, in fine, she sought her pardon and comfort from God in Christ; and died, so far as I understand, praying to and relying upon God in Christ for salvation."

The cases of Margaret Jones, Ann Hibbins, and Elizabeth Morse illustrate strikingly and fully the history and condition of the public mind in New England, and the world over, in reference to witchcraft in the seventeenth century. They show that there was nothing unprecedented, unusual, or eminently shocking, after all, in what I am about to relate as occurring in Salem, in 1692. The only real offence proved upon Margaret Jones was that she was a successful practitioner of medicine, using only simple remedies. Ann Hibbins was the victim of the slanderous gossip of a prejudiced neighborhood; all our actual knowledge of her being her Will, which proves that she was a person of much more than ordinary dignity of mind, which was kept unruffled and serene in the bitterest trials and most outrageous wrongs which it is possible for folly and " man's inhumanity to man " to bring upon us in this life. Elizabeth Morse appears to have been one of the best of Christian women. The accusations against them, as a whole, cover nearly the whole ground upon which the subsequent prosecutions in Salem rested. John Winthrop passed sentence upon Margaret Jones, John Endicott upon Ann Hibbins, and Simon Bradstreet upon Elizabeth Morse. The last-named governor performed the office as an unavoidable act of official duty, and prevented the execution of the sentence by the courageous use of his prerogative, in defiance of public clamor and the wrath of the representatives of the whole people of the colony. These facts sufficiently show, that the proceedings afterwards had in Salem accorded with those in like cases, of that and preceding generations; and were sanctioned by the all but universal sentiments of mankind and a uniform chain of precedents.

The trial of Bridget Bishop, in 1680, before the County Court at Salem, for witchcraft, and her acquittal, have already been mentioned in the account of Salem Village, in the First Part.

In 1688, an Irish woman, named Glover, was executed in Boston for bewitching four children belonging to the family of a Mr. Goodwin. She was a Roman Catholic, represented to have been quite an ignorant person, and seems, moreover, from the accounts given of her, to have been crazy. The oldest of the children was only about thirteen years of age. The most experienced physicians pronounced them bewitched. Their conduct, as it is related by Cotton Mather, was indeed very extraordinary. At one time they would bark like dogs, and then again they would purr like cats. "Yea," says he, "they would fly like geese, and be carried with an incredible swiftness, having but just their toes now and then upon the ground, sometimes not once in twenty feet, and their arms waved like the wings of a bird."

One of the children seems to have had a genius scarcely inferior to that of Master Burke himself: there was no part nor passion she could not enact. She would complain that the old Irish woman had tied an invisible noose round her neck, and was choking her; and her complexion and features would instantly assume the various hues and violent distortions natural to a person in such a predicament. She would declare that an invisible chain was fastened to one of her limbs, and would limp about precisely as though it were really the case. She would say that she was in an oven; the perspiration would drop from her face, and she would exhibit every appearance of being roasted: then she would cry out that cold water was thrown upon her, and her whole frame would shiver and shake. She pretended that the evil spirit came to her in the shape of an invisible horse; and she would canter, gallop, trot, and amble round the rooms and entries in such admirable imitation, that an observer could hardly believe that a horse was not beneath her, and bearing her about. She would go up stairs with exactly such a toss and bound as a person on horseback would exhibit.

After some time, Cotton Mather took her into his own family, to see whether he could not exorcise her.

His account of her conduct, while there, is highly amusing for its credulous simplicity. The cunning and ingenious child seems to have taken great delight in perplexing and playing off her tricks upon the learned man. Once he wished to say something in her presence, to a third person, which he did not intend she should understand. He accordingly spoke in Latin. But she had penetration enough to conjecture what he had said: he was amazed. He then tried Greek: she was equally successful. He next spoke in Hebrew: she instantly detected the meaning. At last he resorted to the Indian language, and that she pretended not to know. He drew the conclusion that the evil being with whom she was in compact was acquainted familiarly with the Latin, Greek, and Hebrew, but not with the Indian tongue.

It is curious to notice how adroitly she fell into the line of his prejudices. He handed her a book written by a Quaker, to which sect it is well known he was violently opposed: she would read it off with great ease, rapidity, and pleasure. A book written against the Quakers she could not read at all. She could read Popish books, but could not decipher a syllable of the Assembly's Catechism. Dr. Mather was earnestly opposed to the order and liturgy of the Church of England. The artful little girl worked with great success upon this prejudice. She pretended to be very fond of the Book of Common Prayer, and called it her Bible. It would relieve her of her sufferings, in a moment, to put it into her hands. While she could not read a word of the Scriptures in the Bible, she could read them very easily in the Prayer-book; but she could not read the Lord's Prayer even in this her favorite volume. All these things went far to strengthen the conviction of Dr. Mather that she was in league with the Devil; for this was the only explanation that could be given to satisfy his mind of her partiality to the productions of Quakers, Catholics, and Episcopalians, and her aversion to the Bible and the Catechism.

She exhibited the most exquisite ingenuity in beguiling Dr. Mather by the force of a charm, the power of which he could not resist for a moment, — flattery. He thus describes, with a complacency but thinly concealed under the veil of affected modesty, the part she played, in order to give the impression — which it was the great object of his ambition to make upon the public mind — that the Devil stood in special fear of his presence : —

"There then stood open the study of one belonging to the family, into which, entering, she stood immediately on her feet, and cried out, 'They are gone! they are gone! They say that they cannot, — God won't let 'em come here!' adding a reason for it which the owner of the study thought more kind than true ; and she presently and perfectly came to herself, so that her whole discourse and carriage was altered into the greatest measure of sobriety."

Upon quitting the study, " the demons " would instantly again take hold of her. Mather continues the statement, by saying that some persons, wishing to try the experiment, had her brought " up into the study ; " but he says that she at once became —

" so strangely distorted, that it was an extreme difficulty to drag her up stairs. The demons would pull her out of the people's hands, and make her heavier than, perhaps, three of herself. With incredible toil (though she kept screaming, ' They say I must not go in '), she was pulled in ; where she was no sooner got, but she could stand on her feet, and, with altered note, say, ' Now I am well.' She would be faint at first, and say ' she felt something to go out of her' (the noises whereof we sometimes heard like those of a mouse) ; but, in a minute or two, she could apply herself to devotion. To satisfy some strangers, the experiment was, divers times, with the same success, repeated, until my lothness to have any thing done like making a charm of a room, caused me to forbid the repetition of it."

Even in her most riotous proceedings, she kept her eye fixed upon the doctor's weak point. When he called the family to prayers, she would whistle and sing and yell to drown his voice, would strike him with her fist, and try to kick him. But her hand or foot would always recoil when within an inch or two of his body ; thus giving the idea that there was a sort of invisible coat of mail, of heavenly temper, and proof against the assaults of the Devil, around his sacred person ! After a while, Dr. Mather concluded to prepare an account of these extraordinary circumstances, wherewithal to entertain his congregation in a sermon. She seemed to be quite displeased at the thought of his making public the doings of her master, the Evil

One, attempted to prevent his writing the intended sermon, and disturbed and interrupted him in all manner of ways. For instance, she once knocked at his study door, and said that "there was somebody down stairs that would be glad to see him." He dropped his pen, and went down. Upon entering the room, he found nobody there but the family. The next time he met her, he undertook to chide her for having told him a falsehood. She denied that she had told a falsehood. "Didn't you say," said he, "that there was somebody down stairs that would be glad to see me?"—"Well," she replied, with inimitable pertness, "is not Mrs. Mather always glad to see you?"

She even went much farther than this in persecuting the good man while he was writing his sermon : she threw large books at his head. But he struggled manfully against these buffetings of Satan, as he considered her conduct to be, finished the sermon, related all these circumstances in it, preached, and published it. Richard Baxter wrote the preface to an edition printed in London, in which he declares that he who will not be convinced by all the evidence Dr. Mather presents that the child was bewitched "must be a very obdurate Sadducee." It is so obvious, that, in this whole affair, Cotton Mather was grossly deceived and audaciously imposed upon by the most consummate and precocious cunning, that it needs no comment. I have given this particular account of it, because there is reason to believe that it originated the delusion in Salem. It occurred only four years before. Dr. Mather's account of the transaction filled the whole country; and it is probable that the children in Mr. Parris's family undertook to re-enact it.

There is nothing in the annals of the histrionic art more illustrative of the infinite versatility of the human faculties, both physical and mental, and of the amazing extent to which cunning, ingenuity, contrivance, quickness of invention, and presence of mind can be cultivated, even in very young persons, than such cases as this just related. It seems, at first, incredible that a mere child could carry on such a complex piece of fraud and imposture as that enacted by the little girl whose achievements have been immortalized by the famous author of the " Magnalia." Many other instances, however, are found recorded in the history of the delusion we are discussing.

That of the grandchild of William and Elizabeth Morse, in Newbury, was nearly as marvellous, and perfectly successful in deceiving the whole country except Caleb Powell; and he got into much trouble in consequence of seeing through it. A similar instance of juvenile imposture is related as having occurred at Amsterdam in 1560. Twenty or thirty boys pretended to be suddenly seized with a kind of rage and fury, were cast upon the ground, and tormented with great agony. These fits were intermittent; and, when they had passed off, their subjects did not seem to be conscious of what had taken place. While they lasted, the boys threw up, apparently from their stomachs, large quantities of needles, pins, thimbles, pieces of cloth, fragments of pots and kettles, bits of glass, locks of hair, and a variety of other articles. There was no doubt, at the time, that they were suffering under the influence of the Devil; and multitudes crowded round them, and gazed upon them with wonder and horror.

The details of the cases in Newbury and Charlestown were dressed up by Cotton Mather and other writers in the strongest colors that credulous superstition and the peculiar views of that age on the subject of demonology could employ. They were almost universally received as proof that Satan had commenced an onslaught, such as had never before been known, upon the Church and the world! They appear to us as simply absurd, and the result of precocious knavery; not so to the people of that generation. They were looked upon as fearful demonstrations of diabolical power, and preludes to the coming of Satan, with his infernal confederates, to overwhelm the land. The imaginations of all were excited, and their apprehensions morbidly aroused. The very air was filled with rumors, fancies, and fears. The ministers sounded the alarm from their pulpits. The magistrates sharpened the sword of justice. The deputy-governor of the colony, Danforth, began to arrest suspected persons months before proceedings commenced, or were thought of, in Salem Village. It was believed that evil spirits had been seen, by men's bodily eyes, in a neighboring town. They glided over the fields, hovered around the houses, appeared, vanished, and re-appeared on the outskirts of the woods, in the vicinity of Gloucester. Their movements were observed by several of the inhabitants ; and the whole population of the Cape was kept in a state of agitation and alarm, in consequence of the mysterious phenomena, for three weeks. The inhabitants retired to the garrison, and put themselves in a state of defence against the diabolical besiegers. Sixty men were despatched from Ipswich, in military array, to re-enforce the garrison, and several valiant sallies were made from its walls. Much powder was expended, but no corporeal or incorporeal blood was shed. An account of these events was drawn up by the Rev. John Emerson, then the minister of the first parish in Gloucester, from which the facts now mentioned have been selected. It is very minute and particular. The appearance and dress of the supernatural enemies are described. They wore white waistcoats, blue shirts, and white breeches, and had bushy heads of black hair. Mr. Emerson concludes his account by expressing the hope that " all rational persons will be satisfied that Gloucester was not alarmed last summer for above a fortnight together by real French and Indians, but that the Devil and his agents were the cause of all the molestation which at this time befell the town."

These wonderful things took place at Cape Ann, about the time that the great conflict between the Devil and his confederates on the one hand, and the ministers and magistrates on the other, at Salem Village, was reaching its height. It is said that it was regarded by the most considerate persons, at the time, as an artful contrivance of the Devil to create a diversion of the attention of the pious colonists from his operations through the witches in Salem, and, by dividing and distracting their forces, to obtain an advantage over them in the war he was waging against their churches and their religion.

We are now ready to enter upon the story of Salem witchcraft. We have endeavored to become acquainted with the people who acted conspicuous parts in the drama, and to understand their character; and have tried to collect, and bring into appreciating view, the opinions and theories, the habits of thought, the associations of mind, the passions, impulses, and fantasies that guided, moulded, and controlled their conduct. The law, literature, and theology of the age, as they bore on the subject, have been brought before us. The last great display of the effects of the doctrines of demonology, of the belief of the agency of invisible, irresponsible beings, whether fallen angels or departed spirits, upon the actions of men and human affairs, is now to open before us. The final results of superstitions and fables and fancies, accumulating through the ages, are to be exhibited in a transaction, an actual demonstration in real life. They are to present an exemplification that will at once fully display their power, and deal their death-blow.

Without the least purpose or wish to cover up or extenuate the follies, excesses, or outrages I am about to describe, into which the community suffered itself to be led in the witchcraft proceedings of 1692,—with a desire, on the contrary, to make the lesson then given of the mischief resulting from misguided enthusiasm, and which will always result when popular excitement is allowed to wield the organized powers of society, as impressive as facts and truth will justify,—I feel bound to say, in advance, that there are some considerations which we must keep before us, while reviewing the incidents of the transaction. The theological, legal, and philosophical doctrines and the popular beliefs, on which it was founded, have, as I have shown, led, in other countries and periods, to similar, and often vastly more shameful, cruel, and destructive results. But there was something in the affair, as it was developed here, that has arrested the notice of mankind, and clothed it with an inherent interest, beyond all other events of the kind that have elsewhere or ever occurred.

The moral force engendered in the civilization planted on these shores, and pervading the whole body of society, supplied a mightier momentum, as it does to this day, and ever will, to the movement of the people, acting in a mass and as a unit, than can anywhere else be found. A population, invigorated by hardy enterprise, and the constant exercise of all the faculties of freedom, and actuated throughout by individual energy of character, must be mightier in motion than any other people. Such a population multiplies tenfold its physical forces, by the addition of moral and intellectual energies. The men of the day and scene we are now to contemplate, however deluded, to whatever extremities carried, were controlled by fixed, absolute, sharply defined, and, in themselves, great ideas. They believed in God. They also believed in the Devil. They bowed in an adoration that penetrated their inmost souls, before the one as a being of infinite holiness: they regarded the other as a being of an all but infinite power of evil. They feared and worshipped God. They hated and defied the Devil. They believed that Satan was waging war against Jehovah, and that the conflict was for the dominion of the world, for the establishment or the overthrow of the Church of Christ. The battle, they fully believed, could have no other issue than the salvation or the ruin of the souls of men. This was not, with them, a mere technical, verbal creed. It was a deepseated conviction, held earnestly with a clear and distinct apprehension of its import, by every individual mind. For this warfare, they put on the whole armor of faith, rallied to the banner of the Most High, and met Satan face to face. In this one great idea, a stern, determined, unflinching, all-sacrificing people concentrated their strength. No wonder that the conflict reached a magnitude which made it observable to the whole country and all countries at the time, and will make it memorable throughout all time. Those engaged in it, with this sentiment absorbing their very souls, passed, for the time, out of the realm of all other sentiments, and were insensible to all other considera-

tions. The nearer and dearer the relatives, the higher
and more conspicuous the persons, who, in their belief, were in league with the Devil, the more profound
the abhorrence of their crime, and the determination
to cut off and destroy them utterly. They believed
that Satan had, once before, " against the throne and
monarchy of God, raised impious war and battle
proud ; " and that for this he had been cast out from
" heaven, with all his host of rebel angels ; " that he,
with his army of subordinate wicked spirits, was making a desperate effort to retrieve his lost estate, by a
renewed rebellion against God ; and they were determined to drive him, and all his confederates, for ever
from the confines of the earth. The humble hamlet
of Salem Village was felt to be the great and final
battle-ground. However wild and absurd this idea is
now regarded, it was then sincerely and thoroughly
entertained, and must be taken into the account, in
coming to a just estimate of the character of the transaction, and of those engaged in it.

One other thought is to be borne in mind, as we
pass through the scenes that are to be spread before
us. The theology of Christendom, at that time, so far
as it relates to the power and agency of Satan and demonology in general, — and this is the only point of
view on which I ever refer to theology in this discussion, — and the whole fabric of popular superstitions
founded upon it, had reached their culmination. The
beginning, middle, and close of the seventeenth century, witnessed the greatest display of those supersti-

tions, and prepared the way for their final explosion. As the hour of their dissolution was at hand, and they were doomed to vanish before the light of science and education, to pass from the realm of supposed reality into that of acknowledged fiction, it seems to have been ordered that they should leave monuments behind them, from which their character, elements, and features, and their terrible influence, might be read and studied in all subsequent ages.

The ideas in reference to the agency and designs of the great enemy of God and man, and all his subordinate hosts, witches, fairies, ghosts, " gorgons and hydras, and chimeras dire," " apparitions, signs, and prodigies," by which the minds of men had so long been filled, and their fearful imaginations exercised, as they took their flight, imprinted themselves, for perpetual remembrance, in productions which, more than any works of mere human genius, are sure to live for ever. They left their forms crystallized, with imperishable lineaments, in the greatest of dramas and the greatest of epics. The plays of Shakespeare, as the century opened, and the verse of Milton in its central period, are their record and their picture.

But there was another shape and aspect in which it was pre-eminently important to have their memory preserved ; and that was their application to life, their influence upon the conduct of men, the action of tribunals, and the movements of society, and, in general, their effects, when allowed full operation, upon human happiness and welfare. This want was supplied, as the century terminated, by the tragedy in real life, whose scenes are now to be presented in WITCHCRAFT AT SALEM VILLAGE.

However strange it seems, it is quite worthy of observation, that the actors in that tragedy, the "afflicted children," and other witnesses, in their various statements and operations, embraced about the whole circle of popular superstition. How those young country girls, some of them mere children, most of them wholly illiterate, could have become familiar with such fancies, to such an extent. is truly surprising. They acted out, and brought to bear with tremendous effect, almost all that can be found in the literature of that day, and the period preceding it, relating to such subjects. Images and visions which had been portrayed in tales of romance, and given interest to the pages of poetry, will be made by them, as we shall see, to throng the woods, flit through the air, and hover over the heads of a terrified court. The ghosts of murdered wives and children will play their parts with a vividness of representation and artistic skill of expression that have hardly been surpassed in scenic representations on the stage. In the Salem-witchcraft proceedings, the superstition of the middle ages was embodied in real action. All its extravagances, absurdities, and monstrosities appear in their application to human experience. We see what the effect has been, and must be, when the affairs of life, in courts of law and the relations of society, or the conduct or feelings of individuals, are suffered to be under the control of fanciful or mystical notions. When a whole people abandons the solid ground of common sense, overleaps the boundaries of human knowledge, gives itself up to wild reveries, and lets loose its passions without restraint, it presents a spectacle more terrific to behold, and becomes more destructive and disastrous, than any convulsion of mere material nature; than tornado, conflagration, or earthquake.

END OF VOL. I.